AN ITINERANT ENGINEER

RICHARD MARTIN

Published in 2016 by FeedARead.com Publishing

For

Hugh, Daniel and Esme

and

In Memory of Jane

Comments from readers

I've thoroughly enjoyed reading some bits of it already and being reduced to fits of laughter several times. Of course I wouldn't believe any of it if I hadn't been there with you on several occasions mentioned. ....I think copies of this book ought to be put in schools to encourage youngsters to take up the profession as we need so many more civil engineers now.

Dave Kilner

I can honestly say that your book comes into the category of "Can't put it down" reading. I love the way you weave humour and fact seamlessly one into the other. So competently put together and an utter joy to read. Many congratulations on a job superbly done and one that should give genuine pleasure to anyone who is privileged to read its pages.

Bill Donald

INDEX

Introduction

My story is only one of many, many, similar stories that can be told by those civil engineers that have travelled the globe, constantly looking for an ever more interesting job. My background and upbringing was not the same as that of most young engineers growing up in Britain today.

It is often said that, in spite of what is taught in schools and universities, nothing prepares one for real life. Education is meant to prepare a person by giving them the basic life skills that one can use later in life to adapt to a situation, and the various influences on that situation. Only by telling others of events and situations that have occurred, can these real life stories be carried into the classroom.

As one gains experience, usually painfully, a more rounded person develops. I was lucky enough to start listening to my elders and betters in civil engineering from a relatively young age.

Some modern graduates have not had this benefit and, consequently, seem to believe that they know it all when they enter the workplace. There is nothing more annoying than watching a new graduate trying to tell a grizzled old foreman the way a job should be done. As time passed, I became one of those more experienced people, and I enjoy passing on this hard earned knowledge to the next generation.

During a game of darts at college, I was asked to keep the score. My mental arithmetic skill was nil and I was made to realise that I had, up to then, done all my calculations on scraps of paper. To be sure of the correct answer, I usually did the calculation three times to confirm accuracy. This did not bode well for a career in civil engineering! However, somehow I managed to cover up this rather serious flaw and enjoyed my 45 years dealing with numbers (although I consumed reams of scrap paper). However, it did need many extra hours of calculations to keep up with my peers. Since retirement, I have heard of a medical condition, called Dyscalculia.

I have never aspired to be a leader of my profession, and I freely admit that I never achieved anything like the excellence my superiors expected of me. All I wanted was to do the best I could on a daily basis, and if it was possible, to enjoy each day

Eur Ing Richard Osborn Martin
TD Hon BA BSc DLC(Hons) CEng FICE

Cornwall 2016

Early years   1877 - 1945

My Grandfather, the Reverend Edward Osborn Martin MC MA, was born in 1877 in Ceylon. He was the eldest son, one of six children, and was a Methodist Missionary in India and Ceylon for many years. His father, my Great Grandfather Edward was also a Methodist Missionary and he handled all the finances of the Wesleyan Ministry in India, and his second child died in Trincomalee and was buried in the foundations of the Chapel that he was building, as there was no other consecrated ground available.

Grandfather joined the Army in the First World War, as a Chaplain, eventually rising to becoming the Senior Chaplain of the Yorkshire Brigade. Several Regimental wives had embroidered a lace Altar cloth with all the Regimental badges of the Brigade. Unfortunately when this was given to me on the way out to Riyadh, Cyprus Airways and Gulf Air managed to lose my suitcase. Grandfather won his Military Cross tending to the wounded in a church crypt during the Battle of Cambrai in 1917. The battle raged overhead, with the frontline moving either side of the church over three days. At the end, the British forces had regained the church and he lead the wounded to safety. When presented with his medal by King George V, he was asked what act of heroism had led to the award. My Grandfather replied, "For making tea, Sir, making tea".

My father was born in the Indian Hill Station of Naini Tal. European wives spent the summers in these cooler towns in the hills. Grandfather studied the many Indian religions, in order to understand how best to convert them to Methodism. This resulted in his writing a book called "The Gods of India", first published in 1913. This book is still used at Oxford University as it details some 360 major and minor deities, and I found pirated reprints for sale in Goa. He served as a Chaplain in Malta until he retired in 1922, moving to Dover before he died in 1937.

My father was sent to Kingswood School, Bath, as the son of a Methodist Minister. Father was awarded his Bachelor of Science by London University in 1931. Here he met my mother, who earned a BA in Geography and was briefly a geography teacher. For five years, he worked for contractors in England, on roads, cement works and housing projects. In 1936, he started up his own house building company in Dover, and I was born in one of his houses, in September 1939, just a few days after War broke out. At the start of the War, he was given Reserved Occupation status and worked for a year with Sir Alexander Gibb and Partners, providing defences for Southampton and the area. He worked on the Royal Ordnance factory at Risley, Warrington, before becoming the Emergency Works Officer for Southampton. In 1941/42, he worked on the construction of the Royal Ordnance Factory in Walsall for James Crosby & Sons. In 1942 he joined Wilson Lovatt & Sons and worked on many War requirements until 1946. These included Airfield runways at RAF Honily and RAF Church Broughton, a steel plant at Darlaston, extensions to factories in Wellington and Newtown, Montgomeryshire, and seven opencast Coal sites. He said that they were exciting times, working against the clock, with shortages of men and material, and under threat of demolition by enemy aircraft.

During this war service, my sister Jennifer was born in Walsall in 1941, and my sister Elizabeth was born in Nottingham in 1943. We lived in some grim houses, under wartime restrictions and shortages. Once, when I was being bathed in a bowl in front of a small coal fire, I slipped out of my Mother's soapy arms, into the grate. My upper left arm was burnt, and I carry the scar to this day. We had a lively Airedale dog, and one day it knocked over a tower of wooden bricks with its tail. I had just built this and showed my objection by pulling the offending tail. The dog's head came round quickly and snapped at me, damaging an eyebrow. In Nottingham, towards the end of the War, my mother ran a Guest House.

Palestine and Iraq   1946 - 1948

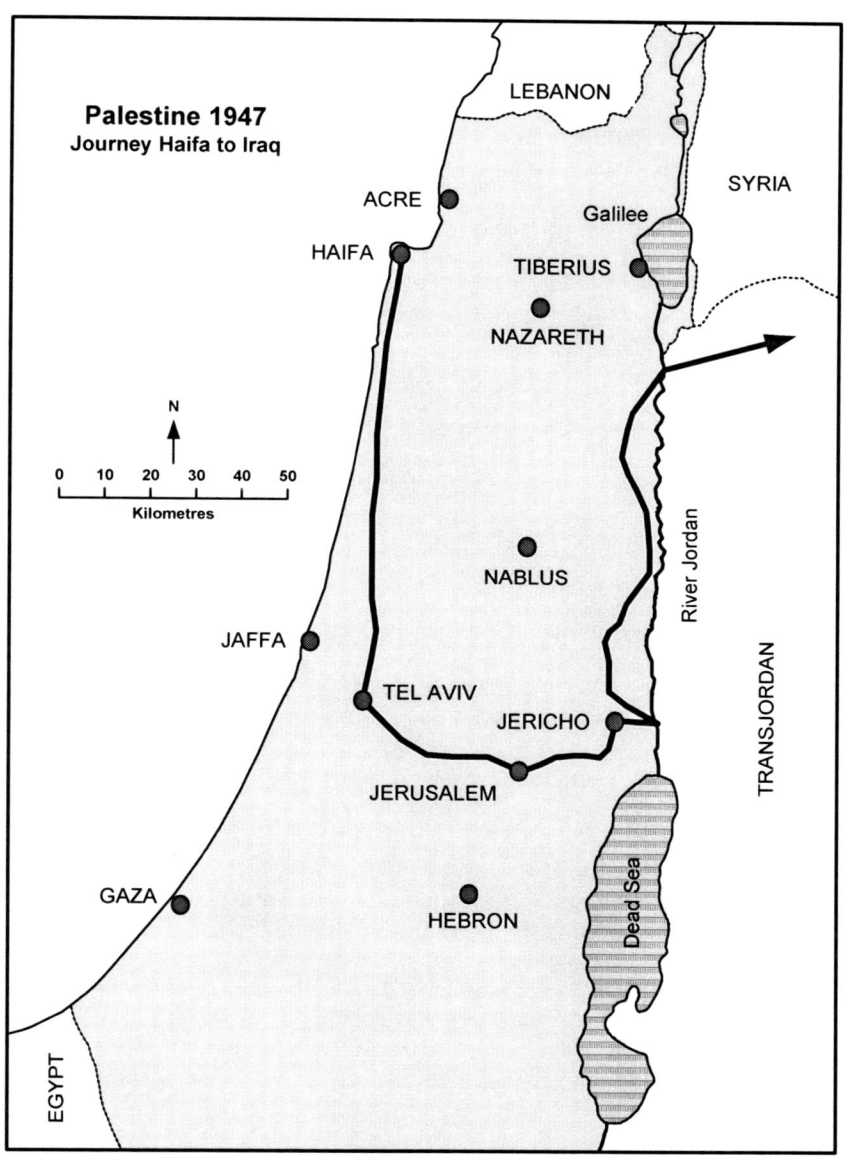

Escape from Palestine 1947

My earliest memories were of the short time we spent in Haifa, in the British run UN Protectorate of Palestine, during 1946/7.

At the end of the War, father had got a job with John Howard and Company, who were the earthworks sub-contractor to the American oil company building the pipeline. This pipeline was intended to deliver oil direct to a Mediterranean port, and thus avoiding the long sea trip down the Arabian Gulf and back up through the Suez Canal.

We lived in an apartment that my father's company rented for us, while he worked onsite on the Haifa – Kirkuk Oil Pipeline which replaced the pipeline blown up in 1939.

I attended a local school in Haifa, but I do remember that I got sent home to learn how to tie my shoe laces before being allowed back into class. I was fascinated by the Arab street scenes and my mother once had to rescue me from the front row of a cock fight in the market.

Living in the same building was Major Roy Farran, a highly decorated wartime SAS officer, whose memoirs are in his book, "The Winged Dagger". It was his job was to combat the Haganah, the Stern Gang and the Irgun; all were fanatical Jewish Independence movements. He had made many enemies amongst these Jewish freedom fighters. His brother, Rex, was visiting him and lived in the flat with him. One day Rex accepted a parcel containing a book bomb addressed to "R. Farran". Sadly, he was killed.

Escape from Palestine

In late 1947, before the State of Israel was declared in May 1948, the Jews prepared for the expected attacks from dispossessed Arabs. Normal life ceased and the company decided to close the Haifa offices for safety. Our family became refugees and fled. My two sisters, Jenny, 5 and Elizabeth, 3, were understandably terrified.

In a dilapidated saloon car, we drove to Jericho to cross the River Jordan over the Allenby Bridge. The journey from Haifa took us down the coast to Jaffa, now Tel Aviv, Jerusalem, and towards the Dead Sea at Jericho. We had hoped for a toilet break at The King David Hotel in Jerusalem but the doors were sealed with sandbags and the hotel was under military control. At Jericho, we found the Bailey Bridge had water running over the deck, and there was continuous military traffic coming into Palestine. The original bridge, which was built by General Allenby in 1918, had been blown up in 1946 and replaced by the Army. We had spent 12 hours just travelling about 100 miles because everyone else had the same idea.

Unable to cross the river, we had to find our way, at night along dirt roads northwards, up the west bank of the Jordan Valley. Eventually, we came to a bridge that we could use, at Bet Shean. We were nearly at the Sea of Galilee and turned East into the desert. Once across, the "road" took us up into the hills of Trans-Jordan. In the early hours of the morning, we found the road blocked by a lorry that had been hit by a rockfall and wrecked, breaking the driver's arm. My father and mother, and the driver pushed the lorry over the edge, into the ravine, and we drove on into Iraq. The route took us from Irbid, Mafraq, and on to Al Rutbah in Iraq, following the pipeline in places. Here, the pipeline route left the main Baghdad road and headed northeast to Kirkuk. The whole journey was some 500 miles, nearly all on desert roads with very few places to get water, or food.

My father's work site was at the H-3 oil pumping station in Iraq. At that time, the country was the Hashemite Kingdom of Iraq, ruled by King Faisal II, although Britain maintained airbases in the country. We stayed there until arrangements were made to get us back to UK. H-3 had a small dirt landing strip, which Saddam Hussein later incorporated into the main Airforce base at Al Habbaniyah with several satellite airstrips spread across the desert, and which featured often in both Gulf Wars. Scud missile batteries operated from this base aimed at Israel.

About 10 miles from the camp was a crossroad with no visible habitation for miles, except for a lonely red British Post box. We never saw a Postman, or anyone empty the box, so we decided to test the system. We put a postcard in the box, addressed to a relative in England. At the same time, we sent an identical card through the company mail system, which was collected by a small aircraft from the landing strip. The card in the Letter box arrived in England two days earlier than the company mail. It showed us that the Royal Mail was able to deliver in those days!

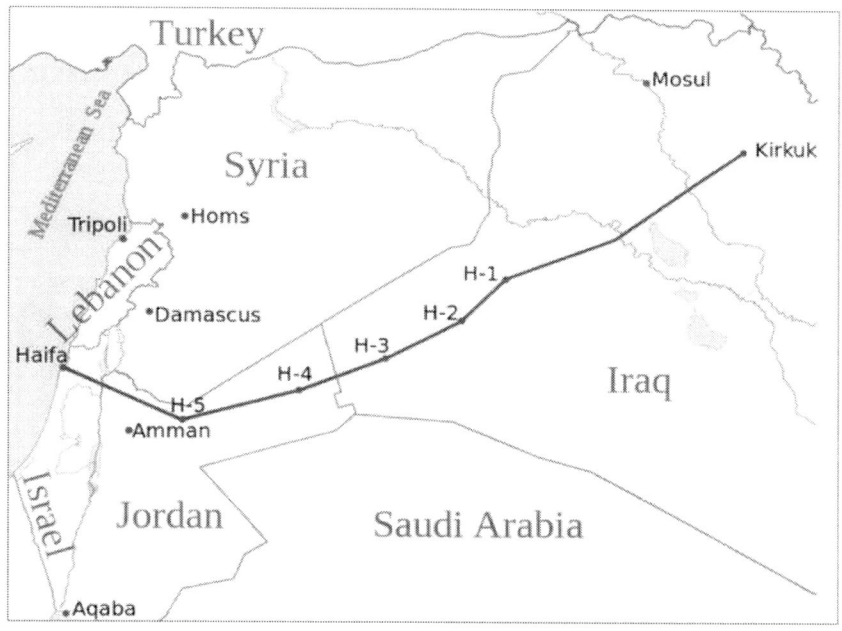

HAIFA – KIRKUK PIPELINE 1947

Before the family got to H-3, a local Bedouin tribe had arrived with the usual herd of camels and set up a large tented camp. In return for drinking water for the camels, the Sheikh invited the senior engineers to a feast. The senior American sat on the Sheikh's right hand and my father on his left. After gallons of Arabic tea,

13

laced with sugar and mint, the Sheikh called out "Jeeb Akle (Bring food)", and the servants brought in a steaming cauldron. The Sheikh's right arm was ceremoniously washed by a servant and he plunged it into the stew. He felt around for a few moments until he found what he was looking for. Holding this round object aloft, he turned to the American and wished him all the foresight, hindsight, and insight that Allah could grant, and popped the sheep's eye into the American's mouth. After another search, he found another tasty item and turned to my father. Knowing that only one eye had been found so far, my father feared the worst. The Sheikh wished my father the remarkable fertility of his prize camel, and hoped that he would have many children, before popping a kidney shaped object in his mouth. It would have been a great insult to the Sheikh to remove the food from one's mouth, so they both chewed and swallowed, with difficulty. I do not know if the American's career improved after this, but my father did not have any more children.

H-3 was some 435 km from Baghdad, and we drove east to the city for a short stay, while arranging the necessary papers for our return to England. We stayed in the company house, which was built round a courtyard and had Eastern toilets. I was given a bed made up by pushing a sofa against the wall in the courtyard area. In the night, and in total darkness, I tried to find the toilet. I did, by getting my foot trapped down the WC hole in the floor. My screams woke everyone.

We were also kept awake by the police whistles. All over Baghdad, pairs of policemen each patrolled an area at night. When they were out of sight of each other, they blew a whistle for the other to hear. If no reply was heard, it indicated a problem and needed an investigation. There was no street lighting. As the police were nervous, the whistles were blown almost continually.

Once all the necessary papers and tickets had been obtained, we drove to Damascus, in Syria, and onto Beirut in Lebanon. Here my mother, my two sisters and I boarded a small freighter for the sea voyage, via Port Said, to Marseilles. We crossed France by slow train to Calais. I was not well behaved on the train. Sitting opposite was a very attractive girl with her naval officer boyfriend. In those difficult times, he had managed to find a pair of silk stockings and she wore them with pride. I had been given an empty matchbox to play with, so I ran this up and down her shins. Mother never let me forget this incident as, I presume, she had to pay for the damage.

We eventually ended up in Nottinghamshire, where my parents had lived during the Second World War. When independent Israel was formed in 1948, the Haifa pumping station was closed down by the Israelis and parts was blown up, along with several lengths of the pipeline. Having had his contract terminated due to "enemy action", Father flew to Southern Rhodesia looking for work.

Rhodesia 1948 – 1950

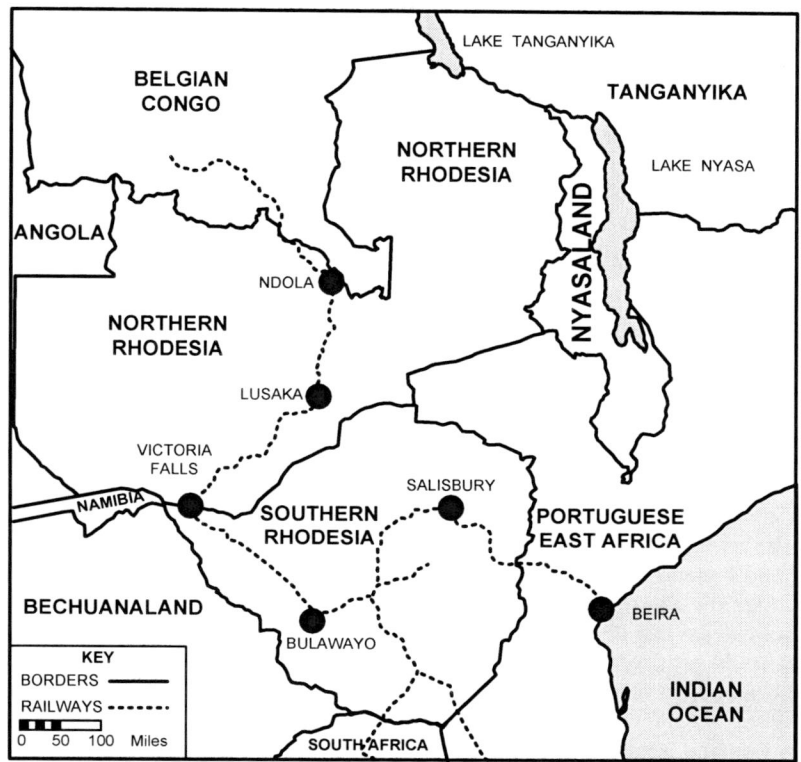

NORTHERN AND SOUTHERN RHODESIA
1948 - 50

In 1948, my father had found work with Costains, who gave him the job of Deputy Agent on the construction of silos for the Rhodesia Cement Company, at Colleen Bawn, some 100 miles southeast of Bulawayo. The rest of the family joined him by flying via Elizabethville, in the Congo. At that time, the Air Terminals at Heathrow were a series of ex-Army tents erected along the hedge by the A4 Bath Road.

I was sent to a boarding school just outside Bulawayo some 100 miles away. I was jealous of my sisters who stayed at home. Whitestones School gave me the choice of learning Afrikaans or French, and I found that there were only three of us in the whole school doing French. The teacher had a strong Afrikaans accent and I later found that this was partly why I was never understood in France. Our uniform consisted of a white shirt, open-toed sandals, an extremely short pair of khaki shorts, known as "broeks" in Afrikaans (the white Rhodesian national dress), and the obligatory sheath knife worn on the belt. What today's 'Elf & Safety' would make of the knife, I dread to think.

Mother set up home in a house built on the construction site and recruited staff from the local village. The locals had no Western skills and needed training. Our laundry was taken down to the local river and beaten into submission using rocks. All the whites were immaculate, after being dried by being spread over bushes. However this treatment was a little too rough for my mother's underwear. She had to make an emergency trip to Bulawayo to replace the shredded garments. Afterwards, she washed these precious items herself.

Typical African Laundry

In the playground, we had an ex- Rhodesian Airforce Hurricane fighter to climb on. Some spoilsport had removed the engine and the guns. We used to go into the bush and climb trees, as all boys do. I fell out of a tree and landed on a very large branch that had broken off an Acacia Thorn tree. The thorns were at least two inches long and I managed to get one to stick straight through my hand and out the other side. Our sheath knives were used to reduce the branch down to about five foot long and we carried this to the school sick-bay. More branch cutting was required before Sister could get my hand into a bowl of warm water. After a short while, she yanked the thorn out and bandaged me up.

In England, school boys used to play with conkers (nuts from the Horse Chestnut tree), trying to break the other boys conker by hitting it with your own. We had no conker trees in Rhodesia, so we used scorpions. Every boy had a matchbox in his pocket with his pet scorpion. To make them fight, two scorpions were put into a jam-jar and the survivor was the winner. One school visited us for a football match, and all the boys had Bushbaby pets tucked in their shirts. These are Galagos, about the size of a squirrel.

One school holiday, I was bored and started a little fire in the bush behind our house on the Cement Factory construction site. Outside of the rainy season, the grass and trees are tinder dry. The fire became a wild bush fire, threatening the construction site. Father stopped all work and every able bodied man was put to beating out the fire. Later, when it was discovered that I had started the blaze, my rather angry father came looking for me. To avoid the obvious result of him catching me, I ran off across the still red-hot scorched and blackened land. I was wearing sandals with a rubber sole. The soles melted off, and a red hot pebble flicked up and landed in my sandal, burning a large hole in my ankle. After a very severe lecture, father told me that I would remember my stupidity each time I saw my ankle. He was right.

We were all taught the correct way to search our bodies for ticks, and how to remove them. They are as much trouble in the grass plains of Africa, as leeches in jungles. Included in the teaching was the story of a new arrival who had found a tick on the back of his calf. After drinking enough "Dutch Courage", he removed it, using a cut throat razor, and left an inch deep crater. Later, in Mombasa, a Vet told me that he was researching the 2,000 different types of tick.

While I was at Whitestones, I caught Jaundice and was sent to the Isolation Hospital in Bulawayo, where I had a complete hospital wing to myself. A day or so later, the rest of the school moved into a separate wing, suffering from Chicken Pox. I finally caught Chicken Pox when I was 22. This was very unpleasant, and it made me wish that I had caught it as a child.

Costains, being well established at the Cement Works, had plant and men available for other small projects, should they become available. One such job was a bridge over a tributary of the River Limpopo, on a minor road between Rhodesia and Bechuanaland (now Botswana). The land on the southern bank was marshy, and unsuitable for a bridge abutment. Eastwards, in South Africa, was firmer ground. My father found the Survey Marker for the country boundary, and moved it a few hundred yards eastwards into South Africa. The bridge and approach roads were built on firm ground and, as far as I am aware, no one knows that the Border between the two countries had changed! Since then, all three countries have gained Independence from Colonial and Apartheid masters and have had enough problems without sorting out this minor adjustment of the map.

I stayed at Whitestones, for three years, while my father was promoted to Site Agent, when his boss became ill and left the country. In my second year at the school, Costains won a contract to provide a large number of housing units for Africans in Ndola, Northern Rhodesia, and the family moved. This move meant that I now had to travel from the north of Northern Rhodesia to the south of Southern Rhodesia for each school holiday, a two and a half day train journey each way. I was only 9 years old.

While boys had to find their own way to school, each term, the girls benefited from a member of the school staff travelling on the train with them. The boys travelled without supervision and parents gave sufficient money to buy the three meals a day from the Dining Car, but we very quickly realised that a profit could be made. The train stopped to take on water a few miles out of town and traders would come out of the bush to sell food and cigarettes to passengers. We bought fruit, bread, jams, sardines, corned beef, condensed milk, and tinned drinks. The trick was to prepare the loaf for the journey, by cutting off one end and hollowing it out. Into the hole went a mixture of jam, sardines, corned beef and anything else that was tasty. During the journey one just ate steadily down the pre-prepared loaf, marvelling at the variety of tastes. Cigarettes came in tins of 50, and one tin was enough for the journey, at 20 a day. As we all had our knives, al fresco dining in our compartments was the norm. The surplus cash came in useful for gambling and buying things from other boys.

Crossing a National Border naked

We also used to play "Truth, Dare or Promise". On one occasion, I found myself naked in the corridor, locked out of my compartment, while the girls were marched past me into the Dining Car by a shocked teacher. On another occasion, I was left standing on the platform at Livingston in Northern Rhodesia, naked, at three o'clock in the morning, watching the train move off to cross the Victoria Falls Bridge and the frontier between the two Rhodesias, carrying my passport and clothes. At the age of 9, I had walk towards the bridge, naked, and talk my way across the border and get through Customs and Immigration. The experience seemed to have done me no harm, and problems that I have met later in life never seemed quite as bad.

The Beyer-Garratt locomotives that hauled the trains in Africa were slow, old, wood burners. Every so often, the train would stop at the side of a pile of cut wood and refuel. Occasionally, herds of buck and other animals would try to race the train, or even try to cross the track in front of the cow-catcher on the front of the engine. If the Dining car was short of meat and a hunter onboard had his rifle, buck was shot and the train waited until the meat was safely on board.

Northern Rhodesia - Ndola

The Ndola African Housing Scheme involved building some 400 single room houses, with external toilets and cooking areas. It needed a large number of bricks, and there was no local supplier up to the job. The Clients' Architect's wife and my mother set up a company to manufacture the handmade clay bricks, called the Marell Brick Company. I spent time watching the clay being dug by hand from pits about 10 feet deep and the same in diameter. The clay was taken to the moulding area in wheel barrows and in headpans along very narrow paths that wound across a moonscape of craters, resembling the trenches of the First World War after a severe shelling. After puddling the clay, using feet, the wooden moulds were filled and turned out for the bricks to dry, before they were placed in crude kilns to bake. The surrounding forest provided the fuel for the kilns. My Mother "cracked the whip" through a very large African foreman. The Foreman sculpted a crude three foot long lion in clay and, after baking it, painted it vivid silver. This had to remain as the showpiece in our home until we left, or he would have been insulted. Looking back, there was probably something abnormal in the Client/Contractor relationship, which allowed wives to set up a company to supply the bricks, but it was necessary to enable the work to proceed. This work showed me just how much "Daughters of the Empire" could achieve in primitive conditions, and I salute my mother and all those stalwarts that have gone before her.

Northern Rhodesia and East Africa had problems with Termites and Soldier Ants. The Soldier Ants would decide to change location (usually because they had eaten everything in the area) and a column about six to eight inches wide, and up to four hundred yards long, would march off in a straight line and whatever was in the way, was eaten. They were omnivorous. There was no way to deflect a column, and I remember the night that a column came through our house. Bedding, books, carpets, clothes, shoes, were all eaten even though we set fire to kerosene puddles to try to divert them. There was a story about a man who fell in a ditch, and all that the ants left of him was the wedding ring on the skeleton and his belt buckle.

The termites were different. They just ate anything wooden, which was most of a house. They moved round a building under the plaster and paint, and hated light, so one was not aware of how much infestation one had, until a roof beam fell, or a door frame dropped out of the wall. In the wild, they lived in enormous colonies. The termites masticated the earth that they dug and this set rock hard when deposited. The termite hills were bulldozer-proof and extended as far down as they showed above ground. Drilling and blasting were sometimes the only way to remove them. Roads were often diverted round an area of termite hills. One particular type of termite seemed to be governed by the Earth's magnetic field and all the termite hills were elongated in a North-South line.

I had severe problems with my teeth while in Ndola, which required the removal of four wisdom teeth under general anaesthetic. The dentist was unable to provide this in his surgery and he made arrangements to use the single operating theatre in the local hospital. I was apprehensive about having my first general anaesthetic, and my mother was worried about the state of the hospital. The dentist collected us in his car and we drove to the hospital, only to be told that the theatre was in use for an emergency operation. We sat patiently in the waiting area, where there was nothing to read or otherwise distract anxious patients. After two hours, the dentist tried to amuse me by opening his scruffy old leather briefcase and tipping out a motley collection of dental tools. He carefully explained how each one was used, with theatrical hand movements. My mother fainted, but only after asking if any of his implements had ever been sterilised. The operation was successful.

Tanganyika   1950 - 1952

Eventually, the Ndola housing scheme was built and occupied, and father had to look for another job. I was safely tucked away in boarding school in Southern Rhodesia, so my sisters and parents set off in a Morris Eight to drive from Ndola to Dar es Salaam in Tanganyika.

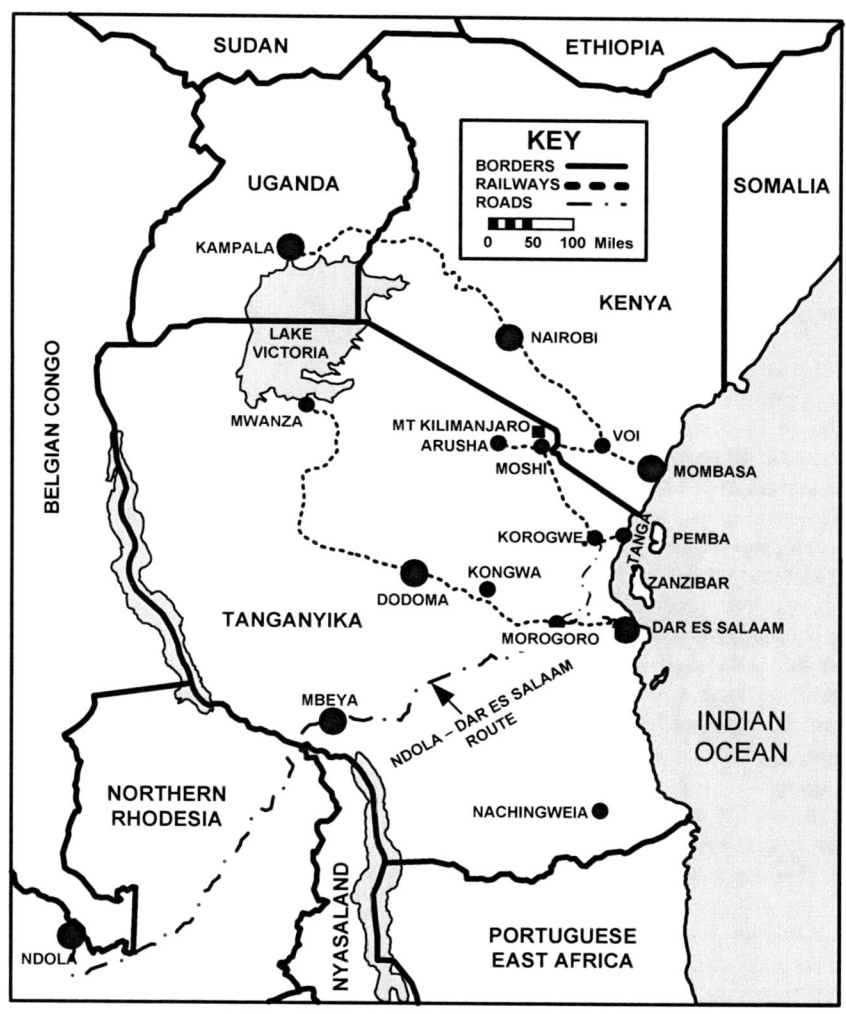

NORTHERN RHODESIA – TANGANYIKA - KENYA
1950 - 54

In 1950, this involved many overnight stays in thatched huts, with rats rustling in the roof, and a total distance of some 1,200 miles along some of the worst roads in the world. The first I knew of this was when the Headmaster asked me which of my

21

friends I would like to spend the next holiday with. A difficult choice, as I had just fallen out with all of them. Eventually, I was put on a small plane to Dar Es Salaam, via Nyasaland (now Malawi). At that time, small companies were running flights using ex-wartime pilots and aircraft. On arrival, the family met me and grabbed my case. When I got to our new home, I found that I had a case containing girl's clothes. Someone else had grabbed mine as they were identical. We eventually swapped the cases when a farmer had brought mine back to the capital from his farm some 400 miles upcountry.

At that time, the UK Labour Government was pouring money into the Colonies. The Tanganyika authorities were recruiting Europeans on a large scale and there just was not enough accommodation. For the first few months, we lived in a makuti (woven palm leaf) building, on an abandoned Army Camp. Dad had got a job with the Public Works Department, and was responsible for building and maintaining roads around the capital. Eventually we moved into purpose built European Government quarters at Oyster Bay, near the beach.

Kongwa School

I was sent off to a boarding school, at Kongwa, in the centre of Tanganyika. A few years before, the Labour Government in UK decided to set up the Groundnut Scheme in Tanganyika, growing the nuts on large scale farms and exporting the vegetable oil to Britain during Rationing. £67M was spent, but only 2,000 tons of oil production ever achieved. This equates to £33,500 per ton, or about 3 pence a nut!! This was due to a total mis-understanding by the Labour Government of the land, the climate, the weather, the local staff, the insects and wild life. It is worth looking up the Groundnut Scheme on Wikipedia for the full history of this typical Labour Party debacle. The scheme was abandoned, to the great relief of the British Taxpayer, and the school took over some of the abandoned buildings. The scheme had turned the area into a red dust-bowl, and there was no longer a working local water supply. Our school uniform was white shirt and shorts. Within a week, we were wearing pink, from the iron particles in the laterite soil. "Dust Devils" (mini-tornados) were the norm, which rose up to 100 feet. A sister scheme was at Nachingwea in southern Tanganyika. This was also abandoned, but only after the Minister was flown out to be shown his mistakes. Millions of pounds of broken-down plant and vehicles had been towed several miles into the bush and left to rot. The pilot was told not to fly the Minister over this very large plant graveyard.

Kongwa School was co-educational and we were to be educated in the social graces expected of "children of the Empire". One evening each week, the tables were removed from the Dining Hall and we were taught to dance. The Headmaster insisted that we learn not only the waltz and quickstep, but also the old favourites such as "The Gay Gordons" and "The Dashing White Sergeant". Music was provided by a wind-up gramophone, and frequently we danced to paraffin or hurricane lamps when the generator failed. For the benefit of the seemingly hundreds of Africans staring in through the open windows, all instruction was given in Swahili. Shouts of "Kulea" (to the left) and "Kushoto" (to the right), "Moja (One), Mbili (Two), Tatu (Three)" echoed, and I still have vivid memories of the windows framing a totally black night, filled with flashing white eyeballs and grinning white teeth. Often, the Africans tried to copy our steps outside, with much mirth and merriment. Needless to say, I have avoided dance floors ever since.

Shortly before my father moved to Nairobi, he built a road to the new Tanganyika Packers Company plant, where local cattle were turned into corned beef. The process was semi-automated, and the animal was pushed forward onto a weighing plate, where stun electrodes came down on the beast's head, and then the trap door opened. One day some new workers had trouble pushing a cow forward, so went round to the other end and pulled on the horns, with the expected result. A token number of cans were removed for the grieving families to bury. There was much debate about the proper quantity of cans, and which set was the correct one to hand to the grieving families for burial. The Christmas Pantomime that year was "Jack and the Beanstalk", and Jack's cow was turned into a crate of corned beef.

An engineer colleague of my father was working about 100 miles inland, on a road project. Once a week, he would send a Land Rover to collect essential spares, official and private mail, fresh food for the workers, and his private shopping list. Mother dealt with the private shopping list and remarked that every week he asked for several bottles of "California Syrup of Figs", a popular sugar based laxative. One week she could not find any to buy. When the vehicle arrived back at the road camp, the staff helped unload but searched in vain for the bottles. A mutinous murmuring started up. They had been used to a tablespoon each until the bottles were emptied, and now they would have to go without. The engineer pretended to look at the letter and list that had come back with the goods, and picked up a jar of Brylcream hair cream. "Memsahib says this is newer and better". They all had a tablespoonful and they never asked for "California Syrup of Figs" again. It saved the engineer a fortune, and the workforce had far less reason for constant trips to the "choo" (toilet). Productivity increased. This story was confirmation, to me, that the African worked better for a boss who could use a bit of "theatricals" and "white man's magic". I was able to use this knowledge to good effect in Nigeria and Kenya later.

One long weekend, we all went to Bagamoyo, the original capital of German East Africa, and the major Zanzibari slave trading port for two hundred years. There are a lot of old ruined Arabic buildings, including the dungeons where the slaves held, and evidence of the trading of salt and ivory. All the major explorers started from here, including Richard Francis Burton, John Hanning Speke, Henry Morton Stanley and James Augustus Grant. Dr Livingstone only passed through after his death, while in transit back to Zanzibar. I climbed a small coconut palm on the edge of the beach, and accidentally dislodged a coconut. An Askari (local policeman) tried to arrest me for theft, but I was released after some negotiations.

On another trip, we drove from Dar Es Salaam to Mwanza on Lake Victoria. We had cabins on a lake steamer for the circular trip round the lake. First we stopped at Bukoba to unload goods destined for Ruanda, then on to Kampala in Uganda. We returned via Kisumu and Musoma, to Mwanza. The weather was poor, and the waves were high enough to make the ship rock like a cradle. Many on board were very seasick. We ate fish caught by the ship's crew, and once the fish was so tough that I had to lend my sheath knife to the Captain, so that he could eat. We saw a lot of hippopotamus, and heard tales of how they would come ashore foraging, and wreck gardens.

We did have a lovely beach holiday at Pangani, a very small settlement just south of Tanga. We hired a beach hut, with several bedrooms, owned by a German couple. This couple had built the hut in 1930, when they were sent by the German Government to plant and harvest coconuts. To induce the locals to help with land clearance and planting of saplings, a bounty was paid. In this master plan, the German Government in Berlin had not included any inducement to allow the saplings to grow to full height and become productive, so each year the bonus was simply paid to re-plant the area all over again. In spite of many memos back to Germany over many years, nothing changed. The couple settled down to a simple but comfortable routine and the locals thanked them each year for the generous bounty. The couple did not even move when Germany lost the Second World War, and had only been to the country capital once in all that time. We used to wait on the beach for the fishermen in dugout canoes to return and buy fish out of the boat. I remember a pregnant shark giving up babies for sale, by a crude slicing open of the stomach.

Dar es Salaam is built round the edge of an inland lagoon, which gave sheltered mooring to shipping. The entrance to the lagoon is through the coral reef, and a narrow passage allows river water to flow to the sea from the lagoon. This narrow passage was tidal, and the Swimming Club was built on one side of the passage. Parents used to drop children off to swim, under a sort of so-called supervision, and collect them again at the end of a day at work or shopping. There was a diving pontoon moored in deep water, and we children swum out to it and sunbathed or dived, well away from parental control. One day a swimmer said that he had seen a six foot long Barracuda moving around under the pontoon. A great debate ensued, as to whether all of us should swim to shore together, because after all, the fish could not bite all of us, or to stay until dark and hope that parents organised a rescue. No one moved. Then I saw my mother waving from the shore. Eventually I dived in and swam as fast as I could. The Devil was snapping at my heels. About halfway, something scratched my ankle. I opened up the turbocharger, way past the red line, and aquaplaned on the froth that I was making. I was still swimming ten yards up the beach. I have never been so scared. I looked back, and saw a tree branch floating past, which must have been my "attacker". I had scratches on my chest from the speed that I arrived on the beach!

Prince of Wales School

In 1952, I had to transfer to secondary education, which was not available in Tanganyika. A place was found for me at The Prince of Wales School in Nairobi. The first year required me to travel by train from Dar Es Salaam to Nairobi. There was a rail track from Dar to Morogoro, then a bus ride to Korogwe in Tanganyika. From here there was a branch line to get across the border into Kenya and on to the main Mombasa to Nairobi line. It was a four day journey, once again without adult supervision.

From Morogoro, the bus we used had two parts. The front part used by senior boys had doors, windows, and soft seats for first class passengers, and the junior boys ended up in the third class open rear part without windows, and with wooden slat seats. The bus journey was about 100 miles and we had frequent stops for breakdowns and refreshments. At one stop, a senior boy spotted an enormous hornet nest up in a tree. He got all the senior boys into the bus, closed all the windows, and used a catapault to annoy the hornets. We juniors had nowhere to go, and all of us were severely stung. I was rescued by the seniors, who managed to remove many of the hornets before they stung me. Another lad ran towards home, some 150 miles away, and was eventually returned to school a week later.

Once we got to Korogwe, we boarded the local train, only for one boy to realize that he had left his watch in the station toilet. The train guard refused to stop the train, so we all pulled the communication cord. The guard ran back for the watch, only half a mile, and the driver tried to find out who had pulled the cord. All 100 of us each had a length of the chain, and it took a long time for him to list the names. We never heard another thing about that "crime". When this local train reached Mackinnon Road in Kenya, on the main Mombasa-Nairobi line that night, we had to wait to join the main line train. Our carriages were shunted and finally connected. During this midnight shunting, an Askari (policeman) caught some of us younger boys "assisting" the coupling of the carriages, at great risk to our lives, and he remonstrated with us. We pretended not to understand his Swahili, so he grabbed a senior boy and lectured him for several minutes without pause. Then he told the senior boy to translate all that he had said, to us. "Don't do it again" the senior boy said, and the Askari was rather put out by this shortened version. During the whole time, he had his rifle in his hand, safety off, and a round up the spout. We thought that the off-hand way the senior boy dismissed the whole matter would make the Askari incandescent with rage and shoot us all. Luckily, he cooled down and we steamed off to Nairobi. The branch line between Korogwe and Mackinnon Road no longer operates, following the break up of the East African Federation in 1975.

In my first year at Prince of Wales School, a new, young, Geography teacher gave the class work to do in the long summer holiday. We had to record all rainfall and hours of sunshine. I handed my work in, and he compared it to that of another boy who also lived in Dar es Salaam. There was no comparison, so he thought that one of us was lying. We were both beaten for not admitting which of us had lied, and for arguing with the teacher. Being new to East Africa, he was not aware that all mail was collected from a box at the Central Post Office in each town. As the addresses were very similar, he had assumed that we lived close together, because, unlike in Africa, UK addresses give detailed locations. I lived on the sea shore, and the clouds sailed over me, without ever dropping any rain. The other boy lived 50 miles inland, at the foot of some hills. As the clouds had to rise over this ridge, this caused them to rain every day, and he noted daily rainfall. Teachers can be wrong, and it took a long while for him to accept his mistake. He had had a practical lesson in Geography, which his University had failed to emphasize.

At Morogoro, there is a mountain which has an almost European climate at the top. When I was young, we made the journey to the top, for strawberries and cream teas at the lovely old colonial hotel. Later, when I returned to East Africa, I found out that the Chinese Army had set up a secret electronic establishment and had commandeered the hotel. The whole hill and surrounding area were off limits.

Kenya   1952 - 1954

In 1952, Dad found a job as County Engineer for Nairobi County Council, and we all moved to the NCC compound at Dagoretti Corner, a few miles outside Nairobi. This meant that, although still a boarder at Prince of Wales School, I could have infrequent weekends at home. On one trip, we took a picnic to the top of the Ngong Hills, taking bottles of water. After boiling the tea, we spent time exploring. When it was time to go, we discovered that the radiator hose had split on the car, so my father contrived an emergency bandage for the hose and we coasted downhill, without the engine, for as far as possible. Once down on the level, we drove carefully home, topping up the radiator from the spare water bottle. Our normal practice at home was to boil drinking water, and store it in the refrigerator in empty gin bottles, as they fitted neatly into the shelf in the door. Only after looking for the gin which was also kept chilled in the refrigerator, did my father realise that we had done the last few miles on neat gin!

Mau-Mau

While I was at school in Nairobi, the Mau Mau started to commit atrocities, and a State of Emergency was declared by the Colonial Governor. All male Europeans were drafted into the Kenya Police Reserve, and all male European school leavers joined the Kenya Regiment, the local Territorial Army equivalent, for active service. School prefects were given commissions, house prefects became NCOs, and the rest joined the ranks. Training started immediately, and pistols were issued to Police Reservists. Women bought their own handguns, and it was common to see holsters being worn by European women in the market, and in shops. As the problem escalated, British troops were sent to assist. Some units were diverted to Kenya while being returned from active duty in Korea and Malaya, to the anger of those troops who were looking forward to leave at the end of a National Service commitment.

Our school was "defended" by the Lancashire Fusiliers, full of "wet behind the ears" National Servicemen. There was a section of 10 men sleeping in each dormitory, and they had to parade each morning. We boys had fun sneaking into their room at night and playing with the Army kit. Some mornings, after the bugle sounded Reveille, a man would find that he had two bayonets on his belt and someone else was without a bayonet, others had lost ammunition, boot pairs would be split up so that sizes did not match (which made us laugh when they hobbled out on parade. The number of bullets in each magazine was varied, with some having an empty magazine. Eventually, they agreed that guarding a bunch of 12 year olds was too much for them, and they volunteered for the safer job of patrols in the bush, chasing actual terrorists.

My father never seemed to get the hang of his Police pistol, and was forever getting a round loaded but was unable to extract it without pulling the trigger! One Sunday afternoon, he pointed the gun out of the window and fired. He had earlier asked a worker to go into the casting yard to release the moulds on some concrete drainage pipes. The bullet seemed to bounce off almost every steel mould. The worker was seen trying to dodge the ricochet. One of the very few times that I have seen an African turn pure white with fear.

Mum used to complain that the milkman was siphoning off the cream before delivery. She could never get any firm evidence, and learned to put up with the watered down milk. However, when the Mau Mau moved into the forest near our home, the milk took on a pink tinge. The milkman had been forced to give them milk, and he had had to top up the bottles with water from the river which carried the red laterite soil away from the hillsides. This information was passed to the authorities but it was a long while before the milk returned to normal.

Father's organisation had a large amount of road building plant, and he was asked to provide plant to dig the mass grave after the Lari massacre. The Mau Mau (it was assumed) had killed some 300 men, women and children. Later investigation showed that, in addition to the Mau Mau element, there was also an inter-tribal reason for the large death toll. The plant was sent, under command of a British road foreman and the work done. But three days later, his wife asked my father to find the foreman, as he had not returned home. He was found dead drunk in a bush bar, trying to wash away the horrors he had seen. He was another victim of Post Traumatic Stress Disorder. He took a long time to recover from the sights he saw that time.

Another time Father had to visit a large Army camp to discuss some job that they wanted doing. He was invited to lunch in the Officers Mess, at the top end of the camp's main street. Some shooting was heard and officers rushed out to see what was happening. A prisoner had killed his guard, grabbed the sub-machine gun, and was running towards the assembled officers. An officer calmly walked to a nearby Land Rover, moved it a few yards so that the Bren gun could fire down the street, and killed the prisoner. Father did not feel like a dessert and coffee after that.

Nairobi County Council

During the school holidays, I went with my father when he visited jobs in outlying areas. This was good experience for a budding engineer, although I had no idea then of a future career. I saw dirt roads being smoothed out by dragging a freshly cut tree along behind a lorry, as there were not enough Graders in working order, and I learnt several other simple techniques. Much of the work was often done using hand tools by gangs of prisoners from the Goal. (Later on, in England, I tried to use labourers in the same way, when waiting for an item of plant would have delayed the work. My efforts were not appreciated.) The prisoners' cheerful camaraderie was a result of the three square meals a day they got while they were residents in "Hoteli King George". Most would have starved without the support of the state, and released prisoners would often snatch a handbag just outside the prison gate and yell "Police", to get arrested again. Government buildings, bridges, and road kerbs were built using the hand hewn granite blocks provided by these prisoners. Even the prison walls were built from these blocks. The UK has a large workforce available in prisons, but "Human Rights" prevents proper and effective use of this captive resource.

Road bridges had to be designed to allow full flood water to pass over the top of the deck "without let or hindrance", and not to be dislodged from the foundations by sixty foot trees tumbling in the water. This, when for 350 days of the year, the river bed is dry, appeared to be a massive over-design. But in flash floods, this over-design is essential. One such bridge, north of Thika, had five spans and the deck stood some 30 foot above the river bed, which was dry the whole time it was under construction. The 100 foot long deck was designed to have the minimum of obstructions to water flow. To stop vehicles going over the edge, a six inch square section concrete upstand, or kerb, was cast at the outer edges of the deck slab, with a drainage gap at intervals. A cheap, lightweight, handrail was bolted to the upstand. Cars were meant to use a diversionary track across the dry wadi bottom during the construction.

Local drivers did not respect road signs and diversions, and at night a car was usually on autopilot coming back from the club or pub. During construction at this bridge site, a temporary barrier was placed across the road to make cars use the diversion. This consisted of a railway line, threaded through holes cut in 40 gallon oil drums filled with earth, but this did not stop one man in a sports car. We found the shattered windscreen lying under the railway line, and we followed the muddy wheel marks across the bridge (the wheel marks were on top of the edge upstand), and across the shuttering ready for the final deck pour. We never found the car, and no one was ever reported hurt. An inspection of the damaged rail line showed that no paraffin red lamps had been deployed. The foreman, when challenged, said that he would not dream of putting them out, and he was keeping them safe to stop the local population from stealing them for use in the family huts! One could not fault his logic, especially as he would have had to pay for the losses. Later, I saw enormous trees somersaulting over the submerged bridge during a flash flood. The following day, the valley was almost dry and all that was necessary was to replace the handrails.

On another occasion, at a crossroad, a roundabout was needed because of the number of collisions. This junction was on the road where Josslyn Hay, Earl of Erroll, was found murdered in 1941. This murder became famous when the book and film "White Mischief" were published. Coming from Nairobi, directly across the junction, the road continued to a pub run by the State Hangman, who had some stories to tell. A roundabout was built, and letters of complaint came to the County Council and the Press. Wheel marks, going straight across the new roundabout, were too numerous to count, mostly made overnight. So, to make drivers go round, Dad filled the centre with large granite boulders, which limited the accidents to night time only, after pub closing time. Complaints kept coming in, essentially saying that the radius of the circle was too tight to drive round at what the locals considered a reasonable speed, so he arranged to prove to the complainers that a long vehicle could go round without crossing any kerb. If he succeeded, it was agreed the complaints would be withdrawn. The demonstration vehicle chosen was a 30 foot long grader. Due to the front and rear axle steering, the demonstration was a success and the roundabout stayed unchanged. It takes an engineer to out-think a Kenyan!

The County Council would sometimes ask Dad to collect debts from the more influential white residents who were tardy with paying Rates. He took me to visit

Michaela and Armand Dennis, who were well known Big Game experts, and who kept two caged Leopards and other Big Cats on the farm. The Denniss decided to "discuss" the debt while leaning on the Leopard cage. One Leopard took exception to this and kept charging at my father and bouncing off the mesh wall. I could see that, at each impact, the opposite side of the cage lifted clear of the ground and the other cat could easily get loose. It did bring the discussion to a rather early end, which I suspect was the intention, and no rent was collected on that day.

Whilst at the Prince of Wales School, I shared a dormitory with a boy called Benetti. He was the son of an Italian farmer, who was well-known as a pre-War mountaineer. During the Second World War, enemy aliens in Kenya were incarcerated in a Prisoner of War camp. In 1943, Felice Benuzzi, Benetti Senior, and some friends got bored sitting in the camp, so they escaped and climbed Mount Kenya. They put up the Italian flag before returning to the camp for the rest of the War. The story of this adventure is told by Benuzzi in his book "No Picnic on Mount Kenya". Another boy was the son of a well-known "White Hunter", who had lost two fingers on one hand. He told clients, who were most impressed, that he had had to force his hand into the mouth of a lion to save his gun bearer from certain death. His son let slip that, during a drunken party, the generator had stopped working and his father had put his fingers in the way of the radiator fan while trying to restart it.

Our school's main rival, was the Duke of York School. Their school cricket ground was named The Nye, after a fast bowler called Jack Nye, who played County Cricket for Sussex before and just after the War. Jack, a Sussex lad, had spent many years in Australia before playing in England. He came to Kenya in 1948, to help build the Mombasa – Nairobi road while keeping elephants at bay in Tsavo National Park by using army Thunderflashes. He became my father's Road Superintendent.

Jack taught cricket to sometimes unwilling boys in Hove before the War. When he received his MBE for services to Kenya, it was presented by the High Commissioner who whispered that he had been one of those unruly boys, who had been "threatened with a good thrashing". Jack met Jomo Kenyatta a number of times and bonded with him when he discovered that Jomo had worked on a Sussex farm in his youth. In 1968, Kenyatta, now the President of Kenya, opened the newly re-built Nairobi – Mombasa Road and a choir sang praises to "Bwana Kiko". Jack was so named because he smoked a pipe. Kiko is Swahili for pipe. BBC2 made a film of this for The Central Office of Information called "The Road that Jack Built".

The County Finance Manager spent over a year selecting and ordering his new car from UK. Daily discussions with everyone, about the choice of make, model, and colour, made all the rest of the staff heartily sick of the whole subject. Eventually the order was placed and the whole delivery sequence was broadcast to the whole world by the proud "soon to be" owner. The car arrived and for a week, seats were offered for suitably selected people to have short rides. Then there was a total silence from the owner, and no car was seen. Had it been stolen? Had it broken down? All was revealed when my mother ferried a bunch of boys to the swimming pool, and the owner's son pointed to a very new white scar on a large tree at the edge of the road, saying proudly "My dad made that mark".

New plant and vehicles for the County Council were ordered through the UK Government and shipped to Mombasa, for rail freight to Nairobi. I was in my father's office when it was reported that a brand new pick-up truck had been wrecked on the way from the station goods yard to the Council Workshop. Apparently, there was no brake fluid, as this had been removed for shipping. No one had thought it necessary to check before handing the keys to a driver! Later, a pair of new small dumpers went missing between Mombasa and Nairobi, but more of this later.

Nairobi had, at that time, a very good Public Transport service. All the bus drivers were Nubians, from Southern Sudan, and they lived in their own separate village, miles away in the hills near our house at Dagoretti. However, soil erosion had left very deep and steep valleys across the whole area. Eucalyptus trees were introduced to stop further erosion, and only steep and narrow paths crossed the area, threading through these very tall trees. Access to the village was only achieved, with difficulty, on foot. One year, the Nubians had a double celebration, to mark a number of years service for the bus company, and the introduction of the first double-decker bus. They invited European dignitaries and senior managers of the Company. Father's Workshop Manager had helped repair some engines in the past and he was invited, so we had a full description of the event. The "walk in" was an hour from a road, and very tiring in the damp early evening heat. In the darkness, a large bonfire could be seen at the top of the climb, through the trees. The trees were Australian (Eucalyptus) Blue gum trees, and these burnt readily, so the Europeans wondered just how a fire crew could even reach the site, let alone get any water onto a fire. Just behind, the bonfire was the new double-decker, the first to arrive in Nairobi, ready to be "christened" at the ceremony. How it got there was a complete mystery, as there were no known roads or tracks. A lot of "Pombe", illicitly brewed beer, was drunk by all that night. The new bus was working on its route early the next morning! Senior managers held a formal inquiry, but no Nubian said a word, and the secret was kept of how the bus had got to and from the party.

I used to wander into the Plant Workshop, not far from my house, and watch the mechanics repair all sorts of plant. An ex-Army Scammell tank transporter had been purchased as scrap. The Plant Manager thought that he could bring it back into service, to carry tracked plant around the County. After a lot of work, the engine was put back into the chassis and an attempt to start it was made. With a diesel, this involved putting some fuel down the vertical air intake pipe and throwing a lighted rag after it. There was an almighty bang and the engine spun. Unfortunately, it spun in the opposite rotation to the designed direction. This caused the very heavy flywheel to fly off, through the granite block wall and a further 200 yards through the casting yard, full of freshly made drainage pipes. "Ah well, back to the drawing board!" Eventually the Scammell did sterling work for a very small purchase price.

During the Mau Mau time, our school Boy Scout troop had had to stop camping out in the forest. An earlier Scout camp was a disaster for me. I had to share a very small tent with a very fat Greek boy called Krusosaniatakis. We were given our rations and told to store them ready to cook in the evening, after games. We slung a rope over a branch and hauled the bag of goodies clear of the ground, and went off to join the others. On our return, I got the fire going, while "Kruso" searched in vain for the food. We eventually found a well chewed bit of rope, but no food, and assumed that the Hyenas had been visiting. This scared us, so we scuttled into the three foot high tent and tried to sleep through the hunger pangs. Then the howling started. "Kruso" stood upright in the tent, and then fled to the latrines, shedding blankets and tent along the way. I was left without cover, with only a single blanket and a groundsheet, trying not to think of Hyenas. I never forgave "Kruso", and I have never forgotten his name.

One evening, during the Mau Mau Emergency, my father invited his boss, the Chairman of the County Council, to dinner. This put my Mother into a spin, deciding what to serve, based on what could be least messed up by the Cook/Houseboy. It also put me into a spin, as our guest was Sir Godfrey Rhodes, Kenya's Chief Scout, and grandson of the famous Cecil Rhodes. I had to promise to be on my very best behaviour, and not to mention my membership of the Boy Scout movement in case I started to monopolise the conversation. Mother organised a five course meal which the cook could manage. She was worried that it was on a Saturday night, and the cook usually got drunk on Saturdays! We had had many Sundays ruined because my Father had to trawl the Police stations looking for the cook. Due to the Emergency, the authorities assumed that anyone picked up by the police was automatically a Mau Mau terrorist, unless rescued by a European.

The day of the big meal arrived and we were all pressed into service to make the house ready. The guest arrived and was offered a drink while waiting for the cook to announce that the meal was ready to be served. A slight difficulty was that the dining room door to the kitchen was always kept locked to stop terrorists bursting in from kitchen, after they had entered via the back door. Every time cook had to bring things in from the kitchen, Mother would operate the door key, while Father pointed his pistol at the door in case of attack. Soup was served, without a hitch, and the fish course arrived without the white sauce. Mother's face was a picture but she said nothing. The main course of roast beef and three vegetables was perfect. The steamed apple pudding was next, and cook was beginning to lose control. Custard was expected, and he had not managed to start making it in time. But, an idea crossed his mind, and he saved the situation. The unused white sauce from the fish course was turned into a lovely yellow custard by adding mustard powder!!! After tasting the mustard-custard, Mother had to be prevented from grabbing the pistol and attacking the cook.

One of my school Prefects was Roger Whittaker, and he was the last prefect to give me "six of the best". His parents owned a grocery store called "Slater and Whittaker" out at Westlands, a suburb of Nairobi. One of my favourite songs of his is "The Good Old EAR&H", which commemorates the East African Railways and Harbours trains that ran from the coast at Mombasa to Kisumu on Lake Victoria and on into Uganda. He really captures the sounds and spirit of the railway.

Another Prefect was Mervyn Cowie. He was the son of the man who started the whole idea of National Game Parks in East Africa, and which formally became fact in 1946. Mervyn, I believe from reading the School Association stories on the Internet, returned to the school to teach. He kept discipline in the normal way. Although deadly accurate with the wooden backed blackboard rubber, he also carried a starting pistol. If a boy was soundly asleep in class, a shot from this gun, fired alongside the ear, made everyone stay alert for a long period. The offender was deaf for a week.

At school we had a new young English Teacher, who also read the News at the local radio station, which was only half a mile from school. We all had home made crystal sets and listened to him, so that we could tease him if he made any mistakes with local names and things. The format was for him to first introduce the "BBC World News", then the "Home News from Great Britain": eventually this was followed by his reading of the "Local News". Local announcements followed, and some music filled in the remaining time before the end of the thirty minute slot. One evening, we heard on the Local News that a European local Councillor had been found dead. The announcements detailed his funeral arrangements. This man was not too popular, and was well known for playing away from home. The teacher had had to choose his "fill-in" music days ahead of the night. This night, we were given the calypso, "He's stone cold dead in de market place. Wife, she hit him on de head with a frying pan". The next day the teacher lost his extra job. He learnt that it always pays to check the music before proceeding.

In 1952, the newly wed Princess Elizabeth and Prince Phillip flew to Kenya for the honeymoon at the famous Treetops Hotel at Nyeri. This hotel was built high in the trees so that elephants could pass underneath on the way to the waterhole. All schools sent contingents to line the route from the airport to Government House, and a great fuss was made of the Royal Visitors by the loyal Colonial subjects. The Kings African Rifles were on parade near where our contingent of school kids sat. The boots shone in the sun, and the khaki uniforms could not have been more heavily starched or ironed. As usual, there was dust in the air; and an officer with a yellow duster would periodically work his way through the ranks wiping dust off boot caps. It was then that I noticed that the Africans were not wearing underpants and that the British Army shorts were a little too short, and far too wide, for the well-endowed Africans. The boot polishing officer seemed to notice this at the same time, and there was frantic activity to tuck away spare flesh in case it offended the young Princess.

After I left to go to school in England, and Kenya was heading for Independence, Jomo Kenyatta was released from prison (as Mau Mau leader) and placed under more lenient house arrest at Fort Hall, some 70 miles north of Nairobi. As a concession, the Colonial Government allocated him a vehicle. He demanded that the road be surfaced and his wish was granted (but mainly so that Colonial officials could visit him in comfort). My father oversaw the job, with Jack Nye doing the work. Later, Jomo was given a second car, and he said that, because of this, the road should be made into a dual-carriageway. This was at a time when no road outside Nairobi was dualled. One cannot blame him for trying, but the road stayed single carriageway.

School in England   1954 - 1956

After just five terms at the Prince of Wales School, my Great Uncle Will (Sir George Martin, ex-Lord Mayor of Leeds) instructed his Trust Fund to release money for me to be educated in England. Uncle Will was childless and all 16 nephews and nieces received money from this fund. Father duly arranged for me to attend the school that he, his brother Harold, and his father Edward had attended. This was Kingswood School, Bath, founded by John Wesley. Many generations and branches of our family have Methodist Ministers or missionaries. However, there is one Reverend on the Family Tree carefully separated out as "Rev (CofE)", so we did have a "black sheep" in the family.

To get to school, I had to fly to England by myself. Father had arranged for family and friends in England to meet me and get me to the school, and get me kitted out. A seat was booked on the Hunting-Clan Airline, later part of Airwork Ltd. This was an ex-wartime Dakota DC3 aircraft, which was not licensed for instrument flying. This meant that we only flew in daylight, and followed known watercourses, railways, and roads. I arrived at the airport, with a large amount of necessary textbooks which well exceeded the weight allowance. The hostess took pity on me and, as she also acted as check-in girl, said that the 15kg of books was normal reading matter for a 3 day flight. I was also, in the African heat, wearing many layers of clothes and a heavy raincoat to save exceeding the weight limit!

We flew from Nairobi, along the railway, to Entebbe in Uganda, where we refuelled and then we followed the Nile to Juba in Sudan, where we landed for lunch. After refuelling again, we reached Wadi Halfa, in Egypt, for our first overnight halt. We were bussed to a charming 1920s colonial style hotel, with a bund at the end of the garden to keep the River Nile at bay, and to keep the crocodiles out of the Dining Room. The Airline insisted that the crew dressed for Dinner, so this meant a long evening gown for the hostess and black tie for the pilots. Sadly, the old Wadi Halfa airfield is no more. The old town and the hotel were submerged under Lake Nasser, formed by the Aswan Dam in 1970. A new town was built on high ground to the east. The next day, we flew via Cairo to Mersa Matruh, some 150 miles west of Alexandria and on the Mediterranean coast. After refuelling, we gained height so as to be able to see Malta and headed there. We spent the night at the Phoenicia Hotel, in Valletta. This grand five star hotel was built in the colonial style in the 1930s and the standards were excellent. Many years later, the staff asked if I had visited the hotel before. I, to their amusement, replied that this was my second visit in 50 years. The final day flying took in Nice and Paris Le Bourget, before landing at Blackbushe Airport, near Camberley. This was used during the War and developed into the main diversion airport for Heathrow, as it had very little problem with fog, compared to Heathrow. Later, in the early 1960s, the Government decided that Gatwick Airport was to be built and Blackbushe was broken up and sold off.

I was collected from the flight by Stanley Comben, an old friend and colleague of my father's. That evening, I discovered that I had lost my wallet and passport. Mr Comben arranged the loan of a bicycle, and his son and I cycled back to Blackbushe. Entering the airfield by the farm gate, we found the DC3, and we opened the door and searched the aircraft. I found the wallet and passport stuffed down a seat and felt a great sigh of relief. Nowadays, looking for lost property on an unattended aircraft, on a security conscious airport, would probably not be possible.

At Kingswood, I was put in the Junior House and a top floor dormitory, with views over the whole of the City of Bath. The rest of the boys had been used to the English curriculum and I struggled to catch up after the African school work. After a year, I was promoted to Upper House, so called because it was the top dormitory floor of three in the main building, and was on the fourth floor. There was a very short time between the wake up bell and the breakfast bell. One ran down many flights of stairs, at the same time trying to fit a tie over a separate stiffened loose collar with studs, and shrug into a sports coat. Although it was pell-mell down the stairs, woe betide you if you did not walk slowly, quietly, and fully dressed and with hair properly combed, into the Dining Room.

I enjoyed the woodwork shop, and was, regrettably, too junior to join the Printing Club. I played Rugby, as a hooker, and once had to play Hockey for my House, because all the other substitutes were ill that day.

Our sports fields were on the top of Lansdown Hill. This exposed area regularly had winds straight from the Russian Steppes, or so we thought, and was the coldest place I have ever endured after a childhood in sunny Africa. The top of the hill was the scene of a Civil War battle in 1643, and was commemorated by a monument erected in 1720 by Sir Beville Grenville. We had to know everything about the construction of the monument, and the wording on the plaques, as it was an integral part of the school punishment system. As a punishment, you were told to run the four miles to the monument and, for instance, count the railings on the south side. If you knew the correct answer, you were able to disappear for a while and then return looking suitably muddy, but not having wasted too much effort. The winter runs in the snow, were the worst, as the monument is set in woodland some distance from the road.

The monument punishment was not often offered to me. As I was a descendant of one of the school's most successful Headmasters (TG Osborn), I would be taken into the School Hall and stood in front of his full length portrait and asked why I was letting him, his family, the school, the Nation, and above all, myself down by misbehaving. In self-defence, I developed a way of defending myself using arguments which gave genuine reasons for not thinking exactly like the strict Methodist that my ancestor was. After leaving Kingswood, Thomas George ("TG") Osborn, went on to found a Methodist Public School called Rydal Mount in 1885. In 1999, Rydal merged with a girls Methodist school nearby, founded by Thomas Paine in 1880, and the new school is now known as Rydal-Penrhos School.

Kingswood had a tradition of not having a fixed half-term break each term. Instead, on two randomly selected fine weather days each term, the boys were given a "Whole Holiday". While we were in Chapel, straight after breakfast, the kitchens prepared packed lunches. In Chapel, the announcement of the holiday was made and we collected the packed lunch and a half a crown coin. We had to say where we hoped to go to, and with whom, and promise to be back by 6pm. We could walk, cycle, take public transport, or beg lifts. A particular friend wanted to play every church organ he could gain access to, and we toured Somerset to this end. While he was playing, I read tombstone inscriptions. This finally took us to Wells Cathedral, where the friend was arrested for using the Bishop's Crosier to break into the organ loft. On another famous occasion, the Whole Holiday coincided with a major break-out from a Borstal establishment. The Police were not amused, with an additional 500 boys on the loose!!

The Music Master had a room high up in the tower of the main building. A, bachelor, he spent his spare time either playing jazz on the chapel organ, or consuming quantities of gin. We boys knew this, as we were asked periodically to carry a large wicker laundry basket, full of empty gin bottles, down the tower stairs. Another master had taught Emperor Haile Selassie's children and strode through the school corridors as if he were still in the Palace.

The school was at the top of Lansdown Hill in Bath, and we used to freewheel our cycles down the very steep hill and leave our bikes near the police station. We returned by bus and the police had to arrange with the school to have the bikes collected.

Various parts of the City were out of bounds, and the limits were strictly enforced. A friend was found with a used and broken match in his pocket in school. He was accused of a whole list of offences. Because of the match, he had been smoking, but to avoid the staff, he had gone into town to smoke. To avoid detection he had not gone in uniform, or worn his school cap, which meant that he had skulked in out of bound streets, and therefore visited a cinema, with a girl, and, worst of all, he had not even requested, or been given permission to leave school. The logic, based on a dead match, was all on the teacher's side. It showed us that one's superiors always had the upper hand, and that there was never any justice for inferiors. Later I realized that this was just like real life.

My father offered me a flight back to Nairobi for the Easter Holidays in 1954. As a teenager interested in all things mechanical, I asked if I could fly in the new wonder aeroplane, the jet propelled De Havilland DC 6 Comet, and my wish was granted. I was duly booked on the joint BOAC/South African Airways flight to Johannesburg leaving on 15th April. Unfortunately, on 8th April, SAA Comet Flight 201 exploded in mid-air after leaving Rome, the second to do so in three months, and BOAC grounded all Comets. The Civil Aviation Authority withdrew the Airworthiness Certificate, pending investigations into the cause. This was the aircraft that I would have used on its next round trip out of London. BOAC provided an old piston driven De Havilland DC-4 Argonaut as a replacement. This was, I felt, a let down but the old Argonaut did, at least, have a proven safety record.

During the holiday in Kenya, Dad let me go out with his engineers on site visits. On one trip, we were a long distance from home, late in the afternoon, and were returning. The driver of the pick-up was explaining to me that on dirt roads, because of the natural amplitude of the suspension, it was best to reach sufficient speed so that the vehicle only hit every third corrugation. Once this optimum speed, about 40 mph, had been found, the ride was much more comfortable and you hoped that nothing would prevent you from continuing all the way at the same speed. In the distance was a giraffe, in the middle of the road, eating the top of a tree. We sounded the horn, flashed the lights, leant out and banged on the bodywork. All this had no effect, and the giraffe continued to munch away. We got closer and slowed right down. There was still no movement from the animal. We stopped feet away and made as much noise as we could. The head turned and a look of distain was sent in our direction, but munching continued. After twenty minutes, our driver got impatient and decided to move the vehicle forward and nudge the legs. This was a big mistake. The heat from the radiator made the animal flinch. A hoof kicked a hole in the radiator, and the giraffe slowly walked away. We were stranded, with darkness approaching. Luckily another motorist arrived and we got a tow home.

On the flight back from Kenya to school, the flight landed in Cyprus. The Emergency was in full swing there and we British passengers had to sit in a special transit waiting room while the aircraft was refuelled. The walls were filled with photographs of British "atrocities" and posters supporting EOKA. The Greek security guards took great delight in refusing access to toilets, while explaining the photographs in great detail.

My first Christmas at school in England was spent with Aunt Neenie. Irene Martin was the youngest sister of my grandfather. She was a formidable lady, who wore metal callipers to support the leg wasted by childhood Polio. A spinster, she taught the piano to generations of children in Bradford. She lived in a grand house in Mornington Villas, Manningham Lane. These fine buildings are now in an area completely occupied by immigrants and are all broken up into bed-sits.

I was introduced to Leeds and Bradford cousins and to Uncle Will (Sir George Martin). He had started work in a Woollen Mill at 16, and could not, then, spell his name correctly. Uncle Will finished up owning the Mill and two others. The cousins introduced me to something I had never seen, - snow. Although I had spent five years in England during the War, I had no memories of snow. It was something that I had only read about in the Victorian novels, and seen on Christmas cards. I took to tobogganing, like a duck to water. My father had arranged for me to receive a bicycle for my Christmas present and on Boxing Day I rode for hours up and down the hills of Bradford. I came home happy and very tired and I seemed to have pulled a muscle in my stomach. Later that evening, the pain got a lot worse. Eventually Aunty Neenie called a cousin, Alan Ambery Smith, a gynaecologist, who diagnosed possible peritonitis and got me rushed to the Bradford Royal Infirmary. Apparently, I had used so much effort pedalling that my insides had got dislodged, and my appendix was eventually found on the wrong side of my stomach, rubbed raw. I came round from the operation to discover that I had contracted Whooping Cough. The coughing played havoc with the stitches and it took longer than usual for the wound to heal. Eventually I was discharged and I went out tobogganing with the cousins, but the operation scar threatened to open again.

Aunt Neenie took me to the cinema as a treat. She had an old Hillman car and always travelled with her very protective Jack Russell dog. Her car's number plate was "MUM 36", and she had police permission to park anywhere in Bradford and Leeds. This was long before Disabled Badges were formally issued. She parked on the pavement in an alleyway behind the cinema and we went in. About an hour later a notice flashed up on the screen, "Will the owner of MUM 36 come to the Manager's office". Aunt Neenie became very embarrassed and refused to move. The notices got more insistent. Still she refused to move. The film was stopped and the Manager came on stage to repeat the request. When there was no response and the film restarted, Aunty Neenie said that we should leave. Outside, her car was surrounded by police. Her Jack Russell dog had defied all attempts by the police to move the car away from a fire escape door, where ambulance men were trying to get a stretchered patient to hospital. The police sergeant offered £25 for the dog, which was a lot of money in those days.

On the subject of number plates, it was the custom for the Lord Mayor's car of most cities at the time, to have a number "1" after the letters which, in those days, designated the town. Leeds City Council decided to retire "MUF 1" and Uncle Will, he felt correctly, refused to allow his new official car to have a number plate reading "MUG 1".

Another family based holiday was taken in Dover. My cousin Peter from Bristol and I went to stay with Nan-Nan, my paternal Grandmother, in her seafront flat. She had a first floor apartment in the centre of the harbour, and had the only fully glazed balcony on a very long sweep of terraced houses. This stood out in all the postcards of the town. The White Cliffs Hotel was next door, and is now the Best Western Churchill Hotel. One rainy afternoon we decided that we would not play on the shingle beach in front of the flat where Nan-Nan could watch over us. We asked permission to go to the cinema. "No. The cinema is a waste of time. The last film I saw was the film of the Coronation, and there was no plot or story". We did talk to the man who lived in the flat above, who was, to us, a very brave and adventurous person. Commander Parris RN once had the job of cleaning Nelson's column, and had climbed to the top.

Some weekends at Kingswood, I would cycle to Hanham, in Bristol, and have a Sunday tea with my cousin Peter and his parents, Claire and Harold. The elder cousin, Michael, was an officer in the Merchant Navy, and I did not meet him until I was working in London.

My other school holidays, while at Kingswood, were spent in Liss, Hampshire. The Anstey family had a large, old, Queen Anne house. Mike Anstey was the Sports Master at Byculla School, a nearby all girls boarding school. During term time some 20 girls lived in his house, and he had overseas students staying in these dormitories during the holidays. Mike had been confirmed dead during the Dunkirk retreat, when he was in the Army. The telegram announcing his death arrived only hours before he jumped off a hospital train and went straight home to his wife. Mike was seen as the PE teacher in the film called "The Happiest Days of Your Life", which was filmed at Byculla School in 1950, with Alistair Sim, Margaret Rutherford and Joyce Grenfell.

Mrs Anstey ran the Nursery School for the Army at Longmoor Camp at Borden, which was then the training school for military railway staff. The London - Portsmouth line ran through the camp in those days. I remember that two officers there were a Major Knight and a Captain Day. When Nikita Khrushchev, the communist leader, visited Britain, he arrived on a Russian Cruiser in Portsmouth. Commander "Buster" Crabb, a leading Navy diver, was thought to have dived to explore this Soviet heavy cruiser when he disappeared in unexplained circumstances. Also staying at the Anstey's was a Jewish boy of Russian extraction. We visited the Army Railway unit, to watch the Khrushchev train go through to London. We only realised how much some Russians hated the man, when the boy started shouting at the train and asking for a machine gun.

One of the other young guests in Liss was a Princess Mujane Attapur, of Iran. She was at school in England and unable to get to Iran during holidays, and I think that she never did return to her country. We played games with the Anstey's and one evening, during a session of "Hide and Seek", I hid in the loft. The ceiling below me collapsed, and I landed on the owner's bed below.

Just after I started school in England, Princess Margaret visited Kenya. Part of her visit included a trip to a "typical" African village. In the usual manner of these visits, months of preparation were needed. My father had to upgrade the 70 mile road to the selected village and electricity was to be supplied so that a hot lunch could be cooked for the Princess.

My father sent a young engineer, with his new wife, to live in the village until the road was finished. Father made periodic inspection visits, sometimes staying overnight with the engineer. On one visit, he took Jack Nye with him and they stayed for a meal. The wife, newly out from England, had tried to teach her cook/houseboy basic cooking, but was certain of only one dish that would not go wrong. Sundowner drinks were served, and then more drinks, then more drinks because cook had not yet announced that the meal was ready. Eventually, the wife excused herself and went in search of the cook. She found him chewing raw meat and spitting the lumps into a bowl. When she enquired as to just what he thought he was doing, he replied "Memsahib, for you and Boss, it is no trouble, but for four people, my jaw hurts". The meal was to have been Shepherds Pie!!! The young couple had had it several times a week, and she said that it was one of the best she had tasted, until she found out just how the meat had been tenderised. The mincer that she had supplied, and demonstrated, had never been used.

Meanwhile, the African village ladies living along the route wanted to look their best. They needed copper bangles, necklaces, and other jewellery. But it was being made from wire stolen from the overhead copper electrical wires that were being erected. It was found that the only way to stop the continued theft of wire was to energise the completed work at the end of each day.

About this time, the Colonial Government were thinking about Independence for Kenya. As a consequence, money from UK dried up a little and some major expenditure was resisted. The main lifeline for the country was the Mombasa – Nairobi road, bringing goods and fuel from the port for the rest of the country. The road surface was collapsing. My father arranged a "Contractor Finance" scheme where Cementation Ltd provided soil stabilization for the worst affected length near Nairobi. The company would be paid later by the Government over a number of years, but the Colony would benefit immediately from an improved road. In the event, by the time Cementation were due for payment, the country had gained independence. The new government said that this arrangement was the responsibility of the previous Colonial Administration, and that Cementation should ask Whitehall for payment. This problem would affect me later on.

Money for schooling was drying up, and I was asked to decide on a career. Mother favoured a Law job, possibly a Barrister. Father elected for a Royal Navy Commission. I had no ideas at all. Whatever was decided, I was to leave Kingswood when the GCE results were known. The Navy and the Law were not what I wanted. Eventually, I told Father that I would like to be a civil engineer. He asked engineering friends for advice, and contacted Loughborough College. Having only just gained seven GCE levels, luckily in the correct subjects, they would put me in the Preliminary Year. This year was designed to bring overseas students up to UK "A" Level in one year, rather than the usual two or even three years. I had to pass this internal examination at the end of the first year, or leave. As they say nowadays, "No Pressure, then".

Holiday in Kenya

That summer, I sailed to Kenya in style on the "Kenya Castle", the pride of the Union Castle Line and only four years old. We had brilliant sunshine and calm seas in the Bay of Biscay, so I sunbathed. When we called at Gibraltar, I was in the sick bay, with the backs of knees badly sunburnt. Other passengers told me what I had missed and I vowed to visit Gibraltar when I could. Then we pulled in to Genoa, where I did go ashore. There was a group of youngsters from Kenya on the ship, and we toured the port together. We had a lovely lunch, washed down by a wine which the waiter called "Stupide". That afternoon, I hired a rowing boat and took three girls into the bay. I quickly found out that the waiter was correct when he had told us that the wine only affected the legs, making one walk like a drunk. It was no way to row a boat, or to impress the girls!!

After Suez, we pulled into Aden. I found myself in the bar of the Marine Hotel, in Crater, with another passenger. He was a much older farmer, who had purchased a vintage Rolls Royce and was shipping it back to Kenya in the boat. "I wanted a car with a wind up window between the driver and the passengers, because it will keep the sheep in the back from licking the back of my neck when I drive round the farm!"

During that summer holiday in Kenya, my father was interviewed by the local radio station. Many of Kenya's roads were gravel surfaced and needed constant maintenance due to corrugation. The suspension on vehicles causes the bodywork to bounce, which in turn displaces the road surface, and the dust blows away. Ridges, or corrugations, appear which shake passengers to bits. Regular grading is done, but unless the surface is properly compacted, corrugations return quickly. My father understood this and he instituted a rolling maintenance programme where a length of road was scarified using the teeth on a grader, the open surface was then watered to bring the material back to the optimum water content, and then it was rolled. This process had been in use for centuries, and Thomas McAdam used this in Scotland three hundred years ago, and the material is referred to as having being "water-bound". The news reporter was terribly excited about this "new" invention and spoke at great length of my father's new process for building "water logged roads". My father was not impressed and warned me to be very careful if I ever spoke to reporters. His reputation suffered a knock for a while.

We drove down to Mombasa to spend a week at the coast. On the way, near Tsavo Game Park, we passed a large American saloon car with a dead rhino embedded in the front. There were no humans around, so we continued to the hotel. That evening, on the radio, we heard that a massive search had been mounted for the missing driver. Blood had been found in the car, and it was feared that he might be wandering in the bush, in a dazed state. Much later that night, a man at the end of the bar finished his beer and said that he had better call the police to say that he was safe and well. He had got a lift in a passing car and had thought nothing more about the accident.

While at the coast, Dad started teaching me to drive and took me along some sandy roads amongst the palm trees. The roads seemed to be about two feet below ground level, which was due to the maintenance grader constantly removing the soft, loose, surface in an attempt to find firmer material. Soft sand was banked up at the sides of the road, so all vehicles kept to the centre. When I met a Police lorry coming the other way, I moved to the side and mounted the sloping soft sand. The car slid sideways into the side of the lorry. My first accident, and for witnesses I had twenty police constables on the lorry!! No damage was done, and the vehicles were separated easily.

Loughborough College   1956- 1960

Loughborough was a bit of a shock, as I no longer had the care umbrella of a school staff or my family. I was on my own, and I had no one to tell me what to do or not to do, or available to give me advice. I did not even have close family in England that I could contact in emergency.

In October 1956, at 17, I was the youngest in the class and a year younger than most UK students going to universities nowadays. Also, I only had the one year to do two years "A" Level work, or leave without further qualifications. Many of the other British students were ex-National Service, and in at least one case, ex- War Service. About 50% were from overseas, mainly from the Far East.

As engineering students in our preliminary year, we were expected to work regular shifts in the College Workshops, as part of an introduction to general engineering. I seem to remember it being one week in four. We clocked on and off, and did a full 40 hour week. The workshop course took us through the making of an electrical motor, starting by making moulds in the pattern making shop, then casting in the foundry, then the fettling of the castings, and so on. I was taught to cut screw threads on a lathe that had been destined for Russia in the First World War, but failed to be sent due to the Russian Revolution. All the markings, cog ratios, spindle settings, and the rest were in Russian script. It made for some unusual screw threads. There were two Russian émigrés maintaining all the workshop machines. They were large men, and carried all their tools in large canvas bags. These bags only contained pairs of hammers, of all shapes and sizes. Nuts and screws were loosened or tightened by using matching pairs of hammers, tapping in unison on opposite sides. It was an amazing skill to watch, but we were never given lessons. All this workshop time reduced the time available for my academic studies. If I passed at the end of the year, the College would give me an internal pass up to the first year of the proper three year Civil Engineering course, so I would not actually have to sit proper A Level papers. However, if I failed the internal exams, I would be out on my ear without any certificates.

For the first three years at Loughborough, I was in digs owned by Mrs Jamieson, a widow, who had three daughters. I shared a room with a Chemical Engineering student from Lincolnshire. He had framed certificates on the wall, all from the Courts and relating to his various juvenile court cases involving alcohol. He had a habit of undressing and kicking his clothes under his bed, to join the rest of his wardrobe. The next day, he would dress in whatever clothes had been pushed out of the other side because, he said, by that time they were clean again!!

Also in the digs, was a Sikh Mechanical Engineering student who had a Morris 8 car with a soft top. It was his pride and joy and we listened endlessly to him talking about it. In the pavement outside the digs were two mature trees and the space between them was the length of his car plus one inch. One day, with six of us bouncing the suspension, we edged the car sideways across the pavement into the gap between the trees until it was tight up against the brick garden wall. Mr Singh was on Workshop training and had to be up early to clock in. Early next morning, there were wails and shouts outside, then silence as he ran to work as he dare not be late. After he had gone, we went outside and put the car back on the road, as it was when we found it. That evening, we listened in complete disbelief to his story about his car being jammed between two trees, and pointed out to him that there was no damage visible on the trees, and that he must have been seeing things! We never let on, and I think that up to this day, he is still unsure that it all actually happened.

At the end of that first year, I managed to get a paid holiday for the whole summer. I went fruit picking for Wilkins Ltd, makers of Tiptree Jams, at Marks Tey in Essex. The tented camp was for continental students to have two weeks each learning English, but was really cheap labour for the company. There were no formal English lessons, and they all tried to learn by talking to me, the only native English person present. The only other full time resident was the Camp leader, who was from Israel. Even the cooks came and went. We lived in tents and all mixed well together. The first task was picking strawberries from quarter mile long rows, in the sun. We could eat as much as we wanted. After the first day, one no longer wanted to taste any fruit! The Jam factory used a lot of sugar, which attracted wasps. The only way to stop them flying was to knock them down into the boiling jam. If you have ever wondered what the lumps in the jam were, now you know!

Later, when the main fruit for the jam factory had been picked, we were hired out to neighbouring farms to gather in harvests. There were so many languages spoken, but French and English predominated. I was a favourite because I was a native English speaker for the others to practice with. However, when we did not want the farmer or his staff to understand, we used French. I was befriended by some Hungarians and I had told them that I wanted to thank the Hungarian cook for her excellent food. They taught me two phrases and I practiced them. The cook was well over six feet tall, but had a perfect hour glass figure. After yet another excellent meal, I went up to her and spoke my well rehearsed lines. Her backhand swipe knocked me clean across the room! Apparently I had complemented her on being a beautiful prostitute and had asked her to lie on her back and make love to the sky! (Always get an independent translation before using a foreign language).

I managed to pass the internal exam and moved up to start the three year Civil Engineering course in 1957. We were lucky in that most of our lecturers had been out in the big, bad, world. The man teaching steel structures owed his job at Loughborough to the way he had planned, in extreme detail, the delivery and erection sequence for the structural steelwork for a factory building on an extremely tight site. Columns were numbered and placed in order on lorries. Each lorry had a convoy number to make sure that they arrived under the crane in the correct sequence. Day One arrived, and so did the first lorry. The erectors found that he had forgotten to order the rivets!!

Our Soil Mechanics lecturer had previously designed a large timber support mat for a 22RB dragline to excavate a bog in the Somerset wetlands. The marshy ground had an extremely low "Safe Bearing Capacity" and needed special consideration. A very large mat was needed to support the Dragline, and he had even designed mats that were required for the low-loader delivering the crane. The crane climbed off the transporter and onto the mat, and then a gurgling was heard, followed by a

44

squelching noise. The operator jumped off the crane as it sank. The next day, the top of the jib was all that could be seen!!

Our Head of Department, Prof J. F. Peck, had designed the turbines for one of the Cunard liners, and it seemed that most of his hydraulics lectures were taken from that experience.

We were shown how to undertake land surveys. The collection of theodolites and levels ranged from 1890s items to current, 1950s, items. The older models came in one or more oak, dovetailed, brass cornered boxes, with stout leather straps for carrying. One set even had a separate box just for the tools needed to assemble the theodolite. One tripod was hewn from a single four inch diameter pole, and had no length adjustment. Telescopic legs make siting a theodolite on sloping ground easy. Some instruments had to be assembled on top of the tripod, and then calibrated before use. On some of the older models, levelling an instrument before taking readings was done by using four, rather than the normal three, adjustable foot screws. Once I had mastered this lot, the junk I had in Nigeria was child's play. But without the college experience, I would have been floundering. Nowadays, it is all electronic gizmos and a whole new world.

At the end of our second year, all the survey kit was taken to the annual survey camp at Clarach Bay, in a deep glacial valley in Wales. As one climbed up to a survey station at the top edge of the glacier-formed 'U' shaped valley, the slope became almost vertical. As the smallest and youngest, I seemed to finish up with the 1890s theodolite, in three wooden boxes (one just for the necessary tools), and the tree trunk tripod. Some wit had glued a matchbox motto to the lid of a box, which read "Don't just look at the hill, climb it".

In the Final Year, for our Survey Practical exam, we surveyed the College Playing Fields, and all the Academic buildings. Our survey had to be plotted on proper hand made heavy paper, carefully wetted and stretched onto the drawing board. All lines were drawn with nibs, not modern pens. The lettering was done by hand, not by stencil. Draughting excellence was required. The finished drawing had to be coloured, using water colour paints. Bill Pegg, the lecturer, could stand at a blackboard with a chalk in each hand and, using both hands simultaneously, write his name first from left to right, then right to left, then from the sides of the board to the centre, then from centre outwards. There were eight perfect, copperplate, signatures. It was impossible to tell any differences, or remember in which direction they had been written. He expected the same standards of draughtsmanship from us. Before the War, Bill had worked on the Trans-Iranian Railway construction and told us that he was fortunate to have survived. The Shah, Reza Shah Pahlavi, came for an inspection, and track-laying was some miles behind the target programme. Iranian engineers worked alongside the British. The Shah looked at the programme, asked what the actual progress was, and where it should have reached by this time. He asked the Iranian engineer to walk the route with him. They got to the end of the actual work, and then continued on to the point where the work should have reached. As an example to the others, the Shah shot the engineer on the spot. It was no use the other engineers protesting the difficulties of blasting a spiral tunnel inside a cliff face to gain height. Excuses are no substitute for doing the work properly in the first place. Some engineers will say that they also have had bosses that had the same attitude as the Shah!

One classroom was built on the roof of a three storey classroom block, but the walls were set back inside the original parapet walls. Looking out of the windows, one could not see the parapet. One student went outside, and when the brand new lecturer arrived, he was seen clinging to the window sill outside with white knuckles. As he was crouching on the original roof, he was able to take one hand off the window sill to bang on the glass, to ask for rescue. After panicking, the lecturer just failed to see the funny side at all.

We often joined in with students of other disciplines, especially during Rag Week. The Schofield Building was our main lecture building. It had a long corridor, with fire doors at intervals. Access at each end was up steps. One morning, lecturers were faced with the large farm tractor, used to mow the playing fields, in the central hall. They found that the wheels could not get through any of the door frames. Mechanical students had realised that the two rear wheels were "dished", and the wheels could be fitted "dished out" for stability, or "dished in" to get through narrow door frames. The lecturers never did work it out. We had to tell them how to remove the tractor. The Aeronautical Department had a Hurricane fighter down on the local aerodrome, which was used as a teaching aid. One night it appeared in the staff carpark outside the main teaching block. It had been towed (wings off), with a bicycle lamp on the propeller, through town and then re-assembled. The police had not seen a thing, although the route used the busy main A6 Trunk Road, long before the M1 Motorway was built.

All the foreign students used to group together and use their own languages amongst themselves. Paranoid English students thought that they were being discussed, and that all conversations in English were being listened to. A few of us ex-East Africa students started using Swahili, in self defence, and this caused the foreign students to use more English. After all, they needed to improve to get better marks.

Loughborough had excellent sports facilities and I took up Badminton, but without a great deal of success. Each night I would play until I finally won a game, and then I felt free to go home! I did eventually get into the college sixth team. Loughborough were UK University Badminton Champions for many years.

Joining the Army

Unlike the other English students, I had no UK Grant to support me. I looked round for an income and discovered that the Nottingham University Officer Training Corps paid attendance money. I promptly joined up. This boosted my income and gave me something to do outside the rather narrow confines of the Student Union. Once a week, I climbed into army uniform and onto a 3 ton lorry for the trip to Beeston Drill Hall in Nottingham. I showed an interest in the Royal Engineers and my training was geared to that branch of the service.

One very cold and wet February, we waited on parade for some dumbo Brigadier to come and inspect us, the drips off our noses turning to icicles. In the rear section, composed of WRAC, was a very plump girl, who was still waiting for her uniform to be made. Eventually the man arrived, very late, and started a slow walk through the ranks, asking inane questions of each and every cadet. It was seemingly hours before he got to the girl without the uniform.

> "And what are you reading at University, my dear?"
> "Theology".
> "Why Theology?"
> "Because I want to marry a bloody Bishop".

She had had enough by then, as had we all.

The OTC Adjutant, a Regular officer, was a very "pukka" South Staffordshire Regiment Captain and wore jodhpurs with brown boots. Each year, we had to qualify on the Rifle Range. Pearl was a student who had just got her WRAC Commission, and was sent to look after the work party in the butts. They had to raise and lower targets, record scores, and paste over the bullet holes. There was a delay at one point, and the Adjutant used the field telephone to ask Pearl about the delay. "Hold on, I am just finishing a row of knitting. I will call you back". The Adjutant was not best pleased.

There was a sort of ulterior motive behind my joining the OTC. National Service still existed in UK, and I did not want to peel spuds for my obligatory two years. A Commission gained via the OTC would make life easier. Also, as Kenya was still under the threat of Mau Mau, I faced a second call up for the Kenya Regiment should I return home. A double call-up liability was not an attractive proposition, and there were probably very few men with this burden. I suppose that I could have decided to run off to some third country and ignore both governments, or just stay on the aircraft flitting back and forth.

Parachute training

Another advantage of the OTC was that they gave me Army pay while attending military courses during college vacations. This was a saving on paying for my own accommodation, and I enjoyed some odd courses, mainly those which were Royal Engineer based. I ticked a box for the Cinema Projectionist Course in York, as I had been told that they practiced with bits of film removed by the British Board of Film Censors, only to discover that I had marked the wrong box! Instead, I went to No1 Parachute Training School at RAF Abingdon. When the taxi came to take me to the railway station, I was on the top floor of my digs. I tripped and fell down the stairs, holding my Army kitbag. When I came to rest, the kitbag flew past me and dragged me down the next flight. My body flew past the kitbag, and dragged the bag on down the stairs. This process continued down several flights of stairs. I arrived on the ground floor feeling rather bruised and dishevelled. Someone joked that I did not need to attend the course, as I had demonstrated the correct way to fall!!

There were four of us from the OTC on this course, but we were split up among all the others for training. The RAF insisted that as Officer Cadets, we used the Officers Mess for meals. The Army thought that we were the lowest of the low, and made us sleep with the other ranks. Morning roll call could not start until we had sauntered out of the RAF Mess after a leisurely breakfast, which did very little to improve the behaviour of the Army Instructor NCOs.

Each morning, we fell in and marched to the ground training hangar, past the Mortuary. Each of us wondered if we might finish up in there! After several days learning how to put on a parachute, and how to roll on landing, we were taken to the tower. Wearing the parachute harness, we climbed to the eighty foot level and moved reluctantly over to the edge of the platform. A braking rope was attached to the back of our harness and we were ordered to jump. It looked an awful long way down. We did quite a few tower jumps, which made us concentrate on the correct way of falling without hurting ourselves. In the distance, we could see the film crew clustered round a parked Dakota DC-3, where Brigit Bardot was filming "Babette goes to War". We never got any closer. She was falling all of about 12 inches onto a stack of mattresses. We would be falling a thousand feet onto hard ground. Life is not fair!! In the RAF Mess, we read that a man had stepped off the kerb in Oxford Street and broken his leg in three places. As the kerb was only about six inches, we mentally calculated what a fall of 2000 times that height could do to a human body, and went off to try to sleep thinking about it.

At the end of the first week, on the Saturday afternoon, the RAF found a Blackburn Beverley aircraft for us to have our "air familiarity" flight. This ungainly animal had a large box shaped body with wide rear doors for freight. Above the body, a sturdy tail boom extended rearwards. It could carry up to 40 paratroopers in the lower freight bay, and 30 in the tail boom. Paratroopers jumped from the two side doors in the freight bay, and through a hole in the floor of the tail boom. There were 60 of us onboard as we stooged in circles over Berkshire, in thick fog and thick cloud, and on auto pilot. We practised standing up, checking each other's straps, shuffling to the door, pretending to jump and then returning to our seats. A RAMC TA dentist officer actually jumped, and panic set in. His chute was seen to deploy correctly as he disappeared into the low cloud. The pilot had no idea where he was, so search teams had no start point. We landed, wondering if he was safe. Eventually he did return. He had landed on the roof of Marks and Spencer in Reading. As he was some eight floors above the traffic on a busy shopping day, no one heard him calling for help until eight at night when traffic noise was much reduced.

One infantry soldier, of limited intelligence, had had great difficulty learning to fall sideways without trying to get his upper leg onto the ground before the leg on the lower side. He kept crossing his legs in mid-air as he fell, which caused him some pain, and the Instructor, apoplexy. After many repeats, the Instructors gave up and warned him that, unless he got it right, he would end up in hospital. When he came in after his Saturday night on the town, he was covered in bruises. He told me, proudly, that he had been practising falling down the stairs of a double-decker bus, but he thought that he now had mastered the problem!

Our first aircraft jump was on the Monday morning, and we were woken at three in the morning. "What a Hell of a time to get up to go and die!" said one man. To encourage us to leave the aircraft, the RAF fed us Baked Beans, with the fried breakfast. With 60 scared souls cooped up in a confined space, the air became foul and all we wanted was fresh air. When the doors opened, it was sheer heaven and we all wanted to get out of the aircraft. RAF psychology worked.

The first jump is a mixture of sheer terror and exhilaration. As I came out of the door, the wind caught me and it was just like sitting in a comfy armchair, attached to the deploying 28 foot diameter parachute. Gravity took over and I swung down below the canopy. Then I saw just how much further there was to fall and I had to resist the temptation to close my eyes and offer a prayer. I quickly checked that the chute was correctly deployed, and that the rigging lines were not twisted. All seemed in order, so I was able to concentrate on the instructions from the NCO Instructor on the ground, who used a loud hailer. I landed properly on that first jump, and we all gathered for a hot tea before getting back for the second jump in the afternoon. The RAF said that the emotional strain of two jumps in a day was the equivalent of an eight hour normal job.

The Drop Zone (DZ) was at RAF Weston-on-the-Green. The Marine in our group had noticed that the DZ was a long narrow strip of land, jammed between a Turkey Farm and the main railway line from London to Birmingham. He told us that we should try to remember how to steer the chutes on future jumps to avoid becoming turkey fodder or rail-kill. Then he dropped his bombshell. The DZ was covered in Fairy Rings, or Pixie Circles, those darker green rings of grass, which are made by pixies and elves dancing in a circle! We must avoid these at all costs, he said, because landing in one would upset the Faery Queen and she can cause you to reappear in a different time zone. Who said that the Marines are not superstitious? If one did land, accidentally, one could apologise to Her Majesty, the Faery Queen, by following a very complicated routine, and, if you were word perfect, she might not cast a spell on you before the next jump. After landing in a Circle, one had to stand up and bow to the North, and recite "I am sorry, Your Majesty, for arriving unannounced. Please accept my apology. I will apologise to your sisters as well". There was much more to the speech, but I cannot remember it. One had to make sure that you have not pushed your backside towards the Queen of the South, while bowing to the Queen of the North, or to the other Queens in any other later bows, as you turn and repeat the speech. Only after bowing to all four Queens in turn can you turn back to the Queen of the North and request permission to leave the Circle, before stepping backwards while bowing. We spent hours rehearsing this, because we did not want any sort of bad luck.

The next day, the three neat, straight, and parallel sticks each of 20 parachutists left the aircraft in textbook fashion. The NCO Instructor on the ground shouted his pleasure at the display through his loudhailer. Nearer the ground, we all saw that we were headed towards a Faery Circle, and immediately took avoiding action, as we had completely forgotten the speech we had carefully learned the night before. We scudded across the sky like a pack of demented dodgem car drivers. The Instructor went incandescent. One man steered straight through another's set of rigging lines, and came out the other side, collapsing both chutes. Chutes bounced off chutes.

One man stepped onto the top of another chute and rode down on top. Chaos reigned. The NCO ran up to the nearest man. He was just standing there, bowing and talking, and not trying to get his chute unclipped, as instructed. NCO asked "What the "blankety blank" did he think he was doing?" "I am apologising to the Queen of the North, Sir". The NCOs face was a picture, and he was lost for words.

We all had to take turns jumping out of the hole in the tail boom. The hole was, from memory, about six feet from front to back. One walked towards the hole and simply stepped into space. As you fell, the aircraft moved forward and you only just fell far enough to clear the rapidly approaching rear edge of the hole. Our Marine ran towards the hole, shouting the Marine war cry of "Geronimo". We watched as he moved at speed, yelling "Geroni......" Then there was a thump as his head hit the opposite edge of the hole. This impact caused him to spin in the air. As his rigging lines deployed, they got entangled with his canopy, producing a "bunch of grapes" which is where the lines run over the top of the canopy and reduce the size, and therefore the support, of the 'chute. Luckily, he had not been knocked unconscious and was able to open his reserve chute.

We progressed to container jumps, where the personal kitbag is attached to your waist when you jump, and then let down on a rope so that it hits the ground before you, and hopefully without injuring you. In the aircraft, the order to stand up was given, and I undid what I thought was the aircraft seatbelt. I discovered that I had undone my parachute harness instead. I hastily thrust as many of the loose ends into the clip that I could find, and hoped that I had found enough of them. All the way down I kept wondering if the clip had enough bits shoved in. On another jump, I was first in the door and we circled for a while with my hands clutching the door frame. My watch strap broke and I made a move to save it, but the dispatcher told me not to as I would have fallen out prematurely. I lost the watch. On my last jump, I did a "straight leg landing". This jarred my lower spine badly, and I fell back hard. This caused my helmet to bang the bridge of my nose. That day I had a clean, new, white, chute. It got covered with blood from the nosebleed. (In later years, the damage to my back caused by this accident got progressively worse.) I staggered to the lorry for the trip to the canteen, where we were all given our Parachute Badges, confirming that we had done eight jumps. The badge is a simple parachute, and is not to be confused with the Airborne Wings earned the hard way, through the "P" Company basic para training.

Iraq monarchy ends

In 1958, I was sitting in the Students Common Room when, to our concern, a policeman entered. He asked for an Iraqi student who was part of the Royal Family, and told him of the 14 July massacre of the King and family by the Iraqi Army. He and his brothers, also at Loughborough, were advised that the Iraqi Embassy was no longer able to support them in England. What happened to them, I never found out, but I don't think that they ever returned to Iraq. A number of years after the massacre, the three ethnic groups in Iraq had failed to produce a cohesive government and this allowed Saddam Hussein to take over the country.

Meanwhile, back at College, we continued studying. In my class, was Roger Boot, son of Henry Boot, the building contractor, and David Coode, son of the Civil Engineering Consultant. We spent long evenings, dosing ourselves with strong coffee, and reading textbooks. Some students were not so diligent. In the year above us, was a very tall Malay, K. Chidambaram, known to all as "Chid". His father had the Caterpillar franchise for Malaya and Singapore, but the son had found drink. He loved his gin. The college authorities finally gated him, and he had to report to the Warden of his Hall of Residence every hour on the hour, to prove that he had not gone into town for a drink. He hired another student with a motor scooter to ferry him to and from the pub, and did his drinking between reporting. Money got short just before his Finals, so he sold me his textbooks, which I still have on my bookshelf. He failed his Finals, and his father managed to get him into Kingston Technical College, in London, to repeat the Final year again. He failed again, so his father disowned him. Very short of money, he discovered a way of getting back to Malaya. He got a Short Service Commission in the Royal Engineers, who were fighting the Borneo campaign at the time, and Chid planned to get a local discharge from the Army at the end of his time in Singapore. I met up with him again in the summer after I left College.

Another one of the foreign students was Dany Chamoun. He was in the year above me. I spent one Christmas week in his digs studying for an exam in the January. We lived on black coffee and Lebanese food. Dany's father, Camille was, at that time, the Lebanese Foreign Minister, and later became Prime Minister of Lebanon. Dany married the daughter of his German college landlady and went on to become the Leader of the combined Christian Militias during the Lebanese Civil Wars. He, and his wife and two sons, were assassinated by a Muslim militia group in October 1990.

Final year

The Final Year of the course started in October, and I went to the Fresher's Ball with my left wrist in plaster. I had spent the summer at a TA Annual Camp, at Perranporth in Cornwall. A visit had been arranged to spend time on Fast Patrol and inflatable boats with the Royal Navy, in Falmouth. We slept in a local TA Drill Hall, sleeping under the snooker table, and went out on the town. The Chain Locker Bar was our favourite, as it was with many seafarers. A merchant seaman would, just before his ship sailed, hand the landlord enough money for a taxi and request that no matter what he said, the landlord was to put him in the taxi back to the ship. The sailor would then drink the rest of his cash as fast as he could before the taxi arrived. There were several sailors in on any evening, and the bar was lively. As a result, I found myself later outside a pub, standing on the shoulders of the College Judo champion, one Ashok Kazakian – later a County Surveyor, when someone called out that the police could be seen. I do not remember why I was on his shoulders, but he ran off and I made a perfect three point landing on the cobbles. A cut nose, a sprained right wrist and a broken left wrist, but I felt nothing and slept well in my sleeping bag that night. The next morning, both wrists had swollen up and I could not undo the drawstring on the sleeping bag. Worse, I could not put on my uniform without help, or use the toilet. A trip to the hospital diagnosed the damage and patched me up, and I returned, still nursing a hangover. The Judo expert said that, as I had a parachute badge, I knew how to fall!!

The wrist in plaster helped to introduce me to my future wife. Jane was one of three brand new teachers that had landed jobs in Leicester and were living in a small village just outside Loughborough. It was their first week as probationary teachers. She taught at Momacre School in Leicester, and I still remember the trouble that she had with one child there. Stephen Purple was the son of the school caretaker. In a "Music and Movement" class, she asked the class of five year olds to pretend to be something in the forest, and act it out in a dance. Stephen lay down behind the piano and slept. When asked what he was doing, he said "I am a fallen leaf".

During the Cold War, the Army set up a special listening unit, manned by Royal Signals Morse code experts. They had to listen, and write down, all Morse Code messages coming from the Communist East. Barry, a Kingswood School friend, was doing his National Service in this unit, which was based near Loughborough. He said that all of his section, except himself, had already completed university and had degrees in various subjects. The corporal had a PhD in Medieval Music, the lance corporals were merely BA or BSc qualified. The corporal used to play the piano in the local pub, singing rude songs gleaned from his researches until his glass showed signs of not being refilled. Then he played Bach fugues until someone noticed. Barry got a weekend pass and invited me to his home in Wilmslow. This is a very posh area in Cheshire, and another friend of his was having a party in a pub to celebrate being demobbed from National Service. This man complained bitterly that he had spent his time in mud and leeches, fighting the Communists in Malayan jungles, while senior officers sipped Gin and Tonics in a comfortable Mess away from the action. We went off to a house to continue the party. Later, the drink ran out and the demob man said that his parents were away and we could "borrow" some alcohol from them. We went to his house, which was locked up properly. The only window he could enter was the small pantry window and he landed on a tray of eggs, and some setting jellies. The pantry door was locked, so he gave up. The next day, Barry and I were invited to lunch by this man, to meet his parents. When we arrived, his father was giving someone a hard time on the telephone, asking for a fingerprint team to come over to the house. Eventually his wife persuaded him that nothing had been stolen, and the cost of the eggs and jellies was minimal. Eventually he agreed to drop the matter. Then an Inspector and his fingerprint team arrived, to take all our prints for elimination purposes. That was when I realised that this was the Chief Constable of Cheshire, and that his son was the would-be thief! Luckily, the Chief Constable had listened to his wife, and he sent the fingerprint team away, to our relief.

A very good friend in my class was Jan Kaminski. His father had flown Spitfires in the War and his widowed mother lived in Chelsea. I lost contact with him after his two years working for Laing Iberia in Spain. Many years later, we regained contact and I made plans to visit him in Cape Town. Sadly, Jan died of cancer in 2006 before I could visit. Jan spent his working life in South Africa, and was Chairman of the Cape Town Opera Company and he took them on European tours.

John Skone, another good friend, after a year with the Port of London Authority, went on to work for Wimpey Canada for the rest of his life, and is still in Edmonton, Alberta. He married Anne, my college landlady's daughter. John also joined the OTC with me, and we went to TA camps together. John was my Best Man, when I married Jane in 1962, in Cardiff.

Eventually, the Final Exams came. Our syllabus had been modified, and made more difficult, to align with a proper university Bachelor of Science degree course. Loughborough had applied for University status and was being examined by the authorities to see if the college was up to University standard. I found the exams hard, and I ran out of steam during the Structures exam. The invigilator noticed that I had only tackled one question, and needed to answer at least one more, to pass. Without speaking, he dropped a Mars Bar on the desk. I ate it, and my mind cleared enough to complete the exam. Our Surveying marks depended on the results of the Playing Field survey and the resulting drawn map. Two Chinese Malay students (Yee and Yeo) actually surveyed the two master baseline stations. Most of the rest of us copied work done by the previous year's students, as they had copied their seniors, and so on. Yee and Yeo compared the previous class's work with their own, and proved that the concrete blocks containing the brass pins of the baseline had been moved. (It was later discovered that this had been done by earlier Final Year students). The other 48 students had to decide whether to re-survey, or submit the work that they had spent so much time on already. I re-surveyed, and without sleeping for several nights, managed to submit my corrected work in time.

Leaving college

In the May of that year, I attended an Army Commissions Board. I had applied for a commission, as part of my big plan to avoid an uncomfortable period of National Service. On the Application form, I mentioned that I spoke Swahili, but there was nowhere on the form to say just how much I actually knew. The Army wanted to check my understanding of the language. The Board consisted of four Colonels, three were Royal Engineers, as expected, but there was also an Airborne medical officer, which made me worry. All was made clear when all the questions were written down, passed to the Medic, who then asked the questions in Swahili. I managed to get through the interview, but when dismissed, I found that I nervously fiddled so much that I had removed my cap badge from my beret and I could not possibly reassemble it, put it on, and salute as required. I did a quick snap to attention, followed by an about turn, and almost ran out of the room. I vowed that I would never, ever, again put something on a form or CV that was untrue or only partly true.

During the previous months, Final Year students had been applying for jobs and most of us had offers, subject gaining satisfactory exam results. The Diploma of Loughborough Colleges was accepted by the Institution of Civil Engineers, so a pass meant that we could become a Graduate member of the ICE without sitting further written exams. I had secured a job, on my father's advice, with Kent County Council Roads Department, under the County Surveyor, Henry Bowdler. This was a two year "Graduate under Agreement" training scheme, which put me through all the different types of county highway work.

The results were announced, and I had gained an Honours Diploma. I was still only 20 years old. A Dinner was arranged for the Final Year Civil Engineering students, and we invited all the lecturers. A darts match was organised to follow the meal and we had two Chinese students, Yong and Yeo, on our team. They had never played darts before. Before they threw, one of us would put a chalk mark where the dart was required to land. They always hit the mark, and our team won.

The OTC summer camp was held in Cultybraggan Camp, near Comrie in Perthshire, Scotland. The camp was an old prisoner of war camp, made of Nissen huts. There was a rifle range and lots, and lots, of heather clad hills to play soldiers on. We were taken to Loch Earn, to practise watermanship on assault boats and pontoons. Some of the pontoons needed to be assembled by men standing waist deep in freezing Scottish water. To make sure that there was no favouritism, the Instructor made us all march into the Loch, up to our necks, so that we were all equally wet. My Commission came through while I was at the camp, and proudly sewed on the solitary "pip" on each shoulder.

At the end of the summer OTC camp, I left Cultybraggan, and travelled by train to Stoke on Trent to see Jane. I had her address, but had not been able to say exactly when I would arrive. I thought that I would surprise her. I left my kitbag in the station Left Luggage and set off. I had her address, but did not realise that the village of Endon was about 8 miles outside town, and I started walking. It rained heavily the whole journey, but I found the house. I was drenched, sneezing, shivering and not feeling at all well when Jane let me in. I collapsed before her mother could walk from the kitchen. I spent two weeks in bed with a bad case of Pleurisy. I did not wake up for two days and finally got to meet her parents for the first time, wearing borrowed pyjamas that I had not dressed myself in. During the recuperation, I proposed to her after asking her father for permission. Jane had passed her Probationary year, and had got a job in Maidstone to be near me.

National Service call up was stopped in Kenya, and in UK, that summer. I no longer had this hanging over my head. Between actually leaving Loughborough and the OTC camp, I was asked to visit two London TA units to see if they would accept me. 131 Para Field Squadron RE (TA) was based in Duke of York's Headquarters in Chelsea. Although I only had a basic parachute qualification, I had hopes of joining this unit. When I saw how big, and fit, these men were, I realised that I would never be up to their standards. It was a relief when the CO said that he did not have a vacancy.

The Kray brothers gang

Another unit that I tried to join was 114 Army Engineer Regiment RE (TA). They were based in Hackney, London. I went to meet the Commanding Officer on a Wednesday evening and, after the interview, was given a tour of the Drill Hall. I was talking to the Quartermaster, in his Stores, when he sent for a driver. When a new recruit joins the TA, he is issued his uniform and other kit. After a cooling off period, if he has not shown up again, it is assumed that he has changed his mind about joining. At this point the Quartermaster wants the kit returned so that it is available for the next recruit. The driver duly arrived with another sapper and the

Quartermaster gave him very precise instructions appropriate for that area of London.

> "Corporal, I want you to go to this address and collect the kit that we issued to this man".
> "Yes, Sir, is it all right if I take me bruvver with me?"
> "Yes, OK. But remember, we only want his kit. You are not to mark him or rough him up. Do you understand?"

Later, I met up with the officers in their bar and met the local Police Inspector. He had just heard of possible reorganisation of the TA and wanted to know about the future of this unit. "You see, we know where the members of the Kray Gang are on Wednesday nights, so it is the only time I can allow my men some time off". If the unit was to be disbanded, he was going to ask for a transfer.

Bomb Disposal

The other unit that showed an interest was 583 Bomb Disposal Squadron (TA), which was based in Rochester, quite close to my new job in Maidstone, Kent. I met the Officer Commanding, a Major Douglas Rabjohn, at Gordon Barracks, in Gillingham, and he accepted me. I was introduced to him by Captain Peter Cunnington, my OTC officer and Loughborough Soil Mechanics lecturer. That was the last time I spoke to Peter until, out of the blue, he telephoned me in January 2010, fifty years later.

King Hussein of Jordan

That summer, I confirmed my job with Kent County Council and found some digs ready for when I started in September. At the end of August, as a newly Commissioned Second Lieutenant, I was required to pass the "Young Officer Course", which for Royal Engineers was held at Gordon Barracks, Gillingham. There was a lot, an awful lot, of drill. This was taught by WO1 Pierotti, who told us on the first day that he was the only non-Guardsman ever to have passed out top of a Guards Senior Drill Instructors Course at Pirbright. He said that he had high standards and that all his students would, however long it took, have those same high standards when he had finished with them. He never swore, but his command of English was amazing.

On the square, at the same time as us, was the King of Jordan, now 24 years old. He had become King at the age of 17 and had an arranged marriage, but later took time to learn the rudiments of drill and other military skills from Britain. From some 300 yards, I heard Pierotti say to King Hussein,

> "You 'orrible idle Monarch, you silly King, you. What are you, Sir?"
> "When I say 'Stand at ease' you bend that knobbly thing half way down your left leg, Sir".

Coincidentally, King Hussein's second wife, Princess Muna, born Antoinette (Toni) Gardiner, was the daughter of a Royal Engineer Lt Colonel. Her father was with a Military delegation to Jordan, and she met her future husband while visiting her father.

Because my left forearm was decorated with two badges, the Bomb Disposal red and gold badge designed by Queen Mary, the Queen Mother, and the parachute badge, Mr Pierotti referred to me as "The Christmas Tree" and he wondered, sarcastically, if I defused bombs while they were still falling.

One day, the Duke of Edinburgh was due to land in a helicopter. Mr Pierotti went straight to the Camp Commandant to say that he refused to allow "a whirly bird" to land on "his" square. We did sword drill in a heavy fog. Mr Pierotti was out of our sight, but the tip of his well polished sword glinted through the murk.

On the camp was a National Service Dental Officer, who would saunter from the Mess at lunch time, diagonally across the hallowed square to his surgery, usually without his hat. "I am saluting you, Sir" called WO1 Pierotti. The dentist stopped and wished him a pleasant afternoon, and resumed strolling. "You should return my salute, Sir". "But I can't salute if I haven't got a hat". "Why haven't you got proper headdress, Sir?" "Don't need it. It is not raining". Mr Pierotti did his best to keep up standards, but there were limits.

The rest of what the Army refers to as "The Knife, Fork and Spoon Course" for new officers, was classroom work on officer duties, military law, Mess etiquette and table manners.

On another course at the same time at Gordon Barracks, was my Loughborough friend, Chid. He was on the Commissioning Course for Short Service Officers. At the end of his course there was to be a formal Commissioning Parade at Brompton Barracks, the Headquarters of the Royal Engineers, in Chatham. We were asked to attend as guests. I had seen Chid wandering around the ablutions that morning, long after everyone else had had breakfast, and I suspected that he would miss the parade. We arrived, and waited for Colonel Eric Kyte, who was to present the new Commissions. Colonel Kyte had commanded 9 Company RE during the War. When volunteers for the new Airborne Engineers were requested on a parade, and he took one pace forward, his entire Company did likewise because of his leadership. To this day, No 9 Squadron RE is the Airborne unit and retains the same number. The small group of about 20 new officers, in No1 blue uniforms, stood lonely in the middle of a vast parade ground. I could not see Chid, and wondered just how he could possibly smuggle himself onto the parade ground and into the squad without anyone noticing. Then, as the car carrying Colonel Kyte pulled up from the right, I heard a clatter as Chid dropped his bicycle on the left. How a six foot Malay could get into the squad of much smaller officers undetected, I don't know, but he did. He was posted to Singapore, to work with moving construction plant to Borneo, so he had managed to get home in spite of his father.

Kent County Council   1960 - 1962

In September, 1960, I started work in Kent County Council Roads Department. The offices were in County Hall, Maidstone. Graduate civil engineers were placed on a two year training programme, consisting of periods spent in various sub-sections in order to gain a wide range of experience in local government highway engineering. I spent time in Major Projects designing major trunk road schemes, Minor Works, designing kerb line changes and bus lay-byes, Private Streets upgrading unadopted roads to county standards, and learning about land acquisition.

In the first months, I was part of a team working on the design of the Detling By-Pass, part of the A249 route from Maidstone to Sittingbourne. The road rose from the low level plain near Maidstone, and up a steep chalk scarp to the high ground towards the north. Contract documents were readied for tenders to be issued in the first week of the New Year. The office Christmas Party was held in our drawing office and all furniture and files were moved out for the event. It was my first office party and a great time was had by all. The next day we returned the furniture and the files, but all the Detling papers, drawings, files, and letters could not be found! We all worked overtime up to and through the Christmas and New Year period, trying to recreate the complete set of contract documents (virtually) from memory. This was before computers were available. We did not have the computer back up copies, which would be available in a modern office, but had found just one or two survey notebooks.

In those days, all calculations were done manually, using slide-rules and Logarithmic Tables. This was well before there were any computers or hand-held calculators to make life simple for engineers. For highway design, we used tables in "Criswell", ("A Handbook of Highway Design", used by all Local Government designers), which gave tables of crossfalls for superelevations at different design speeds of a road. This meant many long hours manually calculating the levels for each point along a road. Unless the results were plotted on graph paper, it was almost impossible to spot a calculation error. A rushed issue of drawings to a contractor could well develop into a claim caused by the delay necessary to produce a corrected design.

My first design

After surviving the Detling debacle, I transferred to the Minor Works section. I was required to survey and design various alterations to kerbs at road junctions, and supervise the construction of these small schemes. I was given my first solo design job. This was a whole bus lay-by to design by myself. Promotion at last! I surveyed and designed the lay-by. Then I found the owner of the land and arranged for the Legal department to arrange to purchase the land. This required me to provide 12 drawings on linen, with the required area highlighted with a pink colour wash. Using County standards, I prepared the Bill of Quantities and specified the construction materials. I sat back and waited for work to start. Eventually, some six or seven years later, it was built! The bureaucracy in local government in Britain as a whole is ridiculous. The work was required immediately, to save lives on the highway. In Nigeria and Oman, the job would have been completed in a week from the first survey day, and in Saudi Arabia it would probably have taken three days because there was more money and plant available.

Meanwhile, I looked after a minor road diversion on the Isle of Sheppey. A length of this road was on the seaward side of the sea defence bund and it had to be ramped up and over the bund. While I was on Sheppey, I used to lunch in Sheerness, overlooking the small harbour. Parking was available on the harbour wall. One day a large Jaguar car reversed into a parking bay, and the rear end projected over the water at the entrance to the harbour. The owner returned to find that his rear end was damaged. It had been hit by a Royal Navy submarine!! I still think of the poor insurance assessor who had to deal with the claim. "Other vehicle involved in the accident – Submarine".

Exhumations

There was a very tight corner in Eynsford, Kent, with poor sight lines, restricted by the graveyard wall and the lych gate on the inside of the bend. It was decided to remove a wide strip of the graveyard, move the gate back, and rebuild the wall. A new pavement and roadworks would make the road safer. I had to supervise the exhumation of the graves affected, and the digging of new graves. The curate had to de-consecrate the work area each morning and, after formally re-burying the day's worth of exhumations, re-consecrate the site at the end of each day. The ground had been disturbed many times over centuries, the soil had turned to a very watery mud, and the excavations just collapsed. We found that coffins had moved horizontally and mingled with other nearby coffins, and all had rotted. Sorting out which bits of which burial matched the church records was a major headache, but virtually all had been dead for more than a century. There were no complaints from relatives. The two Irish labourers took all this in great humour, and rested for tea breaks, on a scaffold board propped up on tombstones. The curate found them holding a conversation with a skull, complete with dangling cigarette in the mouth. He complained, and I had to read the riot act.

Land theft

Private Streets section was interesting, in that I met the public. There are many unmade streets and lanes in the country. The emergency services have to use these to get to incidents, and they complain to the highway authorities for repairs to be done. We respond by saying that we have no power over private land. Only if all affected landowners agree to the work being done and agree to pay for the work, will the County get involved. The county will often act as design co-ordinator and quantity surveyor, to produce a scheme for the landowners' approval, built to County Highways specifications. When the total cost is known, each owner has to agree to pay his or her share, based on the length of the frontage of his property along the new road. We found that owners of houses on a corner plot, with two frontages, often could not afford the double cost and the scheme faltered. Sometimes all but one landowner will agree, and then we had to try to persuade the reluctant owner to agree.

The majority of our work was with developers. We had to ensure that a scheme complied with all the county criteria before we would allow Planning Permission, and we then supervised the construction. We had to do this because the road would eventually become the full responsibility of the County. One developer found a site behind a long row of houses, near Sevenoaks. His proposed access from the highway was past the side of the end house. The gap between the end wall of the house and the neighbouring school playing field fence was about 10 foot less than our absolute minimum requirement, and Planning Permission was refused. At the end of the long summer school holiday, a revised Planning Application was received and I had to check it out on site. There now appeared to be a sufficient width to allow approval for the access road. But how had this been achieved? Close examination revealed that the school fence had been carefully moved back for the whole length of the whole playing field, and by exactly one 10 foot fencing bay along the main road. The Council took the developer to court for stealing land from the school.

Bridge demolition

At the village of Bridge, in East Kent, a road widening scheme was delayed by a redundant railway bridge over the road. The County decided that it would make a suitable training exercise for the Royal Engineers. Demolition of bridges is one of the skills required of a Sapper, and there are not many bridges available in peace time to practise on. They came, drilled holes, filled the holes with explosive, strapped on steel cutting shaped charges, and blew the bridge. When the smoke cleared, the main girders were still sitting on the abutments, and the granite block abutments appeared not to have suffered any damage! Further inspections by senior Sapper officers were developed into "lessons learned" and I attended one lecture on the subject later. Meanwhile, the bridge was now unsafe, roadworks were delayed, and locals were being diverted for miles round the area. Just down the road was a Traction Engine enthusiast, and he reckoned that he had a solution. After getting him permission, and his signing all sorts of indemnity papers, he slung a steel rope round the girders and pulled them down. The Sapper officer in charge of the original blast was present, and was suitably red-faced.

A2 (M) Trunk Road survey

The biggest survey job I had was the A2 Trunk Road, from the Woolwich Borough boundary with Kent, towards Gravesend. I had to survey and plot all the services and street and house access points. At the time this was a three lane road, but with very wide verges. The road was to be improved to dual carriageway (almost motorway standard), and would eventually become the A2(M), and take all the M2 traffic into London. Some 550 properties were affected, and the majority only needed changes to the drives and footpath access. To find the services, I had to contact all the utility providers and meet representatives on site to mark the items for survey. There were a number of manholes that no one could identify immediately, and a measure of detective work resolved the identity of all but one. I had dug strip trenches at intervals, from the garden fence lines to the kerb line, and identified the various pipes and cables, except one remaining cable. This one thin cable was not owned by any organisation that we could think of, so I "accidentally" broke it to see if it was an abandoned and dead cable. On the contrary, it was the NATO HQ to 10 Downing Street "hot line". A pulse was sent down the line at intervals to check that the line was operational. Within minutes, a fleet of cars and vans appeared, the whole area sealed off very efficiently by men in long trench coats and trilby hats, and the line was repaired. If the operation had been done in Soviet Russia, the final act would have been the execution of the technician (to maintain the secrecy). I had kept well away during this repair, not wanting to finish up in some military dungeon. The County Surveyor sent for me and told me that a very senior government official had (not very politely) asked him to kindly take more care when preparing to dig up this bit of road. I was duly warned.

The design of the A2(M) was reasonably straight forward, and required a number of bridges to separate local traffic from the fast, through, traffic. One such bridge required the demolition of a house, owned by a very vocal local opposition councillor. He made his objections known far and wide, by newspaper headlines and protest meetings. He was a thorn in our side. We tried several alignments for the bridge, but all had to affect, more or less, his land. What he really objected to was that the transport café (a "greasy spoon" tar paper shack) next door to him was always unaffected by any of our designs! He had had a feud with the café owner for many years and had tried every tactic in the book to get him closed down. He felt that the café was an eyesore, and that it adversely affected the value of his own property. Eventually, the final scheme demolished the councillor's house (and because he objected to the demolition, he only got the basic Compulsory purchase level of compensation). The café owner, who would no longer be able to trade on the new road, negotiated a handsome compensation for the loss of business. The bridge also affected one of the holes on a small, 9 hole golf course on the opposite side of the road. By careful design, we were able to re-adjust the shape of the golf course.

Later that year my father came to England on Annual Leave, which in those Colonial days was three months. He had arranged to take delivery of a new Morris Mini. It cost him £318 ex-works. As a temporary visitor to Britain, no other taxes were due, as long as he exported the car in under 12 months. He gave me the car at the end of his leave, and I had to pay the Excise duty and all the other taxes before I could register it in my name. This put me in severe financial difficulties, and the cost was about six month's wages.

Bomb Disposal Squadron

I was very active in the TA during this time. I had joined 583 (BD) Squadron, based in Fort Clarence, Rochester. The Drill Hall was at the top of the hill above the city, and had imposing gate posts, which were two bright red painted 500 Kg German Bombs (empty of explosive, I was assured). The Officer Commanding, Major Rabjohn, knew that I had not got a Driving Licence, so I was his automatic choice for the unit MTO (Motor Transport Officer). My sergeant taught me to drive all the vehicles in the fleet, including the BSA 350cc Motorcycle, Bedford RL lorry, Morris 1-Ton lorry, Commer minivan and the Austin Champ (4 x 4). The Champ was a fearsome beast. It had a very powerful Rolls Royce engine and a separate forward/reverse gear lever. All our vehicles were fitted with police sirens, blue flashing lights and the front wings/mudguards were painted a bright red.

Eventually, I had to pass a driving Test. We were able to use a Regular NCO, who was licensed to test Army drivers. We chose a Sunday morning, when traffic was lighter through Chatham and Rochester, and I set off in the Champ with the NCO. In Chatham's main street, I signalled to overtake the marching Salvation Army Band, and while passing the band, I was given the signal for an emergency stop. The Champ does not take kindly to abrupt halts and there was a lot of squealing tyres. The Band scattered, dropping instruments. I fumbled with gear levers and tried to re-start. The NCO, with his best smile, tried to apologise to the Band leader. I remember the Band Leader saying, rather pompously that he "was of the Army of the Kingdom of the Lord". The sergeant replied "Then you are a bloody long way from your barracks". The Band eventually reformed and set off again. The NCO asked me to remain stationary, until the Band had marched away. I regained my composure, and then we set off again. Just in front of the Band, when we caught up with them, was a left turn and I was instructed to take the turn. Once again, there were bandsmen and instruments all over the road. We drove on and the NCO turned to me, with a broad grin, and said that he had always wanted to upset the Salvation Army, and thanked me for the chance! I passed the test.

In the Unit, the Squadron Sergeant Major (SSM) had fought at Arnhem and was a tower of strength. I remember that, when ever we were working in the field, there was always a large cooking pot of Rum and Blackcurrant for all to dip into. We had trouble getting the stains off the aluminium. My Transport section Sergeant had lost his hearing when torpedoed in the Atlantic, and we had to use a sort of sign language. He was small, and I am small. On parade, he stood behind the rear rank of the men, and often I could not see him. To give him the order to march the section away meant my marching to the back of the squad and standing in front of him. Another man had had a serious head injury during the War. A Bailey Bridge panel had fallen on his head and there was a nasty scar from front to back. Because of the thousands of medical inspections that he had attended, he had a habit, when saluting by moving his hand to his head, taking off the beret and rolling it into a tube (badge forward), and holding the beret next to his right ear, all in one very rapid fluid movement. He could do this as fast as a normal salute.

At Christmas in 1960, we held a party for all the children. Presents were wrapped, music and games provided for the kids, and there was the bar for the rest of us. Towards the end of a long afternoon, the kids started asking for Father Christmas. The Second in Command (2ic) was bundled into the Santa kit and given the bag of presents. He sat in a chair and the first kid was brought to him. Before he could say a word, the SSM's son sniffed at him and declared "You're drunk, just like my Daddy". Eventually the presents were given out and families left. The rest of us went back to the bar. Later that evening, we had to pour the 2ic into his Bentley, still in his Father Christmas robes. On the A2, towards Sittingbourne, he was waved down by a walking policeman. He was accused of speeding, and this was before the invention of the radar gun. The 2ic enquired if the policeman had with him "the equipment required under the Road Traffic Act necessary to prove such an accusation?" "And are you fitted with an odometer which has been calibrated in the

61

last seven days? Over what distance have you been following me?" The policeman could not give answers and had to let him proceed. Had the policeman simply opened the car door, Father Christmas would have fallen out. The 2ic was a board member of the Independent Broadcasting Authority and a Justice of the Peace.

In the summer of 1961, the unit exercised its right to march through the City of Rochester, with bayonets fixed and bands playing. We had the Freedom of the City. As part of the parade, the Drill Demonstration Platoon of the Grenadier Guards had been invited to march in full dress uniform. The Guards Officer, a young upper class gentleman, complained to me later in the Officers Mess bar that he felt insulted that his "perfect troops" had to march behind a unit of scruffy part-time soldiers. The Army have a fixed order of precedence, in which the Artillery and Engineers march in front of common infantry units, and there was nothing that he could say about it. Anyway, his unit had not been honoured with the Freedom of the City. Afterward the parade, the Lord Mayor asked us to accept a large barrel of beer that he had set up in the City Hall for the Squadron. The Mace Bearer's daughter became barmaid for the event. When the barrel was empty, she was invited to attend our Pay Parade. In those days, all Other Ranks had to be paid in cash at the end of the attendance. She sat at the pay table with the 2ic's hat on, and winked at each man as he marched up, stamped to attention and held his hand out for the money.

Major Rabjohn was Deputy Head of a Primary School, and smoked a pipe. In London, the Adjutant of the Duke of York's Headquarters in Chelsea was organising Wine and Cheese parties on a very regular basis. He talked wine merchants into providing a free party in the hope that the wine merchant might get the annual contract to supply the Officers Mess. As there were over a thousand wine merchants in London, there were many takers, and we had one free party a week. The Adjutant worked out that he could keep this up for 200 years. Major Rabjohn had a particularly heavy party on one occasion and an Army Staff Car got him to Charing Cross Station. Having caught the train, he fell asleep and missed his stop. He got off the train a few stops further down the line, somewhere in deepest, darkest, Kent. He got home safely, at some very early hour before dawn. A week or so later, his wife noticed a police car taking an interest in his house, and each time she tried to talk to the driver, he drove off. Eventually the policeman found the Major at home, alone. The Major had left his pipe and tobacco with two library books under a park bench in a village some 25 miles beyond his regular stop, and he had been traced from the books. The Chelsea parties continued until that Adjutant was given another posting.

The original Young Offenders Prison was at Borstal, and the village gave its name to the Young Offenders Prison system. The original building was next door to our Drill Hall. The Physical Training Instructor at the Borstal used our large drill hall as a PT gymnasium for his boys in wet weather. The PTI was ex-military and asked if he could train his lads on our miniature rifle range, using our 0.22 rifles. War Office permission was reluctantly granted, eventually. For some months this was successful, until passing cars started to lose windscreens. The boys had been taking rifles out of the range. We were forbidden to have any contact with the Borstal after that.

Jane settled in at a school in Wrotham, a village in an agricultural area. There were a number of Romany families sending children to school while the parents picked hops and fruit in the summer. One bright little girl was sent to school in bare feet. Jane bought her a pair of shoes, only to discover the shoes being worn by the girl's elder sister the next day. She explained that they used the shoes on alternate days. These families had also bought "Tuf" brand shoes, which had a six months guarantee. Due to multiple usage, these shoes became worn out quickly, and were repeatedly being replaced under guarantee!!

Another young teacher asked Jane to go on a shopping trip to London with her on a Saturday, while I was away on training. Sitting in the train, this rather attractive blond-haired lady stared at one of the men in the compartment. Eventually, she reached forward, tapped him on the knee and said "Aren't you the father of one of my children?" She meant one of her pupils, but the looks from the other passengers made her realize the mistake.

At Easter in 1961, the Queen and Prince Phillip were due to visit Rochester to issue Maundy Money to selected parishioners. Our unit was to provide troops to line the route. I was to lead one column and salute as the Royal Party passed. We practised all the moves, and eventually were considered almost up to standard. Then Jane gave me Chicken Pox, which some child in her class had had. For an adult, the illness is quite serious, and I had to miss the parade. I telephoned the Admin Officer at the Drill Hall, so that alterations could be made to replace me. I got a charming official Army letter back, saying that "they were all rather amused". I had recovered enough to attend the Maundy Service, but out of uniform. I did get the chance to line the route, on another Royal Visit. I remember the crowd pushing forward to get a glimpse of the party as they passed. One rather sweaty individual kept pushing his camera into my right ear. As he yelled "Up the Navy" to Prince Phillip, I saluted and managed to knock his camera into the road.

In the summer of 1961, Jane and I toured Ireland in the Mini. We camped in some wonderful country and with friendly people. At the start of August Bank Holiday weekend, the car died and I finally got a local garage to rescue us. The mechanic had been dragged out of a pub, under protest, and towed us to Skibbereen at breakneck speed on a six foot rope. When the engine was examined, he decided that nothing could be done for the three days of the Bank Holiday. He dropped us and our camping equipment in a field, next to a river. We were kept awake by the noise of salmon jumping in the river. The car repair eventually took a week. We drove up the West Coast and into Donegal and Galway, arriving on the last Saturday of our holiday. Miles of open country, not a dwelling in sight, and I had a nearly empty fuel tank. Eventually we reached a croft with a fuel pump outside. Jane had spotted what looked like a shop door at the far end of the building and disappeared. After filling the tank, the pump attendant asked me to go into his office to pay. It was then that I realised that the whole building was one long room. There was a shop at one end, garage at the other, and a bar in between. It took us a while to leave.

Bomb Disposal Training

Weekend training was frequently held at Broadbridge Heath Camp in Horsham. This was the home of the Joint Services Bomb Disposal School and the BD Unit of the Royal Engineers. I had to pass a course to obtain a Bomb Disposal certificate, and I was instructed by RAF and Navy NCOs, as well as Royal Engineers. In 1960, there were still some 4,000 known unexploded bombs buried in the United Kingdom. Most had been graded as Category D, (in open land away from habitation).

We learnt to locate buried bombs, using magnetometer probes to plot changes in the earth's magnetic field when a large metal object was near. Using results from three adjacent holes, it was possible to find the depth, direction, and inclination of a bomb. The probes were put down a pipe jetted into the soil by a high pressure water pump. Everyone got wet, and muddy. The magnetometer was affected by any buried metal, and we found brass bedsteads, old cars, mangles, bicycles in abundance. Each object had to be found, examined, and discarded before we found the bomb. We estimated that some 95% of the metal found was harmless, but it all took time.

Once a bomb, or suspected bomb, had been located, a shaft had to be dug down to the bomb. Because bomb fuzes could be set off by magnetism, all the materials used had to be non-magnetic. Timber sides and frames were held in place with wooden wedges. Hand tools were made of non-magnetic material. Because a disturbance could set a clockwork fuze ticking, the excavation work was done very slowly and carefully. Spoil was brought to the surface using a canvas bucket lifted by a rope suspended from a sheerlegs. Ground water was sucked out by a pump, or bailed into the bucket. It was a mucky, backbreaking, job. The timbering skills that I learnt in training, I was able to apply later in life, particularly at Hendon on the retaining wall excavation.

We learned about the various types of bomb, fuze, initiation device, and the booby traps designed to kill BD technicians. The Army had "liberated" some 8,000 V2 Rocket fuzes from a store in Peenemunde at the end of the War, and we played with these. Britain was very lucky that Hitler did not have time to use up all these extra fuzes in rocket raids. We trained with these "all-ways" impact fuses. A high proportion of German fuzes were clockwork, and the Clock Stopper (a very powerful and heavy magnet) was designed to prevent the fuze from operating by applying a massive magnetic force, pulling all the clockwork mechanism and any striking pin up to the surface of the fuze. From memory, this needed 18 car batteries to provide enough electricity. Of course there is always one idiot in each class, who put his wristwatch near the Clock Stopper, and wondered why the cogs came through the glass face.

The Chief Instructor for fuzes was an RAF Chief Technician. What he could do with clockwork mechanisms was magical, and he had studied the design of every known fuze in the world. Looking towards his retirement, he started training himself on coin operated gambling machines (one-armed bandits) and other arcade machines. After some highly secret "adjustments" he could predict the exact time and amount of any payout. He was intending to buy his own Amusement Arcade with his retirement money. He had a very rich future ahead.

For many other fuzes, it was safer to take the main explosive filling away from the fuze, rather than the fuze from the filling. After a long period in the ground, corrosion prevents fuzes from being simply unscrewed. Also, during filling inevitably a little liquid TNT gets on to screw threads. After a while, this TNT crystallises and unscrewing could potentially rub the faces of two crystals together and cause an explosion. To remove the filling, a trepanning machine is used to cut a circular hole in the bomb casing. Where possible, the hole should be at the bottom so that the explosive can drain out. When the hole has been made, a steam nozzle is inserted and the steam melts the waxy explosive. This is washed out of the hole and allowed to form puddles on the ground. The operator had to use considerable skill to make sure that the steam nozzle did not get blocked by explosive, because the steam generator would stop working. A sudden stop would produce a vacuum in the steam hose, and this could suck explosive back into the steam generator and then (after a loud noise) someone would have to explain where all the bits of the steam generator had got to. Steam made the hose pipe very hot, and the air in the bottom of the bomb shaft got unbearably hot quickly. One officer had a bomb to empty in February, and overnight the ground at the bottom of the shaft had frozen. After a period of steaming out, the frozen ground melted and the bomb started to roll. He had to keep the steam nozzle working and clear of explosive. To do this he had to lay on his back, and the melted explosive solidified onto his uniform. I went down to break off bits, put them into a bucket, and get them hauled up out of his way. The bomb casing was very hot to touch, but we had to hold it from rolling any further. Eventually the job was done and the loose explosive was burnt off in an open area. The officer had to get a new uniform, as civilian dry cleaning would not well work with the TNT that was soaked into the cloth.

About the time of the Birthday Honours List being published, I was the only TA officer in Bomb Disposal HQ at the weekend, and still a lowly Second Lieutenant. Most of the regular officers had gone away on weekend leave, and this left me to be Orderly Officer. In the Mess there were only three other officers. "Archie" Lt Col Bernard Archer, George Cross, another Army Emergency Reserve Lt Col Eric Wakeling, George Medal, and the Chief Instructor, Major Bill Hartley, George Medal. I was in the presence of multiple bravery awards and felt very, very, humble. They had a very heavy evening in the bar, telling stories of bomb incidents, which were fascinating to hear. The next morning, it was a very silent breakfast until there was a roar of anger from behind the newspaper. "Which one of you bastards did this? How did you get someone to print this, in our Mess copy?" Archer had seen his name listed as a new OBE, and swore that one of his friends had "adjusted" the newspaper copy that he was holding.

There is a story about the research undertaken when a new fuze, marked with a "Z", and "40" started to kill people. It was obviously purpose-made to kill anyone attempting to defuse the bomb. Each officer had to report when he found a Z40 marking (or any other never before seen markings). The Home Office team would arrive to record, from a safe distance, every move the officer made, until the explosion. It slowly became apparent that the fuze could only be withdrawn a very little way before detonation. Heads were scratched, but no answers came. At this time, any BD officers' expected life span was about 3 weeks, compared to an RAF fighter pilot having at least six weeks life expectancy. Any one finding one of these bombs knew he was close to the end of his life. This story I heard from either Eric Wakeling or Archie, which may well be true, was about a very studious and abstemious officer who reported that he had a "Z" fuse to deal with and decided, after telling his superiors about the bomb, that he would have an early night. The next day was his birthday, and he intended to start work at dawn when the air is still and there is very little traffic vibration. The others in the Mess had a real drinking session that night and celebrated his birthday for him. In the morning, he set to work, and the fuze came out without the usual detonation! Stuck onto the bottom, was a bit of paper with "Happy Birthday, George" written on it. The others had left the party in the small hours to help him out. On examination, poor machining had provided a "burr" on the edge of a slot in the fuse and the striking pin had been caught up just on the edge of the slot. The Zeus40 problem was actually solved when Bernard Archer removed a complete fuze pocket from a bomb in a burning oil refinery, earning the George Cross.

On another weekend, again as Orderly Officer, I had a telephone call on the Saturday evening from an irate building contractor. He had just been awarded a contract for 400 new homes in Southampton, only to be told that there was an unexploded bomb on his site. Would I please remove it by Monday, or there would be trouble? I explained that it would take several days, after we had arrived, to even locate the bomb, and before the slow process of sinking a shaft down to the bomb. He was not a happy bunny. In the end, the bomb was found and it proved too difficult to remove. As it was a long way from any habitation, it was blown insitu. We left the builder to backfill the massive crater.

The drive down from Rochester to Horsham on a Friday night, long before the M25 was built, took us on the A25 through Redhill, Reigate and Dorking. Evening rush hour traffic was very heavy. One week, I was driving the Commer minibus and it started to rain very heavily. When I switched on the wipers, the siren and flashing blue light also switched on. There was a short circuit on the dashboard, and I had a choice of either having everything working, or nothing working. We needed the wipers, so we drove on, with the siren blaring away merrily and the blue light flashing. When we reached Redhill, the police had stopped all the traffic in the town and cleared the main road for us. The same thing happened in Reigate and Dorking. It was a very pleasant, trouble free, journey through rush hour traffic. I presume that the Police thought that we were returning to Horsham with a live bomb on board.

To get my BD qualification, I had to go on operational call outs. I had to examine the bomb, (or whatever the police wanted us to remove), and write down what I thought it was and how I would deal with it. The Regular Officer Instructor would then say if I was correct or not.

BD Headquarters had a turbocharged Ford saloon car, with the usual red mudguards and the siren, sitting ready in the camp. The boot was full of tools and equipment. The call out crew sat in the Guard Room, waiting for the telephone to ring. A bomb had been found close to St Paul's Cathedral and it was Friday afternoon. The police had stopped the tube trains, in case the vibration set off the bomb. Two Irish labourers, who had found the "bomb", were selling the story to every paper in Fleet Street. Every City Banker was calling the Home Secretary, personally, to ask just how were they meant to get home for the weekend with the roads and Underground trains sealed off? The Home Secretary was putting pressure on the Police Commissioner. The Police Commissioner was, in turn, putting enormous pressure on the Police Inspector on site. On the way into London, the BD car was met by a motorcycle policeman, who was to escort the car all the way to the site. The Captain was driving and had, only the week before, used the same route under police escort. There is one place where the one-way system runs along streets forming two sides of an equilateral triangle, and the sides were about half a mile each. The Captain took the direct route, in the opposite direction to the traffic, along the third side of the triangle, leaving the police escort to take the long way round. It is not often one gets the chance to leave a police escort behind! The car arrived without the escort, to be greeted by a very harassed Inspector, who asked "Just what had kept you" (or words to that effect), and he pointed in the general direction of the bomb.

The student under test went first, into a tunnel being dug away from the site, across a road and presumably for a service connection. He examined the object, wrote down his findings and waved the Captain over. He looked at the "bomb", then at the student's bit of paper. Up to this point no one had spoken a word, and the suspense was killing the Inspector. The BD officers slowly walked over to him and presented the paper. On it was written "Coin operated gas meter". The Inspector looked round for someone to vent his anger on. At that moment, the police motorcycle escort arrived. There was a lot of unprintable language, and the man was sent back on foot patrol duty with immediate effect. With great relief, the Inspector told the Commissioner that traffic could flow again, and the reporters withdrew the cash offers they had made to the two labourers. The gas meter was taken back to the camp and placed in the Black Museum.

In the summer of 1961, the TA was part of a full Mobilization exercise, and some 3000 of us were sent to Germany to "reinforce BAOR (British Army of the Rhine)". The plan had been worked out in great detail, and all our War stores and vehicles were held at stores in Belgium. On arrival, each unit was escorted to a group of vehicles (which hopefully had been fuelled and checked previously) and told to drive them over to collect the stores held for that unit. This included packed rations, tents, bedding, tools and special equipment. Each unit had different lists and quantities, all shown on their Army Form G1098. We signed for the vehicles, and took them away to load stores.

I thought that we had rather more stores than the capacity of the vehicles provided. I checked with the storeman, to find that we had been listed as a regiment, and we were actually only a squadron. We had been expected to take three times the kit. When I was issued with 12 trailer fire pumps, and only had four towing vehicles, the quickest way out of the problem was to accept them, hitch them up and drive them to the far fence and park up what we could not take. If we had not done this, every unit behind us would have backed up. Similarly, pallets of equipment and tools were dumped by the fence. A lot of the surplus food managed to stay on the trucks, and we lived like lords for the rest of the fortnight.

Once loaded and formed up in a convoy, we were escorted out of Belgium, and across Holland, to Germany. The Dutch Maastricht Peninsula sticks down between the other two countries and the Autobahn is continuous for the 60 kilometres across Holland. We had a very large Dutch Military motorcycle policeman escorting our section to make sure that we did not stop in Holland or set foot on Dutch soil. He kept urging us to go faster by standing up and waving his pistol. We were waved through all the Border posts, at speed. Of course, some vehicles were not up to the journey, having been parked up for years waiting for this day. My Champ had many problems, which upset the Dutch policemen. One of another unit's Champs broke down at the German border, so the German police towed it to the nearest British base, which happened to be an RAF unit. The RAF kindly offered to fly the wounded vehicle and passengers to England, but the offer was reluctantly refused. It would have been difficult to explain away a military vehicle in the wrong country.

We reached our "War" location and started learning what our "War" role was expected to be. Apart from acting as ordinary Sappers on minefields and demolitions, we were expected to act as Bomb Disposal. At that time, rockets were beginning to appear on the battlefield, carrying conventional and nuclear warheads. There were also some tactical nuclear demolition devices used by both sides. Any of these new-fangled things could fail to work as designed, leaving someone to have to "make safe". No one had any idea what would be required, but this new problem needed a solution. Senior military planners had not thought this out. The OC reported this problem to the Brigade Commander, and we were instructed to work something out. That is how I got the job of researching and writing the "Standard Operating Procedure for Unexploded Nuclear Bombs (SOP for UXNB)".

Standard Operating Procedure for Unexploded Nuclear Bombs

UXNB could be Battlefield Demolition Devices, Nuclear Shells, missiles or rockets, with a nuclear warhead. Also included in UXNB, were rockets and missiles with conventional warheads found on the battlefield. With any rocket, the liquid propellant was more dangerous to Bomb Disposal personnel than the warhead. LOX (liquid oxygen) would spill into the ground, or lay as a mist over an area, and a spark or static electricity could make it explode. Any liquid fuel trapped in a bent and twisted pipeline could explode if the pipe was straightened when the wreckage was moved. The fuel from Solid Fuel rockets could be set alight, as long as the gas produced could escape easily. Other gases gave us other problems, requiring breathing apparatus. No one had any idea of what constituted a "safe distance" from a damaged nuclear warhead, and how to apply this in a busy war zone. As for the nuclear warheads and demolition devices, I proposed that men in white coats from Aldermaston, suitably protected, came to sort these out! Perhaps they could invent tools and methods for the safe disposal?

The SOP for UXNB called for the first inspection to be done from a great distance, with binoculars. The observer would dictate his comments on a field telephone to his man further back, so that a record was available if the observer died.

Using a radio for this dictation could also upset the electromagnetic field, and cause detonation. Digital cameras had not been invented and the Polaroid camera was only good for distances up to ten feet or so. Camera film would need a laboratory to produce the developed pictures and would not be available. Part of the report was to dictate a drawing of the crash site and the missile, for the note taker to draw out. If you have ever tried to draw as someone dictates, you will understand the problem. One can start at the wrong point on the paper, and go over the edge to get it all in. We never did get the hang of this properly. Later, this developed into a hilarious party game, where one person describes an object and the players have to sketch it. The first to guess the object wins.

Since that time, the whole subject of UXNB has never been mentioned to my knowledge. I can only presume that the subject has been filed under "Too difficult. Discuss later, if at all".

On the way home from the Mobilisation Exercise, we had to return our equipment to the depot in Grobbendonk in Belgium. This left us without transport and we made use of the NAAFI bar. Our unit tipple became the "Drambuie Shandy". The Drambuie cost 4 old pence (1.67p in new money), but the Lemonade was very expensive, so it was used sparingly. The richer lads got a taxi into nearby Antwerp. The next day, there was a Force 7 wind in the English Channel and a few of us were very unwell during the crossing. As one of our officers, Lt Rick White, was a Dover Customs Officer in "Civvi Street", our unit was formed up in three ranks and we just marched straight through Customs and Immigration. 579 Squadron (BD) had a Drill Hall only 100 metres from the dock gate and we all stayed in the bar until we were collected by our spouses. Other units suffered at the hands of Rick's colleagues. We watched from the bar as other units dribbled slowly out of the Dock gates. 21 SAS (Artists Rifles), the London TA Squadron, took up to eight hours to clear Customs. They were suspected of hiding things in the Teddy Bears they had bought for their children. The Bears were unrecognisable when they finally left the docks!

Marriage

In April 1962, Jane and I were married in Dewi Sant (St David's) Church, Cardiff. Jane's parents had moved back to Wales following her father's retirement from teaching mining surveying and geology at North Staffs Technical College in Stoke on Trent. John Skone was my Best Man, and the Bridesmaids were two of Jane's college friends. We hired a cruiser on the Norfolk Broads for the Honeymoon. I had handled some Army boats before, but Jane was a complete novice. She asked a local boatman where she could "park" the boat! I do remember entering Potter Higham at top speed with a jammed throttle, but managed to avoid any damage.

69

In the summer of 1962, the Squadron went on Annual Camp with 114 Army Engineer Regiment, to Lancaster. It was the custom for smaller units to share accommodation with a bigger unit at these camps, and made for inter-unit rivalry. During driver training, including map-reading, some of our vehicles turned right on the Preston Bypass (the original length of Motorway). They crossed the central reservation and disappeared up a slip road. They were spotted by a plain clothes police car. The two blonds in this white Daimler Dart sports car caught up with them and words were had. The Commanding Officer of 114 Regt at that time was also the Chief Engineer of Guinness Brewery. Guinness owned the freehold of about 60 acres in the centre of Lancaster, and had a plush office there, with the black liquid on tap. The two police ladies were invited to discuss the infringements with the Colonel at this office. After a number of glasses of Black Velvet (Guinness and Champagne), the girls were poured back into the Daimler Dart and we heard nothing more. I was out with some vehicles north of Lancaster, when a very long articulated lorry stopped. The driver needed to get to Yorkshire in a hurry and wanted to know if there was a route across the Pennines. This was long before the road was improved. After looking at the map and accepting my advice, he set off. A few days later, I took the same route. On the way up the hill, one could see where he had had to make several attempts at each hairpin bend. Once over the top, the road was straight, narrow and it was gated. The lorry had smashed every gate post on the way down, as it had been too wide to get through. At the bottom we stopped at a pub, and the landlord told us a story about a very unhappy driver who expected to kill an Army Officer if he ever caught up with him!

On the middle Saturday, a regatta was held with competition between our two units. They had three times the number of men to select teams from, so we had to be good to win. The final race was an obstacle course, tackled in aluminium assault boats racing across the River Lune. A pontoon was moored in the centre of the river and the boats had to be hauled up over the pontoon on the way out, and on the way back. The first crew back, with the boat upside down on the bank, paddles laid out in line and all the crew standing to attention, won the race. Lt Rick White was our captain and the boat flew through the water. On the second pontoon crossing, Rick leapt back into the boat but landed heavily with one leg either side of the gunwale. Our team won, but there was blood streaming down Rick's legs. After an emergency operation, he was transferred by train to Ashford Hospital in Kent, to be near his wife. I was selected to escort the stretcher on the train, to look after the catheter bag, and make sure that the ambulances collected him at Kings Cross, and Ashford. Although we had a reserved compartment, three Nuns wanted to join us, until I raised the urine filled bag. At Kings Cross, the ambulance failed to show up and the train was shunted away from the platform. Eventually I found the ambulance and the transfer across London was done. I had been chosen as escort, so that I could visit Jane. The senior officers knew that I had only been married for three months.

More BD stories

In 1936, before the War, the Home Office decreed that the officer in charge of any Bomb Disposal incident was solely responsible for deciding the method of disposal, even if this meant the demolition of property. Small arms ammunition, when found, was normally dealt with by members of the Royal Army Ordnance Corps (RAOC), which is now part of the Royal Logistics Corps.

The RAOC major responsible for the London District had been fined, and disqualified from driving, for jumping a red light while on a call out. He felt that, he should have been treated the same way as ambulances and police cars. As he was most upset, he insisted on following "The Book". Most small items get handed in to police stations, and stay on top of the front desk until the BD officer arrives. Our "major with a grudge" had damaged some 50 police stations by the time we got involved, as he simply placed a guncotton charge on top of the object. We found this out when the police started calling us instead of him, to save further damage.

One police desk sergeant had been seen paying a small boy to take a Butterfly Bomb back to the Recreation Ground, where he had found it. Another sergeant took a grenade that had been handed in, down to the bottom of his station yard and placed it carefully in the rafters of the bicycle shed. The major dealt with this one. He carefully built up sandbags under the grenade, and placed just a few sandbags on the roof. When he blew the charge, a knife edge of blast took the roof off the recently built main building, like cutting the top off a boiled egg.

Many landmines had been laid on the beaches and cliffs of Norfolk and Suffolk. Some were picked up by sea currents, carried through the Straights of Dover, and washed up on South Coast beaches. One such mine arrived at Eastbourne in March 1961. It had been found above High Water level, so the Navy could not be asked to deal with it. It was in an area of sand dunes, some distance from houses, so it was agreed that it would be demolished in situ at noon on a Sunday. The police cleared the dog walkers away and asked residents to keep all windows open. After the explosion, the sea was allowed to refill the crater naturally. What was not immediately realised was that the blast wave had hit the town gasometer, and thrown the top tank off the guide wheels. The tank was jammed, resulting in the pressure in the gas mains dropping. Sunday lunches stopped cooking. The Gas Board had to go round to each house, to make sure that all taps were turned off, before trying to unjam the gasometer.

One weekend, I took some TA BD sappers to Dungeness Point. The Army had a demolition range there, and we had been given a solid fuel booster rocket on which to practise our demolition skills. A rocket works by setting fire to one end. The enormous amount of gas resulting from the intense fire has to get out of the tube. The pressure moves the rocket forward, boosting the missile to over Mach 2 before burning out after four seconds. To demolish the rocket, one makes both ends burn at the same time, cancelling out the blast effect. In theory, the rocket stays put on the ground. To make sure, a longitudinal charge splits open the top of the rocket, allowing more gas to escape upwards, forcing the rocket down onto the ground. We placed the charges and retired to the concrete bunker for safety. I asked the youngest sapper to press the switch. When he did there was the expected bang, followed by an unexpected "Whoosh". Someone had tripped over a bit of detonation cord on the way back to the bunker, preventing the top charge and one of the end charges from exploding. Unsurprisingly, this made the rocket act like a rocket. Where had it gone? I quickly climbed out of the bunker and, looking at where the rocket had laid, worked out that it had headed for France. In the distance, there was a small fishing boat trying to take avoiding action! The rocket fell into the sea. It then dawned on me just how lucky I had been. Had the rocket travelled in the opposite direction, Dungeness Power Station (under construction but nearly completed) would have been badly damaged. The contractor would not have been pleased with me. I was able to use the incident to give a lecture on safety, and the need for checking demolition circuits thoroughly before proceeding.

In the early 1960s, semiconductors and microchips had not been invented. Our Drill Hall classroom had 12 desks with drawers. The contents of these drawers were similar to those found in any housewife's kitchen drawers. To make an IED (Improvised Explosive Device), apart from the explosive and detonator, one has to have a method of initiation. A pressure switch, pressure release switch, pull switch, electrical current, chemical reaction, or heat were some of the ways used. Each class gave me 12 new ideas, using the same household items. Cigar tubes, ball-bearings, clothes pegs and tinfoil all had ingenious uses. Now that we all have access to mobile phones, baby alarms, electric model racing cars, TV remotes and the like, the possibilities become endless. Just think about what our troops have faced in Iraq, Afghanistan, and other similar places.

I had to teach the division of responsibilities between the three Services. Blaster Bates and Bob Newheart recordings were very useful in helping to put across the lessons. Both these gentlemen talked about explosives and responsibilities in a humourous way.

On one trip to Horsham, a resident of St Dunstan's (who help blind ex-Servicemen) was invited for lunch. This was the BD Officer who had booby trapped Brighton Pier during the War, and who returned to dismantle all of his own traps. He had kept detailed records of the hundreds of devices, and sat in an auditorium seat to check his list, to make sure that he had found every last device. The seat was booby trapped and he lost both eyes. He was a remarkable character, and had driven a sports car round a track at speed, with a passenger giving instructions.

A regular occurrence was an official Officers Mess Dinner Night in the Royal Engineers Headquarters, Brompton Barracks, Chatham. I attended several Dinners over the years. These were splendid affairs, with all the officers in red Mess Dress, miniature medals worn, and the Regimental Band playing. The splendid Dining Room could hold up to 500, seated at long tables. All the Regimental Silver, which had been collected over centuries, was displayed along the tables, and valued at over a million pounds. There were many courses, and the table was laid on long strips of cloth in the Regimental Colours. When the table had to be cleared before the Loyal Toast, a Mess waiter stood at the end of each strip. The Band would give a drum roll, and the strips would be pulled off in one clean movement. The strips were up to forty feet long, and moved faster than a whip crack at the end. There was always some junior officer who placed an arm across the strip, and he was usually pulled out of his chair. Earlier in the meal, a junior officer would slide under the table and crawl up towards the senior officer's end of the table. He would tie an officers spurs together with a bootlace and tie the ends to the chair. When the glasses had been charged for the Loyal Toast, the President of the Mess Committee (PMC) would rise and call to his Deputy "Mr Vice, The Queen". This was the signal for all to stand and toast the Queen, but some officers were still tied down to their chairs. When the Port was being circulated, the Band played and a tall and well-built sergeant would walk round with a trombone. He would use the trombone slide to flick ash off the ends of cigars and cigarettes, or flick lighters out of hands, all without missing a note! Later, he would exchange the trombone for a 0.303 rifle with a mouthpiece stuck in the barrel. He had immense strength to be able to hold a 9 lb rifle at arms length and still be able to play. Afterwards, we retired to the Anteroom and drank in the bar. Rowdy Mess games followed.

There is a story about one RE officer which may or not be true. This officer committed some military misdemeanour as a young officer. He was ordered to do a month of Orderly Officer duties in the Brompton Mess. Part of this duty included the daily checking the casks of Napoleon Brandy captured at Waterloo, to make sure that none had been drunk. This Brandy was only ever used when Royalty dined at Brompton. Only officers on the top table with the Royal Guest were served this Brandy. He resolved that he would, at some stage in his career, taste this nectar. Later on, he was posted back to Brompton as a major, and was given the task of organising a Royal Dinner for King George VI. At last, he had a chance to design the seating plan, and carefully placed himself at the end of the top table. He ordered the Brandy to be decanted and made ready. At the last moment, the Royal Party arrived, with one extra person. The Major was forced to give up his seat and he glowered as the decanter passed within feet of him. This only made him more determined to (legally) taste the Brandy. It is said that he became obsessed with this ambition. His chance came at last. Queen Elizabeth was coming to Chatham to honour and accord the School of Military Engineering with the "Royal" prefix. Our man was, by now, the Chief Royal Engineer and was the host for the day. Nothing could stop him having at least one glass of Brandy. At the end of the meal, he turned to his guest and asked if she would like a glass of Brandy. "No, I don't think I will. Thank you", she replied. The wine waiter was told to return the decanter to the cellar by a very emotional General, whose one ambition in life had been thwarted by his Queen. The decanter was diverted to the CRE's room after the Queen had departed, but no one has confirmed this.

M1 Motorway Leicestershire   1962 - 1964

In the summer of 1962, the Graduate under Agreement scheme came to an end in Kent. I had realised that there were no jobs available after the end of the scheme, and I sent off my CV to lots of possible employers. I was invited to several interviews and had a number of offers. One company that I approached (in my innocence) was Cementation Ltd, who wanted an engineer for a bridge job in Hereford. Two Directors interviewed me and one noted my Kenya background and asked if I was related to K. O. Martin. When I said that he was my father, he got up and locked the door. I thought this was strange. They asked me if my father had any property or bank accounts in UK. After discussion, I found out that they were still trying to recover money owed to them by the Kenya Government for stabilizing the Mombasa-Nairobi road, and that my father was responsible (in their eyes) for the debt. Surprisingly, they did not make me a job offer.

I managed to get a job with Sir Owen Williams and Partners. They were the Consultants designing and supervising the next tranche of the M1 Motorway. There were four contracts, over the length from Watford Gap Service Station, to Kegworth where the M1 rejoined the A6 Trunk Road. I was assigned to Contract LY/CH, from Kirby Muxloe to Markfield (where it met the A50 Trunk Road), as an Assistant Resident Engineer.

Our main office was at the site of the Leicester Forest East Service Station, which would be built after we left. The contractor on our section was A. Monk and Co. They supplied some clapped out diesel Land Rovers for site use, which usually froze solid in the winter snows and one had to light fires under the engine before being able to move. The 1962-3 winter was extremely cold. The very cold conditions caused other problems. One day, I took out the 100 foot steel tape which had been left in the Landrover over night. As the tape was drawn out of the case, it stayed in loops. When the chainman pulled, to straighten it, all the loops snapped and I was left with about 20 pieces of steel tape. The metal had become brittle with the cold.

Because Monks were a northern company, they sited their offices at the northern end of the job. Communications between the consultants and contractors had to stretch the length of the site. Most jobs would have insisted on co-location of staff. I was made responsible for all works in the centre one-third of the length, but also had to cover other areas at various times. There were bridges carrying roads over and under the Motorway, and some very deep cuttings, but the majority of the work was in open country.

The initial task was to establish the centreline and reference the vital setting out pegs so that they could be re-established easily. I had a chainman, who (I found out later) had a criminal record. The route took us through a 17 acre wood. The land acquisition for the wood had been delayed, and we had to survey past this obstruction, continuing the line after reaching the other side of the wood. Eventually we got permission to enter the wood for the survey only. All the time I was working, there was a representative of the owner training his shotgun on my chainman from his "side" of the fence line. Eventually the story leaked out. The land owner was in prison, but had not had time to remove the stolen goods buried in the wood. His solicitor had arranged legal reasons to delay the transfer of ownership. My chainman had known about the stolen property, and thought that getting a job on the site would help him to search for it. The delay allowed other gang members to rearrange the hiding places. I think Monks wondered just how to include this story in the Claim for Delay that they wanted to submit!

The Flasher

It was usually bitterly cold and muddy on survey, so one dressed in as many layers as possible. There was no formal protective clothing issued at that time, although Laws and Regulations have helped considerably in later years. There were no radios or mobile telephones in those days so any message had to be sent by telephone from a red public telephone box, or by a note delivered by a driver. One day I told Monks that a concrete pour should not proceed because essential reinforcement had been omitted. As Monks had told me, none too gently, to go away and get lost, I wanted the Resident Engineer to stop the pour. I walked a mile to a phone box, to find the farmer's wife having a long chat with a relative. She popped out and asked if I had any change. My coins were in my clean trousers, worn under my dirty trousers. Without saying a word, I unzipped and lowered my outer trousers and dived in to get at the money. She shot back into the phone box and dialled 999. I offered her the coins I had, but she refused to speak to me, and held the door firmly shut. A police car arrived and I was taken aside and questioned. After a long time, the police believed me and explained to the terrified woman that I was not a "flasher". By this time, Monks had poured the concrete, and I failed to get the work torn down and replaced. I hope that modern communications and external coin pockets on proper wet weather clothing will help avoid similar incidents in future.

Monks had subcontracted the earthmoving to Dick Hampton Ltd. This was my first introduction to heavy muck-shifting, and the characters involved. The first six scrapers arrived on site after driving in convoy from the last job. These were wartime ex-US Army Euclids, with a four wheel ordinary farm tractor towing unit and a cable operated scraper bowl. The lead unit had working headlights. The unit at the rear of the convoy had brake lights. Most of the rest of the units had no lights or brakes! Monks offices were at the bottom of a fairly steep, but narrow, lane lined with dry stone walls. The leading scraper had to drop the bowl into the asphalt road surface to help slow down the following units, which cannoned into each other, and the stone field walls. Not an impressive start to the contract. Later, the bulldozers and accommodation caravans arrived, and work could start. These old Euclids were used for topsoil strip and light work, until they all eventually "died". On site, they were terrifying, as you did not know if the operator could actually stop the machine if he got close to you.

Later on, Dick Hampton invested in more up to date hydraulic operated scrapers. The muck shifting foreman (a German called Peter Altenhoffer) would rush his plant from section to section, at a moment's notice, whenever a hold up prevented him from achieving his weekly bonus volume. In the summer, the lead scraper would churn up dust on the public roads between areas of work. The next in line would follow the brake lights sometimes visible in the dust. He tried to follow the exact path, but was usually a foot or so one side or the other. The third and subsequent scrapers got more and more away from the path. One consequence was that any parked vehicle on road verges was flattened. The scrapers did not even feel the bump! One victim was Hampton's own (self-employed) surveyor, who found that his Minivan was only an inch high when he returned to collect a theodolite from the van! The van and the hired survey gear were his own and not fully insured. The muck-shifting operators were paid a lot more than Assistant Resident Engineers, and could afford big cars. One car developed a broken front suspension and the owner got his colleague to doze the Austin Princess into the borrow pit and bury it. The cost of the spare parts needed to repair the car, were minimal, but the owner just wanted to buy a better car!

My own section office was next to a long skewed underbridge. The abutments and very long wing walls were cast in mass concrete, faced later with "snapped" concrete blocks. The excavations were some fifteen feet deep, and some rudimentary timbering had been provided. A labourer heard the ground creak and groan, and all were evacuated. One older labourer went back into the trench to get his coat which was hanging on a nail. A long timber baulk, which had been standing vertical, fell and hit him on the head. He was pulled out dead, the ambulance took him away, and the police investigated. After all the trauma had finished, Monk's section foremen asked me to fill in the Accident Book, as he was illiterate. I said that I would help him, but that I would only write exactly what he told me, as it was his responsibility to make the entry. We got his name, age, and the date and time easily enough. "Injury?" I asked. "Conclusion of brain", I was told to write. The last column was Remarks, and I was instructed to write: "He made none".

A little later, and several mass concrete pours later, the wing walls were above ground level. One morning, I was looking out of my window when the shutter directly opposite was removed. There, facing me, were the soles of two rubber boots about three foot down from the top of the concrete! Had someone fallen into the pour and no one had noticed? Was there a possibility that he was still alive? How to find out? I had never been in such a situation before and I had to take some sort of action. I had no idea how to cope with this level of major accident. I called my Inspector and we went up to the concrete. The soles had no "give" in them, but that could be because there were either feet, or concrete, in the boots. Then my Inspector noticed little tears in the soles and looked at the newly removed shutter. The nails, holding the (empty) boots in place while the concrete was poured, were still on the shutter. Monk's workmen were having a joke at my expense! After that, Monk's found that I became much stricter in my inspections and I insisted on much higher standards before I would allow concrete to be poured.

On another section, a small road required a bridge to carry the motorway over it. Mass concrete abutments were cast, ready for massive pre-cast beams. These inverted "U" shaped beams were 60 foot span, 20 foot high, and about 20 Tonnes each. Each beam was an inverted "T" section, for later filling with concrete, and the bridge required sixty beams, each two foot wide. The beams arrived on a special truck, with the far end of the beam supported on a separate steerable bogie. The beams were inherently unstable until locked together by the infill concrete. Reinforcement was threaded through holes in the beams.

Temporary tie bars, with threaded ends were put though the holes. This allowed us to tie groups of beams together by screwing nuts onto the threaded ends. Ten beams properly tied together made a relatively stable block. We had a formal road closure over the weekend, to allow us to erect the beams, and our crane sat on the road. We had just placed about 40 beams, when they all lurched sideways, and hung at about 30 degrees to the vertical. Luckily, the temporary tie bars held and were not sheared by the weight of the beams.

Then he appeared, Leicester's best "Sunday Motorist", with his cloth cap pulled down central on his head, and with his wife in a head scarf and clutching an enormous handbag.

He had washed his small car for his weekly run in the country. He had, he told us, paid his Road Fund Tax so he was fully entitled to use the Public Highway at any time. We were in his way and would we please move? We explained that there was about 600 tons of dangerous concrete about to come crashing down on the road. "Not my problem, I am out for a drive, as I have done for many a year, and you have no right to stop me". It took a policeman to finally convince him that we did not want his possible death on our conscience. We eventually managed to get all the beams put back in the upright position again, and the bridge finished without any further trouble. (On a visit many years later, I found that this bridge was no longer necessary as the road had been closed due to further development.)

My Inspector was a keen golfer and he brought his clubs to work. During the time when the various layers of the road were being laid, he would roll a golf ball on the carriageway and watch how it moved. This checked the cross fall, longitudinal fall of the kerb or channel, and surface irregularities which showed up when the ball bounced. When the wearing course was applied, the ball had to roll towards, and into, a gulley pot. If it didn't, the work was condemned.

A large number of the workforce lived on site in caravans. Meat was occasionally "liberated" from local farmers. One time, two inebriated lads caught a sheep and needed to kill it. One held the sheep's neck steady on the ground, while his friend swung the edge of a heavy shovel downwards. He killed the sheep, but also cut off two thumbs.

Leicestershire can get very foggy and I decided on one trip back from Horsham, to ignore the public roads for safety reasons. I knew that the surfacing was more or less complete over the four sections of the M1 under construction, providing a route home in safety. Hugging the edge concrete strip, because it showed white in the fog next to the asphalt surfacing, I set off. All went well until I reached the M6 junction spur. There were trenches and spoil heaps in the carriageway, and the asphalt area had increased in width considerably. I lost sight of the edge strip. The area was about 100 yards in any direction. I drove round all the obstructions but completely lost my sense of direction in the fog. In the end, I decided to park and wait for dawn. This was a good idea that failed.

Bomb Disposal

During my time in Leicestershire, I was still part of the Bomb Disposal Squadron in Kent. In winter, I had more time available for weekend training and would drive down to Rochester, or more frequently, to Broadbridge Heath Camp in Horsham. On another section of the M1 construction, another Assistant RE was also a Bomb Disposal Officer in the TA, so we shared a car on trips to Horsham. He had left McAlpines preparing to cast a bridge deck over a single track railway during a weekend. British Rail had allowed a short "possession" of the track for the crane lifting the concrete onto the deck. We drove back on the Sunday evening, still in uniform. My friend wanted to stop by the job, to make sure that everything was going to plan. Just before we arrived, the deck soffit shutter collapsed, tipping many cubic yards of wet concrete onto the railway line. Mixed into this concrete were scaffolding, reinforcement, and shuttering. The lighting towers were knocked flat and the generator damaged. It was pitch black. There was no lighting, and the 14 workmen panicked. They all thought that the other 13 were still trapped in the wreckage, and were frantically searching for friends. My friend found the foreman, and then gave a loud blast on his whistle. He lined up all the men, checked them off against the register and proved that there was no one missing or hurt. The foreman then took over, anxious to make up for lost time. Some men were told to gather up the wet concrete and take it to some drainage work, waiting for concrete. The foreman was not going to waste anything. Others were told to gather up scaffolding and timber, to clear the rail track. Later, in the early hours, after we retired to the site hut for a mug of tea, there was a loud bang outside and something hit the roof. Some concrete on the rail track had set solid by this time, so the foreman was blasting it off. Where he had found the explosives, I don't know, but we took our tea mugs further down the track and out of harm's way. By dawn the track was cleared enough for the first train to pass safely.

The M1 contract to the north of my own also used Dick Hampton as the earthmoving contractor. In a deep cut, a bulldozer exposed a German 500Kg bomb. The operator left the machine with the bomb up against the blade and ran off to tell the foreman, and to stop the scrapers from approaching. The foreman was the same Peter Altenhoffer that had worked on my section. He told the operator to get back on the machine and just move the bomb to one side, as he needed the excavation completed. Peter said that it was a German bomb and would not hurt him as he was German. The operator suggested (not too politely) that the foreman use the bulldozer to move the bomb if he was so confident. Eventually, Peter agreed to stop the work and call the police and Bomb Disposal. The Duty Captain from Horsham brought his team to the incident. As the bomb was in open country, he elected to blow it up where it sat. The bulldozer was gingerly reversed away from the bomb, after listening for ticking fuzes. It took three days to backfill the crater, and Peter Altenhoffer lost a bonus payment for not completing the cutting in the allowed time. He was not best pleased, and he maintained that the operator had been wrong to refuse a direct order, so he sacked him. There are some bosses that are difficult to work for.

Coldest winter

The 1963/4 winter was very cold, and Jane and I had rented the old School House at Wymeswold, to the east of Loughborough. The school had just one large room initially, but had been converted by adding stud partitions and a ceiling. The plumbing was laid loose on top of the ceiling softboard, and the hot water was heated in the wood burning stove in the kitchen extension. The overhead water tank was situated over the "walk in" fireplace. One day all the pipes froze and each joint in the loft was laid out neatly on top of the ceiling, each with its own icicle sticking out of the ends. Jane called a plumber, who was suddenly overwhelmed with work and he suggest that she get warm by sucking a peppermint, and he would be along in about three weeks! We got some electric fires going to warm the house, but these melted the ice in, and on the ceiling, which started to collapse. The overhead tank was full of ice and I removed this using a cold chisel. The copper pipes in the ceiling were easy to repair, and just needed new copper joints. Meanwhile, the water damage extended to the wooden floors. The rotten floorboards in the entrance hall gave way, and we had to use a scaffold board to reach the bathroom and bedrooms. The landlord agreed to repair the hall floor, and he did by just pouring readymix concrete into the hole! The readymix truck dropped a pair of rear wheels into the drainage manhole in the gateway and was stuck overnight. The living room carpet, after getting wet, shrank about six inches in each direction. This event taught me that Insurance would have been a good idea, and I have been insured ever since.

We loved living in the old school, and it was quiet because of the cemetery behind our building. The son of our farmer neighbour used to shoot crows sitting on our roof. They usually fell off onto our garden, but one did not. During the conversion, the fireplace at the bedroom end of the building had been removed, and the chimney taken away to just above the ceiling. The remaining piece of chimney above the ceiling was still open to the sky, and the dead crow had fallen down. It came to rest on the ceiling, just above our bed. It was some weeks before the smell became unbearable, and we had difficulty finding the source.

After I moved to Leicestershire, I sold the Mini and bought an old Riley 1½ Litre car, with a leather roof and seats. The long sweeping front mudguards and the shiny radiator grill made the car special to me. What I should have looked for was a car in better mechanical condition. Unlike most cars, the (home made) exhaust pipe on my car went under the rear axle. On a severe bump, the axle knocked the pipe out of the clamps and connections. I remember being in a hurry to collect Jane from school, in heavy rain, when I needed to get out and get under the car to re-attach the pipe. I ran the wheels up onto a high verge to give me access, and I lay in the gutter to fix the pipe. The rain water ran down my neck and out of my trouser legs. Jane was not pleased when I collected her from a Coffee Bar, as we had intended to go straight on to some function. A previous owner had fitted slightly larger diameter tyres than the correct specification, and I had not realised. When I had a puncture on the M1, one night, the garage could only find a tyre that was one size bigger again. This worked while travelling in a straight line. The first time I used full steering lock, the tyre chewed up the mudguard. The sewn seams in the leather roof developed leaks. On another trip up the M1, the clutch failed and the car was towed away for repairs. Driving the car after collection, still on the M1, I found that all the clutch bell housing bolts had dropped out, except the top one! Finally, the engine gave up while I visited a friend. The car remained in his drive until I replaced the piston rings. Shortly after that, I sold it (to the great relief of friends and family).

Eventually the section of M1 was nearing completion. I submitted applications to about 50 possible employers, and arranged 15 appointments into a week, which I took as leave. Most offices, in those days, were in Victoria Street, London. I managed to have three interviews in one building in the same day and met Interviewer No 1 in the lift on the way to Interview No 3. When he asked what I was doing, I told him that other offers were better than his. His offer letter showed an increase on the figure previously discussed! However, one had to be careful when claiming expenses for all these interviews. Another interviewer had asked me if I was any good at setting out. I replied (jokingly I thought) that I was a bit better than my father, in that he had built a bridge in the wrong country. The interviewer was not amused.

M1 Motorway London   1964 - 1966

I was successful in getting an offer from Marples Ridgeway Ltd, for a job as Section Engineer on the Hendon Urban Motorway (M1) in London. This would be my first job with a contractor, and I was going to have to get my hands dirty for the first time.

I found a flat in Mill Hill and we drove down at the end of September, 1964. The flat would not be ready until the next day, but we had been invited to a Mess Dinner in the Duke of York's Headquarters, Chelsea. I had booked a posh hotel in Chelsea for that night, and the doorman who opened Jane's car door was given the plastic bowl straight from our kitchen sink, full of cleaning items. There was no room in the car, after loading up all our stuff, so Jane had sat holding it the whole way from the Midlands. We went to our room and changed. I was in full Mess kit, red jacket, black bow tie, boots and spurs. In the lift, American tourist gave me a tip, thinking I was the bell boy. This was an auspicious start to the new job.

Marples Ridgeway had a reputation for tendering for the technically more difficult and "one-off" jobs, and this one lived up to the promise. Unlike motorway jobs up to that time, this was not in open fields, with no need to worry about utility diversions. This motorway was to be carved out of the slope on a railway cutting, and through a built up area. The whole site was on London Clay, which swells and shrinks depending on how much rain it had absorbed and whether the sun was shining on it. In a wet November, this clay was worse to cross than the Belgian battlefields of the First World War. For most of the route, the motorway ran parallel to, and on land belonging to, the East Coast Main Railway line. As the railway was in a deep cutting, there was a long slope up to the houses above. Our job was to put a retaining wall in the back gardens of the houses and then dig out the slope, giving a flat area between the railway and the new retaining wall for the motorway.

On arrival, we first had to establish the main and section offices. A derelict piece of land belonging to London Underground was to be the main office location, south of Mill Hill Broadway. We found, by accident, that an old rail track bed lead us from there straight into Edgware tube station. We drove up and parked in the space left for Platform 6 and headed for a café in the High Street. The Ticket collector would not accept that we had not arrived by tube, but by vehicle. We had to take him to see the car, before he would allow us to get our coffees.

Retaining walls

The long railway straight from south of Mill Hill Broadway, up to nearly Scratchwood Service Station, was straight. This made the setting out of this length relatively easy. I was given the section starting immediately north of the A41 Trunk Road. The first survey job was to establish the centreline pegs and reference these with secondary pegs. Reference pegs were vital, because the only site route for plant on this section ran down the centreline. The operators seemed to take great delight in seeing how many pegs they could destroy in a day!

The eastern side of the new motorway was to be the thirty foot high retaining wall supporting the houses above. This wall was designed with a 1 in 36 slope on the exposed face, (and a 1 in 18 slope on the rear face). The toe of the wall was to be exactly three feet below the surfacing level, and the centreline was on a vertical curve. The top of the wall had to be exactly one foot wide and one foot above the existing (but variable) garden levels for the houses. The centreline started a horizontal transition curve half way along my section. We were to build this wall in 25 foot long sections. Setting out each section was, therefore a long and painful daily essay in mathematics. There were no calculators, or computers, in those days!!

The first job was to dig the trench for the wall. This needed to be some 40 foot deep, in London Clay. This clay swelled and shrank, depending on how much rain or sun it received. To avoid the collapse of the trench, the excavation sides were fully supported by boards trapped behind rolled steel joists (RSJs). I was very grateful for my Bomb Disposal training, as bomb shaft construction was in many ways similar to the trench supporting system that we used.

Because the vertical RSJs were not exactly in line, and not exactly vertical, each horizontal strut was a different length. As the hardwood was so expensive, and replacements came by boat from South America, an instruction was given that a saw cut could only be made after my Section Agent and the Project Manager had countersigned the request. One day I needed a 5 foot length, and duly obtained permission to cut a 12 foot timber. I marked the timber and left the gang to move the compressor close enough to the timber, to power the air-driven saw. I retired to my hut, directly across the trench, and left them to make the cut. I heard the saw working and looked up. A 5 foot length had been cut off. Good, I thought. Then I watched in horror as the carpenter scratched his head and measured the remaining piece. It was not the 5 foot he was expecting, but 7 foot long. Before I could stop him, the extra 2 foot had been cut off. When I reached him and showed him that we now had two 5 foot long pieces, he realised his mistake.

The timber strutting across the trench was placed at six foot vertical intervals, as the dig progressed. The actual digging was done using a Case Traxcavator with a Four-in-One bucket. By removing the safety cab, and buying a safety helmet for the operator, the machine could just get under the strutting, but the operator had to remember to duck.

The main concrete pours for the base units were about 180 cubic metres in volume. We expected the two suppliers to have difficulty with their batching plants at some time during any pour, so we gave each plant an order for half the amount. Inevitably, one plant either broke down, or ran out of material, and the remainder of the order was switched to the surviving plant. Because of the heavy day time traffic in London, the pours started in the evening and usually finished just before dawn. On one pour, a truck failed to appear and the plant confirmed that it had left full and should be expected. A few days later, I heard the story. The truck driver had suspected that his wife was entertaining another gentleman when he was on the night shift. Over a period of weeks, he had parked near his home and observed two shadows on the bedroom curtains. He worked out which cars belonged to neighbours, and which were visiting. Eventually he had had enough, and he reversed the concrete truck up to a sports car with its soft roof, and filled it with 6 cubic metres of concrete. A lot of concrete also went over the road and footpath. Then he parked the truck and waited for his wife's gentleman visitor to leave the house, which he eventually did, but on a bicycle!!! The sports car owner was a little upset, as was his insurance company.

M1 – HENDON URBAN MOTORWAY
Climbing Shutter finishing the top of Retaining Wall

Marples Ridgeway had a boffin for a Technical Director. Mr Jackson designed the infamous "Climbing Shutter" for this wall.

Two complete machines were made, and I had one of them. The principle idea was for two shutter blades to rise slowly as the concrete was poured, using the legs of the machine as tracks for the guide wheels on the backs of the blades. The blades rose about six inches an hour, and used less than half a cubic metre of concrete in the hour. We achieved a high quality finish on the visible face, by having two masons attending to the concrete as it appeared below the blade. In the winter, we had two braziers in the trench to keep these men warm. One day, I went down and there was one man who was not trowelling. He had a bottle of milk in one hand and a bottle of whiskey in the other. Whiskey for the cold weather, and milk to pacify the ulcer caused by the whiskey! The pour was continuous for some 36 hours. A very slow process, but the machine had to be watched very carefully the whole time.

On the long pours, boredom could set in. Once a pour started, it had to be finished, whatever the weather. One night, in winter, there had been light rain continuously. To get to the machine, one walked across the twelve inch wide timber struts. There was no handrail or safety ropes. The timber tops were coated with slimy clay and mud. At about midnight, a row broke out between the foreman and a labourer. They were screaming at each other, and threatening to dismember each other in the most imaginative of ways. This took place while they, and I, were standing on the strut. I was, unfortunately, between the two men. I looked down some thirty feet at the array of long vertical starter bars ready for the next pour, and realized that when we all fell, they would have to remove us in pieces. Somehow, I managed to talk the men into continuing the conversation on firm ground, and moved clear. The West Indian labourer eventually went and sulked in the tea room for the rest of the shift. In the morning I arranged for him to be transferred to the adjacent section, away from this foreman. He had been working on the new section for less than a day when two police cars arrived to arrest him for something else not related to our job. He managed to stab two of the police before they subdued him. I am still asking myself if he was carrying a knife when he was arguing with the foreman.

There were some lighter moments on this section. Down at the foot of the slope was a British Rail workers hut. My foreman rigger, Ron Dorricott from Anglesey, commandeered the hut as it was due for demolition, and started using the stove. When the railway staff saw the smoke, they kept delivering fuel. One very wet, foggy, and windy night, I had arranged to take Jane out for the evening. We had dressed up, but I had to check that all was going well with the arrangements for the next day's work. I parked my car just above the path down to the hut and went to talk to Ron, the foreman in charge of the Climbing Shutter machine. He offered me a mug of tea, and then he realized that Jane was waiting in my car. He got the tea boy (a Donegal lad of about six foot and fifteen stone) to take a mug of tea to Jane. There was little or no lighting where I had parked, and it was drizzling. Suddenly a large figure loomed up against her car window, and it went very dark. A shovel sized hand rapped on the glass. Eventually Jane lowered the window. "A cuppa tay for ye, Mam". With that, he took his greasy cap of the top of the mug, which he had used to stop the rain getting into the tea, and still steaming, placed it back on his head. He licked his thumb and forefinger and ran them round the lip of the mug, to clean it for the lady. Jane took the mug and he lumbered off. The mug was still full when I returned.

During the trenching operation for the retaining wall, we had the occasional accident. One man tried to use a long ladder, which had been tied up vertically to stop anyone using it. Due to the slimy wet clay on his boots, he slipped and used the main verticals of the ladder as a rail track for his hands and feet, and used his jaw and nose on the rungs to slow himself down. Another, more serious, accident happened when about two cubic yards of clay fell onto a labourer from a great height. We dug him out and got him into the site Landrover to take him to Edgware General Hospital, only half a mile away. It was far quicker than waiting for an ambulance. I was sure he was dead. At the hospital, I jumped out to get a trolley and the accident team, while the driver reversed up to the door. I got back to the vehicle, to discover that the "body" had vanished. He was out on the main road, virtually fully recovered. It appears that he did not want to be admitted to hospital in case his Income Tax "fiddle" came to light. He was about 16 or 17, and when he arrived from Ireland, Mary at Paddington had sold him a set of documents showing that he had six children. This meant that he could make a large saving on Income Tax deductions. This fiddle was commonplace in the industry in those days, and the loophole has since been removed by various Government means.

We had official contact, for road closure reasons and so on, with the local police station. Our favourite pub was across the road from the police station. Angus McKay, a foreman, often visited his granny in the Highlands. She distilled a wicked Poteen and Angus would bring back a bottle or two when he had a weekend away. This was a highly alcoholic clear liquid. A bottle of "Doctor Angus" was always kept in the pub safe. The Police Station Sergeant was teetotal and was frequently called to ask the contractors to be a little quieter while in the pub. The General Foreman decided that the Sergeant should learn to laugh a little and invited him to a drink. Before long, (with the help of Doctor Angus) we had him on a table top, with his arms round the Foreman, singing at the top of his voice. His Inspector was not amused.

Steel tapes do lie

The section immediately to the south of my section was absolutely straight, and the rail track was the base line for the setting out. The site was incredibly muddy. The new retaining wall was to be some 120 feet offset from the rail track, and the wall line pegs took a great deal of effort to place. The setting out team needed five or more chainmen to hold the tape clear of the mud, to pull each others boots out of the mud, and to wipe the steel tape clean when a measurement to a peg was needed. After several weeks of wall building in the wet winter, the ground dried and a survey check was done. The wall was found to have been built ten feet closer to the centreline than it should have been. The engineer was taken to task for this error. In his defence, he produced the steel tape that he had used, and explained that only about a foot of tape could be cleaned at any one time. The tape had been misprinted at the factory, and had the 20' to 30' markings repeated twice!!! He got away with the error, and there is now a section of the M1 without a hard shoulder. The whole time that this engineer was building the retaining wall along his section, a family of Blackbirds would fly from the nest in a tree to inspect the Climbing Shutter. Eventually, the frame reached the garden next door to the tree with the nest. That night, the birds flew round the machine for a while making a horrible noise, and disappeared. The next day the nest was empty and abandoned. During the move of the Climbing Shutter to the bay opposite the tree, there was an accident and the frame demolished the tree. The Blackbirds had known it was going to happen!

Identity parade

Frank had other problems on his section. One morning, a very angry local resident (a blue-rinsed Jewish lady) telephoned our site Agent to complain that the labourers were not using the latrines provided. One had poked his naked bottom through the temporary fence and deposited something in her garden. The Agent was ordered to remove the offending matter immediately, and the labourer was to be sacked immediately, or a formal complaint would be raised to Head Office. The first part was swiftly dealt with, but the section foreman asked the lady if she could help identify the perpetrator, as none had owned up out of some 30 possibles. He suggested an identity parade. "But I only saw his naked bottom". "Well I can arrange for all the men to bend down naked for you". Eventually, no one was sacked, as she refused to examine some thirty bottoms.

Sandwiches in the sewer

In Mill Hill, we had to divert many main services in The Broadway, to allow for bridge abutments to be built. One diversion involved a 54" diameter live main sewer. By using temporary stop-ends, we replaced this pipe in eight foot pipe lengths. It was a difficult and dangerous job. One Friday (pay day) the temporary stop-end gave way and the trench filled up rapidly with raw sewage. Luckily it was lunch time and the gang were in the Bookmakers shop across the road. I was looking at the hole, when one of the labourers reached past me with a stick with a nail through it. He was trying to fish for an overcoat that had been hanging on a nail. It was now floating on the sewage. I said that there was no need because the insurance would replace the coat and refund the wage packet that he had lost. "No, it's not my wages that I've lost. I need to get my sandwiches out of the pocket".

At the end of the first December in Mill Hill, I was invited by Monks to attend the grand opening of the Leicestershire M1, in the presence of the Minister of Transport. I was given time off, as the Mill Hill Christmas Party was to be held on the same Saturday night. I drove up early, in thick snow, and was asked to stand with three Monk's staff by one of our bridges so that I could meet the Minister. It was very, very, cold and the Minister was late. When he did come, he gave a long homily about Drinking and Driving, while we stood and shivered in the snow. By then, all we wanted was a hot toddy! The party in the Flying Horse was a great reunion and all drinks were free. I left and drove down the newly opened Motorway. I arrived in London in time to take Jane to the Marples Ridgeway Christmas party, which was great fun. As I was on TA duty in Horsham on the Sunday, Jane and I left the party early (after midnight), taking another engineer's wife home as well. He had decided to stay at the party. I drove on to Horsham. In the extreme cold that morning, with an extreme hangover headache, I spent the morning teaching sappers how to start and stop a very large, unsilenced, diesel engined, air compressor. The whistling from the air taps still haunts me. When I returned to work, I noticed that the engineer seemed to have been gardening all weekend. His hands were black and torn. He was staring at them unable to think how they came to be in that state. Later, we discovered that many of the new saplings planted by the council in holes in the pavement were missing. A number of houses with pristine lawns now had a new sapling proudly growing in the middle. He maintained that it was not him and that he could remember nothing.

Major trench collapse

Our Wedding Anniversary was due in April, and a booking for a meal on the Saturday night had been made, when the deep trench started to move on the Thursday before. The main horizontal timbers holding the sides apart started to creak and groan. One of the brackets supporting the end of a 12" x 12" timber bent the centre of the bracket down through 90 degrees. This bracket was a length of 15" x 15" RSJ, and was held at each end to the vertical RSJs. The bracket was only six foot long, so the force was considerable. The timber had been packed tight using folding wedges, but it appeared that the sawn end of the timber was not square, putting an uneven force on the bracket. After the first timber failed, even more load was transferred to adjacent timbers, and a progressive collapse followed.

We rushed to place more timbers in the trench, wherever we could. There were only so many timbers available and emergency purchases of 30' long 12" x 12" hardwood timbers are not easy to find. Meanwhile, cracks had appeared in the back gardens of the houses, and major settlement took place as the ground subsided into our trench. On the Saturday morning at 8:00 am, the company had three Solicitors going door to door, getting ready for householder claims!!! We did what we could to save fish ponds, green houses, and patios. One glass greenhouse had 30 inches of wedges under one corner, and no glass was broken. An ornamental pond slid from one level down to the next level with out cracking, nursed by labourers. The fish were collected and returned (with a water refill) after each move. The man who bred world famous racing pigeons had an enormous aviary across the whole width of his garden. The foreman set the tea boy to work, banging on the walls, to keep the birds flying. This, he had told the boy, would reduce the load on the foundations, and save the trench from collapse!! We paid a large claim for the owner's lost sales when the birds refused to produce eggs for many months. His birds had been ordered from Japan and other countries.

Although our flat was closer to my site office than the main site offices, I did not get home for those five days and my wife was none too pleased about the Anniversary meal. After five days of non-stop work, we halted the collapse, and none of the houses near the trench developed cracks.

M1 – HENDON URBAN MOTORWAY
Completed Retaining Wall

That summer, Jane and I took a camping holiday in France and Spain. We intended to meet up with Jan Kaminski, who was working for Laing Iberia in Barcelona and Zaragosa. We eventually found his site office in Barcelona, only to be told that he had recently been transferred to Vittoria near San Sebastian in northern Spain. This gave us a reason to traverse Spain, enjoy the scenery, and find Jan. We drove through Andorra and camped there for two nights. Eventually we found the Vittoria site, only to be told that Jan was in UK on leave! Back in Mill Hill, we found a note from Jan asking where we were as he had travelled especially to see us.

In 1963, Kenya had decided to abolish the Nairobi County Council (against all sane reasons, as all the press coverage at the time stated), and my father was lucky to get the job of Engineer to the Central Rift Province. He was the Kenya delegate to the Pan-African Highway conference in Addis Ababa, to discuss international co-operation and the building of the East-West Highway from Mombasa to Nigeria and beyond. He came back from Ethiopia with a bottle of VAT69 Whiskey, which had a label in Coptic script. I used to re-fill this bottle with regular whiskey and then offer it to friends, and watch the bemused faces.

Edgware School

Jane got a job teaching in Edgware, as Head of Infants at a Primary School. The local population had been re-housed in prefabs just after the end of the War, after being bombed out of the East End of London. By this time, the prefabricated homes were showing signs of wear and morale was low. A consequence was that family discipline had deteriorated. Jane advised me to keep the car windows closed and the doors locked when I went to collect her from work. Once I was harassed by a gang of 10 year olds, who wanted to slash my tyres. They only stopped when Jane told them who I was, and I was well looked after by these mini-thugs on subsequent visits. On site, we were still using kerosene road lamps to protect excavations. These frequently went missing. Eventually the mystery was solved. There was a small paragraph, on the bottom of page 7 in the local weekly paper, which read "School burnt down for fifth time". The Education Authority had given up on re-building the school in non-combustible materials some years ago, and simply installed temporary buildings each time. One evening, shortly after some exam results had been issued, Jane was interviewing parents in her classroom. A man staggered in, brandishing a bottle. "Can't you see that I am busy? Go and see the Headmistress in the other building", said Jane. The man meekly left and the Headmistress was hit over the head with the bottle, and had five stitches across her forehead.

Army training

I continued with TA training at Rochester, but the unit had become a victim of MOD budget cuts and was now reduced in size and reformed as 590 Specialist Team (BD) Royal Engineers. Officer training continued at the School of Military Engineering in Chatham.

Scratchwood Services

M1 – HENDON URBAN MOTORWAY
Scratchwood Services Bridges

After my retaining walls had been finished, I transferred to the Scratchwood area to build the two service area overbridges. These were pre-stressed post-tensioned decks, resting on slender piers at the rear of the hard shoulders. I adapted the "Climbing Shutter" to form the piers. The piers were narrower at ground level, than the width at the deck, so I had to allow for a taper at each end and the piers had "boat shaped" ends. I designed the two wooden shutters, with the boat shape, which were trapped inside the Climbing shutter blades. It worked well and saved time on conventional concreting methods.

Scratchwood is next to Mill Hill Golf Course, and the Motorway took a little of their land. At this point, the motorway was on an embankment. During the filling of this embankment, twin engined scrapers were used, with push assistance from bulldozers. Episode 96 of "The Avengers" was being filmed in a bunker close to the site, and the plant operators used to park up to watch the filming, and to see Dianna Rigg playing Emma Peel as she emerged from a secret door in the sand bunker. While the machines parked, the engines were still running, and the vibrations upset the cameramen and the sound recorder technician. Lots of waving was done, asking the machines to move away, but the operators just waved back.

One afternoon, I was the only person in the main office when the Resident Engineer came in to tell us that the main embankment at Scratchwood had started to slip, and could spill over onto the Golf Course. He had had a liquid lunch, and I had a little difficulty understanding just exactly what he wanted us to do about this problem. I got a piece of paper and sketched the area, marking the slip area. He said that we had to immediately move all plant to the area and remove the embankment. I made this note on the paper. I then asked him to sign and date the paper, as my boss would not believe me. He did, and I set off to issue the instruction to the earthmoving sub-contractor. The correct procedure for dealing with a clay slip is to overload the area above the slip circle, to force the moving part to find equilibrium. The RE had ordered, in writing, the exact opposite. After two weeks of very costly work, paid at daywork rates, the RE was persuaded to reverse his decision and allow us to overload the slip. Because I had got the instruction in writing, all our costs were paid, and the instruction also supported our claim for extension of time to complete the contract. It always pays to get instructions in writing.

One of my friends on this job was Tony Fillingham. He was the chief surveyor and had a team of Italian surveyors that Marples had repatriated from a job in the Sudan. Tony was large and a miner's son from Nottingham and his principle chainman was even larger. The chainman worked weekends as a bouncer in an Irish Dance Hall in the East End of London. One night we returned to my flat and I invited them in for a coffee. It was late, and Tony did not want to disturb Jane. Tony and I stood outside on the pavement while I tried to persuade him to come in. Meanwhile, I sent the chainman up to put on the kettle. He fumbled his way up the stairs in the dark, making some noise. At the top my diminutive wife hit him with a frying pan and he fell back down the stairs. Jane was not pleased, and the next time I asked these two hulking great men for a coffee, they both politely refused in case they upset Jane again. The chainman even suggested that she could have a well paid job at the dance hall as his assistant on the door.

After a year in the Mill Hill flat, Jane and I had had enough of the Jehovah's Witness training scheme as their offices were close by. The constant visits resulted in a lack of sleep on a Sunday morning. We found a flat in an old Victorian house in Finchley. Jane got a job in a Primary School in Golders Green. The school was built of brick and had a tiled roof. The chances of this school burning down were much reduced. Just before Christmas, Jane asked if I could find some holly and ivy to decorate the school. We were clearing some vegetation ready for stripping the topsoil, and there was plenty of holly and ivy available. I asked the ganger to sort out a few bits for Jane and deliver them to the school in the site van, and left him to get on with it while I went off to speak to the Site Agent. About two hours later, I was called to the telephone. Jane was furious, and explained that a full 10 tonne tipper load of branches (including small trees) had been tipped in the playground and the staff could not get the cars out! The ganger was sent back to remove the surplus. At the end of term, the school had the Christmas Party, and had arranged with a nearby Old Folks Home to supply a Father Christmas to hand out presents to the kids. The old man had gone out for a walk and could not be found. Jane telephoned, asking for help. As a way of making up to her for the vegetation mistake, I sent the ganger to punish him. It was a great success, except that the ganger had decided that he needed quantities of Dutch courage before he would step inside the school gates.

Tony's job often meant measuring off from the outside rail of the East Coast Main Line. One day, when the earthmoving was in full swing, a chainman was holding a pencil on a nail embedded in the railway sleeper. Tony was focussing his theodolite on the pencil when a train went by and removed the chainman's head. He had not heard the train, or warning shouts, because of the very loud noise made by the engines of the earthmoving machines. Tony was very badly affected by this, and left the company.

Richard Biffa

When the embankments had been completed, topsoil had to be spread on the slopes. Several sub-contract "chancers" bought very cheap, clapped out, unregistered, tipper lorries to run between the top soil heap and the slopes. Occasionally a tipper would roll over and the wreck was hauled back to a land fill area on the site and buried. One of these sub-contractors was Richard Biffa. He must have made money on our job, as his waste disposal empire sold for a fortune several years later. Richard took two of us out for a meal in a very upmarket West End restaurant. We arrived in style, in one of his unlicensed tippers. The doorman, in top hat and long scarlet coat, rushed forward to move us away from his prestige establishment, only to be given a screwdriver wrapped in a large banknote. The screwdriver was the ignition key, and the doorman was asked to park the tipper carefully, and not to get it scratched!

Another of these tipper owners was illiterate and wanted me to help him to tender for replacing the brickwork in some Victorian sewer manhole shafts, in the Archway area of London. We set off in his shiny new Bentley and I carried a tape and notebook. The first manhole lid came up easily and he climbed down about twenty feet. I noted the measurements that he dictated and his comments on the state of the Victorian brickwork. The second manhole lid was more difficult to lift, but we managed it. The third shaft was full to the brim with septic sewage, so we just replaced the lid. The last manhole was the lowest in the pipe run. It was dry at the bottom, so he climbed down and started poking the bricks at the bottom. Suddenly there was a gurgling noise, and then a flood of sewage. It over took him on the way up, and he popped out like a cork. He did not want to dirty the new Bentley, so I had to fiddle in his filthy pocket and find his keys, to take the car back to the site. He walked off and caught a tube train home. I understand that London Underground had to remove the complete train from duty while they cleaned it.

Port Talbot Harbour   1966 - 1968

In October 1966, Marples Ridgeway won the contract to build the New Harbour at Port Talbot in South Wales, for the Steel Company of Wales. I was appointed as one of the three Shift Bosses, and moved to Porthcawl. Jane was about three months pregnant and I looked for a suitable house to rent. I found a charming old cottage at Ton Kenfig, overlooking the sand dunes and the sea.

After building the offices, the major job was to construct the eight mile haul road from the Steel Company quarry, down to the beach. At that time, this was the longest haul road in Europe. We were being supplied with rock armour from this quarry, free of charge under the contract. The forty foot wide road had to be capable of handling 80 tonne gross Caterpillar 769 dump trucks. There was only one crossing of

Port Talbot Harbour - CAT 769 Dump Truck on Haul Road

a public road, and traffic lights were installed, however these were manually operated (in those far off days). The weather was not kind to us, and the length of the road across farmland was particularly boggy. The first five miles of this road from the harbour ran parallel to the beach through the Margam Dunes. The area is one of the last remnants of a large sand dune system that once stretched along the coast from the River Ogmore to the Gower peninsula. Some of the dunes now cover the site of a submerged ancient town and castle, and only the castle tower remains above ground. It was said that the bells in the submerged church would ring on a stormy night.

After the sand dunes, the road turned inland at Sker Point, and passed Sker House. This house was immortalised by R. D. Blackmore in his story "The Maid of Sker", but the book was not a best seller. This was based on the true story of Elizabeth (Bessie) Williams, who fancied a young carpenter but was not allowed to marry him by her father. She was imprisoned by her father until she agreed to marry a farmer in 1766. The farmer died only a few months after the wedding, but Parish records show that she later had four children, one of whom died in infancy. The Williams farm house was now "The Maid of Sker" Public House, and the room where Bessie was imprisoned could be viewed.

On my first weekend off, I drove back to Finchley on a wet and cold Friday night. We had moved from Mill Hill to avoid the Jehovah's Witness training school. On the North Circular Road, in heavy rain, I was stationary at the traffic lights when a car ran into the back of me at speed. The other driver had just won the "Salesman of the Year" award from Gillette. He had been celebrating and kept trying to bribe me with the whole contents of his sample case. My car had been written off. I got home much later than expected and tumbled into bed. I was woken by a torch shining into Jane's face and a burly police sergeant asking her if she had heard the burglar reported by a neighbour. The policeman was very cautious as the neighbour had told him that Jane was alone and pregnant. He completely ignored me. He would not even talk to me, until Jane eventually persuaded him that I was genuinely her husband, and not just any spare man. My wallet had been taken from the lounge, and the window was still open. The thief had got away, but the Borstal Offenders rehabilitation house in the same street was checked out. Jane was teaching with the wife of the local Inspector and our thanks were passed on to the sergeant for his considerate behaviour.

After Jane moved from London over Christmas, we settled in at Ton Kenfig. Jane was now close to her parents and her brother's family in Cardiff. They were also looking forward to the new baby. Our landlord was Dr Tom Miles, an Anaesthetist working in Cardiff. He and his wife worked in our garden most weekends. They would start at opposite ends of a flower bed, and work until the vacuum jug of Martini was empty. The rest of the very long garden was kept under control by ten geese, who took exception to our Dachshund, "Chui". One summer Sunday afternoon, Tom decided, after the usual jug of Martini, to donate two geese to the City of Cardiff and put them on Roath Park Lake. The geese did not like the forty mile journey in the small car, and objected by pecking the back of his head. Eventually he got to the lake, and was promptly arrested for stealing geese from the lake!!

We had fourteen CAT 769 dump trucks. Three had open flat load beds for carrying large rock pieces, and the rest were standard rock bodies. Empty, they weighed about 30 tonnes and were 15 feet wide, 27 feet long. Tyres were some five foot diameter. They were a delight to drive, with air brakes and hydraulic power assisted steering. Most cars at that time had none of these advantages and were very heavy to operate.

The first actual job to start was the construction of the mile and a quarter long outer breakwater. Once this had sufficiently advanced, and was giving some protection, the jetty and the inner breakwater could be started. The whole process was weather dependant, and one quickly learned the hard way just how powerful Nature could be when angry. In order to assist predictions of weather changes, we gave four hourly reports to the Met Office of wave height, direction, and wind speed. In return they gave us daily predictions projected from our information. This allowed us to make safe before major storms, and to generally plan the work. As my brother-in-law and his wife were keen golfers, they kept asking for detailed forecasts when visiting golf courses near Port Talbot.

The breakwater had a central core, protected by two layers each side of larger rock. The slopes extended down below sand level by about six feet, and rested on a trench filled with medium sized armour rock. The bottom of this trench was given a layer of core material. Three to six tonne rocks form the inner armour layer. The heaviest rock was on the outer layer, and this outer armour consisted of rock weighing a minimum of eight tonnes each. The biggest we ever received was up to twenty tonnes and was the size of a large saloon car.

At Port Talbot, the tidal range is some eighteen feet, and the receding sea exposes 1,200 feet of sand between high and low tide marks. As the sea recedes, the sand dries out and the wind creates sand storms. The sun beats down on the wet sand and reflects upwards, and the glare hurt the eyes. The basic rock breakwater was to be built up to one foot above high water level, and then a massive concrete wall is formed on top. However, during construction we had to contend with an average of twenty foot waves at high tides before the concrete wall was built to protect us! Although one engineer did get washed off into the sea, he was rescued. The Project Manager called him into the office the next day and accused him of wasting his time in the water. He could have taken some soundings while waiting for the Swansea lifeboat to arrive!

Our first job was to dig the thirty foot wide toe trenches each side of the breakwater and fill them with rock. This was done in forty foot lengths, during each tide.

The final length of this trench on the seaward side was done at maximum low spring tide level in March, and at night. It was on my shift, and I carefully planned the operation. I made sure that all plant had been serviced and in working order, and that enough 3 to 6 tonne sized rock armour was available in a stock pile at the start of the breakwater. The plant followed the tide down the beach as it receded. The D8 Caterpillar bulldozer started the excavation by pushing out sand to make the hole. When the hole filled with sea water, and it was too difficult for the dozer, the 22RB dragline completed the dig. After finishing, the dragline moved away from the trench and parked at the side of the trench, to the seaward end, clear of the rock dumping operation. I called up the three pre-loaded CAT 769 dump trucks and they tipped rock into the trench. The heaps of rock needed to be pushed evenly into the trench and this was done by the dozer. After more rock was tipped, the dozer went further across the trench, spreading rock. Then the dozer found that it was resting on a rock, with the tracks completely clear of any support. It was trapped. The operator tried all sorts of movements, but with the tracks out of contact with any thing solid, it was to no avail. The rising tide started to flood back. A steel rope from the 22RB was attached to the dozer, with great difficulty because men had to clamber across one metre diameter rocks, in water, in the dark. The 22RB reversed and pulled the dozer until the tracks made contact with solid rock. We had only filled half of the trench and had to work in ever deepening water to finish the work. Wet sand, when vibrated, turns into quicksand. The throbbing engines of the dump trucks, dragline, and dozer, gave large vibrations. I had to constantly make sure that all the plant kept moving on the beach to prevent them from digging themselves in. During this time, I had visions of explaining to the Project Manager just how I had managed to drown five major items of plant, but luck was on my side.

On one of the other Shifts, one dump truck turned circles on full lock on the wet beach while waiting to tip his load. Following his own wheel marks, he had dug a deep trench for his wheels and he became bogged. The Shift Manager tried to pull him out using a dozer, but with no success. The truck was recovered the next morning, in full view of the Project Manager. Fish were found in the cab and the air intake pipe. The engine was stripped down immediately and all traces of salt water flushed out.

The truck was back at work within days. The Shift Manager had an uncomfortable time on the carpet in front of the Project Manager.

PORT TALBOT BREAKWATER
Lima 2400 + Rockgrab - NCK 1405 - CAT 769

The main armour rock was placed by two LIMA 2400 cranes. These had massive four pronged grabs, and were capable of placing a 10 tonne rock at a radius of 100 feet, using a jib of 160 foot. Hugh Delap, the site Chief Engineer, developed a simple mechanism and technique for placing rock to line and level, under water, and at night. He used a "bomb sight" fixed in front of the operator's eye, so that he could watch a steel ball clamped to the hoist rope a known number of feet above the grab. I had to position this crane on a stable platform of rock at a known position on the breakwater, at a known height, with the centreline of the crane parallel to the breakwater centre line. Hugh knew the seabed level opposite the crane position, and could calculate the volume of rock required to fill the slope. This was translated into a chart showing the number of rocks to be placed in a small "square". The operator placed rock into the square until the steel ball failed to descend below the bomb sight. Each "square" was located by using the crane's jib radius indicator, and the horizontal angle indicator, in the operator's cab. It was always satisfying to see the formed slope appear, as the tide went out and exposed the new work. Of course, not all the rocks are the same size and shape, and the degree of interlocking varied. Sometimes a little rearranging of the rocks was required to smooth out the slope.

At the furthest end of the breakwater (the nose), during construction, the dump trucks would tip "Core" material. This was material straight off the crusher conveyor belt and was from 12 inches down to dust. But it was also unwashed, so it had a high clay content. Every so often, as work progressed, a turning area had to be formed so that the dump trucks could turn and reverse the last few feet to the tipping point. A "Banksman" would guide the truck backwards and tell him to stop at the correct place for him to tip. As the tipping point was moving with each load tipped, we did not have a large timber or concrete beam for the rear wheels to touch at the tipping point. The Banksman was vital, and in all our day or night working, no truck ever fell into the sea. One Banksman had been invalided out of the Coal Mines after being crushed by a reversing underground train. This man was guiding a truck back when he slipped and fell under the rear wheels of the dump truck. The wheels travelled up his legs to very nearly his waist. I made the truck move forward, off his legs, and called for the Emergency services. The road bed was pitted with twelve inch deep holes between rocks, and his legs followed the shape of the ground. I was making his head comfortable when a labourer decided to help by pulling off the rubber boots!! I had to punch him in the face to stop him. The Banksman did eventually recover, after multiple breaks in every leg bone, but not enough to return to normal work. I met him a year later at the Opening Ceremony.

Behind the breakwater nose, stood the leading LIMA 2400 crane. This placed the intermediate rock armour, each weighing 3 to 6 tonnes, on both sides of the freshly tipped core material. The Crane picked up the armour with the grab, by dropping the grab heavily onto the rock to spring the tines open. This was dangerous, as the grab could bounce and fall sideways, so personnel stood well clear. The second LIMA 2400 stood behind the first crane and this placed the main rock armour, which weighed nominally 6 to 8 tonnes. Some rocks weighed up to 20 tonnes, as blasting was not an exact science. Both cranes were fitted with the "in-house" bomb sight technology.

There were three Shifts, each working eight hours. Starting at 6:00am, and changing at 2:00pm and 10:00pm, each team spent a week on "Mornings", then went on to "Afternoons", and then "Nights". I preferred Nights as senior management were least likely to visit, and other daytime only people were absent.

Because highly skilled LIMA 2400 operators were in short supply, these men worked 12 hour shifts. We had to humour and coddle these men. One, Harry, we knew was an alcoholic, but a brilliant operator. We searched him at the start of each shift, and checked his crane, to make sure that his two large bottles of "Blackcurrant Cordial" were not anywhere on the site, but he managed to hide the bottles most days. At the end of the shift, he often had to be carried off the job!

Secretary of State for Wales

One day, we had a visit from the Secretary of State for Wales. Mr Thomas later became Speaker of the House in Parliament. It was very calm day, with no wind and a flat sea. The entourage and the attendant TV cameras proceeded down the breakwater, while the Resident Engineer and Project Manager explained the work. The whole entourage stood and watched Harry, the crane driver, pick up and place a few rocks, and shouted up to him that they were impressed with his skill. Then the Secretary's safety helmet blew off his head and landed upside down in the sea and floated away. Harry quickly used his 4 tonne grab to pick up the helmet and handed it back to the Secretary!! It was all recorded on TV for the News programmes, and Harry was thanked again by all the top brass. Then the foreman shouted up to Harry "You couldn't have done that sober, could you?" Harry came out of the cab, waving a large wrench, and asking the foreman if he would kindly repeat the allegation. The TV cameras were still rolling! It was quite a day, and I made friends with the BBC reporter.

Later, after a major storm had washed away weeks of work, the reporter brought his cameraman down to interview me. Waves were still about 20 to 30 feet high and the only semi-safe place to film was on top of the A-Frame above the crane cab. This is some 30 feet above the top of the working surface and the nominal high water mark. A wave plucked both of us off the crane and dumped us on the working surface. I came to when the receding sea water swung his camera against my helmet! Jane was at home and she found out about the incident when relatives in Cardiff saw the film on TV News and telephoned her. He like filming me because I was quite short and, standing against rocks and waves, the job looked much more impressive. We were lucky, as we could have been washed into the sea. Jane was pregnant with Hugh and did not really like me being away on the Night Shift, as there was no one senior to watch out for me. Sometimes I would drive home to see her, telling the gang that I was inspecting the quarry. Once I took a CAT 769 dump truck.

Unlike all my previous jobs, we had site communications. We used PYE radios, and had two networks. The Shift Manager was one of the juniors on the main site network, and also the boss on the Shift network. This meant that the Shift Manager carried two radios. These were 10" x 6" x 2" and weighed about 2 kilos each. Batteries did not hold a charge for long, so one also carried a spare battery, which was the main part of the weight of a radio. Carrying them made you fit. We all wore one piece green waterproof suits. There was not much room inside the suit, but it was necessary to have the radio set inside to keep it dry. In my case, I had to fit two radios inside the suit, with two microphones protruding from the collar. I did get strange looks in a bank once, when I went to draw out some money.

Some of the Dump Trucks were fitted with a radio, and so were the two LIMAs. Later, we set a radio in the Steel Company of Wales Quarry weighbridge to help control the Dump Trucks. On the daylight shifts, the Project Manager would notice that there was little or no movement on the breakwater and yell down the radio to the Shift Manager to ask why. We found that if we asked the crane operators to move the jib up and down now and again, he was usually fooled into thinking we were working. However, there were times when all the trucks were still on the haul road or waiting in the quarry, and that meant there was nothing to do on the breakwater. I was lucky to have a Shift Engineer who had just returned from Tanganyika, and was Welsh. When the Project Manager called me, I called Dai in Swahili, and he told the foreman and crane operators in Welsh to get the jibs swinging. The Project Manager could listen in to my network, and he never worked out what we were doing!

After a few months, the Steel Company Quarry started to run short of the quantity and sizes of stone that we needed, and we arranged to take stone from an adjacent private quarry, Gaens Quarry which is now owned by English China Clays. The official contract required us to use the Steel Company Quarry, and they got upset when we went to another supplier. We pointed out that to the Steel Company quarry that their production of rock had slowed down and it was delaying our work. There were two reasons for this lack of production.

Firstly, the Steel Company was highly unionised. In order to handle the very large rocks we needed, they had purchased a new Yale 404 wheeled loader with a rock grab instead of the usual bucket. This was a monster machine which could handle 20 ton rocks, but the Union insisted that the operator with the most seniority in the company drove the machine, rather than the most capable man. It turned out that the senior man was approaching retirement and had never driven anything remotely approaching the size of the Yale, and was terrified. But, supported by the Union Representative, he took forever to finally admit that he was too scared to drive the machine. In fact, he eventually accepted sick leave for the remainder of his working life, leaving the way clear for a younger man.

Secondly, the Quarry Manager was an ex-Merchant Navy master mariner, and he had plotted a survey of the quarry on graph paper. This large drawing hung in his office, and the ever changing blasting face was marked up at weekly intervals on this chart. I went out to look at the row of holes being charged for the next blast, and had a look at the rock face. Back in the Manager's office it became clear that (to keep his drawing neat) he was blasting to the graph paper lines, rather than the geological fault lines in the rock. The result was that we got large rock at one end of the face and dust at the other end. It took people much more senior than me to convince him to change his blasting layout, but eventually we started to get reasonable supplies again.

Of course, there were the usual plant breakdowns. One day I noticed that all the 3 to 6 tonne stone was arriving painted white! The Yale loader in the quarry was broken down, so the larger stones could not be loaded. They had had to collect up all the stones that had been painted and used to mark out the roads in the quarry. On another occasion, a large rock was lifted by the grab and revealed a length of Detonating Cord protruding from a drilled hole. The charge had mis-fired and could explode. This was quickly dumped in the sea.

When rock supplies started to slow down from the Steel Company quarry, I would divert the dump trucks to the other supplier, Gaens Quarry, by using the radio. It was diplomatic not to pre-announce my intentions because the Steel Company would raise objections and production would slow down while we argued. I would send my Swahili speaking engineer to the quarry and he could tell me the situation before we gave orders to the drivers, without the Steel Company really understanding what I was doing. All went well until they produced a Swahili speaking manager!!!

The breakwater was one and a quarter miles long, and had three changes of direction. To complete the harbour, a smaller breakwater was to be built on the other side of the new jetty. The expected progress was based on some 36,000 tonnes of rock placed each week. Once we all got familiar with the job, there was little else to do but invent ways of increasing production and try to beat records set by the other two Shift teams. When production reached 45,000 tonnes a week, the tyre fitters could no longer keep up with the number of blow-outs and punctures. As each tyre cost about three months of my salary, I was told to slow down.

A by-product of the increase in production was the fierce competition between the Dump Truck drivers. All loads had to pass over our weighbridge, at the root of the breakwater. The weighbridge was at the bottom of a short but steep slope and at an angle to the road. The trucks would race down this slope to be first in the queue. My site hut was close to the weighbridge and headlights of the trucks aimed directly at my office door. I could foresee a race between drivers resulting in one forcing the other off the road and into my office. My nerve broke one evening. I moved a crane off the breakwater, picked up my office and moved it 50 yards away from danger. I was vindicated a little later. Bill Legg, the elderly General Foreman, drove up the haul road to stop drivers because of the icy conditions. His method for stopping a 70 ton truck was to stop his vehicle just in front of it! There were some spectacular near misses!

The harbour had been sited in direct line with the opening between the Cornish coast and The Mumbles peninsula. This direct line was the direction of the prevailing South Westerly winds. The next landfall was the coast of Brazil, and wave energy is calculated using the distance from the last landfall. There were long discussions during the design phase because of the potential wave damage. The Steel Company wanted this location because ships could unload direct on to a conveyor belt feeding the blast furnaces. If the Harbour was placed a few miles East, to save wave damage, then the iron ore would have to be "double handled" onto rail trucks to get it to the furnaces. Hydraulic models were built and tested, and the designers concluded that the new harbour would survive. Not only would it survive, but the rock armour need not be as large as the 40 tonne blocks used on similar breakwaters on Britain's coast. On a February night, in a storm, one was working at one foot above High Water Mark, and dodging 20 foot waves. Even on calmer days, a three foot wave could cover the running surface at high tide. As this was long before Health and Safety legislation, and Construction (Design and Management) Regulations (CDM), we were just told to get on with the job.

We had three major storms while I was working in Port Talbot. The soft open, unprotected, core material at the end was gouged out by the waves. This was taken shorewards along both faces of the breakwater and deposited on the finished rock armour slopes. The intermediate sized armour had rested on the core, but became unsupported and, in turn, this was also picked up and strewn along the sides of the breakwater. Up to 100 to 150 feet of finished work would be destroyed in a storm.

PORT TALBOT HARBOUR
MAIN BREAKWATER
Showing storm damage bulges

After one storm, in which the crane operator had been isolated in his cab for 48 hours, it took another day to build a path to rescue him. The sea had removed all the clay and smaller rock, leaving deep holes between the 10 ton boulders.

After a storm, we had two concurrent tasks. Firstly, we had to "clean" the damaged end and start tipping rock again. Secondly, we had to remove the deposited rock and re-adjust the rock armour that had been covered and or displaced. After the first storm, the insurance company paid for the hire of a third LIMA 2400 crane just to repair the damage. Recovered core and intermediate rock was taken forward to the end and tipped. The repair crane then set about realigning the rock armour.

Another problem was the volume of clay on the breakwater, which arrived clinging to the rock. The quarry overburden (topsoil and clay) was not completely stripped off before a blast, and the rock/clay/soil mix was loaded into the crusher and sent to us. Senior management decided to run trials on which size of pump and jetting nozzle would clean off the unwanted clay. Each attempt would gouge out large volumes of the top of the core, which was the running surface for the dump trucks. As the core lumps were about twelve inch size, it made walking and driving small vehicles impossible. We had on the breakwater, a wide, flat, tray we had used for placing core material by crane. I hitched this 12'x 12' x 2' tray onto a LIMA crane and filled it with sea water. When the tray was about 50 feet above the roadbed, it was tipped and the 7,000 litre deluge removed the clay, leaving the roadbed in place. There was no need for pumps and jetting nozzles.

As we made progress, the supply of large rocks slowed down. We looked for alternative sources. As there was a rail siding virtually on site, we got rock from Derbyshire. One or two rocks were chained down on each rail flatbed. A quarry on the Mumbles, the far side of Swansea provided some rock. This was carried by a contractor who purchased ex-British Road Services flatbed articulated lorries. Most of the Swansea stone was moved over night, as traffic was less and accidents caused by rocks rolling off a truck were less likely to involve a car! One of the downsides of this arrangement was that the Swansea prostitutes travelled in the lorries after the town had gone to sleep. They would move from cab to cab while the drivers were waiting for the crane to unload them. One "lady" tripped in the dark and cut her ankle. She came to my site office and asked for the First Aid box. We patched her up and gave her a cup of tea. But that was not enough. She had been injured at work and demanded that I make the necessary entry in the Accident Book, as required by The Factories Act. She was insistent. Eventually, the only way to pacify her was to make the entry, which I managed to do in pencil (and I erased it later).

Long before Britain fell into the clutches of the Health and Safety tsars, our company encouraged safety on sites. We also provided First Aid courses, to ensure that there was an even spread of First Aiders across the three shifts. A cash addition to the hourly rate meant that we had plenty of volunteers. A wrinkly old crane operator, known to all as "Dai Fang", came to me proudly waving his First Aid Certificate and asked for the increase in pay. He was a very heavy smoker, and had just one tooth. This heavily nicotine stained weapon hung from his top jaw. Apparently, he was qualified in "mouth to mouth" resuscitation!!! The mere sight of him would bring any patient back to life instantly.

For minor jobs and to help with maintenance of the larger cranes, we hired a 22RB crane. The owner operator needed a large van full of spares parts, tools, and oxy-acetylene cutting gear to keep it working. Often, when expected to arrive for the night shift, the police would arrest him because they thought that he needed the tools for a bank raid. His sidekick offered us all some pork one night. He would bring the beast to the site and we could all cut off lumps to take home. Two of them went up the valleys and stunned a pig with a sledgehammer, and bundled it into the van. On the way back, down the steep and bendy road in the dark, the pig woke up. It was very angry and managed to get out of the passenger side door before they could stop!

The occupants and the van were somewhat damaged by this, and we did not get the promised pork.

On another occasion, a dump truck driver asked if he and some friends could have a few days off. His school friend, Richard Burton (the film star was born in Port Talbot) had invited them to a party in the Dorchester Hotel in London. It was, apparently, a very good night and my gang mixed with several film stars.

Union troubles

More rock was found in Ireland. A 500 tonne coaster was hired to carry the rocks from Waterford to Port Talbot. The ship arrived and was berthed in the dock, along side our crane. The only way to get the rocks out of the ship's hold was to use a rock grab on a crane. We had months of experience of handling rock, and were ready to start unloading just as soon as the Customs and other officials had finished. Then the Dockers Union insisted that dockers, and only dockers, could unload any ship in the port. It took the gang of dockers an hour to clock on, dress in protective clothing, and walk to the ship. They looked into the hold, scratched their heads, and talked. Time dragged on. The Ship's Captain (and owner) had another cargo to collect in Newport in two days time, and was worried about missing the tide to get out of the dock. The dockers climbed into the hold and ordered our crane driver to lower the grab onto the first rock. They attempted to pull the four fingers open and place them over the rock. The grab does not work that way. It has to be bounced onto the rock, which would be very dangerous for the dockers in the confines of the hold. We tried to explain to the dockers, but they knew best. After hours of trying, they gave up and went to discuss the problem with the Union Representative. We went to speak to the Harbourmaster. No rock was moved that day. The next day, the Captain gave an ultimatum. Either we unloaded the rock, or he was taking it all back to Ireland, and he would have to lose the valuable return cargo from Newport. The dockers refused to continue to unload, and refused to let us unload for them. The ship caught the next tide and no more stone came by sea!!!! We could have unloaded the ship within four hours, but the Union stopped us. If only Maggie Thatcher had been around then.

In the summer, the tyre fitters would swim in the sea until they were needed. These men were two of the plumpest men I have ever seen. They worked for Michelin, and looked just like the company logo. Their site transport was a very small Mini pick-up. The seats had been removed to get their bodies in through the doors! One night, they drove past my office and right down to the water's edge at approaching low tide. There were two young ladies with them, carrying the alcohol and rugs. I was called some time later, to find four naked bodies in my office, covered only with small rugs. They had gone back to the sand dunes for privacy and had lost track of time. The pick-up, with all the clothes was under about ten feet of sea water. I told them that next time they should consider parking above high tide level.

With three major cranes on the breakwater, maintenance had to be done insitu. There was a standing instruction that all cranes not actually working, had to have the jibs lined parallel to the breakwater centreline. This was to make sure that, in the event of an accident, the jib did not fall into the sea and pull the cab with it. It also kept the massive counterweight at the rear of the cab clear of the access route along the breakwater. One day, the maintenance Landrover was parked opposite the tea cabin, an old railway goods van without wheels. The third LIMA was not being used, so the operator decided to grease the cogs on the main jib lifting drum. The crane assistant stood in the engine compartment, slapping grease on each cog tooth as the eight foot diameter wheel turned. The operator went for a cup of tea, leaving the engine running and the jib slowly lifting. A while later, the jib lifted past the vertical and crashed back to earth from a great height. The eight foot wide lattice landed astride the Landrover, with the two mechanics sitting inside. The Landrover was not touched, but the frame of the jib prevented the doors from opening! A very lucky escape, but the crane assistant had been thrown across the exhaust manifold, burning his chest, before he was dumped out of the rear doors and ten feet down to the ground. Because the jib had been aligned with the breakwater, repairs were simplified, even though the loss of production was costly. The crane operator disappeared when the crash happened, and eventually a letter came from his doctor saying that he was no longer mentally fit to return to work.

TA in Swansea

I had transferred from Bomb Disposal to 108 Field Squadron RE(TA) in Swansea. One evening Jane and I were returning from the Drill Hall along the dual carriageway towards Port Talbot, when I found that, exiting a roundabout, one of our lorries had deposited a 10 tonne rock onto the road. I found a telephone box and told the Shift Manager on duty. He had to mobilise our Yale 404 rock grab and an empty lorry to collect the rock.

My new TA unit just did normal Royal Engineer training. We had been given a MACC (Military Aid to the Civil Community) task. A large, derelict, country house had become a death trap. All the floor joists, on all three floors and the basement, had been removed by chain saw. Sheep were dead in the basement. Could we please blow it up and bring all the walls down to ground level? We spent two days on the job one weekend. The house was famous for having the famous batsman Dr W. G. Grace stay there for a local cricket match. This was the only recorded time that W. G. scored a duck. After drilling and placing the charges, we retired a safe distance and blew the building. Not all the walls fell completely down, so we used our Michigan tractor to push these down and level the site. Then we discovered that part of the basement extended out beyond the walls that we had seen. Grass had grown over the wooden roof of this area, but it was not strong enough to support the Michigan shovel. We spent a few anxious hours recovering the shovel, and returned home very late on the Sunday evening.

In October 1966, a coal slag heap at Aberfan descended on the village, killing 144 (including 116 children). The TA unit sent all its vehicles and some sappers to help out. This was a terrible tragedy, which has taken the village many years to recover from.

Free Wales Army

I had a sergeant in 108 Squadron who was keen to learn his trade and get Army certificates. The top grade in his trade was "Combat Engineer Grade 1". To get this, he needed six months at the Royal School of Military Engineering, in Chatham, and I arranged for him to get a place on the course. He attended the course and got high marks. At this time, in the mid - 1960s, the British Government was becoming increasingly worried about the IRA, and the new Free Scotland movement with its military wing. The one thing they did not want was a problem in Wales as well. On his return, my man joined the Free Wales Army. They sent him to the Brecon Beacons, to demolish a National Grid pylon. He cut all four legs very close to the ground, and the pylon sunk down slightly but carried on working. He had been trained to cut each leg at a different height so that it would buckle and collapse, but had forgotten his training. The Government wanted the Free Wales Army removed from the picture and instructed that this case be laughed out of court and the FWA ridiculed. A senior Barrister, Major Tasker Watkins VC QC, was sent down, with the promise that he would be made a Judge if he was successful. He had won his VC in a bayonet charge, serving with The Welch Regiment after D-Day. Needless to say, Tasker succeeded in winning the case for the Government and much ridiculing was done in court and the media and nothing more was heard of the Free Wales movement. My Brother-in-Law had invited me to a party at the Cardiff Golf Club shortly after the case had ended and Tasker was there celebrating his promotion to the High Court. I was introduced to Tasker. Later in the evening we sang Army and Rugby songs together. All the evening I was hoping that I would not blurt out the fact that I had trained the sergeant! I could just imagine the response. Tasker went on to become Sir Tasker Watkins VC GBE QC, Deputy Lord Chief Justice and was for 11 years the President of the Welsh Rugby Union. There is now a statue of him at the entrance to the Millennium Stadium in Cardiff. Strangely enough, his official WRU car was often parked outside my Mother in Law's house. The driver lived next door.

Major Quick, the OC in Swansea, insisted that one had to be in uniform to collect Army pay. The Other Ranks fell in on a Wednesday evening, at the end of training, and names were called out in alphabetical order. One night, the pay parade was proceeding laboriously when Major Quick entered the room. He spotted that Corporal Williams was not in uniform and stopped the paying out to yell at him.

"But I am in uniform, Sir!"
"No you are not."
"Oh yes I am, Sir. This is British Rail Drivers uniform and I am driving the Fishguard to Paddington Express. Can I be paid next please, instead of alphabetical order? If you don't hurry up, my train will be arriving late in London, Sir."

Another officer worked for British Telecommunications and was in charge of external civil engineering works, usually done by contractors. Some time before I met Peter, he had had to remonstrate with one labourer, in a trench that he was meant to be digging. This man was always falling asleep. He got the man fired. Tom Jones had been spending his nights singing and was not fit for work in day time.

Royal Monmouthshire Royal Engineers (Militia)

Within six months of my joining the Swansea unit, the TA was reorganised, and the unit became part of the Royal Monmouthshire Royal Engineers (Militia), or RMonRE(M). This is the senior TA unit and the only Militia unit, and it actually has a chapter of its own in the Army List between the Regular units and the rest of the TA. It was recorded in The Royal Muster of Military Units in 1539. The Honourable Artillery Company in London claim to be the senior reserve army unit. Although formed in 1539, the HAC were disloyal to the Crown when fighting for Cromwell's Parliamentarians and cannot claim continuous loyal service. Our officers claim that the RMonRE(M) was much older, having descended from the archers that fought at Crecy and Agincourt.

The Regimental Headquarters were in The Castle, at Monmouth. The main dining room on the first floor has mementos dating back to the 1700s. There is a wooden shield with two duelling pistols fixed to it and a brass plate commemorated the gift in 1750. About 100 years after the shield was presented, one Mess Night, a pistol was removed and pointed at the brass plate on the shield. The trigger was pulled, and the shot left a dent in the plate. Both pistols had been mounted fully loaded! A second brass plate was added to tell this story. The dining room is the full length of the building, but was not originally that size. One end had been partitioned off and hastily prepared for Oliver Cromwell to use as a bedroom. There is a very fancy plaster cornicing, with hanging loops of flowers and leaves, supported by leather straps inside the plaster. Hidden between two bunches of flowers is a face with Cromwell's wart on the nose. The plasterer was a Royalist.

Mad Italians and my new son

In February 1967, Jane moved to her mother's home in Cardiff as she had high blood pressure. She needed to be near the Gynaecologist and the hospital. Hugh was born on 19th March, with no complications. There was a sticky moment when we went to register the birth. I had forgotten that there are two ways to spell our chosen name for our son. The Registrar sent us out to choose between Huw and Hugh. I prevailed and Hugh was registered. In hindsight, I should have agreed to Huw, with all our Welsh connections. After recovering, Jane and Hugh came back to Ton Kenfig. Hugh was a normal, noisy, healthy baby. To get Jane some respite, we asked a neighbour if she would baby-sit on Wednesday evenings for us to go out. She loved looking after Hugh, and spent her time polishing everything we owned until it gleamed. As Jane got more used to Hugh, and was coping better, she found that she did not want to go out every Wednesday. But we felt we had to because we would upset the baby-sitter if we did not! To give Jane more freedom, she re-started driving lessons. (The first attempt in Leicestershire failed when the Examiner groped her, while promising a pass). We used the haul road on Sundays, when there were no large dump trucks to scare her. Eventually she passed her driving test and she was able to visit her family in Cardiff whenever she wanted.

The company had recently completed a contract in Sudan. The only man left in Sudan was the Project Manager. Although the company had been paid for the work done, the Sudan Government would not allow any money to be sent out of the country. This rule did not apply to profits from agriculture, so the company bought and ran a large farm (I think the crop was coffee). The Project Manager, a civil engineer, had to learn how to be a (successful) farmer, and stay until the money was back in UK. From Sudan, a surveyor was transferred to Port Talbot. He was an Italian, and a heavy smoker. He was allocated to my section, and had digs in the town. The company were still trying to arrange his work permit when he set fire to his digs by smoking in bed. After the hospital had sorted out his burns, which had required four weeks in bed, he was discharged. No landlady would accept him, and his previous landlady was still recovering from her burns. The Project Manager pleaded with me to accept him as a lodger. Jane and I were very reluctant as he could cause another fire, but we finally accepted him. He, and his room, was searched several times a day for matches, lighters, and cigarettes! He repaid us by making Anchovy pizzas, which we detested. Eventually, his work permit application was refused and he went back to Italy.

TA Camp in Germany

We went to Germany for our summer camp, at the Bridging Camp in Hamelin (home of the Pied Piper). For the first week we worked on bridging. On dry land, we practised Bailey Bridging at night without lights.

We also trained on the Light Floating Bridge (LFB), which is a pontoon bridge. The pontoons arrive in sections on lorries and trailers, and have to be assembled in the water. A mobile crane is used to unload the lorries and place the pontoons in the water, and to recover them back onto the lorries after use. We built a bridge on a river and were just finishing off the final tasks when, from nowhere three RAF Jaguar jet fighters came down the river. They had to climb slightly to fly over the bridge. The noise and jet blast was terrifying. Several sappers leapt into the water and had to be rescued. The Instructors had laid on the flight for a bit of realistic training. After that, we had to dismantle the bridge and put it back on the trailers. My Troop Officer, Lt David George, also worked with me on Port Talbot Harbour. We were both standing by the crane, watching the Regular Army crane operator, when the crane failed to lift a pontoon. The jib smashed down on the pontoon, and the crane toppled over onto the lorry. The operator jumped clear and ran to the jib. He took a split pin out of his pocket, saying "This will get me out of the shit", and attempted to replace it in the Safe Load Indicator. David and I both knew all about Safe Load Indicators on cranes, and realised that the split pin had been removed to stop the alarm bell ringing when the crane was overloaded. This particular pontoon had a leak and the hull was full of water, making the unit much heavier than the capacity of the crane. We had to give statements to the inquiry, and at the subsequent Court Marshall, the operator tried to say that he had really said "This will get the shit out of it".

The second week was a tactical exercise, moving around Germany and camping in the forests. Some of our sappers had to remain in camp as a Rear Party, to support the Adjutant. Before we left on exercise, the Regiment was paraded and the various rules were read out to us. One particular rule was in the Part Three Orders and fixed to every notice board. This detailed the out of bounds streets in the town, especially behind the Railway Station – the Red Light area. The British Army and the German

Police agreed that we should avoid trouble while we were guests of the Host Nation. We had several Williams in the squadron, so they were known as "Williams D" or Williams A". One sapper, Williams DD, nicknamed "Double Dense", was one of those left behind, because he would have been a liability on the exercise. After he had finished his duties, he was spotted copying things off the Part III Orders. He was allowed to go into town but arrived back in good order. He went every night after that, until one morning he returned towing an elderly dyed blonde female into camp, who he had met in one of the streets listed on the Part III Orders. He went straight to the Adjutant and explained that he had met the love of his life and wanted to marry her straight away. The Adjutant was a little flustered, and noticed that the Colonel had just driven into camp. The Adjutant said that he needed to discuss this with the Colonel. Williams was pleased, and then spotted the Colonel and rushed up to him, believing that he was the Padre! Wasn't it lucky that the Padre was available just when he was needed for his wedding? My OC, Major Quick, was hauled back to camp to sort out the matter.

The second summer at Port Talbot, the TA Regiment again trained in Germany, at Hamelin. By this time David George had left Marples Ridgeway, and had got a job with the World Bank, supervising the building of the new Limmasol Harbour in Cyprus. The Consultants again were Rendell Palmer and Tritton, and David was delighted now to be in charge of them, after his time under them at Port Talbot. When the date and place of the Summer Camp were known, David called me to find out exactly where we would be on the afternoons of the first and the second Fridays. This was because, as a non-UK resident, he could buy a Tax Free Mercedes car. However, it had to be delivered to a German address to get the tax benefit. Eventually, Regimental Headquarters produced the Grid References for two clearings in the forests and I passed these to David. Mercedes accepted the addresses and confirmed the order. The only problem was to get David to Germany from Cyprus. The Iron Curtain was still in existence and David flew via Bulgaria!! Not only did a British Officer go behind the Iron Curtain, he did it with his Army hat and boots tied to the outside of his luggage! He had no problems and arrived safely.

The Troop reconnaissance vehicle was a Ferret Scout Car, issued without the machine gun for the turret. It was crewed by a commander and a driver. Officers had been issued with Sterling submachine guns, which we carried everywhere. David wished to thank me for getting the details for Mercedes, so we drove off for a drink in the Ferret. He found a pub and he introduced me to Steinhager liqueur which is 80^0 proof. I really liked it and consumed more than a sensible quantity. Leaving the pub, I was map reading and we took a wrong turning and finished up on an Autobahn heading away from our bivouac area. We could not find anywhere to manage a U-turn, and travelled for miles. Eventually we did, and David drove back. Sitting in the turret, I realised that I no longer had my Sterling sub-machine gun!! We got back to the pub and found it still hanging on the hat stand in the bar.

German Law requires all heavy vehicles not to use the public highway on Saturday and Sunday, so we had to find a bivouac area and stay put from Friday evening until Monday. We drove into a small village with the lads (mostly valley coal miners) singing Welsh songs. An impromptu Male Voice Choir had arrived. The tail board of the truck dropped and a rugby ball bounced out. The villagers realised that these were not the usual soldiers they had been used to. David, our German speaker, got involved and, in return for free beers and sandwiches, we agreed to sing in the pub. No one slept in a tent that weekend. The German hospitality was excellent.

At the appointed hour of the first Friday, at the Grid Reference in a dense pine forest, the car transporter arrived with a Mercedes van full of mechanics and salesmen. The car was unloaded, checked over, and given to David. They asked me to contact RHQ to confirm on the radio the next location for the following Friday. When this was done, the Mercedes team drove off. We debated adding camouflage to the brand new white saloon, to match the Army vehicles hidden in the woods. After all, the car would have to hide in the forests with us for the next seven days. David thought that this might invalidate the Warranty, so we reluctantly desisted. A week later, in another wood, the Mercedes van appeared and the team performed a full service on the car. Not all car companies in Britain can manage this level of service! After the camp ended, David drove from Germany to Athens and took a ferry to Cyprus.

Dredging problems

Once the breakwater at Port Talbot was long enough to provide some protection, the harbour was dredged to allow the Iron Ore carriers to enter. A Dutch Dredging company did this work. The Ore handling equipment for the jetty had been ordered, and the building of the jetty had to start on programme to save heavy delay payments to the Handling Equipment company. The jetty was built on steel tube piles. These piles were 120 foot long, 30 inches diameter, and had a conical driving shoe on one end. Bill Legg, the General Foreman, lined up the piling rig and got everything ready for the following morning's very low tide. He was going to place a pile at the edge of the water, as a guide, and drive the other piles as the rig retreated shorewards. Bill was one of the old school, who had been brought up on the old steam driven plant used pre-war.

That night, the dredger ran aground on the beach, straddling the jetty line. The next morning, Bill and I drove to the jetty to start the piling rig off on the journey, only to find our way blocked by a ship. Bill drove up to the ship, parked, and got out. He shouted up to the deck but got no reply. The crew were going nowhere until the next high tide, so they had gone to sleep. Bill found a 7lb club hammer and started pounding on the steel plates of the ship and demanding that it be removed from "his" site immediately. Eventually, a tousled and bleary Captain leant over the side and explained in rather colourful language that the ship was stuck, high and dry, in the sand and that no one could do anything about it until the high tide.

On another occasion, in very thick fog, I was feeling my way along the breakwater at night. The site lighting was reduced to little yellow pin-pricks. It was very quiet, when suddenly there was a crash just beside me. I yelled out, and a voice replied with a Dutch accent "No need to worry. I am just landing some illegal immigrants!" The dredger had gone aground again, because the crew could not see in the fog.

Later on, when the piling was underway, and a strong point established, the jetty progressed beyond the low tide mark into deep water. Piles were assembled on land, and dragged down the beach. A plate was welded over the open top of the pile to make it float. At high tide, the floating pile was dragged along the jetty and tied up near the piling rig, ready for use. After one storm, it was found that one of the piles was missing, having broken the ropes holding it to the jetty. A small boat went looking for it in the Bristol Channel, which is a very busy shipping lane. It was not found and it was thought to have filled with water and sunk. It was not underwater near the jetty. Where had it gone? Three weeks later, it floated back into the harbour. Where had it been? More to the point, how had it missed sinking a merchant vessel? Only an inch showed above water when it floated, so it would have been difficult to see. I don't know if the coastguard had been told, and whether they had informed shipping. A 120 foot long steel arrow would have made a hole in any ship.

Army training

In Swansea, we shared the Drill Hall with an RAMC Field Hospital unit. The film "Zulu" was given a special showing in Swansea, attended by the Mayor and other dignitaries, because the men who fought at Rourke's Drift were the South Wales Borderers. They had been led by a Royal Engineer, Lt John Chard. We were the nearest RE unit, so we officers were invited to attend in best blue uniform. All went well at the reception until one of our officers stood up suddenly under a tray of full sherry glasses and drenched the Lady Mayoress!

I was lucky enough to find time to attend a Regular Army Stores handling Course, held at Long Marsden near Stratford Upon Avon. This was where the 100 miles of Bailey Bridge was stored, and repainted at regular intervals.

Another interesting course that I attended was the Joint Services Nuclear Biological and Chemical Warfare course near Salisbury. This was designed to train the officer responsible for NBC warfare in each unit, on how to train his unit in NBC defence and how to fight under NBC conditions. We wore gas masks most of the time so that we could understand the limitations caused by protective clothing. I remember the first time that I heard "Gas Gas Gas" being shouted during training. One had to find and put on the gas mask without taking a breath. The sergeant instructor had lit a smoke stick and stuck it in my mask, preventing me from lifting it up to my face. When I did, I took a deep breath and took a lung full of smoke. I reeled out of the classroom and staggered across a patch of grass before demolishing a barbed wire fence. I had never felt so ill, but it was a valuable lesson to learn about the dangers of gas and smoke. I made several friends on the NBC course, and one proved very useful later.

Father retires

My father had recently retired from his job as Director of Public Works in Swaziland. One of his jobs had been to build a high granite block wall round the prison. Although he wanted buttresses at intervals to make the wall more rigid and stable in high winds, budget restrictions applied. He was told not to have the buttresses. He was awarded the MBE for services to the Swazi Government. This was announced in the local newspaper on the same day that the prison wall blew down in a gale. The headline read "Director of Public Works gets MBE for allowing prisoners to escape." There was an inquiry, and because my father was unable to produce any written evidence that he had been forced to leave out the buttresses, he was ordered to pay for the repair (from his final salary settlement). The moral of this story is "Get it in writing".

My parents left Swaziland and caught a ship from Capetown, to return to UK. During the journey, Uncle Will died in Leeds, and Dad inherited a part of the estate. Under the Tax Laws at that time, this would come to him tax-free if he remained out of UK for a further 12 months. As they had retired and could afford the time to sit out the wait to save a large sum of money, they left the ship at Lisbon and rented a villa in the Algarve. The only problem remaining was that all his money was in UK Banks and the Wilson Government restricted Britons from taking more than £300 a year out of UK. They were almost destitute, so I was asked to deliver cash by spending Christmas with them. Jane and Hugh looked forward to the trip, and I stuffed pound notes into my shoes and set off for Heathrow. After checking in, on 23rd December, I briefly collapsed in the Departure Lounge. It was a sudden bronchial attack of some sort, and we missed the flight. I called my friend from the NBC course, and he very kindly collected us and took us to his home in Stanwell, very close to Heathrow. John was Duty Officer at RAF Uxbridge, which handled Royal Flights and this gave him connections with Civil Aviation. He fixed us up with a flight to Lisbon on Christmas Eve, and we did not have to pay anything for the change of tickets.

My parents had not given me an address, (mail went to a Post Office for collection) and had arranged to meet us at Faro Airport. My parents did not have a telephone number for us to use. We hired a car in Lisbon and drove south in the night, hoping to find my parents. After a lot of detective work, we were reunited and the holiday could start. Dad suggested a drink of the local Red Wine and I could only describe it as "Chewing Wine". It left a hard red crust on the lips. I assumed that that was all my father had in the house, and I offered to buy a bottle of (drinkable) wine. Dad said not to worry as he still had another five gallons in the kitchen!

The next morning, my mother offered Hugh a glass of orange juice for breakfast. Hugh was horrified to see her take a few oranges off a tree in the garden and squeeze them. This could not be proper orange juice as there was no cardboard carton in sight! Hugh enjoyed the sun and the sand, and Jane loved the fish.

We would go to a small fishing village and watch the boats unload the catch onto the sand. An auctioneer would stop by each catch and sell it. The lucky buyer had to protect the heap from the feet of the crowd surging onto the next sale. We watched the local restaurant owner collect his purchase and went to have a meal.

PORT TALBOT HARBOUR
MAIN BREAKWATER
Completed with concrete wall

Eventually, the breakwater construction reached the end and Marples Ridgeway had to close down the rock placing teams. I was selected to transfer to the new Marples Ridgway – Sudrohrbau Joint Venture building gas pipelines.

After I left the final concrete top wall and roadway was added to the breakwater, and the rock slope finished off.

113

Pipelines   1968 - 1969

The company had formed a Joint Venture with Sudrohrbau, a German company based in Ingolstadt, near Munich, to take advantage of work for the Natural Gas distribution system. In 1968, I was selected to join this team in Essex for the 24 inch pipeline from east of Wickford to the east side of Southend on Sea. Marples staff were responsible for all non-pipe work, while the Germans handled all the technical pipe work. While I was the Marples senior site engineer, my German opposite number was Hans Neidermier.

Southend on Sea

I travelled to Essex, and Jane and Hugh went to live with her mother in Cardiff. The company had come to an arrangement with the owner of a large rural hotel, and all staff lived there. In the late 19th century, there had been a proposal to build a road between Hullbridge and South Woodham Ferrers, including a new bridge over the River Crouch. A Victorian speculator built the hotel, to take advantage of the new passing trade. In the end, the bridge was not built, and there was this large hotel perched on a river bank at the end of the road. Our German welders took a while to get used to living in the hotel. When one ordered a Scotch Egg at the bar, the parrot would hop along, lift the cover, and pass the egg to you in his beak.

The clients on this job were The North Thames Gas Board. They supplied the pipes and arranged the easements through each property.   The pipes were longitudinally welded steel pipes, and NTGB were responsible for the structural strength of this weld. The route was mainly in agricultural land, but did cross the River Roach, a wide tributary of the River Crouch.

London Docks strike

The Germans had shipped all the specialised plant from Munich. The crawler side-boom cranes and welding sets had arrived safely, but the "Igel" had not cleared London Docks. The Igel was an ex-US Army 12 wheel heavy truck, converted to carry two 40 foot long pipes on cradles, and to handle the pipes using the mounted hydraulic crane.

This machine was critical to progress, and was sitting on a barge in the middle of the River Thames during a Dock Strike!! I was sent to get it. This was definitely Mission Impossible.

Another engineer, Peter, lent me his pre-war Bentley, and the very large driver of the Igel travelled with me to Tilbury. The driver was massive, spoke no English, and looked threatening in his heavy long black leather coat and leather hat. I drove into an eerily empty port and found HM Customs. I had the paperwork for the Customs clearance but I had to get the "Igel" onto dry land for the Customs officer. Through a hatch in the wall, I tried to negotiate the release of the truck. I was getting nowhere, when the telephone inside the office rang. It was Peter wanting to talk to me about the next job of the day after the truck had been released. His timing was impeccable and he never told me just how he managed it. (This was in the days long before mobile telephones). This telephone call impressed the Customs man, and he directed me to the Port Office. On arrival, again Peter telephoned just as I was about to knock on the sliding window. The man opened the hatch and asked if I was Mr Martin. I said I was, and he thrust the telephone out to me. I had a talk with Peter, and told him how far I had got in the process. The Port man told me that the truck was on a barge moored in the centre of the Thames, and it needed a tug boat to bring it under the crane for unloading. But, he said, the Docks were on strike and that I should return when the strike had ended. He let me know that there was an emergency crew in a tea room, but that they were unlikely to help me. I found the tea room and my German driver loomed up behind me. Luckily, the emergency crew were bored, and agreed to unload the truck for me. We were soon able to check the truck over for damage, and complete the paperwork. It only took about four hours. Without the "stage props" of the Bentley, the large leather coat, the lack of English, and the telephone calls, we could not have managed it.

Pipeline work

The trenching was simple, and the pipes were delivered along the "trace" by the Igel. The pipes were supported clear of the ground, on "skids" (4" x 4" x 4 foot oak timbers). Welding of the pipes proceeded. X-Rays of all welds had to be done before we were allowed to wrap the joint against corrosion. I had a small team digging road crossings ahead of the main trench work. We would identify any buried services, dig the trench, place a "sleeve" pipe, and backfill the trench in the same day, if possible. We had five large steel sheets to place over the trench to allow vehicles to cross during the work. At the end of one day, I told the ganger to load all the tools and the road plates and take them to the next road crossing. I went to check the new site at the end of the day, to be sure that all was correct for the early start the next day. The five steel sheets were missing. There was no damage on the ground, so they had not been tipped off the lorry. The Project Manager called the Police, who found them at the nearest scrap merchant. He had paid a man who had driven my truck, and said that he looked like my ganger. This man was found and arrested. I got my plates back, but had to spend time at the Police Station with my boss, making statements. It was some hours later that the man was charged. After his court case and sentencing, his lawyer demanded his overtime payment for the time from the theft up to the time of his being charged!! We refused to pay the money, but admired his cheek.

The welders on the project were mainly German, but there were a number of British welders who did the more complicated "Tie-in" welds. These men were very well paid. So much so that one came to me for permission to be absent one day. He told me that he was off to buy his wife a Nursing Home, for cash!

The route took us through an orchard. The owner was very concerned about damage, even vibration damage, to his trees. The German Foreman (Herr Langwasser) said that he would ignore this man. The man appeared with a rifle, and when I told Langwasser that he was on the Olympic Rifle Team and would not miss, co-operation was agreed. Herr Langwasser was large and, when angry, would pick up one of the oak "skids" in one hand and chase the person that had offended him.

116

It was about this time that Michael Bentine, the Anglo-Peruvian old Etonian member of The Goon Show, invented the "400 year old" pub game of "Dwile Flunking". The job passed a pub and the regulars challenged the Germans to a match on the Sunday. They agreed, before they found out that it involved being struck with a floor cloth soaked in old beer slops. They took it in good fun, but everyone had a sore head the next day.

The pipeline had valve chambers at intervals, which had to be concreted round the pipework. The chamber had to be waterproof, to avoid corrosion affecting the operation of the valve. One of these chambers was in a ploughed field alongside the main road out of Southend, towards what is now the Southend Airport. There were no hedges or fences on this section of road, and the chamber was on a slope rising from the road. We had trouble with a leaking joint in the concrete base slab, and had tried everything to seal the leak. We resorted to an underwater sealing technique. At evening rush hour, the road was crowded. Drivers suddenly became aware of a fully dressed Scuba diver, complete with air bottles, rising from what looked like a furrow in the ploughed field. The car crashes were blamed on us, but the police said that the drivers had taken their eyes off the road!

The river crossing was the first time that I had been involved in towing a pipe across water and sinking it into a trench. I learnt a lot about buoyancy and the effect of river currents. The task went smoothly.

Opening of Port Talbot Harbour

Jane and I were invited back to Port Talbot to witness the opening of the Harbour by the Queen. There had been extensive preparations. A new route had been constructed to take the Royal cavalcade and official visitors to the marquee. This needed a Bailey Bridge and Lt David George and the Swansea Squadron built this. The jetty was not fully complete in time for the Visit. The in-situ deck slabs had not been cast in some bays. The 4 metre by 4 metre openings were hastily covered in thin plywood and sprayed with a cement wash, to make them look complete. After formally opening the Harbour, the Queen climbed into an open topped Land Rover and toured the site. The driver tried to take her along the (very unsafe) jetty, but we managed to prevent the accident from happening.

As the official guests left the reception afterwards, a car went off the side of the dock and sank. David George dived in and tried to rescue the occupants. There were two couples in a small car, and this had got tangled up in some broken piling underwater. David made many attempts, but sadly failed. The dead were the Harbourmasters of Barry and Cardiff and their wives. David was awarded a Queens Commendation for his rescue attempt.

Jane and I met up with all the members of my Shift and the ex-miner who had had his legs broken was there in his wheelchair. He said that he never wanted to work in construction again and was going to get an office job when he finally healed up. Apparently there had been an argument after the visit between two labourers, who both wanted to take home the W.C. that had been provided for the Queen.

Slough

North Thames Gas Board gave us another contract, based on our performance at Southend. The new job was between Gerrards Cross, Slough and Southall. Once again, NTGB supplied the 24 inch diameter steel pipes. This part of the route went through agricultural land and the estates of landed gentry and stockbrokers. The model, Jean Shrimpton, lived with her parents here and had a length of pipe on their land. The route also went past Pinewood Studios. Often a scene from a "Carry On" film was shot on the leafy road which ran parallel to the trench.

After passing the village of Iver, the route reached the M4 at Slough. From there into London, the route followed the M4, switching from side to side when obstructed. The centreline of the trench was 10 feet outside the motorway fence line. This made delivery of the pipes by the "Igel" truck very easy. It parked on the hard shoulder of the M4 and swung the 40 foot long pipes off the truck cradles straight over the fence. Of course, the offside pipe has to be swung in a circle, across the three lanes of the busy motorway, round the front of the cab, three foot above the road surface, before crossing the fence!! We all had German registered vehicles, with left-hand drive steering, and Munich number plates. We found it easier to deliver pipes at night when traffic was reduced. The Metropolitan Police patrols were very unhappy with this process and often tried to stop us. When they arrived, no one spoke a word of English and we just ignored the officers until the job was done, and we all drove off in our German registered cars. We had an Irish lad with a Landrover, who dispensed tea from an urn on the tailboard. He caught up with us one evening and gave the policemen each a plastic mug of hot tea each while they tried to remonstrate with us. I have fond memories of two lonely and frustrated policemen, drinking the tea, as we all drove off.

All the welded joints had to be X-rayed. The company that was doing this work was incapable of keeping up with our rate of progress, and we could not wrap or bury the pipe until they had approved the weld in each joint. Ill feeling between us and the X-ray company staff increased. The law specified safety distances for the filming process, and the number of warning signs that had to be put in place before the radioactive Caesium source could be used. The safety distances crossed into the middle lane of the M4 Motorway, and affected all traffic into Heathrow Airport. The Police decided, after taking scientific advice, that moving vehicles would not be greatly affected, so stopping traffic on the M4 was not necessary. The cost to the police and the Gas Board of halting traffic for each weld inspection would have been enormous!

One particular weld inspector gave us plenty of problems. Often he had to return to a joint after his first x-ray failed for another attempt, causing increased frustration. One day, he was seen struggling to move all the warning signs to the pipe joint area. This needed three trips on foot. The van which dropped him off went on to another job, leaving the signs and the radioactive Caesium source on the road verge. A foreman picked the source up and delivered it to a local police station, as a bit of lost property. A major panic ensued, which eventually resulted in the inspector being sacked and filming rates improving.

As on the previous pipeline job in Essex, my role was all the advance earthworks, temporary fencing and road crossings. There was one rail embankment crossing near Iver. We had to drive a sleeve pipe through the embankment. This was done by the thrust boring sub-contractor, and this required me to visit at night to check on progress. Several times the Swansea to Paddington Express had whistled at me, as Corporal Williams was the driver and had recognized me! One night the police came to us and asked if they could borrow our floodlights as a train had struck what could have been a trespasser on the track. We set up the lights and a number of policemen formed a line across the area and they searched. They found body parts and placed them in plastic bags. The bags were brought back to the Incident van and the body was assembled to check that all was accounted for. All was going well until the third leg was found! The whole place was searched again and most of the second body accounted for, except for the head. All the time, trains were passing and light from the carriages shone down the embankment slopes. There were iron railings at the bottom, and just as a train passed, a policeman looked up and caught sight of the carriage lights flashing on the eyes in the head stuck on top of the railings. He became a gibbering wreck, and never worked again.

Thrust boring

The route crossed the M4 twice, and this was done by thrust boring. The first thrust bore was successful. The sleeve pipe was fairly straight and level and daylight could be seen from the other end. The second bore was a disaster. The bore was just west of Junction 3, at Cranford. The motorway rises on embankment to meet the bridges over the ground level roundabout. Access on and off the motorway is provided by slip roads rising from the roundabout. The bore started on the south side of the motorway, below the original ground level. Eventually the bore broke through on the north side, three feet above the slip road level, and frightened motorists. It was some fifteen feet above the correct level! The thrust bore company was forced to make another attempt at their own expense, which was successful. There were some angry letters to the Managing Director of the Thrust bore company, and counter claims for "unforeseen ground conditions", which were rejected. I later met the Managing Director at my Professional Interview. He was one of my two Interviewers!

Bailey Bridging

At Cranford Church, access was needed for the normal pipeline crews and plant to cross a Graveyard with heavy tracked machines. This was refused by the Church authorities. An alternative access, directly off the roundabout, required a Bailey Bridge to cross a wide stream. A specialist company supplied the bridge and the supervisor to oversee the erection. My men acted as labour. The supervisor had, he told me, recently retired from the Royal Engineers. The job should have been simple for him. But it was a tight launch site, and the bridge had to be pushed uphill during construction. These two problems defeated him. While waiting for someone to notice his difficulty, he kept adding panels and trying to push forward on the temporary rollers. Eventually he found that he could no longer push the bridge. I took over, and I used two labourers, one foreman, and a 22RB crane to complete the job. After that successful build, I took down, moved, and re-erected the bridge five times, with the same small crew. The supervisor had been trained to use a Troop of 40 men for this task.

Heavy digging

On the north side of the M4, where the M4/M25 interchange now stands, we ran into great difficulty digging the trench. We knew that we were going through gravel beds with a high water table, so there were many large pumps in use. Many of these gravel pits had been excavated and then used for waste disposal. At one point, the large Hymac backhoe was taking enormous swings down into the trench, and the bucket was bouncing back into the air. We hired a diver, who found that we were in an area of Landfill. The excavator was trying to cut through old earthmoving machine tyres, and they acted like a giant trampoline. The only way to dig the trench was to use underwater oxy-acetylene cutting gear, because of the steel cords in the tyres. After many days, the work was completed. The ground water had been turned black by the burning tyres. Hovis had a big bakery, some distance away, which used ground water extracted from the same gravel bed. Apparently a large amount of bread had to be thrown away as it had a funny grey colour.

Hugh's accident

Jane had arrived in London and was looking for a house to rent. She called me to say that she had heard from Cardiff that Hugh had had an accident. My Mother in Law had just made a pot of tea when the doorbell rang. She put the tea pot on a high shelf and went to answer the door. Hugh, as soon as she had left the room, climbed up and pulled the tea pot over and he was badly scalded. He had severe burns on his forehead and down his left arm. Hot tea was trapped in his woolly sweater, and Mother in Law picked him up to comfort him, trapping the heat in the elbow joint. The doctor thought that the damage to the elbow would prevent him ever straightening his arm, or allowing him to use the muscles in his forearm. After he was patched up, we transferred him to Wrexham Park Hospital in Slough and we both spent time at his bedside. I was able to do some work by using the site radio system from there. The doctors in Slough were very good, and the elbow problem got sorted. He still has a ravaged arm and a scar on his head. He was proud of the scar on his arm because "It was just like Daddy's". Eventually we found a house to rent just off the A30, across the road from Heathrow Airport. The noise from the aircraft, the A30, and the filling station next door made life unpleasant. My sister Jenny and her husband Ian lived in Chertsey, not too far away. Jenny had two children the same age as Hugh and we spent a lot of time together.

Jane had an old Ford car, which was constantly breaking down. I found a cheap source of spare parts. A scrap merchant had a car breaking yard near the site. We had to dig in the gravel bed near his yard, and he suggested that we dump the spoil in his yard to firm up the ground, to save carting it miles to a tip. Whenever I wanted a spare part, he would let me find and take what I wanted in return for some gravel. I kept Jane's car going very cheaply.

The final length of pipe went through Southall, with its big Asian population. Most of the Asian families had left East Africa and did not have any connection with the Indian sub-continent. However, a common second language was Swahili and I had to talk to people to explain when I was intending to dig up roads and move heavy plant past homes. This was three years before the massive influx when Idi Amin threw Asians out of Uganda in 1972. At the end of that year on the pipeline job, I spoke some German, a little Irish-English, and Swahili. My normal English had vanished, in spite of my living and working in my own capital city!

The North Thames Gas Board Resident Engineer was not easy to like. In the middle of one crisis, with plant having fallen into the trench and blocking the road, his priority seemed to be to get me to clean mud off the road. My priority was to save the plant and open the road to traffic, and then I could spare time for non-essentials like mud. There was a heated argument and he threw me off the site. I was happy to leave, because it meant my first early night at home for some weeks. I was reinstated the next day, without an apology.

Drowned in mud

Sometimes a weld photograph is re-examined some time after the date that it was recorded. A result of this late checking is that the pipe often had already been lowered into the trench and partly backfilled. On one occasion, the Resident Engineer ordered that a weld be cut out and re-welded to his satisfaction. The weld was found to be some 80 feet from an open end and buried in the trench. It was agreed that more weld could be added to the inside of the pipe, rather than lift the pipe out and cut it open. The pipe was 24" internal diameter and a welder agreed to attempt the task, in return for a very large sum of money. A trolley was made up for him to lie on, and measured ropes were attached so that we could locate the offending weld. By pushing one shoulder forward and the other back, the welder could move in the pipe. Towing the welding cable, he set off. We stopped him at the correct distance and he found the weld. As soon as he struck the weld, this consumed all the oxygen in the pipe near him and he blacked out. This had been expected and he was hauled out safely. A great deal of time and effort had been saved.

After a length of pipe has been welded and buried, it has to be pressure tested. The test pressure is between three and six times the expected working pressure. The pipe to be tested has steel plates welded to the open ends and the pipe is filled with water. Large capacity, high pressure air compressors are attached to valves fitted in the end plates and pressure is built up. The test requires that the pressure is maintained for twenty four hours, without a noticeable drop in pressure at any time.

At the western end of our contract, in the agricultural area, there is a valley to the north of Pinewood Studios. A pressure test was arranged for the half mile length. This was going well and I was monitoring the pressure gauge at the top of the hill, when I noticed the Resident Engineer (RE) and the Gas Board Land Agent walking along the trench line. Just as they got to the lowest point in the valley, there was an almighty roar as the pipe split open just behind them. Thousands of gallons of water, under pressure, mixed with the field soil and rose up in a mushroom cloud. The sky turned dark brown, and I saw the two men trying to run in the sea of mud. The cloud seemed to hang, and then it fell. After a few moments, two muddy creatures started to crawl towards us. The RE demanded a change of clothes and said emphatically that I would pay for the replacements. He believed that one of the circumferential welds that we were responsible for had burst. He was not a happy bunny. Later, it was proved that one of the longitudinal welds, that the NTGB were responsible for, had split and we were vindicated. He paid his own dry cleaning costs.

The RE and the Land Agent were found to have manipulated the choice of route, to get back-handers from grateful owners when massive extra work was done. Fences, walls, roads and other work that was not strictly necessary, was billed to NTGB. After sentencing, they both served two years.

Meanwhile, a TA summer camp was due. My unit was assigned to clearing up Battlefield damage during and after a major exercise in Germany involving the Bundeswehr. Tanks were used and the tank tracks chewed up fields and roads. Whenever possible, I would try to prevent damage before it happened and sometimes stopped a tank to remonstrate. A German tank stopped, the main gun swung down to point at me, a terrifying vision. The hatch opened, and a Panzer officer climbed out. Lt Hans Neidermier had been my opposite number on the pipeline job!! It is a small world. When he arrived in England, he could hardly speak two words of English and I helped him. Hans was the typical blond Aryan giant and when we both needed an item of plant at the same time, he always politely offered to fight me for it! At the end, he spoke fluent English and I was reduced to a sort of basic pidgin English/German/Swahili mix.

The Joint Venture had had many delays and it was proposed that I move to our Head office in Victoria Street to assist with the claim preparation, although there was much more work still required to complete the works.

Before I left the site for head office, Jane complained about the state of the garden in our rented house next to the Heathrow boundary. One Sunday, I took four labourers from the site and we cleaned the whole area up. On site, to prevent weeds growing up in pump chambers, NTGB required us to saturate the areas with the weed killer DT245. This chemical, now banned, was known to the Americans in Vietnam as Agent Orange. Without me knowing, one lad sprayed our garden with this highly toxic chemical. In Vietnam, forests have taken over forty years to start recovering. Years later, each time I flew back to Heathrow I could see the garden as we landed. For the next thirty years, the garden still looked bare.

London (again)   1969 - 1970

Claim against North Thames Gas Board

In 1969, I started work in the company headquarters, as part of the team preparing the claim against North Thames Gas Board. The job had taken three times as long as NTGB had predicted, and was still unfinished. There had been several incidents where the longitudinal pipe weld had been found to be faulty, and there were a number of questionable site instructions given by the RE. I was tasked to look at all the site diaries, notes, site instructions, and other papers. To clarify points, where possible, I interviewed staff. All this detective work was needed to ensure that our claim would stand up.

Liverpool briefly

I was also sent to help out in Liverpool, on the approach roads to the second Mersey Tunnel. The Climbing Shutter was being used again for retaining walls. Ron Dorricott, my rigger foreman was again in charge. He had made his home in a derelict pub on Scotland Road. This pub was due for demolition by us under the scheme. Ron invited me to share his humble home. There was a rat (called Henry after the site general Foreman) who popped out from behind the fireplace, looking for food. This was the first government job in the UK to be paid to erect security fencing round a site. Thieving is a major sport in Liverpool, and the client (now the Highways Agency) agreed to pay for security fencing to save delays. This did not deter the thieves. The client was asked to pay extra for security lighting, and then they agreed to pay for security guards. Eventually, underfed Alsatian dog were given to the guards. Still the thieving went on. The order came to remove the human guards, and just leave the hungry dogs. On my first night there, I was sitting in a pub with Ron when the door opened and a seven year old boy came in. He was trying to sell an Alsatian dog that he had stolen off our site!

Just outside our pub, there was the new arch over the entrance to the new Birkenhead tunnel. In order to gradually get drivers eyes used to the change from tunnel lighting to normal open air light, this section of the arch (carrying the rebuilt Scotland Road), had glass blocks set in the surface. These allowed light to percolate through to the road below. One day there was a banging noise outside, so I investigated. There was a very young lad (about 8 years old) sitting on the pavement with a lump hammer, cold chisel, and a gallon of gloss white paint. He was breaking a hole through a glass block. "What are you doing?" I asked. He replied, "When I get the hole finished, I'm going to pour white paint on the windscreens of the cars underneath".

My stay on the site came to an abrupt halt. As a setting out engineer, I had to erect wooden profile boards to help control the shape of the excavations. I reached for a suitable timber, broke it in half with a hammer and proceeded to nail it onto the upright peg. This was a highly Unionised site, in a Unionised city, and I was not a fully paid up member of the Union. I should have asked a carpenter to do this kind of work. Everyone walked off site. I was advised by the Site Agent to return quickly to London.

The Ritz Hotel

Once, while in the London Office, I was given a bundle of drawings to take to our job on the London Underground, at Green Park Tube Station. From time immemorial, tunnellers had always finished a shift with a drink in the nearest pub. We were in donkey jackets and rubber boots, and covered in clay. That day the foreman decided that a drink was needed and we all trooped off to "the nearest pub". The doorman at The Ritz Hotel refused us entry, for some reason that we could not understand, and we had to find somewhere more hospitable.

Watford printing works

When I got back to London, the Claim was nearly finished. It just required printing and binding. I was sent to a printing firm in Watford to supervise and assist producing ten sets of some fifteen volumes of documents. It was fascinating to see how a printer worked. After six weeks, and proof reading changes, the documents were ready. This was an interim Claim, for work only up to the time I left site. Work on site was still not complete. The sum that we claimed was three times the original Contract Sum. The covering letter was signed and our commissionaire was told to deliver the documents to North Thames Gas Board on a Friday afternoon. The Chief Quantity Surveyor told the commissionaire to bring the NTGB cheque back that night. (A bit of wishful thinking, I thought).

Renting the Queen Mary

The company were actively tendering for all kinds of work. We felt that we had the expertise to construct the Ekofisk Oil Drilling platform, and we prepared a tender. This was a 300 feet high concrete structure that had to be built for use in deep water. While one engineer was sent off to Scotland to find suitable sites for fabricating this massive concrete structure, I was sent to find temporary accommodation for some 4,000 personnel. I approached Cunard to ask about redundant liners, and got a reasonably good hire rate for hiring RMS Queen Mary for a two year period. She had been retired in 1967, and had carried a maximum of 16,000 American troops during the War. Although she was configured for 2,150 passengers in comfort, we would have to get many more aboard. We did not win the Ekofisk contract.

TA Training

TA training at weekends now took place at Chickerell Camp, Wyke Regis, near Weymouth. This is the Royal Engineer Wet Bridging Camp. Below the accommodation, there is a wide concrete "hard" where floating bridge equipment of all kinds can be launched into "The Fleet", a stretch of water separated from the sea by Chesil Bank. Apart from the Light Floating Bridge (LFB), we also trained on the Heavy Floating Bridge (HAFB), and the Heavy Ferry. Both of the latter being designed to carry the Main Battle Tank (MBT).

The Heavy Ferry is made up of several sections for transport, driven by four jet propulsion units that have 360^0 steering. To operate the Ferry, one had four separate helmsmen, each with a dedicated throttle man, a total of eight men. The skipper of this nifty craft had to co-ordinate the speed and direction of all four power units, in order for the craft not to spin out of control. When there was a tank on the ferry, the skipper could not see all of his helmsmen at the same time, unless he stood on top of the tank turret. Even more fun was taking a tank across a river at night, without lights. My niece, Claire, married a Royal Navy Commander, who had been No 1 on the Aircraft Carrier HMS Illustrious. He had been telling me how difficult it was to steer his ship. I told him that he had better come and practice on the Heavy Ferry before trying to make me believe him.

At one camp, a General came to inspect us. I had had the Heavy Ferry in the water early and had been going up and down the river, while waiting for him to arrive. I learnt which settings for steering, and the different engine revs, on each of the four engines, were necessary to hold the ferry onto the bank (for unloading a lorry) while the river current was pushing against the sides. I ordered the General off the ferry until he had donned a kapok lifejacket, then we took off up river. I gently turned the ferry into the bank, dropped the ramps, drove off the lorry and returned the General to home ground. I had made it look very simple, but it was anything but simple. When the General returned his lifejacket, it fell into the water and sank like a stone. So much for Army 'Elf and Safety.

The one bad thing with any military training is that, at the end of the day, the kit has to be returned to the Stores and all accounted for. It adds hours to a task, and you are doubly tired at the end, especially when you are handling heavy bridging equipment.

At the end of each Annual Camp, we had to return some extra vehicles to a Depot in Taunton. We shared the camp with a Regiment and they had about three times the number of vehicles to return. Great preparations were made, to ensure that all our vehicles arrived together and ahead of those from the Regiment. At dawn the next morning, I found that a 1-Ton truck was missing. I sent the rest off to Taunton and started to search for the truck. The Regiment had taken it across the water and left it on Chesil Bank! They were determined that they would be first to hand back their vehicles! I had to build a pontoon, cross the water, load the truck and get it back onto the mainland. Then we had to catch up the rest of our vehicles and pray that the Regiment had driven more slowly. The Depot would only start accepting vehicles when the whole complete group had arrived. That was a nightmare drive, and we arrived to find that the Regiment had had a low-loader stuck across a roundabout. We had beaten them!

Bath   1970

Marples Ridgway decided to move the Head Office from Victoria, London to Bath during early 1970. I was still in the Temporary Works Design office, so I also had to move to the West Country. Jane and I got a flat in a converted Barn in Monkton Combe, south of the city. On the same landing was another very friendly couple. He was a Flying Officer in the RAF, and flew C130 Hercules from RAF Lyneham.

Professional interview preparation

During this time, I was given several Temporary Works tasks to design for sites. This was the time, I thought, to complete my preparation for the Professional Interview for membership of The Institution of Civil Engineers. Having spent so much time out on site, I was some three years behind my contemporaries in gaining Membership. My first designs related to the temporary formwork under a section of the elevated motorway junction between the M5 and the M6, otherwise known as Spaghetti Junction. This section was on marshy ground between a canal and a 132,000 Volt overhead electricity line. We needed a method of moving the temporary formwork. I drew up three separate schemes, costed them, and provided a method statement for the use of each. These designs were used, in discussion, to defeat the RE and make him allow a reasonable method of re-using the shuttering system. I had designed something that would not work and would never be used. However, it was accepted by the examiners of the Institution when I submitted it.

I spent many long evenings getting my papers ready for the Professional Interview for Membership of the Institution of Civil Engineers. We took on a young apprentice draughtswoman for the Drawing Office. She was attractive, and her lunch breaks were getting longer. We all walked into Bath to buy sandwiches for lunch. Eventually the Head of the Section had had enough of her late returns and challenged her. "Why were you late back from lunch?" She replied "The man that was following me was walking very slowly".

I submitted my papers for the Professional Interview for Membership of the Institution of Civil Engineers. I had to wait to see if they were up to standard and whether the Institution would call me to the Professional Interview.

TA training went on and I was given command of the Troop based in Bristol. Numbers were down, so we organised a recruitment drive. The Permanent Staff Instructor had been newly transferred from Germany and he was full of enthusiasm. We toured towns south and east of Bath on Saturday afternoons. One day we had more than 30 lads sign up. The PSI was very pleased with himself. Then we found out that they had all been let out of a Mental hospital for the afternoon. The PSI became the butt of several jokes.

Dover Cliffs   1970 - 1971

"Painting the White Cliffs of Dover"

Once I had submitted my application for membership of the Institution, I was asked to take over as the Site Agent on the Dover Cliffs Stabilization Project, in Kent. This job had been running for a year, when the Agent was offered a job digging mining shafts in Australia. My brief was to close down the job, and not to take longer than three months. As it was a Cost Plus contract, I took a full year to close the job down and I made money for the company.

Dover Cliffs Stabilization

Dover Castle sits on top of massive chalk cliffs, with the town extending along the foreshore below. There are many houses on the cliff side of the road, which runs along above the shingle beach inside the harbour. At the time, this road was the only link to the car ferries to France and Belgium. The chalk contains flint stones, and as the weathering proceeds, the flints fall out. Some flints drop the full 250 feet height of the cliff and make a mess of the houses below. As owners of the cliff, the Ministry of Ancient Monuments (now English Heritage) decided to stabilise the face of the cliff, to reduce the number of claims for damage. There were two companies interested in the task. Marples Ridgway and a local scrap merchant. The scrap merchant stated that he would let his boy down on the end of a rope, fixed to a Landrover. Raising and lowering was simply controlled by driving forward or reversing the vehicle. The Ministry decided that, although this was considerably

129

cheaper, we should have the job on our better safety proposals. As the actual work required was unknown, and had to be decided on a day to day basis, the work was to be paid for on a Cost Plus basis. The original estimate was for three months work. Closer examination showed that considerably more time was needed and I arrived a year after work had started.

Working the cliff face

On top of the cliff were two 10 Ton Henderson Derrick cranes. These were electrically powered. Most of the work on the cliff face was carried out by men standing in a large skip, lowered by the Derrick. As the skip was mostly lowered below the operator's sight line, we had radio communications between the foreman in the skip and the crane operator. However, there were problems. The only radio frequency that we were allowed to use was completely dominated by the extremely powerful BBC Long Wave radio mast less than a mile away. The previous agent that I took over from had discussed this with his father (who worked in the Radio Licencing Office in London). His father recommended a cheap Japanese system that could be found on sale illegally, and we survived using this banned frequency.

Once a month, the Ministry Architect would appear for a site visit, to sign off the accounts, and we would give him a tour of the cliff in the skip. He was a particularly

Ministry Inspection Team

nervous 60 year old, and always very anxious that he should not miss the train back to London. On one visit, the foreman ordered the crane operator to lower us over the edge of the cliff and we commenced the cliff examination. While we were occupied, the foreman switched his radio for the old and broken set that we kept for repairs. The sea mist came in and covered the cliff top. All one could see was the hoist rope disappearing into the cloud. The Architect indicated that he had seen enough and that we should return him to terra firma. The foreman attempted to speak to the crane operator, but with no success. He tried shouting, but got no reply. He banged the radio on the edge of the skip, to try to get it working, but without success. All this took time, and I tried to tell the Architect that the crane operator would have to lift us up when he went home at the end of the day (much too late for the London train), and that we would pay for his hotel. Eventually, the foreman threw the radio out of the skip in disgust. The Architect's face was a picture. Eventually, a voice was heard calling to us and we were lifted to the cliff top in the cloud. When I finally got the Architect back to the site office, and had given him a strong cup of tea (not a mug, he was an Architect!), he would have signed his own death warrant if I had had put in front of him. All he did sign was the monthly Bill of Quantities, so that we could get paid, and he never ever queried anything that I put in front of him after that day.

Fitting the Jib on a Derrick

The two derricks moved along the cliff top in a leap-frog manner. One was used to dismantle and then rebuild the other in the new position. Massive concrete blocks, with holding down bolts, had to be cast in large holes. These blocks counteracted the weight of the jib and load. New 415 volt three phase electric cable connections were needed for the power supply. The biggest difficulty was the installing the crane jib and the hoist rope. These items hung over the houses below while they were being assembled and were a considerable danger to the occupants. Just before I arrived on site, a very large lump of chalk had fallen on the Public House. Luckily, it fell on a Sunday morning, before opening time and it only demolished the external Gents toilet. A rule was then established by the Ministry that during crane building (and other dangerous work), occupants (if they wished) could move into temporary accommodation at Government expense. This offer was enthusiastically accepted, and the hotel bills were excessive. I merely passed these on, with our added percentage. But it was better to be safe than sorry.

When we moved the cranes to cover further areas of the cliff, the Ministry took the opportunity to clear away old concrete left over from the War. It was decided that drilling and blasting would not be appropriate. However some of the slabs were quite thick, and breaking them with the normal jackhammer was painfully slow. We investigated ways of increasing production and someone suggested "hydraulic feathers". A hole is drilled and the feathers are placed in the hole. Under hydraulic pressure, the feathers expand sideways and exert pressure on the concrete. The idea is to drill a line of holes, at calculated distances apart, and split lumps off the main block. The company representative came to show us how to do the work. When the first hole was ready, we all retired to a concrete bunker (last used by Winston Churchill to wave two fingers across the Channel) and switched on the hydraulics. There was an almighty bang and a short while later the broken bit of concrete splashed into the sea, just short of the harbour breakwater, nearly a mile away. We reduced the distances between holes and the edge of the slabs, and had no further mishaps.

Battle of Britain film

During my time in Dover, the film "The Battle of Britain" was being made. This required lots of Spitfire flying over the cliffs. The aircraft no longer had proper radios, and the pilots were given instruction by small walkie-talkie radios. They suffered the same radio blackout that we had, due to the extremely powerful signal from the BBC Long Wave mast. Further, the two crane jibs were lowered to the ground to prevent them being included in the filming. The film company came to a financial agreement with the Ministry because I was prevented from working.

Professional Interview

From Dover, I went up to the magnificent building on Great George Street, Westminster for the Interview for Professional Membership of the Institution of Civil Engineers. Some time before the actual interview, one had to present a portfolio of drawings, calculations and other details, describing ones experience. At the interview one had to talk about technical problems one had encountered and how these were solved. The two Interviewers then asked a series of questions based on the papers that had been submitted. Finally, they had to set an essay subject, based on the interview, for the two hour written exam held after the lunch break. The subject of thrust boring came up, and I criticised the sub-contractor that had worked on the pipeline jobs, mentioning the claim we had against the company for the poor work. One Interviewer then introduced himself as the Managing Director of that company, and I thought that I had ruined my chances completely. I stood by my comments and the other Interviewer quickly changed the subject. Outside, I met three other engineers that I knew and we had a rather liquid lunch, and we were the last to arrive back into the exam. That afternoon, 200 of us sat at desks in the Great Hall and looked at our individually selected subjects. Mine was "Pipeline construction, with particular reference to Thrust Boring". I knew who had selected the subject and he was going to tear my effort to shreds. I started by listing the headings of my essay, down to and including Thrust Boring and the final summary. I wrote steadily for two hours, in great detail on all the preceding headings, and ended by starting the first line of the Thrust Boring paragraph. I made it look as though I had run out of time just as I reached the subject. I passed, and the essay (without the Thrust Boring bit) was recommended for publication. I never found out what the Thrust Bore man thought of my effort.

President of the Institution

Certain sections of the chalk were less stable and weaker than other areas. I thought that these areas could benefit from rock-bolting. To support my idea, I engaged Sir William Halcrow, the Consultant that had worked on the geology for the Channel Tunnel. Sir Alan Muir Wood was the senior Partner and he often visited the site, to check on his staff. He concurred and his report was submitted to the Ministry and accepted by them. We started drilling to place 20 foot long McAlloy high tensile rock bolts. In an untethered skip, drilling was difficult. Even to tether the skip, drilling and bolting was needed. The drill bit has to be forced onto the surface, but all that happened was that the skip swung away from the cliff face until the weight and force balanced. This often left a ten foot gap between the face and the skip. Eventually I "proved" to Sir Alan that the only time that conditions for drilling were perfect was when the wind was at more than Force 6, and from the South West. The wind helped force the skip onto the cliff face, and drilling was easier. As we were paid on Cost Plus, I "discovered" that this wind event only took place on Sundays, when we paid workers at double rate! Sir Alan Muir Wood later became President of The Institution and he introduced me to the Inspector General of Railways (at a Royal Engineers Headquarters Mess Dinner) as "the biggest bull-shitter he had ever met!" Praise at last.

Sometimes the McAlloy bars did not go as deeply into the hole as we required, and a certain amount of surplus had to be cut off with an oxy-acetylene torch. The offcut became very hot, and despite heavy leather gloves, one piece fell. We searched for it but did not find it. The next day, a Hover Ferry Hostess found it. She had rented a room in one of the houses under the cliff. The piece had dropped through the roof, and the ceiling, and landed on her bed. It was hot enough to burn a hole through the bedding and the mattress! Luckily, she had been mid-Channel when it happened.

The McAlloy bars were much longer than the width of the skip. Considerable balancing skills was required to feed the bar into the drilled hole, and then to grout the bar into the chalk. Furthermore, too much grout pressure could dislodge the chalk from the face. We placed steel mesh over the area covered by the bolts, and placed large plates over the bolts to transfer the bolt load into the mesh. The whole area was then covered with sprayed concrete. This was another area of problem for the Ministry Architect. In winter, green lichen grows on the chalk. This dies off in the summer, leaving a white surface. The Architect tried to insist that the sprayed concrete was green in winter and white in summer! The Architect thought that the unchanging grey concrete was detrimental to the aesthetic appeal of this well known tourist attraction, and that it would affect visitor numbers to the Castle. I don't think that I ever really convinced him that he was asking the impossible, but he was an architect after all!

Marples Ridgway had completed work on the Sewage Treatment Plant at Hastings. The company had handed the site over to the Client and departed, but a 20 foot long wooden rowing boat had become wedged in the new concrete outfall on the beach. I was asked to take a team to Hastings and remove the boat. We agreed that this was best done during the March Spring tides. There is nothing more bracing than working on a sewage outfall in cold, wet weather. We removed the boat, in pieces, and normal flow resumed.

Jane moved down to Kent with Hugh, and we rented a bungalow at Capel, high on the cliff top between Folkestone and Dover. We suddenly got lots of visitors, who found that it made their Channel Ferry trip easier. Another drawback was that, in winter, no Doctor would make house visits due to the dangerous icy hills. When Hugh was ill, Jane had to drive into Folkestone on very icy roads.

A publican friend at St Margaret's Bay had a framed horseshoe behind the bar. It was a shoe from a Derby winner. Against his wife's wishes, he had placed £1000 on a rank outsider at 100 to 1. Eventually he listened to his wife and cancelled the bet.

The horse won. The brass plate on the frame read "Do not listen to your wife". When I met him, he was divorced.

Due to the continual chalk falls, we had fixed a temporary protection fence at the foot of the cliff. This caught the chalk we trimmed off, and the natural falls. It was set up in the back gardens of the houses. The cliff face was covered in netting, (made to special order in Bridport) to control the pieces of chalk and flint as they fell. On a quiet Sunday afternoon, I was showing Jane and Hugh round the site at the top of the cliff, when we heard voices. Some young boys had climbed all the way up the netting, and were trying to enter the air intake duct to the secret Regional Centre of Government bunker under the Castle. The only way to get them off the cliff face was to make them finish the climb to the top. We took their names and gave them a ticking off, and made them walk the long way back to the bottom. My office was in the abandoned Napoleonic era Barracks, just to the East of the main Castle Walls. There were a number of abandoned anti-aircraft gun emplacements and defensive positions in the area. One day, I heard a number of small explosions and went to investigate. Two labourers had found a handful of old 0.303 ammunition, and were hitting it with a sledgehammer!! Just below the Barracks, was the field that Bleriot landed in on his flight across the Channel from France. The spot is marked by a concrete cross.

One day, I was at the foot of the cliff watching the gang removing chalk from the back gardens when some elderly American Tourists came off a Ferry. They looked up at the 250 foot high cliff above and asked a labourer how long the cliffs had been there. One man replied, "I started work here in January, and they were here then!" Later, we fixed permanent fencing along the foot of the cliffs, to catch future falls.

I always had trouble with my mileage claim on this job. The Head Office Accountant had seen the site plan and worked out that the site was 40 foot wide and half a mile long. Why did I claim eight miles to go from the top of the cliff to the bottom? I tried to explain that successive Kings and Queens, over a period of some 800 years, had continually improved the defences of the Castle and this governed the route that I had to take. My Regimental Headquarters were in Monmouth Castle, and I would receive Army correspondence addressed to me at Dover Castle. Military mail was from "Monmouth Castle to Dover Castle". Only the Lord Lieutenant of Kent shared my Dover address!

At the end, it was my sad duty to close down the site and pay off the work force. By this time Marples Ridgeway had been taken over by the Bath and Portland Group. The founders of the company had hoped that their sons would take over. Captain John Ridgeway, having rowed across the Atlantic, retired to a Scottish Island. PC Marples was content with being a Metropolitan policeman. I received orders to pay off the General Foreman on grounds of age. This was a very highly experienced Tunnel expert, who was extremely fit. I found him in the stores. He reached out and picked up a 45 lb Jack Hammer in one hand and gave it to me to hold while he read the Head Office letter. I just could not see what the logic was in letting him go. He wanted to go on working until he was no longer able, and he was fit and able but well over 65.

Dawlish Warren Sea Defences 1971

After the Dover job, I was asked to cover for the Agent on the Dawlish Warren Sea Defences project in Devon, while he went on three weeks leave. Jane returned to live with her parents in Cardiff for this time. The job required the installation of wooden groins and Reno mattresses on the foreshore to control the erosion by the sea. The work was held up because the supply of very expensive greenheart timber was delayed. The client was pressing for the work to be speeded up. When I checked up with the UK supplier, he could not tell me when I could expect the timber. By careful questioning, I discovered the name of the importer and asked him about our order. Eventually, I discovered that our order was still on the quayside in Brazil, having been dumped to make room for some other cargo. Meanwhile the work of protecting the beach with stone filled Reno Mattresses progressed.

Dawlish is at the mouth of the River Exe, and directly across from Exmouth. The Exmouth Police telephoned to say that they had recovered some items that could have been stolen from my site. Although I could see Exmouth across the estuary, and it was a mere one mile away, the road journey was 20 miles each way. The police had recovered small tools and petrol driven concrete vibrators. The thieves had used a small boat for the theft. The worst part of that job was travelling at weekends back to Cardiff through the tourist traffic.

Germany and Army helicopters

Before my next posting, I went to Germany with the TA. We went to again to Hameln, home of the Pied Piper, and worked on our bridging skills. The BOAR role at that time was for our Regiment to prepare bridges over the River Weser for demolition in advance of a Soviet attack. While the troops were struggling with Bailey Bridging in the Hameln Camp, officers drove off to survey bridges and decide where to place demolition charges and place firing points. Regular RE officers then considered our reports, and compared them to the Army ideas for each location. The differences in the schemes were discussed, and often one of our ideas found its way into the Battle Plan. Quick recces were often done from a helicopter.

One night several of us found our way to a German village with a night club. A lot of alcohol flowed and I ended up talking to another British officer that I had never seen before. The club management threw him out when he had had too much to drink, and I hitched a ride in his taxi. I was more amazed when, instead of taking him into the main barracks, the taxi dropped him at our tented camp. We staggered up the hill, having been challenged by the guard, who happened to be from my own Troop, and found our tents for the last hour of sleep. I was told that I was first up in the Sioux helicopter to recce a bridge for demolition, and I recognised my pilot as my partner from the night before! The Sioux was a two-seater glass bubble with a lattice boom for the tail rotor. Two skids kept the bubble off the floor. My pilot took off and we found the first bridge over the river. It was a steel truss bridge about 100 feet long. The pilot suggested that I sketch a side view and kindly hovered above the water while I filled the notebook with details. This attracted the attention of local pedestrians and some car drivers stopped to look. He then suggested that the opposite side may have differences and we flew over the top and hovered on the other side. The crowd got bigger, and more cars stopped. After that, he suggested that I needed an end elevation view and we landed on the road, stopping traffic, while I sketched. We took off again and landed on the road on the other end of the bridge, to make more notes. It was a busy road and the German public had become alarmed by the pilot's actions. The Police arrived in a Volkswagen Beetle and wanted us to stop work and go away. The pilot ignored the Police and then dropped to water level under the bridge so that I could sketch the cross girders supporting the deck, because this would be where I would need to place demolition charges. The Police started shooting down through the rotor blades to attract our attention, so we flew away. When we got back to the camp, a senior German policeman was talking to the Colonel. My pilot was removed for questioning, and he later had his pilot's wings removed at a Court Martial.

The second week of the camp was taken up by attempting to build a Heavy Ferry at night on the fast flowing River Weser. In factory fresh conditions, the ferry can move at about 6 knots, and the Weser in flood can match this. Our tired old ferry had weeds clogging the water intakes of the propulsion units. We had with us the Editor of The South Wales Echo newspaper, and he was writing a story on the TA local units. As the separate pontoon units were lowered into the water, strong ropes were attached to them, tied onto parked lorries, so that they would not float away in the dark. Men had to stand on the pontoons and lever two units together and fix the pins holding the units together. The river was flowing fast and the rain was driving down. I was talking to the Editor, when a shout went up. One unit had broken away and disappeared down the river. A very irate Sergeant Instructor ran up to a Sapper near me. "I told you to watch that rope" he shouted. The Sapper replied "But I did watch it. I saw where it went. It went that way". The German River police prevented the unit floating over a weir and towed it back to us, still with the two sappers onboard.

The Padre's wound

It was on the same exercise that something happened that went down in Regimental history. We had a young curate as a Padre and he did his best to be one of the boys. However, he did get embarrassed at times, and went far into the bushes when he needed to relieve himself. Once he went too far, and disturbed a wasp. It stung him in mid-flow and there were screams of agony. He was sent off to get medical attention. Later, he saw the funny side and was heard (so rumour has it) praying that God should "remove the pain but keep the swelling". Thereafter, we all referred to "The Padre's Wound". A year later he introduced his new bride to us, and someone asked her if God had heard the prayer.

Gloucestershire 1971 - 1974

A417 Over Causeway

After the Dawlish Site Agent returned from leave, I was asked to help start up a new road contract in Gloucester. The A417 was the most southerly crossing of the River Severn between England and Wales, before the Severn Bridges were built. The road followed the old Roman causeway across the swamp between the West and East branches of the River Severn. This route was also used by all the major Utilities. There was a main gas distribution pipe, 144 telephone ducts, water supply pipes, and a section of the Defence Fuel Distribution pipeline. The National Grid had a 132Kv underground line across the site. This site was the bottleneck on the route to South Wales.

Our contract required the single carriageway to be upgraded to dual-carriageway, complete with new bridges across both waterways. However, the main problem was the alluvial bog that covered the area. The material extended downwards for many metres. The designers decided that the embankments had to be overloaded (an additional six foot of earth on top) and left until settlement had stopped before removing the extra soil. Dovetailing all the utility diversions, traffic diversions, and earthworks into the programme was thankfully not my job.

As the advance engineer, I had to set up the offices, get telephones installed for ourselves and the Resident Engineer, and liaise with the County Highway Engineers. Jane and I decided that we should stop being nomads and buy a house. I spotted a house on a new development in Hempsted. This was on the west of the Gloucester Ship Canal, and only accessed across bridges which could be retracted for ship movements. Jane approved my choice over a weekend visit. Earlier, I had visited British Telecoms and ordered a number of telephone lines for the site offices. As an aside, I had asked how long it would take an individual to get a line into a home. The Estate Agent proudly showed us to the house, and was surprised to find a note from the Telephone Engineer saying that he had called to install my new telephone, but that we were not at home. We had not even made an offer to buy the house at that point. There are times when British Telecomms can work miracles.

I was to be one of the two Section Engineers, and I was responsible for the Earthworks. I had to install depth gauges, fixed to the interface between the original ground and the underside of the new fill. Weekly readings of levels were taken as we placed and compacted the fill. A metal rod of known length, inside a plastic sleeve pipe, allowed this to happen. Some embankments had to wait a minimum of 52 weeks of settlement, and others required 72 weeks. During the waiting time, all the service diversions had to be achieved. The 120 new telephone ducts were bundled in groups and surrounded with concrete. There were 6 banks of telephone ducts. The new gas main was laid in a trench, as was the local electrical distribution cables, and the water supply. The Defence Pipeline was isolated from the fill, in a concrete box duct. The same treatment was given to the oil-filled 132 Kv cables. While all this work was going on, the traffic had to be kept flowing along the site.

Marples Ridgway Ltd was now firmly controlled by the Bath and Portland Group, who decided that all work would be sub-contracted. Our Estimator in Head Office had worked out the necessary margins and dictated the rates that any sub-contractors would be allowed to charge. It did not work out like that. The sub-contractors had worked out what they were willing to do the work for, which was in every case far more than our Estimator had allowed!! Our site Agent got very annoyed with the Estimator, who would not allow us to let contracts at what he considered excessive prices. No work could start with out a sub-contractor. The Estimator was forced to accept that he had made a mistake, and he was demoted and given to us as the Site Quantity Surveyor. Head Office had to find extra money for the job. No wonder, with this obviously low price, why we were awarded the contract. The estimator had no concept of current prices, and he expected us to suffer for his mistakes.

The initial setting out involved placing main reference pegs on the flood plain between the two branches of the River Severn. When a high tide in the estuary coincides with heavy rainfall run-off in Wales, a phenomenon known as the Severn Bore occurs. A standing wave moves upstream, some 2 metres high, causing local flooding for a short time. My setting out party was in the middle of the flood plain when the Bore appeared. Most of us made it safely to dry land, but one chainman spent the afternoon standing on top of a wooden fence post, waiting for the water to subside.

We had let the earthworks contract to the lowest bidder (out of the necessity to save money), and this quasi-legal outfit gave us a number of problems. Their Site Agent was working for no salary and living in a caravan on site, to pay off a debt to the company owner (a man with a hard reputation in the underworld).

I frequently had to visit the borrow pit where the fill was being loaded onto lorries. The boss had hired all sorts of "MOT failure" lorries, and was running them on the public highway. He issued dire threats to the owner drivers and paid them a pittance for each load (after deducting "fines" for all sorts of imagined misdemeanours). There was always a feeling of being under siege in the borrow pit site hut. One particular row between the Contractor and a driver lead to the driver storming out and reversing his lorry into the Contractor's new Volvo Estate car. The driver stormed back in and said, "If I were you, I would move the Volvo in case I hit it on the way out!"

The Fairground

On the north side of the original causeway, a number of houses had been built, and access had to be maintained. Behind these houses, was a large area used as a winter home for the Goose Fair. In the winter, this group returned from a long summer tour of UK towns and cities, to rest and recuperate. There were all kinds of showground rides and stands, together with all the accommodation caravans and the generators. Our new road was to be built at a much higher level than the existing showground site. A ramped access road was designed, which was needed by the showground people to get the vans and trailers back onto the highway at the end of the winter. I had to set this out and referencing pegs needed to be placed between caravans and dodgem car trailers. I got to know several of the show people. Later, when the kerbs were being placed, I received a Site Instruction to lower the kerb between the Hoopla stall and the Haunted House. Hardly a description fixed by immovable objects, as these were both mounted on trailers! This friendship with the showground people certainly paid off later in the summer, when they set up in Gloucester. I was my son's hero, and all his school friends envied him. Who else had a father that could get him free rides on the Helter Skelter and the Dodgems? One Romany family had retired from the show, and had a small plot of land between the railway and our new road. I sorted out the access for their vehicle and they were grateful. Thereafter, while we lived in Gloucester, each year they sent me a Christmas Tree.

Christmas week was quiet, as the contract sent most workers away for two weeks. This quiet time was the best period to install two large metal Armco culverts across the width of the site. This then required very careful placing of the fill on either side of the culverts. Too much on one side and the shape of the culvert bulged towards the unfilled side. I worked the full two weeks, as I could not trust the earthworks contractor to do this delicate work without supervision.

Piling inspections

There were three major bridges on the project. Due to the very deep alluvial mud strata, support to the abutments was provided by deep bored piles. These one metre diameter, 40 metre deep excavations, had a wider cavern "belled" out at the bottom to spread the load of the pile over a much wider footprint. Before the pile could be concreted, the whole excavation had to be examined and signed off. The inspecting engineer was lowered down in a bucket, with a lamp on an extension cable. One day, the Bridge Section Engineer was not available, and I was delegated to inspect. With trepidation, I entered the bucket, having extracted promises from the piling sub-contractor to pull me out if I screamed. I looked up as the bucket dropped downward. The view of the sky through the circle at the top reduced to a pinprick. The bucket reached the bottom and I tried the lamp. It would not work. Although there had been some light from the top, it suddenly went completely dark. Some one had put the cover over the top. I felt a panic attack coming on, and yelled for help. There was silence, except for the echo of my voice. Eventually, the lamp lit, and the cover was removed. I did the inspection, and called for the crane to hoist me up. Then the rain started. On the way up, I got drenched. When I finally got out, I looked round and saw that there had been no rain anywhere else. The piling gang were all grinning. They had been urinating on me! Apparently, this was done to all "first time" inspectors, as an initiation.

Jane worked as a supply teacher for various schools in Gloucester, more or less full time. We had very good neighbours. The Flory family had four daughters eventually, but only had two when they bought the house next door to our house in Hempsted. Roger Flory had worked for a major aluminium extrusion die manufacturer, as a salesman. He and two friends from this company decided to set up a company making and selling extrusion dies. They all mortgaged everything they could, and Roger set off trying to get contracts. He travelled across Britain, Egypt and Iran. He slept rough to save hotel costs. Contracts were won by promising early deliveries. This often meant a dash to Heathrow, while the metal was still cooling, to catch a cargo flight. Cash flow was a problem, and sometimes Jane fed Jill and her daughters. There came a time when I offered to buy Roger's Morris Marina car for a little over book price to help out. The company survived, and Roger later visited us in Cornwall in his Lamborghini!!

Jane shopped in Gloucester, and had commented on a man often seen in ladies changing rooms dressed as a woman. This man was well known to the police. Dressed as a woman, he would try to pick up long distance lorry drivers in a pub near the Gloucester Canal. There were several late night splashes when irate truckers found out the true facts and tossed him into the canal. When the Bridge Section Engineer finally finished the last bridge, we needed to (yet again) divert traffic onto the finished bridge. As the Traffic Police Inspector had worked well with us, the Agent invited him to formally cut a ribbon to declare the route open. The ribbon was tied to handrails at the apex of the bridge, and our official party approached from the west. The Bridge Section Engineer approached from the east, with our cross-dresser, dressed as a lady, who he had asked to cut the ribbon. They arrived at the same time and stared at each other. The Inspector had been trying to arrest this man ever since he joined the Force many years ago, and he was not best pleased.

Jane had a Hillman Imp car while we lived in Gloucester. When we had a TA Dinner to attend, or I had a late evening training session to attend, Jane would drop me off and spend the evening in Cardiff with her parents and collect me on her return. One evening we had a Mess Dinner, and I was in Mess Kit (red jacket and spurs on my boots) when Jane collected me. I slumped down in the car and fell asleep, but Jane woke me to say a police car had been following her for some time and would not overtake when it had been possible. She was beginning to panic. After another mile, the police suddenly overtook and forced us to stop. Both constables rushed to our doors and made sure that we could not escape. We wound down the windows and asked why we had been stopped. They were looking for a Borstal absconder. They had seen a diminutive driver, who was driving cautiously and nervously, and assumed that they had found the lad. Jane thanked them for the compliment about her age, and two very embarrassed constables returned to the search. Strangely enough, the very next day, Jane was followed home from Hempsted School by a police car, which carefully blocked her car in our drive so that she could not escape. The very young constable had made the same mistake as his colleagues of the night before. Jane was at least twice his age, and he blushed beautifully. The Hillman Imp had an intermittent oil leak, which no garage could find. Eventually, we did run out of engine oil on a long journey and a small crack was discovered in the aluminium sump, which only opened up when the engine was hot.

Territorial Decoration

By this time, I had 12 years Commissioned Service with the TA, which qualified me for the Territorial Decoration (TD). Having just had all my uniforms stolen from my car during a visit to mother-in-law, I had to borrow a Service Dress uniform for the medal presentation. The Adjutant, Captain "Tubby" Linham was a very strict and competent APJI (Army Parachute Jump Instructor), and did not like the fit of the borrowed uniform. He dryly commented that I would look better when I had grown up into it! A ceremonial parade was held at Monmouth Castle, and the Lord Lieutenant presented medals to several of us. During this period I was a Troop Commander, based on our Bristol Drill Hall, and I reported to the Squadron Commander in Newport. One of our duties was to inspect a grave and make any repairs. Lt Col John Chard RE won his VC at Rourke's Drift in South Africa, and was buried in the churchyard at Chard in Somerset. Later that summer, the Regiment exercised its right to "march through Monmouth with bayonets fixed and bands playing". We formed up at the foot of the town, near the river, and marched steadily up the long hill, to the Castle. My sword got heavier and heavier as we marched. The Mayor was saluted at the Town Hall. Cramp set in and when we dismissed, I could hardly grip the sword hilt to do the final salute. The festivities continued with a full dress Mess Dinner, to which the Lord Lieutenant, the Chief Constable, the Mayor, and others were invited. Accommodation was scarce and the dance went on until the last man dropped. We had taken sleeping bags and camped in my car for the remainder of the night. The entrance to the Castle is up a narrow alley off the main street and a police constable had been told to patrol this area, because the Chief Constable was present. After the visitors had driven off, he got bored and started examining parked cars. He found us asleep, and woke us up. He decided that I was "drunk in charge of a motor vehicle". I explained that I was parked on military land, was in military uniform, and that he had no jurisdiction. I suggested that he stand at the end of the alley, on the public highway, and if I drove out he could arrest me. It was a bitterly cold, wet, night, and I was glad to get back into my sleeping bag. When we left the next morning, the constable had gone.

The summer TA camp was held in Germany again. We were to be part of a major bridging exercise. We were introduced to the M2 Rig. This self-propelled bridging unit could travel on roads at normal convoy speeds, then enter the water down a 30 degree slope, float and deploy propulsion units, and link up with other units to form a bridge strong enough to take a Main Battle Tank. It had a crew of three and each unit was worth (in 1972) about £250,000. The convoy set off with six of these expensive units and all our other plant and vehicles. Capt John Mann was in the lead Landrover. We were all very tired and the exercise area was restricted to four map sheets. We went on and on for hours, continually eastwards, towards the Iron Curtain. Eventually, a motorcycle managed to get John to stop. When asked where he was, he did not know. We found that we were two map sheets beyond the exercise area and only 30km from East Germany. The Communists would have loved to have captured these highly secret bridging units. The Landrover driver was a terrified young Sapper. He was scared of asking the way, or even talking to the officer. So at each junction, if John's head lolled to the left, he turned left, and if it lolled to the right, he turned right!

Later that year, I managed to get an attachment to a Regular RE unit for a two week period. The Squadron was at Hameln Bridging Camp. As soon as I arrived, the Officer Commanding disappeared to recce a task for the unit, and his Second-In-Command went off to skipper the Regimental boat at the Kiel Regatta. I became the senior officer. The children in the British Forces School in Hameln, although their fathers were Royal Engineers, did not know what Daddy did at work. I arranged for classes to watch a Bailey Bridge being constructed. Training continued until the weekend, when the three remaining young officers had organised a two day river race between Troops. Aluminium Assault boats and inflatables were used and there was a night's rest on the river bank. What I did not realise was that the start was next door to a pub, the overnight campsite was at a pub, and the finishing line was opposite a pub. How any of those 120 men failed to have an accident was a miracle. Some said to me afterwards that they had not even noticed the weirs on the river!

I attended an Officers training weekend at Chatham, and I met a Major who had just returned from being the Training Officer for the Malayan Engineers. I asked if he knew of my Loughborough friend, Chid. Oh yes, he knew him! He was well known in the Malaysian peninsula and there were many stories told about him. His first job, after being Commissioned, was to assist with the Borneo campaign. In Singapore, he was instructed to put 4,000 oil drums in a Royal Navy Landing Craft. This he did, and sent it on to Borneo. When it arrived, someone complained that the drums were empty when they should have been filled with Diesel fuel. Chid's defence was that he had not been told to fill the drums!

Later, after his Short Service Commission ended, Chid joined the Malay Territorial Force. During an inspection by a very high ranking officer from UK, this officer inspected the troops on parade, stopping occasionally to speak to soldiers. Chid stood out because of his tremendous height and the officer stopped opposite him. "And which kampong (village) do you come from?" "Kampong Chelsea, actually, Sir", Chid replied in his best cut glass accent.

In 1963, Malaya joined with Sabah and Sarawak to become the Federation of Malaysia. As part of the celebrations, there was a military parade at the sports stadium in Kuala Lumpur. Leading the parade was a number of tanks and, as they passed the new Head of State, Tunku Abdul Rahman, they saluted him in the correct way by lowering the main gun and swinging it towards him. (This salute copies the movement of an officer's sword when he salutes). Chid was leading the Malay Engineers in a Ferret Scout Car, armed with a Browning machine gun in the turret. Chid should have merely stood to attention in the turret and saluted as he passed. But having seen what the tanks in front had done, he thought that he should copy them. He grabbed the machine gun and turned it towards the Head of State, causing enormous panic and virtually emptied the stands! Chid was definitely someone who caused people to remember him.

Herefordshire - 1974

Hereford County Council

The Over Causeway contract was coming to a close. The company had won a road contract in southern Iran but I was not prepared to accept a bachelor contract at that time. I looked for work, and was offered a job as a Senior Engineer in the Herefordshire County Council Roads Department. This meant a 30 mile drive to Hereford each day, but this was preferable to uprooting the family from Gloucester and Hugh from his school. The work was not very interesting except for one scheme which had to link up with a road crossing into Wales near Hay on Wye. The Welsh had a totally different set of rules and specifications and I had to work out compromises with the Welsh engineers. I found out that my old Section Agent from the Mill Hill M1 Motorway days was working in one of the Hereford offices and we met up. At the end of my first year in this job, the unexpected amalgamation of two English Counties happened and we became "Herefordshire and Worcestershire". This resulted in some duplication in the new combined Roads Department and I took voluntary redundancy when it was offered.

Cold Stores

A fellow RMonRE(M) officer suggested that I join the small company that he now worked for, in Ledbury. This company manufactured and erected self-contained controlled atmosphere cold stores for fruit and vegetables. The company was taking advantage of the new EU farm policy of giving large grants to farmers to purchase and use these cold stores. Essentially, these were 10metre cubes that had one large door for the fork lift to bring in pallets of produce, and a computer controlled gas system linked to the freezing unit. The produce would be chilled, and certain gases extracted, to give the produce a state of suspended animation until required for sale. Then the temperature would be raised and certain gases introduced to ripen the produce in time for the sale. Different fruits required different temperatures and gases. I got the job and we erected units on two different farms. After three months in the job, the EU farming grant system was changed. Brussels decided that all grants could only be given to "farming co-operatives". No UK farmer wanted to rent space in a cold store from a co-operative (or even to co-operate with a neighbour), so there were no more orders and we all got paid off.

Once again, I was job hunting. Lots of CVs were typed up, adverts chased up, agencies contacted, and telephone calls mounted up. I went to at least forty interviews, including one with Sir Lindsay Parkinson & Company. This company had recently hit the headlines when "flying pickets" had invaded their Shropshire site, and clashed with workers. The Building Workers Union had called a National Strike for better pay and conditions, but not all workers and sites were willing to come out on strike. The Union sent the flying pickets to smaller sites to "encourage" workers to strike. Edward Heath was the Prime Minister at the time and seven ringleaders were arrested and tried. Des Warren and Rikki Tomlinson (now a TV actor) received prison sentences, and became known as "The Shrewsbury Two". Parkinsons wanted me to be the Section Engineer on the site which had hit the headlines with some of the worst violence in the Union's fight to cause a National

Strike of all Building Workers in Britain. Although the violence was in 1972, industrial relations on site were still at an all time low point the following year. So I declined the job offer.

Early on a Sunday morning after the interview, the Managing Director of Sir Lindsay Parkinson telephoned to ask if I would like to work in Mombasa. He had turned over my CV and saw that I spoke Swahili and had lived in Kenya. We talked some more, and it turned out that the Project Manager in Mombasa was turning down new work because he did not have spare engineers, although he was getting these job offers because his was the only company in Kenya with heavy piling equipment. Later I discovered that the Project Manager did not want the extra responsibility as it interfered with his golf and drinking. I was duly offered the Mombasa job and prepared to travel out. Jane was to remain in Gloucester until the end of my three months probationary period, in case I failed to make the grade.

Mombasa   1974 - 1976

Not wanted on site

I was to be the senior to all staff under the Project Manager, and to be available to be a Project Manager should a new contract be awarded to the company in East Africa. Or that was the plan until I met the Project Manager, who had his own ideas. I travelled down to London and the company, after getting the necessary Work Permit, fitted me up with multiple inoculations and an air ticket for the flight to Mombasa.

I was seen off at Heathrow by my sister Jenny and my brother-in-law, Ian, who gave me a bundle of newspapers and magazines for the journey. After boarding, I checked the bundle and discovered a copy of "Private Eye", with a cartoon of Idi Amin on the cover. We would be landing in Entebbe and the secret police would be searching the cabin. I did not appreciate Ian's sense of humour and had to destroy the cover.

I arrived on a Saturday and was met at the airport by "Big John", the General Foreman. He took me to The Castle Hotel on Kilindini Road. The company used this hotel for bachelor staff. John would not answer any questions about the Project Manager and suggested that I wait to find out when I started work on the Monday. I thought that this was worryingly strange, and wondered if I had made the right choice in accepting the job. That night, two or three other members of staff, and their wives, visited the hotel to look me over but kept themselves separate. I got increasingly more worried. On the Monday morning, John drove me onto the site and ushered me quickly into the presence of the Project Manager. There was no handshake of welcome. Instead he just looked me up and down. I was wearing brand new khaki shorts, socks and a white shirt, which was the normal East African dress. Then he said that he had not wanted any extra staff, that he had disagreed with Head Office, and had told them not to send me out to Kenya. I was beginning to feel very worried. He asked if I had yet unpacked. When I said that I had, he said that that was a pity as there was not much time left if I was to get the noon flight back to UK. Eventually, he decided that he would test my man-management skills and decide later if I was to return to England. "I have the only air-conditioned office on this site. You engineers work outside in the sun. All the labour force is refusing to work. Get them back to work". I was dismissed.

Others in the building had heard him shouting at me and helpfully turned their backs as I left the building, as they did not want to be seen siding with the new boy. I did not know where to turn. Then I decided to walk round the site to think about my future. At the first trench there were a group of workers. I greeted them in broken Swahili which I had not spoken since my pipeline days in Southall, and asked why they were not working, but I could not understand the replies. I walked on to other groups, and slowly, more Swahili came back to me. It was extremely hot and humid. My milky white legs and arms stood out like beacons, and I was the picture of someone fresh from England. The site was about a mile long and half a mile wide. The site had been made level by cutting out a hillside, and the white rock face reflected the sun onto me. I was getting sunburnt. Once I got to the gang at the far end of the site, I had to face the lonely walk back to admit defeat. Half way across the site stood a bulldozer with a cab. It would give me some shelter from the sun, at least. I climbed in and asked the operator why he was not working and he gave me a long answer in Swahili. Something surfaced from the depths of my memory, and I asked him what pair of monkeys had had the accident that resulted in his birth. It was like turning on a light switch. His smile widened, he shook my hand, and leapt out of the cab. He ran to the nearest group of workers, shouting "He's one of us. He speaks our language. We have a good boss here" and slowly the word was spread. Tools were picked up and work resumed. I began to feel much better and returned to tell the Project Manager that I had passed his test. He had to accept me, but from then on our relationship became even more frigid, and remained so until I left the country.

We were building two new berths in Mombasa harbour for East African Railways and Harbours (EAR&H), to a design by Coode and Partners. Apart from the actual steel and concrete wharves, there was a vast area of rail tracks and Customs storage sheds to be constructed. I was given responsibility for all the non-wharf works. The site had already been landscaped and all the underground services were almost completed. The next job was to build all the foundations for the sheds and put the hard surfacing on the area. Rail tracks snaked between the sheds and onto the wharves. The whole area was protected by high pressure fire mains.

Having survived my first day, the Plant Manager was instructed to purchase a car for me. He took me into Hughes Motors, the Ford Agent for East Africa. I was told to sit quietly in the waiting room, while he dealt with an Indian salesman. I looked around and spotted a familiar face. Peter Hughes had been studying Automotive Engineering at Loughborough when I was there. I went into his office and we talked about old times. Peter had been sent down by his father to look over the Branch, and it was sheer coincidence that I saw him. The Plant Manager was horrified when he could not find me, and was most embarrassed to find me with Peter. The story got back to the Project Manager, who was a control freak. He would allow no one to speak to any organisation outside the site. This was yet another black mark against me.

Our work routine included an early start with a short break on site for lunch. The bachelors then, work permitting, drove back to the hotel at the end of the day in several cars. One man commandeered a table on the verandah overlooking Kilindini Road, and ordered beers for us all. Others in the car would go into the bar and order beers to be served on the verandah. The car driver, after parking at the rear of the hotel, would walk through and order more beers before sitting down. The next car followed the same routine. With this slick, much practised routine, we had at least four rounds of beer per car on the table before we had finally sat down. Our beer of choice was "Tusker", brewed by Coast Lager Ltd. The verandah overlooked the street, and a horde of beggars descended on us every day. Wood carvings and other items were thrust in our faces. One day, a walking stick was offered. A colleague took it and examined the carved handle very closely. The beggar thought that he had a sale, and said how much he wanted for the stick. "But this is so well made. It is worth much, much, more!" The beggar looked flustered, and our man found even more points to praise and re-doubled his original massive price. This went on for several minutes, the price rising to astronomic proportions, until the beggar snatched the stick and ran off in total confusion. The beggars, we came to find out, were run as a commercial operation by a well dressed Mercedes owner. He housed and fed them, in return for a percentage of the daily sales income. They were often mutilated soon after birth, so that they could not walk or even stand. Some used home made trolleys to get around. The Swiss hotel manager had one particular favourite, and made him a job offer as a lift attendant. He would get food and lodging, on top of a wage and a uniform. A special seat would be built into the lift for him. The beggar turned down the offer because he would be better off as a beggar!

While I was in the hotel, I noticed a Royal Engineer Warrant Officer living in a nearby house. I did not get a chance to meet him and could not find out what he was doing. Later, in Oman, Mike Holliday told me that he had been sent out to recover old cannon from the sea and return them to Fort Jesus, the old Portuguese fort which is now a museum. Mike had also been at Kongwa School at the same time as me, and had served in Bomb Disposal!

We were on the coast, with beautiful sandy bathing beaches. Most afternoons, once I had my company car, I went to Nyali Beach and parked near a footpath between two villas which lead to the beach. Frequently, a rusty old Ford would park next to me with four middle aged European ladies dressed in some sort of white clothing. There was a flurry of what appeared to be white bed sheets, and then they appeared in swimming costumes. They paddled and sunbathed, and on one occasion one lady ran after an African lad who had stolen a handbag. Her 100 metre dash on hot and soft sand was worthy of an Olympic medal. The rugby tackle was executed perfectly, as was the clip round the ear after she had secured the handbag. I did not think too much about these women until after Jane arrived.

Eventually, it was reluctantly agreed that I had survived the probationary period and could bring Jane and Hugh out to Mombasa. One of the foremen had resigned, so a house became vacant. I cleared out his junk, but kept the Hurley stick that he had left under the bed. I thought that it may come in handy when we had intruders. All houses had metal grills welded to all the windows which, therefore, had to open inwards. The bedroom half of the houses had a stout, lockable, door separating this area from the more public living area and kitchens. This was my first introduction to "Fortress Architecture". Usually, there was a three metre wide strip of gravel immediately surrounding the house. This meant that all visitors made a loud crunching noise as they crossed the strip, and one could hear a burglar approaching. This strip, and the drive, was "owned" by the guard dog. African visitors had to shout from the road to attract attention, so that the dog could be controlled.

With Jane arriving shortly, I needed a Cook/Houseboy. This essential servant had to be above reproach, and a recommendation from a trusted previous employer was vital. One just did not advertise or approach a job agency for staff. Written references were carefully phrased in a code. One that my mother received many years before read "This man is an excellent pastry cook. He is so light fingered". I was lucky to find that our Plant Manager and his wife were leaving and I was invited to meet Joseph, a Luo from Kisumu on Lake Victoria and I took him on. Joseph worked for us the whole time that we were in Kenya, and never let us down.

The Plant Manager had a much loved cat that they wanted to send to England, and the carpenter foreman was asked to make the travel box required by the airline. This proved difficult. The dimensions did not make sense to the foreman carpenter, who was used to making boxes for concrete. We drew an isometric picture to help explain, and the carpenter's face lit up in understanding. He went off and returned with his masterpiece. On a rectangular sheet of plywood, he had nailed another piece of plywood cut to the outline of the isometric sketch. The cat was expected to travel between the two layers of plywood. Eventually a British foreman had to make the box! The Plant Manager was from Kings Lynn, and spent his previous annual leave there, meeting old school chums. One day he had far too much to drink and his drinking friend offered to see him home safely. A brand new Police Station had been built since his last visit, and his friend was a sergeant in civilian clothes. They entered this gleaming establishment, and the Plant man felt at home in this new bar. He ordered a Gin and Tonic from the helpful barman! The Desk Sergeant promptly arrested him.

Jane was interested in finding a job and I wrote to The Loreto Convent in Mombasa, on her behalf, saying that both my sisters had attended another Loreto Convent School in Eldoret. The Mother Superior replied that subject to interview, there was a job available. Jane was pleased but asked that I find a car for her as she needed to get to work and ferry Hugh around town. I found a blue Volkswagen Beetle. This had a good engine, but the body work was the same as all other cars on the coast. The high humidity, combined with the salt laden air, meant that there was a huge amount of rust. I only managed to seal the deal the day before my family arrived. They had had a very bumpy flight. Hugh had been sick all over Jane, who had had no chance to change clothes during the long transit stop in Nairobi. She was tired out and at the end of her tether. I was so pleased to see them both, after three months of working for the Project Manager that I ignored her feelings and suggested that we pick up her car on the way to our new home. She had never driven in Africa before; the car was new to her, and she could hardly focus on the road. She followed me home, while I had Hugh in my car. It was an unforgivable thing to have done to her, but later, (much, much, later), she agreed that being thrown in at the deep end had been for the best. Jane had arranged to rent our Gloucester home while we were away, and this paid for the mortgage.

Mother Superior

I took Jane to the Convent for her Interview and not only did she get the job, but she also enrolled Hugh at the school. In the garage of our house was a full sized Table Tennis table. I ask Jane if the Convent would like the table as a free gift. They said that they would be delighted to receive it, and I arranged to borrow a pick-up truck to deliver it on the Saturday afternoon. We arrived to find a welcoming committee of two Nuns and a Priest standing at the front of the school. The taller Nun seemed to know me and spoke to me as though I had known her for years. I must have looked blank.

148

"Don't you recognise me?" she asked.

Suddenly I remembered where I had seen her before.

"No, not with your clothes on", I replied.

The Priest and Jane both looked shocked. We explained to the others that we had swum together several times. It is not often that one gets the chance to say something like that to a Mother Superior!

The Resident Engineer, Michael Leonard, had his two sons at the school. His wife, Margaret, and Jane became firm friends.

White Man's Magic

To get material for the sub-base layer for the project, we had been given a quarry to use. There was a slight problem, in that the haul road went through a small village and the route was virtually blocked by a vast Baobab tree. We wanted this tree removed. The villagers said that the Baobab tree was sacred and could not be harmed. All this happened shortly before I arrived in Kenya. Another engineer conducted the negotiations, which seemed to be getting nowhere. It was all down to getting past the problem of the sacred nature of the tree. Then our engineer had a brainwave. He told the Headman that in his country, England, we also had our own Ju-Ju magic and that he would try to use this to speak to the spirit in the tree and ask the spirit to move to another tree. If it worked, would the Headman agree to allow the tree to be removed? "Yes, if I can be convinced that the spirit is happy in his new tree". The engineer typed up a Local Government Compulsory Purchase Order, in flowery language. This was mounted in a varnished wooden frame and taken to the tree. Four wooden boxes were made and several bottles of whiskey were placed in each of them. One bottle was kept for the ceremony. In front of the whole village, as witnesses, the Order was read out in a loud voice, speaking firstly directly to the tree, and then repeated again to the four points of the compass. The framed order was carefully fixed to the tree with long copper nails. It was explained that copper had magical powers, unlike the steel nails. The boxes were buried at the four corners of the square marked on the ground, surrounding the tree. Lastly, the whiskey was dribbled along the line marking the square, as a libation for the spirit. It was all very impressive. The engineer told the Headman that it would take time for the spirit to move, but this strong English Ju-Ju would work. He would come back in a week's time. When he returned the boxes had been dug up and the Headman gave permission to remove the tree. The African responds to a bit of play-acting far better than he does to force or reason, and I often would act the fool to get something moving when working in Kenya and later in Nigeria.

To marry in the asphalt surfacing with the neighbouring existing surfaces, I had to clear a lot of rubbish away. Much later, I discovered that I had removed the Customs Fence securing the Port. The Chinese Ambassador to Uganda had been expecting delivery of his new official car, a top of the range Mercedes. It failed to arrive, but was found a year later during a Police raid in Sudan! No one else seemed to notice that 500 metres of fence was missing while I was in Mombasa. During that clean up, I found a gang of about 20 men sitting and sleeping on my work area. I shouted at them and got them moving a large heap of new railway sleepers. After eight hours of hard work, one of these men diffidently came over to me and told me that they were all dockers, working for EAR&H, and they were not employed by our company. I said that it served them right for looking lazy. They took good care to find better hidden places to sleep after that.

I had two locally employed English foremen, both called Steve. "Thin Steve" was emaciated, and was a plant operator by trade. He had previously cleared land for sisal plantations, spending weeks alone in the bush on his bulldozer. Once a week, he was given a few vegetables, some water, and 10 rounds of ammunition for his rifle. The rifle was his protection against wild animals, and for his supply of meat. He had done this for years, living a very lonely existence and he had little conversation. In contrast, "Thick Steve" was a well built man with two Kikuyu wives, and a large family back on his "shamba" (farm). He had walked the 300 miles from Nairobi to get the job! Behind the site, there was an old road, and I asked Thick Steve to remove all the post and wire fencing before we commenced earthworks. Many months later, when Steve was paid off, he begged me to lend him a site truck to take all this fencing, which he had carefully hoarded, back to his shamba.

Another locally employed foreman was Jimmy. He worked on the concrete gang, so I did not have much to do with him until we started constructing the sheds. In conversation, he asked me if I was any relation to K. O. Martin. I told him that he was my father. He told me about the theft of two dumpers off a disused railway siding many years ago. He had pushed the railway truck into a siding and re-coupled the train before it continued to Nairobi. After he had two years use from the dumpers, he felt guilty and put the dumpers back on the railway truck, which had been hidden in undergrowth all this time, and hoped that someone would find them! Jimmy liked a drink. He had a very vicious Alsatian dog that guarded his house. One long Easter break, Jimmy came home on the Friday night to find a thief in his bedroom. The dog had him up against the wall and would not let him move. The thief pleaded to be let free as he had stolen nothing. Jimmy agreed and said that he was free to go. "But what about the dog?" "He was here when you came, so you are free to leave". Jimmy went to sleep and went out to the pub for the next two days. In that time neither dog nor thief moved or took their eyes off each other. Eventually, Jimmy reluctantly called off the dog.

While I was still living as a single man, Jimmy and others took me for a pub crawl on Kilindini Road. We were in a bar close to the dock gates and Jimmy was explaining that, to be safe, one had to stand with one's back to a wall to avoid being robbed by a pickpocket or, worse, being attacked from behind. He was standing against an ornamental block wall, with hand-sized holes! At the till, a rather drunk European sailor was demanding the correct change from the barman at the till. The barman was distracted by the sub-machine gun being pointed at him by an armed robber. The drunk insisted on being served first and insisted that the robber wait his turn. A shot was fired, which went through a fleshy part of the drunk's leg, but the drunk finally got his change and allowed the robber to talk to the barman. The till was emptied, the robber left, and "resumed service was as normal as possible". We were much further into the bar, and could not get out without passing the robber at the till, so we just stayed still. This was, I was lead to believe, normal behaviour at the lower end of Kilindini Road. On another occasion, we entertained a new Director out from London to a visit to a nightclub. This was in an old shop, complete with the plate glass window. A fight outside resulted in the Director being struck on the head by the whole sheet of glass.

More problems with the Project Manager

After a few months, the Project Manager went on leave. He was extremely reluctant to hand over authority to anyone, especially me, but several faxes from London forced his hand. I was warned by others not to make the same mistake that happened the previous year when he left on holiday. That time, the then General Foreman was so pleased that the Project Manager was no longer in Kenya that he gave everyone a paid day off work! While I felt the same way, I resisted the temptation. My first problem rose during one of the major concrete pours on the wharf. I checked that we had enough cement in the silo, sand and aggregate in the bins, and that the mechanical plant was ready. The sand and aggregate required for the pour was more than the site storage capacity, and the supplier was well used to running a delivery during a pour. On this day, his tipper developed a fault and a flat bed lorry was used. This meant that all the aggregate had to be unloaded by labourers with shovels! Later, his loader broke down and the lorry had to be loaded by labourers as well. A very similar situation developed with the sand supply, and this meant finding forty labourers, and shovels, so that the lorry could be loaded and unloaded. We monitored the whole supply chain and staggered towards completion of the pour. Then the cement silo was found to be empty. Cement can "arch" in a silo and leave a large but undetected void. Looking through the hatch at the top, the silo had appeared full. Our site was the only one in the country using bulk cement supplies. Bamburi Cement Company only supplied bulk cement for export, to ships in the port. Because of the "export" link, we dealt with a department that needed an Export Licence for each order. While I could order a load of cement, the Project Manager had not registered my name and signature with the company for the Export Order to be finalised. He thought that if I failed to get more cement, he could sack me for incompetence. I talked to the company and managed to get a delivery of bagged cement, and work continued. Towards the end of the pour, the water supply stopped! What else could go wrong? There were water storage tanks in the port for firefighting, and we "borrowed" enough to complete the pour, to my great relief.

Later, I found out that the whole town water supply had been affected, as a hippopotamus had blocked the intake pipe in the Tsavo National Park. During this pour, we had run out of sand, cement, aggregate, and water! These sorts of problems do not usually happen in Britain.

While the Project Manager was on leave, a more serious problem came up. He had not settled the account with Shell for the site fuel supply, and they would not send any more fuel until they were paid. He seemed determined to trip me up and had taken the site cheque book with him. I asked our Office Manager to arrange a meeting with Shell. I managed to persuade Shell that he had inadvertently taken the cheque book to UK, and that Shell would be paid on his return. We showed the site bank statements to prove that funds were available. We got our supply and work carried on.

On his return, the Project Manager found that work had progressed in spite of the problems that he had caused. The company were invited to tender for a road contract north of Nairobi, and he took the opportunity to send me to report on the site and the difficulties that would affect the price. This was exactly why Head Office had employed me. He used my report to put in inflated prices to ensure that we did not win the contract, and that his life would not be complicated.

The Project Manager kept all our Passports, Birth and Marriage Certificates, and our qualifications in the safe in his office. Kenya required that we had originals of all these important documents with us at all times. The inevitable happened. An armed raid resulted in the safe being removed, blown up, contents destroyed and one of our guards dying from an arrow wound. Without these documents, no one could travel to UK until replacements arrived.

Teflon

On a lighter note, an engineer's wife had just returned from an extended visit to England. She told ladies at a coffee morning that she had bought a new lot of saucepans and that the box had arrived just that morning. They were the first of the new Teflon Coated type, and definitely the first to arrive in Kenya! She was so pleased with them and could not wait to get back home to see them out of the box. William, her Cook/Houseboy was waiting for her. "Why for you bring dirty black pans into my house? It very hard to get black off but I manage it!"

Jane and Margaret Leonard joined forces for the weekly trip to the vegetable market. This was a large covered building, with stalls selling a vast range of local produce. The humidity, combined with the need to spray the produce to keep it fresh, meant that there was always several inches of water on the floor, mixed with rotting leaves. Wellington boots had to be worn and the smell was foul. As one arrived, several small boys would jostle to get the job of carrying one's bag. The boy would ensure that you only shopped from stalls owned by his family. You were not expected to choose better items from a rival stall. After a few visits, a particular boy was "yours" for all subsequent visits and prices could be adjusted downwards for a regular customer.

We inherited a feral cat that had taken to living in our villa. He did not like being handled. One evening on our return from a meal at the Club, Jane picked him up and cuddled him. The cat swung a claw and caught Jane's eyeball. In agony, we went to a Sri Lankan eye doctor. After his examination, the eye was bandaged and had to be kept in the dark for two weeks. He would make his final diagnosis when the bandages came off. Drops were put in the eye daily, and we kept our fingers crossed that no permanent damage had occurred. During this period, Jane still had to visit the vegetable market, but could not see properly. Margaret Leonard still talks about Jane carefully selecting a very large bunch of really hot chillies, thinking that they were carrots. Eventually, the bandages came off and there was no infection or visible damage. Jane's eyesight was normal, although a residual scratch remained on the lens. Jane wanted to celebrate, so we went for a meal to the Club. When we got home, Jane went to cuddle the cat! I managed to stop her before the whole sorry saga repeated itself.

Armed burglary

We had a lovely black Labrador as our guard dog, and the gardener looked after him. At Easter, we had a few days holiday, so I booked a hotel on the beach south of Mombasa. We left Joseph in charge and had just settled down to the evening meal when I got a telephone call from him. Could I please come home and talk to the police about the armed robbery. We cancelled the rest of the stay and drove home, wondering just how much stuff had been stolen and who had been hurt or killed. Joseph met us and explained that he had gone for a shower in his own quarters at the back of our villa before dusk, so that he could spend the night in the house. When he came back he was confronted by three Africans, one waving a shotgun, who were all laden with things taken from the house. The dog was barking furiously and had been hit by one of the thieves. The house had been locked up, but the thieves had sent a child in through the tiny bathroom window, which because of the size did not have the usual metal grill. The child found the keys and opened the doors. We checked and found that a TV, radio, and the music centre had been removed. The Police eventually came, and said that we seemed to be the third house in the road attacked that night. The first house had lost a loaded shotgun, so it was lucky that Joseph had not been in the house. We found the music centre in the ditch outside the house and it was unharmed. Jane remembers the Police returning to take statements, while I was at work. As the constable got out of the vehicle, his unlaced boots fell off. Hugh's school uniform had been stolen and the Police wanted to interview an eight year old boy about the theft, without his parents being present! Jane told them to get lost.

Jane had the Reception Class at the Convent. There were about 20 children from about ten nationalities. As Kenya was now independent, rich Kenyans favoured Convent education. There were Japanese, Chinese, Indians, and children from several European countries. Jane decided to discuss Ethnicity and Origins with these five year olds. To get things moving, she knew she could rely on young David Leonard. So she asked him "What are you? Where do you come from?" "I'm a Paki Paddy" he replied. Jane struggled to keep a straight face. He was Irish but born in Karachi. Forty years later, Jane met David again and reminded him of the incident. Margaret Leonard told Jane about David's birth in Karachi. After the birth, she was offered a bath. Wonderful, she thought. The bed was pushed along concrete paths from one end of the hospital to the other, and left in the shade outside the bathroom. Many hours later, the nurse returned to apologise that there would be no bath, because some one had stolen the bucket! When Mike arrived to collect Margaret and David, the baby was locked into the accounts section safe until the full bill had been settled in cash.

A new young Scottish engineer had recently joined us and his probationary period had ended. When his wife was due to arrive in Mombasa, the Project Manger deliberately sent him off to do a site survey for another tender. As he would not be at the airport to meet his wife, he asked the General Foreman, Big John, to meet her. I was with John when we went to the airport and on the way he turned off the road towards the top of our borrow pit. There were two Africans just starting to put up a makuti (woven palm frond) hut in a clearing in the bush. John told them to hurry up as Memsahib was coming. We met the new wife, and collected her luggage from

Customs. After enquiring about her flight, we found out that she had never been south of Hadrian's Wall, let alone into Africa. We set off, with John saying that he hoped that she would like her new home and that he hoped that it would be finished by the time we arrived. We turned off the asphalt road and went into the bush, to the makuti hut. It was still in need of a roof, and John got out and tore strips off the two builders. The new wife heard him say that Memsahib was very angry that it had not been ready for her, and that he doubted whether it would be ready for nightfall. Her face was a picture. John, after a few choice swearwords, got back to the car and told new wife that, as her house was not finished, there was no alternative but to find a hotel for her. The hotel already had her booking, and it took weeks before she would talk to John. Secretly the engineer saw the joke, but had to look upset about the trick.

Assassination attempt

To produce rock to protect the sloping bank under the wharves, the company operated a quarry some distance inland from Mombasa. The quarry manager frequently had to visit site, to meet the Project Manager. One day, my car was in for service and I needed to borrow a car for a trip into town. The quarry manager very kindly lent me his car without any fuss. Mombasa Town is on an island. There are just three ways a vehicle can reach the town. To the north, there was Nyali Bridge, and to the south the Likoni Ferry across the mouth of the port. The main access is by the causeway on the Nairobi Road. President Jomo Kenyatta was visiting the town and, on the way to a function at the main hotel on the island, a bomb was detonated close to his cavalcade. It destroyed a tree but no one was harmed. I was unaware of this when I ran into a Police road block on the causeway. Eventually it was my turn for inspection. When I asked why we were being searched, the corporal told me he was searching for explosives. I was ordered to open the boot. It was full of very new cardboard boxes. The corporal was satisfied and told me to drive on. By this time my knees had turned to jelly. I could hardly stand, let alone drive. Stamped clearly on each box was the logo of the ICI Nobel Division. I was carrying 200 lbs of best blasting gelignite, more than enough for an assassination attempt on the President. Once in town, I telephoned the site and asked the quarry manager to come and collect his car. I was definitely not going to take it back through any police check points while it had that cargo!

Most Sundays were spent visiting one or other of the beach hotels, where if we booked lunch we could swim in the hotel pool all day without charge. Occasionally we would visit a game park. Both Tsavo East and Tsavo West were about an hours drive away. We would leave early and spend two three hours in the early morning watching the game feed. When the animals found it too hot to eat, at about 10 o'clock, we would go to a Game Lodge. Hugh would swim in the pool while we watched, sipping long cold drinks in the shade. After a big buffet lunch, elbowing our way through the tourists, we would spend the cooler hours of the afternoon watching more game. As a special treat on the way back home, we would take Hugh to the Drive-In Movie Theatre in Mombasa. The films were projected onto a white painted concrete wall and the sound was meant to come from earphones plugged into a post by the car. Not all posts worked, so we and all of the other movie-goers drove round testing the posts until we found a working post. Accidents and fights

154

sometimes happened. Thick Steve was the only man I knew who could make a profit from a visit to the Drive In. He had bought a very large American soft top car, and he took his six or seven kids. He arrived early and sent them all off searching for bottles thrown away the previous night. The value of the returned "empties" paid for the night!

Call me "Mzee"

In common with other younger engineers, I found that Kenyan workers would only obey my orders if they felt like it. It was very frustrating. I had noticed that my sideburns were beginning to show grey hairs and carefully removed all grey bits each day. This meant shaving higher and higher up the face each day. Soon, the shaved areas would meet at the top. I was forced to acknowledge my age and let the grey hairs grow. A Kenyan worker noticed the grey hair and called me "Mzee". This is an honoured title for a respected elder. From then on, every order was obeyed without question. Why had I tried to hide the grey hair all that time, I asked myself.

Lamu

Head Office in London instructed the Project Manager to put in a tender for repairs to the jetty at Lamu, far to the north of Mombasa. I was dispatched, with Jane and Hugh, to spend a week gathering data. I knew that the roads were very poorly maintained north of Malindi, so I made sure that Jane had a shovel to put in the boot. We arrived at the jetty in Lamu and waited for a boat to ferry us to the island and our hotel. There was a boat but the police were escorting their delivery of beer and we had to wait our turn. I looked at the dilapidated jetty, which was leaning at an alarming angle, and took some photos. The jetty was used to load cattle from the hinterland onto a small cattle steamer, which took them to Mombasa for slaughter. Eventually we got a ride on a boat and crossed to the island. There, we stepped out straight onto the beach and walked up to the main square. Sitting outside the police station was the only vehicle allowed on the island. There were no roads on the island and the old Arab town streets were, at most, five foot wide. When I asked where our hotel was, I was told that it was about half a mile away along the beach, but that we would have to sit in a bar and wait until the tide went down. There was an extremely slow pace of life, geared to tides and walking speed.

While Jane and Hugh explored Peponi's Hotel, I made contact with local dignitaries and took notes for the tender. At the jetty, I met the skipper of the cattle steamer. He was Dutchman, who lived in a total alcohol daze. If you smelled his ship, you could understand. Terrified cattle spent two days on the boat, which seemed not to have any way of properly washing away deposits. On the return journey, all the offal from the slaughter house was loaded aboard, to be disposed during the return trip. The sharks followed the boat in both directions, and had never been so well fed. I watched a loading process as the job included design of improved facilities. Then the skipper waved a gin bottle at me and opened the throttle. Unfortunately, he had not released all the mooring ropes and he pulled off the last remaining proper bollard. He sailed on, totally unaware of the damage that he had just caused!

155

On the return journey, dark clouds could be seen coming in across the Indian Ocean. There was a long stretch of road made from the local Black Cotton soil on the road north of Malindi. Black Cotton soil is hygroscopic and swells enormously when wet. There were some long stretches with deep ruts caused by heavy vehicles, and I knew that my car would have great difficulty when it rained. Ahead of me, in the distance, I could see a large bus, full of passengers. If that got stuck, I would never be able to pass it. I raced to overtake the bus, with one eye on the approaching black cloud. Jane and Hugh were holding on for safety, and Jane refused to accept my reason for the speed. I had to be in front of the bus before we got bogged down, so that the passengers could help push me out. Eventually we overtook the bus, and a little later, the rain completely washed us out. As expected, the car got stuck. I asked Jane if she had made sure that the shovel was in the boot. She said it was, as it was with Hugh's toy bucket he used for sandcastles. She meant Hugh's plastic spade! I was not best pleased, but set to, digging under the car with a bendy little spade. I would have been better off using a metal teaspoon. The bus arrived, and being unable to pass, the passengers got out in the rain and moved us forward. I was very appreciative and gave out the remains of my beer as well as some cash. We arrived back in Mombasa covered from head to toe in black glutinous mud. It was simpler just to stand in the shower fully clothed.

A Director flew out from London to supervise the tender preparation. He had absolutely no conception of the problems of working in a remote area in Africa. On his list was the Agent's saloon car for travel on Lamu Island (where there are no roads). He asked about port facilities, in relation to unloading heavy materials. I showed him photos of labourers carrying sacks up the beach from a beached dhow. When I told him that there were at that time a maximum of 15 hotel beds on the island and that we would need a self-contained camp to live in, the costs started to mount. This was before we had even considered the actual rebuilding task! Our eventual tender price was not accepted, and a cheap bodge repair was done. I would have loved to have lived on Lamu for a year, but it was not to be.

Railway engineer

On the cargo area, we needed someone with railways experience to take charge of the track laying. An engineer suddenly appeared. He had southern Africa rail experience, and this part of the job seemed to be child's play to him. He was a jazz fanatic and talked about nothing else. His favourite tune was Glen Millar's "The Chattanooga Choo Choo". Eventually, the story came out about why he was suddenly available to us. At that time, there was trouble between Apartheid South Africa and neighbouring African States. Eventually, after a lot of diplomacy, President Kenneth Kaunda of Zambia and President Vorster of South Africa arranged to meet in Botswana, to discuss the problem of white rule in Southern Rhodesia. It was suggested that the meeting be held in a railway carriage, similar to the surrender meetings held in railway carriages at the end of the World Wars. To achieve this, some track had to be laid at the selected location and our friend was the project manager who drew up the design. Any project needs a title to place in the title block on the drawing. With his love of music, he had called the project "The Chattanigger Choo Choo", and this was his downfall.

Hugh and the broken leg

I eventually persuaded the Project Manager to allow me to take a week of local leave over Christmas and booked hotels in Nairobi, and at Treetops Hotel, near Nyeri. This was where Princess Elizabeth spent her honeymoon and learnt that her father had died. We were all looking forward to the trip. On Christmas Eve in Nairobi, we visited the Animal Orphanage. Jane stroked a Cheetah through the wire cage, to Hugh's horror. On Boxing Day we set off very early as we had to meet the Treetops vehicle, to be transported into the Aberdare National Park. Shortly after leaving Thika, I lost control of the car on a stretch of badly corrugated road, and we rolled into the forest. Jane was thrown from the front seat and she landed on Hugh, breaking his thigh. I suffered a cut ear, leaving blood all over the interior. We eventually got Hugh out of the upturned car, and I waited for a passing car and help. We were very lucky when the first car happened to be a European. He took Jane and Hugh off to hospital, promising to send someone else to help me. In those days, all Europeans would drop everything to assist a fellow European in distress. Regrettably, it is no longer always like that. Eventually another car arrived and I was taken to a school compound and given a hot drink and news of my family. The first man had driven past the local hospital in Thika, and straight on to the Nairobi Hospital, some 70 miles away. He was still with Jane when I arrived some hours later. Meanwhile, my rescuer had arranged a lift for me to the hospital. My driver was a Ward Sister at the hospital, who had been spending Christmas with friends at the school. After making sure that Hugh was receiving treatment and had been given a bed in the ward supervised by my driver, Jane and I got a room in the Nairobi Club.

Murder charge

The next day I hired a car. With the limited funds I had, all I could afford was a 600cc Daihatsu "Dudu". Dudu is the Swahili word for insect. I had been told that I had to report the accident to the Police. On arrival, the Thika Police said that the accident had occurred about 200 metres outside their area, and that I would have to drive 20 miles further to a small Police Post. I found the Police Post, and saw that my car was inside. It was midday, and there was no one in the station. After a wait, I spotted a constable in the yard and spoke to him. I identified myself as the driver of the car and asked if I could make a report on the accident. This proved a little difficult as his knowledge of written English was poor, so I took the forms from him and completed them. He then announced that they had examined the car and several witnesses to the accident, (although there were none to my knowledge), and announced that, as one person had died, I was to be arrested for the causing the death! They did not seem to know who had died. This was not looking good. I asked to speak to his superior. No, the Inspector could not be woken up just to talk to a murderer. Eventually I prevailed and the Inspector came. I explained the blood from my cut ear, and that Hugh only had a broken leg and was in Nairobi Hospital expected to make a full recovery. "No, we have you on a holding charge until he dies". I protested that I had had to wait two hours before a car rescued us, and that I had seen no "witnesses" in that time. "We are keeping them safe for the Court case". Eventually, after many hours of persuasion, they agreed that I could return to my family. They said that they knew where I worked and would re-arrest me later. I was free to go. I asked if I could rescue some of our possessions from the car, and permission was granted. The two rear wings had been folded over the boot lid, so I asked if there was a metal bar that I could use to lever open the boot. Under the charge desk, they found a four foot metal bar, with a label "Murder Case 397 – Exhibit A". After opening the boot, I very carefully wiped my prints off the bar.

Dead body in my car

Having loaded all our loose things into the very small car, I set off towards Nairobi. There is a long, steep, incline near Thika, in a cutting. Looking up from the bottom of the hill, I could see a problem. There were about 100 people on the road near the top of the road. I drove up slowly and tried to push through the crowd. Someone put a hand on the bonnet of the car, and this was just enough to kill the engine. The crowd explained that a woman had been knocked down by a car and they begged me to take her to the nearest hospital. I realised that if I arrived with her, I could be accused of being the driver that had knocked her down, and I had just survived one brush with the Police. I asked if the driver of the vehicle was available to travel with me, as he could tell the hospital what had happened. The driver was produced, a bit beaten up by the crowd but still able to walk and talk, and I told him to get into the car. Others had, by this time, managed to get the 20 stone African woman into the back seat of the two-door car! It was a very steep hill and a very small engine, with a very large load. I had to ask for a push to the top of the hill. We were nearly at the top of the hill when we were stopped and a bloodied bundle of rags was pushed onto the back seat. We set off again and the driver told me that he was genuinely sorry for the accident, but that the woman had just turned and stepped out into the road without warning. He was a senior manager with East African Airways. I got to Thika Hospital and found the place deserted. Eventually we found and woke up some staff and they came, reluctantly, to help. The woman had died and rigor mortis was starting. She had to be unbent before we could get her out of the back seat. She was very heavy. Then I realized that the bloody bundle that I had been given was her child, who had been strapped on her back. The child was also dead. As soon as I got the other driver out of the car, I took off as fast as I could, leaving him to explain to the hospital and police. I did not want get involved with a second car accident in two days. I was very, very, shaken, but managed to get to the Club and unload our possessions. I had two double brandies and then returned the hire car. There was no one at the depot, so I posted the keys through the letter box. I had not had time to remove the two pints of human blood, swilling around on the floor, but the hire company never mentioned this to me!! Eventually I got to the Ward. Jane's initial reaction was "You are late. You are drunk". Although I tried then, and many times later, Jane never accepted my story. And I never did tell her the worst bits.

Every three months after the accident, two policemen from this station would travel down to Mombasa, to interview me. I realized that they had kept the "murder charge" on file so that they could justify claiming expenses. Needless to say, the Project Manager was not amused at the loss of a company car and felt inclined to believe the police story about the "murder".

Running an airport

As soon as Hugh was comfortable, Jane and I flew to Mombasa. We arranged for Hugh to be transferred to the Mombasa Hospital and got ready to collect him. We were booked on the only flight from Mombasa to Nairobi on New Years Day, a Public Holiday. As all our possessions were loose, we took three suitcases, nested inside each other, and a blanket to keep Hugh warm. In the Departure Lounge there was only one other family. They had just sold a hotel and they were off to South Africa to start a new life. She was holding a new baby and the toddler was crying. Outside there were two Fokker Friendship aircraft. Our bags were loaded and we were asked to board. After an uneventful flight, we arrived at Nairobi. The Airport was virtually deserted and no bags appeared. There was one official still in the arrivals area so we reported that our bags were missing and had to complete Claim Forms. Then the farce started.

> "What is missing?"
> "A suitcase", I replied.
> "Contents of suitcase?"
> "A suitcase", I said again.
> "No, we have the suitcase. What are the contents?"
> "A suitcase".

Eventually, she managed to understand. The hotel man had lost all his worldly possessions and his paperwork took for ever.

The hotel man and I roamed round the corridors looking for anyone in charge. The Station Manager was absent, but we checked the schedules and realised that the other plane that had been in Mombasa had flown to Dar es Salaam with our bags! The hotel man's wife was beside herself. The baby wanted a feed and the food was in another country! We found the empty Communications room and eventually the hotel man managed to send a telex to Dar es Salaam asking that they send all our bags back. A plane did arrive and we did get everything back. At this time, there were only us passengers and the pilot left in the building. Even the night watchmen were missing. We had operated Nairobi Airport, as civilian passengers, for about ten hours. It makes Heathrow security seem a bit over the top!

We got Hugh onto the flight back and his stretcher was strapped in. During the flight, the Captain came back to talk to Hugh. Hugh asked how the plane was flying if the pilot was talking to him, and forcefully suggested that he return to the cockpit for the safety of the passengers. Hugh was doubtful about the standard of some pilots. On a previous trip, returning from Nairobi, we had to land at Malindi before ending up in Mombasa. On that flight a senior British pilot was on the jump seat, with a Kenyan pilot under examination doing the flying. On approach to Malindi, we seemed to be too high and had to dive steeply. While this was happening, passengers could see first the airport fence on the left, then a brief view of the runway, then the fence on the right, then again we swung back to the left again. As we were in a steep dive, the curtain between the cockpit and the passengers swung forward over the pilot's eyes, and the senior pilot wrenched it off the rail. We landed rather bumpily and taxied to the stand. There was absolute silence as everyone said grateful prayers to a whole multitude of deities. Then a voice broke the silence. Hugh said to me "Daddy. Is that man a learner?"

Hugh had many weeks in the Mombasa Hospital, and we got to know the Irish orthopaedic surgeon, a Mr McVicar, quite well. He smoked cigars, and the Matron had a strict No Smoking policy. When ever Matron appeared, Jane suddenly found herself outside on the Fire Escape clutching a cigar! This surgeon spent half of his time working for young beggars to have surgery at his expense, so that they could return as much as possible to normal. When Hugh was discharged from hospital, he could not put weight on the leg, but was told to spend time swimming to build up his muscles again. We made arrangements with hotels for him to visit daily, and hotel staff were only too pleased to carry him from the car and onto a reserved lounger at the pool side. This is how he met Bjorn Bork the Tennis player, and Julie Felix the folk singer, when they stayed at the Nyali Beach Hotel. There was a comic moment when the giant aircraft carrier USS Enterprise visited Mombasa. She was too large to enter port through the coral reef, so the ship's boats ferried small groups ashore. One group of about 20 new Midshipmen arrived at the hotel, all in crisp white uniforms carrying identical rolled up towels under the left arm. Hugh was bored with swimming lengths and had started seeing how long he could sit on the bottom at the deep end. A very alert Midshipman had noticed him going down, but had not seen him rise. He shouted to his friends and 20 caps and towels were dropped as they all dived in to rescue Hugh. Hugh came up to see what the confusion was all about and then dived under to watch the fuss. 20 very wet Midshipmen, with egg on their faces, got a cheer from the audience sat around the pool.

Idi Amin

Towards the end of my first year in Mombasa, we had to extend the bunkering fuel pipes from the existing wharves to join up with the new ones in our contract. Examination showed that new pipes were also needed for adjacent existing wharves. To do this work meant that ships could not use the existing wharves while fire mains and oil pipes were out of commission, causing a loss of revenue to the port. The port agreed to the extra work, but set a very tight dead line for completion of the work. I was offered a years salary as a bonus if I met the dead line. We were progressing very well until the last weekend, where all that was left to do was replace some slabs over the pipe trenches. On the Sunday afternoon, I drove to the site to make sure that all was in order for a speedy completion the next day. I was stopped by four very large Africans in sunglasses and flowered shirts, and wearing Colt 45 revolvers. The flowered shirts told me that these were Ugandan Special Police. Idi Amin, then President of Uganda, had purchased some Soviet light tanks and had started to unload them onto my unfinished work! A diplomatic row erupted and Kenya denied the right for the tanks to move across Kenya.

The ship and the tanks stayed in Mombasa for another year and I failed to get my bonus. I hold Idi Amin personally responsible for the loss of the bonus. This incident contributed to the break up of the East African Federation.

Father's death

My parents had finished the year in Portugal, to avoid tax on Uncle Will's money, and had bought a house in Cranbrook, Kent. Father spent his time brewing home made wines and Mother tended the garden. Father developed Parkinson's Disease and I got a telephone call from Mother to say that he had been taken into Sevenoaks Hospital and that I should return home to see him. The Project Manager did not believe me but asked Head office to check, which they did. He unlocked the safe and gave me my passport and booked me on that evening's flight to Heathrow. I needed an Exit and Re-entry stamp in the passport before the travel agent was allowed by Kenya Law to release the ticket. This stamp could only be issued if I could show that my Income Tax was paid up to date. I trotted off to the Tax Office and they agreed to look for my file and start the calculations. I had not been in Kenya for many months, and had paid tax at an emergency level, putting me in credit. The file still had to be found and dealt with. The staff reported that the file was missing. After finding a senior tax official, I was allowed into the main office to help search for the file. I eventually found it in a pile of files used to replace a broken chair leg. By that time, the lunch break had started. It took two hours in the afternoon to get the calculations done and the stamp in the passport. I had telephoned the Immigration Office to warn them of a possible delay, and the official said that he would stay on after the official closing time of 4:00 pm. His office was a 20 minute drive across town. I got to the gate, but the night guard refused me entry because the office had closed! I ran back to the car and blew the horn and I saw a window open and an African wave to me. Between us, we managed to convince the guard to allow my passport to get the stamp. I only just made the travel agent before they closed.

I spent three days and nights with my parents in the hospital. The night I took Mother home for a rest, Father died. We went to the hospital and "did the necessary", as they say in Nigeria. On my return, I reported back to the Project Manager, who was with a visiting Director who happened to know my father. The Project Manager had wound me up and when the Director asked what my father had died of, I replied "He died of the same thing I am dying of - Parkinson's Disease". I was working for Sir Lindsay Parkinson & Company.

Hunter's Lodge

We arranged to have a short stay in a new Game Lodge with the Leonard family. We travelled to the western edge of Tsavo, to a new game lodge called Hunters Lodge. We had to park across the river from the Lodge, and cross over in an inflatable boat. It took several trips, and the return journeys were full of American Tourists leaving the Lodge. One sent his wife and luggage ahead while he recorded the trip on his video camera. She managed to fall in the river, and people started to shout "Beware, crocodile". She scrambled out very quickly, and we all thought that she would have to fly all the way to the USA still dripping wet! The Lodge was a series of large tents with camp beds, and a few Makuti, palm frond, huts. Mike and Margaret had one hut with their daughter, while Jane and I had the three boys in our hut. After a game tour in an open topped vehicle, we ate in the dining room and put the boys to bed and returned to the bar. Later, after we had retired, I was woken by a rhythmic crunching noise. It was like nothing I had heard before and I thought that a lion was trying to eat his way into the hut. I feared for the boys, two of which were not mine but were under my responsibility. The "windows" of the hut were bits of canvas rolled down over a simple opening. I grabbed the torch and carefully lifted the canvas. Six inches away, I saw the eye of an elephant that was chomping away at a small tree. Each time his jaw moved, the hut shook. I quickly switched off the torch because I did not want to annoy the elephant, and told Jane and the boys to remain very still and quiet. Eventually the elephant moved away and we tried to sleep.

The next morning we found enormous footprints actually touching the hut. We told everyone at breakfast, but one lady topped our story. She had a tent with camp beds, and had retired to bed long before her husband. The men in the bar had seen the elephants wandering through the camp and had decided to stay in the bar all night, for safety. This lady felt someone fondling her rather intimately and thought that it was her husband, only to discover that it was a roving trunk!

At Christmas we visited the Lodge in Tsavo. I took Hugh to bed early so that I could make sure he was asleep before putting out his presents ready for him to find in the morning. Jane stayed in the bar, watching a young male elephant at the water hole. However, when Jane decided to retire, a warden spotted a leopard in the open corridor to our bedroom block. She had to stay in the main building for the rest of the night!

Kenya Law put difficulties on expatriates in many different ways. On final departure, the limit of all money and goods that one could remove was limited to a total value of 2,000 Kenya Shillings (at that time about £100). We were paid in Sterling, in UK, and had a small local currency living allowance. Locally employed people, like Jane, often saved up more than the limit, so "arrangements" were made with others to "export" the surplus. My parents were still working in Kenya after independence and had accumulated cash and property from Colonial times and afterwards. A colleague of my mother's suggested that, as she and her husband wanted to stay on in Kenya, we took over her Swiss bank account and other savings, in return for my parent's cash and property. A deal was struck and, later when sorting my mother's estate, I found lots of Swiss Stocks and Shares! On his final departure, my father got his tax clearance stamp in his passport but he was stopped as he boarded the flight. An official pretended to find fault with the tax calculation. My father handed over the deeds to an apartment and was allowed to leave Kenya. Soon after I arrived in Kenya, I needed to buy Jane a car, so I needed extra cash. An Indian supplier had a son at college in England who wanted money for his rent. I wrote a letter to my UK Bank Manager instructing him to put £250 in used notes into an envelope and send it to an address in Essex. I gave this letter to the Indian, who gave me Kenya Shillings in return. He posted the letter, and his son eventually got the cash. During the next visit to my Bank, the manager had words with me about ethics!

Another problem was registering the birth of a baby. If one was not careful, the baby could end up becoming a Kenya Citizen and have to stay when the parents left the country! One friend was Danish and his wife was English. Both Embassies had to register the birth within 48 hours of the birth, to avoid this problem. As the birth was going to be 300 miles from the Embassies in Nairobi, this could be very difficult. We suggested that the wife get to England for the birth, and she had the baby there. Another engineer and his wife were both British, but his Birth Certificate recorded his birth address as C/o GHQ, Iraq, during the Second World War. This address was not sufficient for the Kenya Authorities, so she also left early and had her baby in England. Another couple in Kenya were still trying to get their 8 year old daughter out of a Zambian Orphanage, having fallen foul of the same problem there.

Mombasa Tug Berth

After the first year, the Harbour Board asked me to quote for building a new Tug Berth Jetty, which had been designed by Bertlin & Partners. The Project Manager was away on leave again, so I submitted a price after getting London Head Office to check my figures. We were awarded the contract and I started to make plans to transfer plant and men to the new work. The tug berth was principally precast units, post-tensioned, supported on steel piles. I set up the precast yard in a very congested area under, and between the tracks of, the Henderson derrick. The piling was to be done by a 38RB crane on a pontoon. The Project Manager had a 38RB parked up and idle. I asked for it and was told that I could have it, but was not to damage any of the permanent works already completed! The next day, I arrived to walk it to the new site, to discover that he had asphalted a large area, totally surrounding the crane! Damage was inevitable, and he knew that he could sack me for this. Luckily, the rest of the site staff were on my side. They came in late in the evening, laid protective matting, drove the crane clear of the site, and told me so that I was prepared for the morning row. I had similar problems with smaller plant, but in the end, I managed to get enough plant to survive. The Project Manager retained control of site cash, so all purchases had to be approved by him and he took delight in delaying payments to critical suppliers.

Bertlin's Resident Engineer arrived in style. He had been working for Sir Alexander Gibbs, on bridges in Scotland and this was his first job overseas. He got a room at the Mombasa Club until a house could be rented for him. He came onto site clutching the Fly-Fishing rod that had been a leaving present from his last job. His fishing expertise, in the water of the harbour, was treated with scorn by the locals, who did much better with a short string and a bent pin.

I had two British foremen with me on the Tug Berth, one a Geordie Irishman with an incomprehensible accent, and a Piling expert. The piling went well, with piles being driven into coral. Due to crane limitations, the piles were in two halves, the top being welded onto the bottom after it had been partly driven down. Sometimes a "set" would be achieved before the pile had barely entered the coral. Other times, a void in the coral would be found and we scrambled to stop the pile from disappearing from sight! There were two mooring dolphins to be built about 40 feet from the main jetty. To position the pontoon, anchors had to be placed on the harbour bed, which was covered with all kinds of junk. We were delayed by a particularly nasty eel living in a sunken pontoon. Any attempt to work on the anchor, which was inextricably embedded in the pontoon, was met with fury.

Welder's gloves were bitten off. Eventually we had to abandon that anchor and buy a replacement!

One day, during a tea break, the telephone rang. It was Jane in a terrible panic. A few months before, our Labrador guard dog had attacked the garden boy, biting his throat. We had her destroyed, and the vet found a massive brain tumour. We had replaced the Labrador with a three year old German Shepherd bitch called Sheena, and Jane said that our new dog had apparently savaged some sheep which she thought belonged to the President. The sheep were grazing outside President Kenyatta's Palace near where we lived. She did not think that any of the Palace guards had seen the dog, or the attack. My two foremen suggested that she recovered the dead sheep for sale in the market, and keep quiet. They said that there must be at least 20 other similar dogs living in the area, so she could blame it on one of those! We were all laughing at her, which did not improve the situation. We heard nothing more about this attack, so Jane eventually relaxed.

Rabies was endemic in Kenya and all pets were inoculated against this deadly disease. It became too much of a problem when it was found that the local monkey population had also acquired the disease. The Government decided to shoot all monkeys to prevent humans from being bitten. The Police and Army set about the task with gusto. Anything that moved was shot, even children playing in bush villages! Eventually an order was given to halt the killing.

The Foreman carpenter, from Newcastle, was very enthusiastic and his African workers really wanted to do their best for him. The only problem was that they could not understand a word he said. I had to listen from the office window, and be ready when the African foreman came to ask me what he had said. He lived in shorts and "flip-flop" sandals. Eventually, he trod on a nail which went right through his foot. One Sunday, it was his turn to supervise the people working overtime, but I dropped in to have a word before I took Jane and Hugh to a beach hotel for a swim and lunch. Just as I was leaving, I noticed that the pontoon, with the 38RB was no longer tied up and was floating away. I watched him put a rope between his teeth and swim out to collect the pontoon. He liked a drink and throwing empty beer bottles. As each bar has to have a photo of President Jomo Kenyatta, these became a target. One night he damaged a photo of the President and we were fortunate enough to get him out of Kenya before he was arrested for insulting the President! (This is a crime worse than murder in Kenya). This left me without a European foreman, or a diver. I had to learn to use the Scuba equipment overnight. One dive before lunch left me covered in old oil and other sludge disposed of by ships. I decided to drive home in just my underpants, to get a shower. Unfortunately, the President was in town and all cars were halted and the occupants ordered to stand in the sun and wait for him to pass. It was embarrassing and very hot for the next hour.

I had a good Indian fitter on site, and he spent a lot of time replacing the rusted floor panels on Jane's VW Beetle, and repairing all the other faults. It was like painting the Forth Bridge, a seemingly never ending job. Once, Jane went round a roundabout and the passenger fell into the road because the door catch rusted off. In the wet season, the front floor panel would drop down and scoop up rain water from puddles and direct into the passenger's lap. Due to the high humidity, the pressed paper glove box of the Beetle dissolved and dropped off and we decided to weld up the glove box lid to stop Hugh and friends "posting" things directly into the luggage compartment at the front of the car. One day, Jane was stopped at a Police search on Nyali Bridge. The corporal insisted that she open the glove box. She tried to explain but he insisted that it be opened. He grabbed a bayonet from one of his men and jammed it into the crack and levered it. The bayonet snapped off, and a Superintendent was called over to get Jane to pay for damage to Police property. The Superintendent listened to Jane and waved her on her way. At the end of our two year stay, not only did we still have the bayonet still lodged in the glove box, but we also sold the Beetle for more than we originally paid for it.

One of the advantages of working in the port was that the fire main was never shut off. When the rest of the town suffered water shortages, I took home gallons of water. The Dock Police searched vehicles all the time for goods stolen from ships and bonded warehouses, but never seemed to notice my water containers.

The Tug Berth was being built for Harry Brown, the Harbourmaster. He controlled the whole Kenyan coast. He often came to the site and we got on well. I met his signaller, an ex-Royal Navy Yeoman of Signals. Ships visiting the port would send requests to enter port, by Morse Code in those days. Some ships wireless operators thought that the shore operator would be an inexperienced Kenyan, and send very slowly. The ex-RN man would send a reply which included "Send faster. Three mistakes in your last message". He would get them going faster and faster, until they completely lost control! Harry took me to see Kenyans being trained as divers using the old heavy suit and metal dome helmet. The divers were needed in the port for setting anchors for buoys and searching underwater. The suited man would be lowered on a hoist into a tank while he became accustomed to the suit. One man we watched held his breath as he saw the water level move up the face mask. He did not draw breath until we lifted him out and unscrewed the faceplate!

During White Rhodesia's "Unilateral Declaration of Independence", UN sanctions included preventing fuel oil from reaching Rhodesia via the Portuguese port of Beira in Mozambique. The Beira Blockade ended in 1975, when Mozambique gained independence. I was sitting in Harry's office when three frigates from the "Beira Patrol" made an entrance to the port. The ships were from France, USA and the Royal Navy. They all wanted to show how smart they could perform manoeuvres, so that they could brag about seamanship skills in the bars on Kilindini Road afterwards. National prides were at stake. The French came in first and steamed up to the trot, the mooring opposite the wharves. With lots of shouts and bugles, they arrived at the buoy and attempted to drop the "buoy jumper" by small boat, onto the buoy. A seaman is required to fix the rope onto the buoy. The frigate over ran the boat and sunk it. Eventually the frigate got moored, but facing inland. Any Navy will tell you that a ship must be moored facing out to sea, for a quick get away. The Americans then came in and there was even more whistles and loudspeaker orders. In a similar way as the French, the American frigate was eventually moored facing inland. Then it was the turn of the Royal Navy. Harry muttered a prayer that the British pride would show the others just how it must be done. The frigate came in, spun round in its own length, and moored up facing outwards. Not a sound was heard. No whistles, bugles, loudspeakers or sunken boats. Perfect!! Ashore that night, the Royal Navy told the other sailors how it should have been done. There were a lot of fights.

I had a number of heavy lifts to do, which needed the Dockyard Floating Crane. "Jumbo" was attended by two old steam tugs and the whole team needed a day to get up steam before working. The Project Manager had used Jumbo often, but was charged three days hire each time, (mobilise, lift, demobilise). Harry used to let me use Jumbo free and call it a training exercise. When the Project Manager found out that I was not paying for "Jumbo", relationships got even worse.

I had an Indian assistant engineer, a Jain. The Jains are a very strict Hindu sect, and they were not allowed to injure any animal. A lot of our work included working in and under water, but he dare not enter the water in case he upset the fish! This meant that I had to do all the diving.

Jane had a large circle of friends amongst the teaching community. Some were wives of other engineers, on other jobs in the area. Others were wives of teachers in schools nearby. A Danish water engineer had an attractive English wife who worked with Jane. After my Resident Engineer found a house to rent, he asked his new young wife to join him and she travelled out with the daughter from his first wife. The two women were about the same age. I invited them for a meal, and asked Jane to invite another couple to balance things up. The RE telephoned to say that there had been a power cut, and could his ladies use our house to get ready? We agreed and, while they were upstairs, we got the table laid and sorted out Joseph in the kitchen. Our other guests arrived, the Danish engineer and his wife. When all our guests met for the first time, I detected a sudden hostile atmosphere, but poured drinks. We chatted, mainly to tell the new ladies about life in Mombasa and places to see. We waited for Joseph to announce that "Dinner is served, Memsahib". Eventually there was a series of bangs and clatters from the kitchen and Joseph appeared. He stood to attention and said, luckily in Swahili, "The cooker is f****d". He had all the rings, the oven, and the warming cupboard switched on, and consequently all the fuses had blown. We sorted that and ate. The RE and his ladies left soon after. Then the engineer's wife told us that the RE had been propositioning her for weeks!! No wonder there had been a frosty evening.

Border closed

The Tug Berth contract was paid from the Headquarters of The East African Railways and Harbours Board (EAR&H) in Dar es Salaam. In the middle of the contract, the East African Federation broke up and borders were closed. My job was in Kenya and the payment came from the wrong side of a now closed border. The Project Manager would not be pleased, but he was in the same boat, with the same client. I discussed the problem with the Port Engineer and came up with a proposal. He had access to revenue from Port dues and could pay Parkinson's from Kenya, and once the Final Account was agreed, he could attempt to claim back any balance from Tanzania. I had to visit the Dar Es Salaam Headquarters of EAR&H to get their agreement. I flew to Dar, via Seychelles, as direct air flights had been stopped. The

Northern Irish Troubles were just starting up and I was in the Immigration queue behind three Irish Nuns. They had their passports stamped with loud shouts of "Freedom Fighters", and then mine was stamped with the Immigration official saying "Filthy British". I got the agreement from the EAR&H and returned. The Project Manager was, for the first time, pleased with me. By this time, Parkinson's had been taken over and we were now working for Fairclough Limited and the Project Manager was trying to ingratiate himself with the new management.

Other contractors would sometimes borrow, or lend, equipment to each other on an informal basis. This was not the Project Manager's way, but I found that it worked for both sides. After the Piling Foreman left, I needed a qualified diver and I employed an Englishman who was trying to run a tourist attraction. He had a large tank with glass walls, which he filled with fish and turtles from the sea. He also had some snakes. Hugh liked visiting because he could take the python out and play with it. I was asked to help him feed the fish and turtles during a busy tourist invasion, as his assistant were sick. I had a wet suit and heavy welder's gloves. I was given a box of prawns and had been told that the sand shark was off his food. I had to put the shark under my left arm and try to screw a prawn into its mouth. That was the easy bit. The turtles tried to eat the prawn box, my fingers, my ears and my toes. They have very powerful jaws. This tourist attraction owner was asked to dive by another contractor who was trying to set out navigation buoys in the entrance channel to the port. I loaned them a Theodolite to help triangulate the placing of the buoys. The contractor's engineer was ex-Bomb Disposal and had lost a calf muscle when a car bomb went off in Belfast. When I went to collect the Theodolite, I heard that this man had just been killed. He had gone spear-fishing and had speared a very large grouper. The fish took off at speed and he had been unable to release the gun from the wrist strap, and had been towed through some steel piles.

A colleague's daughters had four guinea pigs and entrusted them to us while they went on leave. Two promptly died. I found that the English butcher could supply replacements. Each week, I would drop a cold box and a shopping list at the butcher on the way into work, and collect the meat in the box at lunch time. One day, there were two mature ladies in the butcher when I settled up. There was a shoe box on top of my cold box, which squeaked. The butcher told me to remember to "Boil them, 20 minutes per pound". The ladies were horrified. Later more guinea pigs died and got replaced. We could no longer remember what the original colours were and had to come clean and tell the mother. The girls did not notice, and eventually went off the idea of owning the pets. Hugh showed an interest and we were given them. Joseph, our houseboy, had arranged for his nephew, Oweno, to replace the gardener. He now became Head Guinea Pig man, and the numbers kept increasing. Gardening duties reduced and grass gathering took over as the main task. When we finally left Kenya, we had to find homes for 42 Guinea pigs.

The Bush telegraph does work. We had proof. Up at Lake Victoria, the homeland of the Luo tribe, there was an outbreak of Cholera. The Government put the area into quarantine to suppress the news as the death toll rose. The week before, Joseph had asked for a few days off to visit Rose, his chief wife. He returned to tell us that there was no problem with the Cholera Epidemic, and that he got round the road blocks easily, by walking through the bush. So much for the Government quarantine, which was designed to prevent the spread of the disease. He had known about the problem long before it had been made public. It amused me that Joseph told Jane that he was a staunch Christian and only had the one young wife in Mombasa. This was meant to impress Jane. Separately, he told me about his senior wife, Rose, who ran his shamba up near Lake Victoria. I wondered why Joseph had not realised that Jane and I might compare notes.

One of Jane's teaching colleagues was married to a teacher at Shimo La Tewa Secondary school. Jane often took Hugh and the two Leonard boys to play with the teacher's children. The school was some 30 miles north of Mombasa and the only other buildings in the area was the Bamburi Cement Works. This was a desolate area. One afternoon, just an hour before sunset, the derrick managed to derail one of the bogies which supported a 20 ton counterweight. My foreman rushed in, in a panic, and asked me to help unload the concrete weights. Just then the phone rang, and Jane reported that the Beatle had run out of fuel on the deserted bit of road outside the Cement Works and she wanted to be home before dark. I stopped the foreman from stripping the counterweight, because it would take several days to rebuild the crane after we got the bogie back on the rails. I quickly sent the fitter off with some fuel and went to look at the derrick. I realised that the derrick had pulled the bogie off the tracks, trying to lift something beyond its capacity. By putting the hook back on the same thing and pulling, the derrick was able to lift the bogie. Using two Turfors (steel rope hand winches) the bogie was pulled back over the tracks and it was lowered down. The job was done in 15 minutes. I arrived home at the same time as Jane. Had I listened to the foreman, I would have been there all night.

The job came to an end and we handed the site over to the Harbour Master. We had to find a new home for Sheena, the Alsatian. Jane's teacher friend asked if she could have her, and we agreed. On our last weekend, we handed her over. On the following Monday we asked how Sheena had got on in her new home. There were two staff houses at the school, built close together and last thing at night, the dog was let out for a last walk but did not come back immediately. The husband called "Sheena" repeatedly, until the husband in the other house came out and punched him. It came out that the dog's new owner had had a fling with the wife in the other house, and she was also called Sheena.

During our time in Kenya, Hugh had built up a collection of carved wooden animals. These were made for the tourists and there were stalls all over town and at all the hotels. During the "Rainy Season" Hugh decided to look for the one animal to complete the set of East African animals. All the stalls, on the central reservation of the main road, were covered with tied down plastic sheets. The stall holders were sheltering from the rain in shop doorways. Hugh set off and started lifting the plastic sheets on stall after stall, searching for the missing animal. Eventually a stall holder could no longer stand watching his stock being ruined by rain water, as the shoe polish washes off the wood easily. He asked Hugh what he was looking for. "A Fisi" he replied, using the Swahili word for Hyena. "A fish? I have plenty fish to show you". "No" says Hugh, "I mean a Hyena". "But we don't make that nasty thing. Tourist do not buy". The stall holder agreed to have a Fisi especially carved for Hugh and we collected it the next weekend.

168

The President's daughter

As Jane was the only formally qualified teacher in the school, she was asked to test Teacher Training students on their final teaching practice. One such student was the President's daughter and Jane was torn between ensuring professional standards, and making sure that she did not get us kicked out of the country, or worse, if she criticised. The girl said that she would be teaching the Crucifixion, presumably as this would go down well at a Convent School. The preparation for the lesson was rather sketchy, but Jane let her proceed. This student walked into a class of five year olds with some bits of wood, a hammer and some nails. When she asked for a child to come forward, Jane stopped the lesson and told the girl that she had failed the test, for terrifying the children. The girl looked at Jane and said that it did not matter because "Daddy was making her a headmistress next term".

The day before we flew, we handed the house back to the company and emptied all our beer bottles with friends. I got the deposit money back from the brewery and during this last party we seemed to have bought a tortoise from a passing street trader. Friends drove us to the Mombasa Beach Hotel for our last night. I went to check in, and Jane wrapped the tortoise up in a raincoat, because she did not know what else to do. The hotel staff were mesmerised by a raincoat moving away from the Reception desk across the marble floor towards freedom. Jane finally gave a friend a farewell gift of a tortoise. The next day we flew to Nairobi and had a week in Masai Mara Game Park. We saw some wonderful scenes and it was in the height of the wildebeest migration. Thousands of these animals kept running south to Tanzania, while we drove round for eight hours. We came back to the same place where they were crossing the road and there were still thousands more galloping across. The plains were grey with the sea of animals.

The Entebbe Raid

After the game park, we returned to Nairobi Hilton for our last night. An Israeli friend from Mombasa, who had provided galvanised fittings for the Tug Berth, bought us the evening meal. He suddenly stopped eating and listened. He had heard a lot of Hebrew being spoken and got up to ask what was going on. It appeared that half of Mossad were in the dining room, all in blue blazers. It was 3rd July, 1976, the eve of the Entebbe Raid, and Nairobi was the nearest friendly airport. It was said that British Airways would not be able to fly because their first stop would normally be Entebbe and it could coincide with military action by the Israeli Special Forces. We tried to keep this secret from Hugh, and we thought that we had succeeded. Hugh had made friends with the hotel staff and toured the kitchens and all of the lifts. The raid actually took place just after midnight, but information did not reach us until late the next afternoon. We were advised to check in at the airport in the morning and our friend took us, so that he could talk to the Israelis that would be at the airport. In the car, Hugh asked us about the hostages in Kampala. He had been reading newspapers with the hotel staff. So much for secrecy! At the airport, Kenyan military vehicles were patrolling with Israelis in blazers manning the machine guns. Eventually, BA announced that there would be a delayed departure and that we would not be stopping at Kampala. The raid was successful, except that the Israeli Commander died, together with four hostages. The Commander was the elder brother of Benjamin Netanyahu who has since been Prime Minister of Israel twice.

We had let our house in Gloucester while we were away. The first tenants let the garden grow wild and had nailed up the windows to stop their children running away. We got these people out and found perfect replacements. A school teacher had emigrated to New Zealand, but he had inherited a title and had to return to England. They loved our house and made us a handsome cash offer for the house and contents, so that they could stay in the area. Unfortunately, we were homeless and jobless and we had to refuse the offer.

The day after we moved back in, the milk lady just looked at me and said "The usual two pints?" We had never been away.

Gloucester (again)   1976

I started another round of job hunting while Hugh returned to the Hempsted School, and Jane got a job at the same school. I sent out many letters and CVs. I attended a small number of interviews, most of which I discovered were linked to tender bids for jobs. If these companies did not actually have the job, then neither did I. Some were genuine jobs but I had a gut feeling that they were not for me. Streeters of Dorking wanted someone to put new sewers through the old town in Jeddah, Saudi Arabia. I turned this down, and later I found that Streeters had gone bust because they had no idea just what was involved. I was offered the job of head office engineer in Abu Dhabi for a company run by an excitable Italian. He said that he had once before hired an engineer from Kenya, "But he spent all of his time lying in bed with a bottle of gin and screaming in Swahili". His company had won a contract to air freight cement to a new airfield at Thumrait in Oman. The Sultanate was fighting a war with the Yemeni Communists in Dhofar. This was a "cost-plus" contract, and I would be entitled to "tentage according to one's rank" together with my own platoon of soldiers for my protection. I turned this job down, but many years later, I worked on Thumrait Airfield. I heard that the engineer that actually took the job made a lot of money in back-handers. Owners of all sorts of aircraft fought to get him to hire them, as the rates were very high. The need for the cement was extremely urgent and an awful lot had to be flown in using small aircraft, some of which failed to return. I was called back to meet the Italian Managing Director, who made many promises, but none in writing.

I was interviewed by Taylor Woodrow International, and was offered a job in Nigeria. I suspected that this was only because I had grown up and lived elsewhere in Africa, and that others without this experience were not staying long in Nigeria. I was proved correct. Staff turnover in Nigeria was high, as some people just could not stomach the conditions.

At about this time, my brother-in-law, Ian Paton, was Financial Director of Collins Radio, with his office near Heathrow. This company supplied high quality radios for aircraft. Nigeria had ordered a Boeing 747 for the President, and the Inspector of Army Signals, Brigadier Murtala Mohammed, was sent to negotiate the details of the contract with Ian. The installation of the radios was done at Heathrow and stage payments were received from Murtala during personal inspection trips. One day, Ian and Murtala were poring over a document in Ian's office when a Telex was delivered by a secretary. Ian passed it over, saying "I think that this is for you, Mr President". A coup had been successful. On a subsequent trip to Lagos, Ian was asked by Murtala if there was anything that the President could do for Ian before he returned to London. "Well, yes there is. I have an old school friend working in Lagos but each time I visit you, I am escorted to and from the airport. It would be good to meet him". "Give me his name and I will make sure that you meet him". The Nigerian Telephone system had never worked, but the ex-Inspector of Army Signals knew how to get at least one line working. Ian's friend worked at a junior level in the back room of a remote suburban branch of Barclays Bank. The manager heard the telephone ring and could not believe his ears. Telephones just did not work in Lagos. He answered and was greeted with "This is the President. I want to talk to your assistant". Blind panic set in, but eventually a Presidential limousine took Ian to meet his school friend. His friend asked him to never again wish for anything in Nigeria! The strain was too much for him to stand.

Later the aircraft was nearly ready to be handed to the Nigerians. A test flight was arranged to check the radios in use while airborne. Someone suggested, while they were flying, that it would be good to check the radios over Nigeria, to see how they coped with tropical conditions. The aircraft landed at Lagos, and none of the crew had passports as their jackets were still on the backs of chairs in Heathrow.

> "Where you from? What you want in Nigeria?"
> "We are testing the President's aircraft".
> "Which President? We just shot one".

Murtala Mohammed was shot on his way to work that morning. It was about three weeks before Ian located the aircraft and the crew. Families in UK had been frantic.

Jane managed to get a job in Hempsted School, where we lived. Hugh attended the school as well, so they travelled together. Hugh got on well, but Jane noticed that although his reading was well up to standard for his age, his written work was not as good as she had expected. She took her concerns to the Headmaster, who convinced her that, as she was a teacher as well as a mother, she was over compensating. Jane agreed to let the matter rest.

Nigeria 1976 – 1983

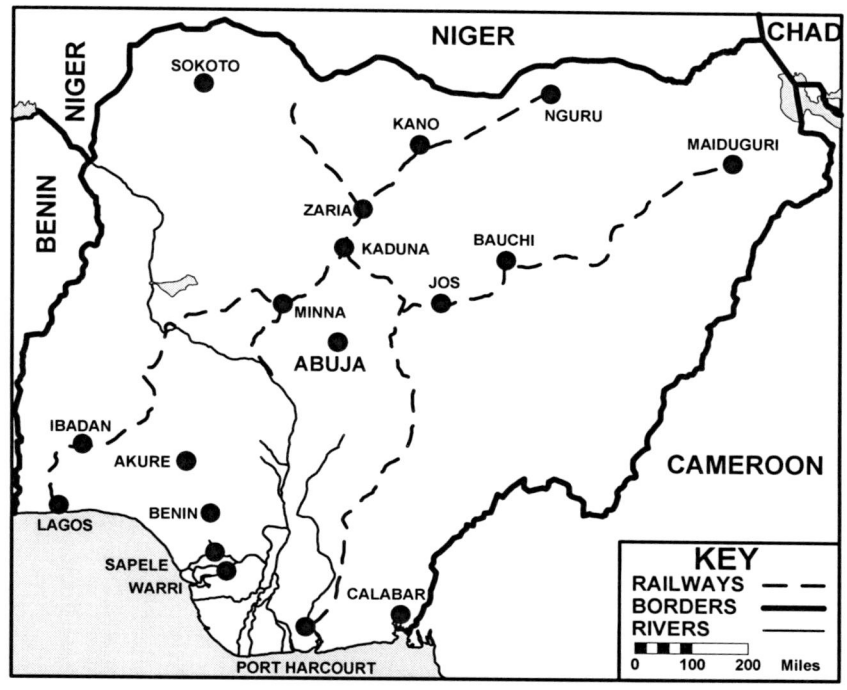

NIGERIA 1976 - 1983

Nguru 1976 - 1977

In March 1976, my Brother-in-Law saw me off at Heathrow. There was a colourful bunch of travellers at the Check-in desk. One was an African in full national dress, with two enormous necklaces, down to his feet, made up of 50 toilet rolls. Ian bet that he would finish up sitting next to me on the flight. He was right; the Ghanaian was taking essential supplies back to a country that had none for sale. I wondered what I should have been taking with me.

Three of us arrived in Nigeria on the same flight, to be met by the company's Fixer at Lagos Airport. It was hot and sweaty. The humidity only made the vegetation rot and this increased the smell. There were other unpleasant and unidentifiable smells. The other two were put on flights to other cities, and my flight to Kano left late afternoon. I had been allocated to the £8 million Nguru Barracks Road Project in Borno State, where the roads were to have a "Bitumen stabilised sand base course". I was met at the airport in Kano and went to share a house with a grizzled old foreman and his Nigerian "wife". He was many years past retirement age, but elected to stay on in Nigeria as he could no longer tolerate living in Britain.

The next morning I met the Project Manager, Mike Brown. His initials were M. A. N. and the Nigerians called him "Man Brown".

I studied all the literature available on how to use "bitumen stabilized sand" as a base course. The material had been suggested because there was no quarry, or stone products, within 200 miles of the site, whereas sand was readily available. This site was on the border with Niger, and in the great sand sea left behind when Lake Chad evaporated over millions of years, leaving a completely flat area stretching over 500 miles. Initially, until the site accommodation was erected, our staff were based in Kano, getting all the plant assembled. There were some 25 miles of "bitumen-stabilized sand" roads to build. This included a 12 mile link road from the barracks to the railway station in Nguru.

My worst flight ever

One day, a Lagos based Director came to Kano and we hired a single engined aeroplane to fly to Nguru for a visit. There was an abandoned RAF wartime strip near the site. We took off in high spirits, in clear weather. No sooner than we had climbed above the airport, a massive sand storm blew in. The sand completely filled the horizon, up to 10,000 feet at least. The pilot tried to return to Kano but we were enveloped in very turbulent winds, with sand scouring the windshield. The control tower advised all aircraft that the airport was now closed. The pilot struggled to simply keep us flying and the rest of us were airsick. Mike Brown stopped himself from being sick by smoking a large cigar, but this had the opposite effect on the rest of us. He was not popular! Eventually, we spotted the white lines of the runway some distance below us, but at right angles to our track. Seconds later, we were back in our own sandy hell. There was no radio contact with Air Traffic Control. The next sighting of land was when a hill flashed past only just under a wing tip. Eventually, the sand storm moved on, and we found the airport again. The winds were still very strong, but fuel was getting low. We landed with the fuselage at an angle to the runway and danced along on one main wheel, hoping not to perform a "ground loop". No one has ever been as relieved as we were to have landed safely. The pilot was still shaking that night when we went to his hotel to thank him for his skill. This was, by far, the worst flight that I have ever had.

There were two foremen already on site in Nguru, erecting our accommodation, and living in a rented bungalow. I was sent up to take charge and met Steve and Wally. Steve was a hardworking man and progress was being made. Wally was a diminutive Glaswegian who liked a drink. The bungalow was next to a large pond, with only a sand bund built to keep out the crocodiles (although I never saw one). It was very hot, and being on the edge of the Sahara, very dry. There was only one vehicle, so I stayed in at night while the other two went into the village. Two Italian engineers were building all the Army accommodation on the site and lived in the adjacent bungalow. Wally and Steve could never agree to return home at the same time in the evening, so there were arguments. Eventually a four wheel drive Ford Tractor arrived on site and Wally got his own personal transport.

Our accommodation consisted of two blocks of five bachelor rooms, a mess hall (kitchen, dining and lounge), the office block, and the Project Manager's house.

Wally had set the foundations to all except the Mess hall above ground, as the area flooded during the rains. The resulting floors were not level and this gave problems with doors opening. My room door had to open outwards because the floor inside rose steeply from the doorway. Wally was unrepentant and said that it was all well up to Nigerian standards. The carpenter, when about to fix the last door, asked an exasperated Wally which way he wanted it hung, was told to hang it from the top! The carpenter did as instructed! The Nigerian carpenters asked me for more "screwnails". This word describes how a woodscrew is driven into wood with a hammer. No self-respecting Nigerian used a screwdriver.

NGURU CAMP - NIGERIA
Note difference in floor levels - Mess Hall at rear

The last building to be started was the Mess Hall and, to save time, Mike Brown decided to leave out the elevated foundations. I still remember the tide marks halfway up the billiard table legs, after the rain storms that he had decided would not possibly flood the camp!

As the buildings became habitable, we set up the kitchen and hired the best domestic staff we could find locally. The cook (when sober) produced filling, if bland, meals although we tried to supervise and advise him. The cleaner-cum-laundryman was a very hard-working Hausa. All the previous day's laundry would be piled on the sideboard in the dining room at dawn, in piles sorted by type. One had to sort through to find one's own items. We called this system "First up, best dressed", as early risers had the choice of items. A late breakfast meant that you were left with Wally Brown's reject underpants! The laundryman had one other fault. Periodically, and without warning, he would disappear, (to his home village we discovered eventually), for a week or more and then return to demand that we sack his replacement. A young strong and willing labourer became our Mess waiter. When it came to clearing the empty china plates after a meal, he folded each plate in half and put the two halves together to make them easier to hold. As we rapidly began to run out of plates, Musa was hastily transferred to my Materials Laboratory. His strength was much more useful in compacting concrete and asphalt samples.

We were short of all sorts of tools and equipment, so we had to find solutions. To provide labourers with shovels, I went to the market and found that scrap car doors were set in the ground to form animal pens for market day trading. I bought several of these and had the local car mechanic cut shovel blades from the metal of the car doors. These were nailed onto broom stick handles. They were strong enough to dig in the loose dry sand of the area. To help me to give orders, I thought that a little of the local language would be useful. I asked for the Hausa words for flat, straight, level, horizontal, and vertical. The answer was "We have no need for these strange ideas, so we have no words". Nigerian buildings often have foundations and floors that follow the slope of the land. We needed to hire some tipper trucks and I found some in the town. The Hausa owner was willing to hire them to us. He brought his father along to help discuss the price. The Hausa are Muslim, and there are a lot of Arabic words in the language resulting from the

175

influence of the Koran. They were a bit flummoxed when I seemed to be able to understand the prices they were discussing amongst themselves, as Swahili uses the same Arabic numbering. I was able to get a much reduced rate for tipper hire, when they had hoped for much more.

Using the tippers proved a little difficult at times because of the highly erratic deliveries of fuel to Nguru. Petrol seemed to arrive more often than diesel, because cars and petrol generators outnumbered the diesel vehicles. However, a delivery arrived and was put in the underground tanks at the filling station. The pumps needed electricity, and the local diesel power station was undergoing a major overhaul. Diesel engines were being stripped down, and there was no power during daylight hours while the lone Brit laboured over the massive Blackstone engines. I came to an arrangement with the Blackstone Mechanic, where I would line up all my tippers at the pumps, and he would temporarily switch on one generator long enough for me to fill my trucks. By the time the town realised that the electricity was back on, and that the diesel pumps were working, we had driven off and all the lights all went off again! This was my first introduction to that wonderful Nigerian institution – NEPA. Officially, the Nigerian Electric Power Authority, but everyone knew that it stood for "Never Ever Power Available".

Visas and prostitutes

After a short time on a Temporary Work Visa, I had to get my permanent Work Permit. This could only be done by visiting an office of the Nigeria High Commission outside Nigeria. The company used the one in Ghana, and I was sent off to Accra. Nigeria was gearing up to host the "First Pan African Festival of Music and Culture", being held in Lagos. There were two of us and we were met by the Taylor Woodrow Ghana "fixer" and we drove to the company flat. On the way, the traffic constable on duty at a junction stopped our car. He came straight to the rear window, ignoring the driver, and stuck his hand in my face. He demanded my Driving Licence. I told him that I was not driving. It turned out that it was the way they all asked for "dash" in Ghana. After two days, we duly got our Work Permits and were taken to the Airport to catch the last flight of the day back to Lagos. We were sitting on the aircraft and wondering what was causing the delay. I was sharing the two seat row with a very overweight African lady who was clutching a large enamel bowl of dried fish. The smell was atrocious. The pilot announced that there was a delay at Lagos. We waited for a bit longer. The pilot, a Canadian, came on the loudspeakers again. "Ladies and gentlemen, you will not believe what I am going to tell you, so I will just let you listen to Lagos Tower". A very, very, harassed Air Traffic Controller was telling the pilot of a plane carrying the President of an African country to "Land in another country and take a taxi, we are full up!"

All the Presidents and dancers, musicians, and hangers-on for every country in Africa, and their Press packs, had turned up for the Festival. There was literally, no space for another aircraft anywhere in Lagos Airport. The pilot asked us to all disembark, and return at dawn the next day, to try again. The Airport was closed, lights were off, Immigration officers at home in bed and we had to climb out over the security fence. Some people who lived in Ghana had cars in the carpark, and we got a lift back to the company flat. The Houseboy, having seen us depart, had stripped the beds and all the sheets were soaking in the bath! We went outside and found a taxi to get us to a restaurant for a meal. The taxi driver insisted on buying the beers for the rest of the night. Ghana was a lovely country, and a complete opposite to Nigeria. The next morning, we returned to the airport, where Immigration officials could not understand why we already had exit visas stamped in our passports.

We returned to Lagos, to find a chaotic situation. The roads were blocked by striking prostitutes. The Nigerian Union of Prostitutes had been asked by the government to help host all the foreign visitors and make a success of the Festival. The NUP reasoned that this meant that they were all now, temporarily at least, government employees. So where were the government cars, houses and salaries? The government refused to talk to the NUP. I was lucky to get away to the north and back to the refuge of the site.

The lost Brigadier

Eventually, the accommodation was in occupation and plant had arrived. It seemed that the whole of Nguru wanted a job. There were about 300 applicants pestering me for work, while Mike was still in Kano. The State Governor of Kano State was also the Commanding General for the Infantry Battalion in Nguru, and he decided to have an inspection. The troops were on parade, in best uniforms, and waited in the sun for the General from early morning. I realized that the General would have to drive past our offices, and through the 300 job applicants, who were blocking the road. I spoke to the Adjutant, who instructed the Military Police Platoon to "move the men" out of the Barracks. Using the standard Nigerian whip, a stripped down electric cable with metal washers on the ends of each wire, the men were quickly formed into three ranks and made to run the twelve miles back into town. All I saw was the column of dust disappearing into the distance. Six hours later, the General arrived and the Battalion was still on the parade ground in the baking sun. By this time, the map reading officer was under arrest for getting them lost in the six foot high grass covering the whole area. Apparently they had strayed into the neighbouring country of Niger and had to talk their way out of a Diplomatic problem. One consequence of a visit by this General was a follow up visit by the State Governor of Borno State, in which the barracks was sited, to find out what the Kano Governor was doing trespassing outside his area of responsibility. The Borno Governor's escort of some 25 armed men were a menacing bunch, and we saw them often.

Plant started to arrive, including our 8 Mercedes tipper trucks. The Plant Manager, an ex Merchant Navy engine room man, was told to go and make up a list of spare parts so that we could order them up in advance. From a handbook, he made the list, multiplied the quantities by eight and we ordered the parts. Only after the first breakdowns, did we discover that we had two slightly different versions of the same truck. Our man had ordered from the parts book of the single truck of its type. The other seven trucks had no spares on site! It pays to check. This Plant man spent most of his time on his personal appearance and said that he would never go home with a woman unless she owned a trouser press and a shoeshine machine. He always wore brilliant white shirt and shorts, with never a hint of oil or grease, which showed the rest of us that he never got his hands dirty and left all the engine repairs to his deputy. He was forever combing his hair so one day we stole his pocket comb, and, after hours of "searching for it", we produced an African style comb from the market. His fit of sulks lasted weeks. He was eventually sent back to UK.

The company purchased some new Landrovers, and these were driven to the site. The route followed the embankment of the second longest railway straight in Africa, some 200 miles. Before the Second World War, the British Government realised that the area to the North East of Kano was suitable for ground nut cultivation. A railway line was built to help develop the area, and an oil mill built. Over the years, the groundnut crop deteriorated and the mill was reduced to extracting oils from all sorts of unsuitable plants. The land the railway passed through was virtually flat as far as one could see. In the rainy season, the land would flood and the road track moved from the flat, up the sloping side of the railway embankment to stay clear of the flood water. One of the Landrover drivers decided to use the opportunity to illegally carry paying passengers between villages on the route, and crashed. He killed a passenger and several others needed major surgery. We recovered the vehicle from the Police eventually, and wondered what to do with it. The engine had done only 600 miles, but the chassis was bent out of shape! I took our mechanic, an ex-REME Commando, down to the market place where camels were held for auction. Armed with a tape measure, we took down part of the walls of the stockade, which was made of old vehicle chassis planted vertically in the ground. Out of a choice of about twenty, we found two chassis that matched our requirements and we re-built the Landrover. This extra vehicle came in very handy.

The official contract drawings were still in Imperial measurements. They had been signed off by a certain Brigadier Obasanjo some years before Nigeria went Metric. However, no one wanted to ask the current President, the same man, if we could change the drawings to Metric units! From somewhere, a much worn Imperial level staff was found and sent to me. I had three surveyors and three dumpy levels, but just the one staff. The land was flat for hundreds of miles around, meaning that only very small level differences need be measured. I separated the three parts of the telescopic staff and gave a piece to each surveyor. They said that they could not use the staff sections, "because there was no zero". Levelling is done by subtracting from each other any two readings off a staff, so a zero was not required. Eventually, they accepted this as another bit of "white man's magic".

I had to prepare working drawings, and decided on a single centreline level for virtually all roads because of the flatness of the land. This made it very easy to spot a kerb that was above or below level. I also kept the roads as long straights wherever possible. My surveyors marvelled at my ability to spot an incorrect peg from a great distance. More of the White Man's magic! Sometimes I had to send some instructions to the surveyor setting out ahead of the concrete gang. The first time that I wrote out an instruction out and handed it to my driver, I instructed him to return to the office as soon as he had delivered the message. A short while later, I realised that the vehicle had not moved, and the driver was sitting outside. When challenged, he said "You say go and come back, so I save time by not going".

Arrested by Military Police

Working on a Nigerian Army Base is not without problems. The Army were waiting for their Officers Mess to be built by the Italian contractor, so our Mess Hall became the Officers Mess. This was not a formal arrangement, and they felt that they did not need to pay for drinks! In the early days, I got on well with the Major commanding the Battalion. One Sunday morning, after a night in the bar, I was woken by thunderous crashes on my door. Wearing only underpants, I staggered to the door. Two armed Military Policemen grabbed me and thrust me, face down, into the back of a Land Rover. We drove at speed over the rough ground, as this was before the roads had been built. Army boots pressed down on my back to make sure that I did not escape. At the Major's house, I met Steve, who had also been arrested. We were frog-marched inside and held at gun point, up against the wall. After half an hour, with no explanation, a civilian came and started to measure us. Was this for coffins, we wondered? The measurer jotted his findings down on the newly painted wall, using ball point pen. Then a door opened and the Major came out. He seemed a bit upset, but it seemed it was only because the wall now needed repainting. He explained that he wanted to present us with Nigerian robes, and needed our measurements. His lads had been a little too enthusiastic in the interpretation of his orders. The major apologised to us and spoke to his soldiers. What he said, I don't know, but they were gentle with us when they took us back home. Later Steve and I were invited to a party, in our own bar, and we were made honourary Nigerian Princes. I got the blue robes, while macho Steve looked very uncomfortable in the pink ones.

To dig the long trenches for culverts through the embankments, we used a wheeled loading shovel. A culvert trench near the officer's married quarters seemed to be taking time. The foreman asked the operator why this was. "I can only dig in the morning. In the afternoon, my back hurts." The Army retired to bed in the afternoons, coming out again when it got cooler. The Second in Command could not sleep with the noise of our machine, and instructed his guards to stop the noise. This they did by whipping the operator!

We started trials of the bitumen stabilized sand base material. The sand, when dug, was moist enough to cause explosions in the asphalt plant, due to the heat making steam in a confined space. Sand was dug and spread in the sun, turned over and re-spread, and eventually found to be dry enough to use. We dug several borrow pits and dozed the sand up into heaps. These heaps were higher than the sparse and straggly trees of the area. The local children took advantage of being able to see right out to the horizon for the first time. The look of sheer wonder on the faces was worth the trouble of having them invade the works. We decided to leave one heap for the town to use as a look out and kids playground! When we cleared the vegetation from the borrow pit area, we found many poisonous snakes, the Gabon Viper being the most deadly. Large yellow scorpions were plentiful. Spiders measured up to four inches across, and were said to be bird eaters. We had been helpfully advised by the Company Doctor, that after being bitten by a snake, to bring the snake to the surgery for identification so that the correct anti-venom could be used. We preferred the other advice given by an old Africa hand. He said the victim should be given a full bottle of whisky to drink. The victim would then either survive or die happy.

Scott Wilson Kirkpatrick had submitted a Paper to the Institution of Civil Engineers, suggesting that the best mix used 4% bitumen, so we used that as a guide. The resulting mix was full of air voids, and looked like Aero chocolate. It was possible to lay it using an asphalt paving machine, but it could not be rolled until the temperature dropped considerably. Rolling and consolidation took place after a wait of a minimum of two days after being laid. Without this delay, the roller sank through the mix and had to be dug out. We had to roll and compact the base for several days, to remove all of the trapped air. I found that, where the finished levels were not correct, the mix could be sculpted to the required shape using a grader in the same way one removes surplus butter from a piece of bread. The best time of day for sculpting was just after noon, when the sun had warmed up the surface.

The base course was laid between concrete haunches, backed by filled verges. The haunches were extruded by machines running on rails. The concrete mix for this extrusion process needed careful monitoring and the Resident Engineer insisted that a number of concrete cubes were sent for testing each week in Kano, over some 200 miles of very bumpy road. Some cubes did not survive the journey. Depending on the results, adjustments were made to the mix each week. It was many months later, when the road had nearly reached the town, some 12 miles away, when the concrete mixer supplying the haunches broke down. There was a spare mixer near my Materials Laboratory and this was pressed into service. My Lab Technician came to me, panicking, because he could no longer make the concrete for the weekly cubes! He had been making a special batch of concrete for the cubes every week, from his personal mixer, since the start of the job, and none of the concrete used on the site had ever been tested!

Early on in the contract, and to celebrate the occupation of the living accommodation, the Managing Director and other Head Office staff flew up to inspect the site. They handed me a 16mm Film Projector and screen. They had arranged that we should have a rented film each week to watch. That first night, I realised that they had not brought the spare spool, on which the film is wound after it has been through the projector! I positioned a large cardboard box under the projector and showed the film. While the MD and party were drinking in the bar afterwards, I was trying to disentangle the box of film and wind it back onto the spool. I had to have a spare spool and asked the MD to make sure that he sent an extra empty spool with the next film.

There was no spare spool the following week, and our audience had grown to include several Catholic Priests and Nuns, and all the Army Officers. Someone told me that there was a disused open air cinema in town and I found the man who used to operate the cinema. In the projection box were many old films, but the only reel that matched my requirements was an old Chinese Communist propaganda film. This was quickly removed and thrown away, and I arrived back just in time to show the new film at the advertised time.

It seemed that almost anything could be found in the town. The Lebanese couple that operated the Oil Mill had spent every leave, for many years, in Europe trying to buy a hand operated pasta machine. During the site clearance for the new road, I had to demolish a shed some 50 metres from their bungalow. The shed contained 50 pasta machines of the exact make that they had been searching for all those years!

At great expense, the company purchased a second-hand billiard table in Liverpool and shipped it to us. The 1,000 mile road journey proved to be the most difficult bit. Only 12 miles from camp, the lorry hit a bump and some of the slate slabs shattered. In our spare time, we lovingly re-built the table. All 12 expats worked, for once, as a perfect team, for this most wanted addition to the Mess. To replace the slate slabs, we used two layers of marine grade plywood, all carefully screwed together, with all screws properly countersunk and filled, and then we assembled the baize cloth and the cushions. During the first game, it was realized that, although we had cut out for the corner pockets, we had forgotten to cut out for the two side pockets! We made the alterations and reassembled the table. We found that, immediately under the spot were the black ball is placed, someone had used a round head screw, which left a small bump. This was not altered, as it gave an advantage to the home team players. The ball could be redirected by the bump! In the wet season, we had to play in rubber boots because the building flooded. The Project Manager was often reminded that he had not allowed us to raise the floor level when we built the Mess hall.

Surface to Air Missiles

The company had a contract with a light aircraft company, which allowed mail, personnel, and vital spares to get to remote sites quickly. The airstrips were maintained by the staff on the nearest site. At Nguru, there was a strip some 5 miles out into the bush, which had become somewhat overgrown since it was abandoned by the RAF at the end of the Second World War. I cleared the strip, and smoothed it out, ready for the weekly flights. When the aircraft was approaching, the pilot would call us on the radio and request that we meet him. This depended on someone actually being near our site radio set, the generator actually supplying electricity, and a vehicle being available for the journey. Once, on returning from leave, I hitched a ride with the German pilot but we failed to raise anyone on the radio. The site knew the schedule, so we just hoped that someone would come. We sat in the baking sun for hours. Two Fulani horsemen rode up, very interested in the aircraft. The pilot was keen on the horses, so he tried to set up a deal where the Fulani took the plane, and he took the horses. He explained that the horsemen had to wear the pilot's shirt because it had the magic wings and gold bars, without which the bird would not fly! The pilot fancied the Fulani shirt, which sensibly was open at the sides from the underarm to the hem. It was much cooler than an ordinary shirt. Eventually, the Fulani declined the swap and rode off, and still there was no company vehicle. The pilot decided to take off and "buzz" the camp to produce a reaction. He did, in that the Army thought that they were under attack and dug out the surface-to-air missiles. Someone did notice and a vehicle was seen moving towards the airstrip. When I arrived, there was a diplomatic row going on between the Army and the Project Manager.

The Major commanding the Battalion was selected to attend a Staff Course at Fort Bragg, in the United States, prior to his promotion. He was to take his wife, who pointed out that she needed a good evening dress for formal dinners. There were no dress shops within 1,000 miles and he asked me to buy a dress for his wife when I went on leave. I still remember the look on the face of the sales assistant in one of the several Knightsbridge shops we visited, when Jane who was a Size 8/10, rummaged through the racks for a Size 26 dress. Eventually, we bought an electric blue, sequinned, number which we felt would be appropriate. The Major was very pleased with the dress, as it was so "OTT" as to suit a large Nigerian lady.

When the Major was about to leave, he arranged for a Farewell Lunch, and I was chief guest. He scoured the town for chairs and filled the largest room available in the unfinished building contract. The rains had recently finished, and there were many smaller ponds still drying out. A miracle of nature in the Lake Chad basin is that fish survive, possibly as eggs underground in moist soil during the hot dry season. After hatching and while in the rapidly evaporating pools of water these fish grow at an alarming rate, and the last to be caught is enormous. I watched four men carrying the fish for our lunch, and they were struggling. The head was about a foot in diameter. The Major had the cooks prepare a Nigerian delicacy – Peppered Fish Soup. We entered the room and I was ushered to the only armchair. Soft drinks were passed round. Bowls of fish soup were given to all and I waited for mine. The last plate came, with the whole fish head standing proud. I was expected to eat all the flesh on the head. The peppered liquid was hot enough to burn my mouth. Embarrassed, I toyed with the fish head, hoping that the Major would see my discomfort. Eventually I decided to copy other guests and slide my plate under the chair. No such luck with the armchair and I was forced to ask the Major to dispose of it.

Spying charges

When the Major left, his Second in Command took over the battalion. Captain O. A. S. Benson was not liked by anyone. Up until then, the Army had sent a bus into town for families to shop, and charged a small sum. This money was placed in the Regimental Fund. As the driver, fuel, repairs, and all other expenses were paid by the Army, this should have meant that the fund kept increasing. Shortly after Benson took over, the fund was found to be empty. The Adjutant queried this with Benson, and promptly got put in the cells for his troubles. We liked the Adjutant and realized that he had not been seen for a while. One of us, innocently, asked if he was away on a course, or if he was away for compassionate reasons. "That is a Military Secret. You are spying". We were all placed under house arrest, our camp was inside the Army Camp, and I was abruptly taken in for questioning. My boss was away on leave. After a night in the Guard Room, there was more questioning.

I had upset Benson earlier that week for failing to hire unnecessary extra labourers from his wife. I had said that I did not have the authority to hire extra men, for which the company had no need for. I had realised that this was a form of blackmail and I resisted lining his wife's pockets. During the next few days my cell in the Guard Room looked out onto the exercise yard. A prisoner was made to squat, a lorry tyre was placed round his neck, and he was forced to "bunny-hop" along a gravel path for about 25 metres, and back. The sun was directly overhead. After several laps, encouraged by a Military Policeman with a whip, he was allowed a break. He collapsed onto his back and the Policeman produced a glass of ice cold water for him. Condensation glistened in the sun. This was poured down onto the ground just past his head. "Right, you've had your break. Get up and start moving!" I could see that I might have to start learning to bunny-hop! My expat staff got worried when I disappeared, and started asking more questions. They thought about reporting my disappearance to the Police in town. Benson began to realise that he had done something wrong and that the story would eventually get back to his Brigadier in Kano. Towards the end of the week, he was asking me to help draft letters to the Brigadier, to get him off the hook. I was freed after seven days and resumed work. The others had continued working without me as there was nothing else to do, being confined to camp, so we made progress. I only told Head Office about the situation later, as I had not been physically harmed. I was very pleased to read a year or so later that Captain Benson was given a 2 year hard labour sentence in a Military Prison for embezzlement.

As there was no quarry, or rock, within 200 miles, all aggregate was delivered by rail from Kano. The stone was loaded onto flatbed railway trucks, and had to be off-loaded manually in Nguru. A train of 10 flatbeds needed a very large number of labourers to scrape every stone out and onto the ground, and then to load our tippers to carry it to the site.

We started making trial mixes of asphalt wearing course and an "expert" foreman arrived to operate the paving machine. He said that he had been trained in Liverpool by the TV stars of "The Boys from the Black Stuff". The first real wearing course to be laid was at the main gate, linking onto the main public road. It looked horrible, with all sorts of bumps and hollows. I challenged the foreman who had operated the paving machine and he said it was because he could not stop laughing at the very smart Army guards. They had highly polished boots, chromed helmets that shone, white belts, gaiters, and gloves. First thing in the morning, it was very cold, so they had topped off the uniform with towelling bathrobes in pink and a knitted tea-cosy on top of the helmet!

There were a few other expatriates in the area and they visited our camp. One Irish man was installing a water supply scheme for nearby villages. He had been issued with a High Frequency radio to contact his Head Office, and this needed an aerial to be erected on a fixed bearing. He had no compass, so he waited until a Muslim started praying, facing the East, and noted the direction by placing ranging rods in line with the man's spine. From this he calculated the correct angle for the aerial. Needless to say, this was a failure.

The weather in the north of Nigeria was full of violent extremes. We suffered violent sand storms, horrendous rain storms, and unrelenting sun. During the laying of the base and wearing courses, weather was a critical element. We would prepare an area for the base course, spraying the tack coat of bitumen between the kerb haunches. A sand storm would appear from nowhere and the whole depth between the haunches would fill with blown sand. Working on the wet bitumen tack coat, we would start to dig out the sand. As the sand storm departed, the same winds would

183

bring a rain storm which turned all our efforts to mud. We started cleaning up, helped by the bright sun the next morning, only for the cycle to repeat! Luckily, there were days when we beat the weather and progress was made. Another problem was working at night, laying the base course. The heat in the mix reduced more quickly at night, allowing work to proceed. Work was done under floodlights, which attracted all the insects in Africa to the work area. Most got stuck under the rollers. In the locust season, the top layer seemed to be locust bodies, rather than base course. Areas had to be dug out and scrapped. Herdsmen, young boys, used to drive herds of goats across the road, and we discovered that goat droppings were extremely corrosive to fresh bitumen, leaving large holes! We did not have these problems in England.

As light relief, two of us would spend two nights in the company house in Kano every third week. On the rota, I was paired with Wally Burns. He really enjoyed Peppered Chicken, bought from a roadside stall where it was cooked over a charcoal fire, but more of that later. The big hotel in Kano had a good restaurant and bar where aircrews stayed. During the Hajj season, Nigeria would hire several aircraft, complete with crews, to ferry Muslim Hajjis to and from Jeddah for the annual pilgrimage. Nigeria, having suffered from complaints in previous years, decided to standardise the luggage each hajji could carry. Each was given an identical small suitcase, painted in the Nigerian colours of green and white. This made the luggage more identifiable to the Saudi authorities. However, on return, most of the identical suitcases had lost the labels, and the many illiterate owners failed to find their own. This resulted in a mountain of unclaimed suitcases at Kano airport. Worse, most hajjis, knowing that they still had to travel across Nigeria to get home, had bought food for this part of the journey. The suitcase mountain became a health hazard. A particular problem was the birth of millions of tiny fruit flies found in decomposing pineapples. Taylor Woodrow were contracted to dig a big hole and bury the lot! The flight crews, Air Tara from Ireland and Iceland Air, had bets with each other to see who could do the fastest round trip delivering pilgrims as the Hajj started. Serious discussions took place on tactics for loading and unloading passengers in the most efficient, and imaginative, ways. This included a low pass at Jeddah with the doors open and the crews throwing pilgrims out, to save time in landing Cabin crew had to learn phrases like "Do not light your paraffin stove until the seatbelt sign has been switched off" in several Nigerian dialects. After the end of the Hajj, Nigerians would straggle from Mecca down to Jeddah for the return flight. Aircraft could not take off until every seat was filled. Again, bets were made about the longest wait in Jeddah. One crew took 13 days to fill the seats.

Kano was also the home of the Nigerian Airforce Flying School. They used Russian MIGs and had a completely independent Air Traffic Control tower. The international civilian airport was very close and many "near misses" happened because the two Towers would not speak to each other. Taylor Woodrow had a contract to add facilities to the airbase, including a mortuary. They had been having difficulties getting acceptance signatures for each facility, and this was affecting payment of invoices. Instructions were given that no keys were to be released until the Airforce signature had been obtained. One Saturday, the Group Captain took off in his MIG, but the engine "flamed out" half way along the runway. He ejected at ground level, and landed on his head, killing him instantly. The aircraft rolled to a stop, undamaged. A party of six officers, with the body, approached the newly completed mortuary, asking if the body could be placed inside. The supervisor refused until he had his Airforce signature. The Airforce signatory was the dead Group Captain! A stand-off took place, while someone was dispatched to produce written authority for another officer to sign. At the main gate, we were building a plinth for a MIG to stand as a "Gate Guardian". The MIG would be placed on the plinth some ten foot off the ground. As this was the minimum height for the correct use of the ejector seat, it was proposed that a metal plate be added with this information, as a training aid for future pilots!

Before I left Nguru, we suffered a monster storm. We all hid in the Mess and watched all sorts of objects being picked up and hurled for vast distances. At the entrance gate to our compound, we had built a wooded sentry box for our guard. The bottom was weighed down with several concrete blocks. During the storm, the sentry box was seen bouncing along the road for about 50 yards before coming to a halt in a ditch. The guard could not be found straight after the storm and did not appear for work for some days. We assumed that he had left his post early and was safe. No, he had stayed in the box and ridden inside it as we watched! He had a broken arm. The boss was on leave, and we watched the corrugated iron sheets of his roof of his house being ripped to shreds. Personal items were sucked out and flown away. When the storm abated, we went over to the office block. A complete roof truss from the boss's house had speared down through the office roof, and was embedded in the floor, only feet from the radio but damaging the aerial. We were unable to report the damage and ask for help.

Minna   1977 - 1979

In 1977, I was transferred from Nguru to Minna, Niger State to be the Chief Engineer on the Minna Roads contract. At Independence, Nigeria had been split into six States. In subsequent years, further splits on tribal lines increased the number of States to nineteen by 1977. Each new State required a State Capital with a Governor's residence and administration centre. This meant that small towns with dirt roads had to be upgraded to suit the new status. Minna was a brand new capital and Taylor Woodrow won the contract to provide some 30 kilometres of asphalt roads. Other contractors provided water supply, electricity distribution, and telephones. This had been a small outpost in Colonial days, and there were a number of Colonial bungalows on the only hill, placed round the high level water storage tank. I used to go up in the evenings and sit in the shade and unwind from the stress of the day. I could smell the Africa of my childhood, the paraffin and wood fires heating the evening's meals. The sounds of the Africa I that I remembered drifted up from below.

A supervisor and his wife were the first people on site and lived in a mobile home while the accommodation was built. She cooked meals for up to 20 people three times a day, as there was no restaurant in town. A hotel had been opened, but only the bedrooms were in use, and the generator needed our fuel and attention. A Swedish company were building our prefabricated bachelor units, four ensuite rooms per block, and six bungalows for married staff. They also built four bungalows for the Resident Engineer and his staff. We took occupation of our new homes after three months of camping in the hotel.

I shared a hotel room with our elderly quarry manager. The mattresses were Nigerian-made foam rubber and these had been stood on end in the sun for a long time before arrival, causing them to bend in the middle and set solid in a curved shape. A mattress would touch the bed frame at each end, but show two foot of space under the centre! The pillows were built to Nigerian requirements. The Nigerian normally sleeps with the head supported on a wooden block, and these pillows had the same degree of comfort. We opened up the pillows and removed half of the stuffing and sewed them up again. We hid the surplus stuffing in the cupboards. Each day replacement pillows arrived. We started to take our adjusted pillows to work with us, so that we could have a night's rest. The Hotel Management wrote us a letter asking us to desist, or face expulsion. This letter was handed to our Quarry Manager on his arrival at the end of work. The quarry manager asked the receptionist for a pen. "Is there one "L" or two in bollocks?" he asked me before signing. He wrote a one word reply on the back of the letter and signed it. The receptionist took the reply to the manager and returned to tell us that our apology had been accepted!

The State Police Commissioner had very strong relations with a French contractor who had built several roads in the State and who he had expected to win the contract. If the French contractor had won the job, it would have been highly beneficial, financially, to the Commissioner. He took offence at our presence and conspired to make our life difficult. Each evening our water tanker was "arrested" for some imagined reason and we went without showers and cooking water! I found that, when I stopped to look at a length of road, I was "moved along" by the police. Worse, we negotiated some land for a quarry so that we could produce our aggregate but this was close to the Police Rifle range, and was actually behind the Butts. Small arms training intensified, with rounds landing in and among our plant, and threatening the explosives store. The Quarry Manager produced a handful of bullets that had bounced off the machine he was hiding behind. Something had to be done, and high level talks in Lagos produced results. A new Commissioner was appointed, and he promptly declared the whole of the town a construction site and threatened dire penalties to anyone causing a delay to the contract.

I was not aware of the change of Commissioner the next day when I approached a traffic policeman on point duty, in a battered old pick-up. The pick-up had a column gear change, but the bolts holding the steering column to the body were missing. Just as I approached, the policeman spotted an attractive young Nigerian motor scooter driver and without warning, gave her priority. I tried to stop, and change gear, but swerved and hit the wooden box the policeman was standing on! He rolled away in the dust, picked himself up and dusted himself down and tried to

clean his white over-sleeves and gloves. Replacing his white covered cap, he turned and slowly marched over to me. I could feel the full weight of the whole Nigerian Police force was about to descend on me. When he got to my vehicle, he drew himself up to attention and saluted. "Sorry Mastah, Sorry Mastah. I be stupid. Please forget!" He had obviously listened to the new Commissioner's orders that morning!

From then on, we had perfect co-operation and it was a joy to work with the Police. Of course, there was the odd policeman who could not forget his normal way of behaving. One stopped our Plant Manger on some pretext and requested a bribe. The Plant Manager said that his cash was in the office and would he accompany him? On arrival at the Plant Yard, the policeman was refused payment and ejected from the vehicle. There was a standing company rule that the yard gates could only be opened after a "chit" had been signed by the Plant Manager. It was some hours before the policeman was released back to duty.

Slowly plant and equipment arrived. Usually it arrived at the end of a day while we were sitting outside the caravan having a beer. It was like Christmas, as we checked the delivery ticket to see what had come and for whom. I got a D8 Bulldozer long before my first Theodolite, so I used that to define the centreline of the main dual carriageway! Once, a dishevelled driver appeared in a taxi. His articulated truck had got wedged in a railway bridge. The road crossed the River Niger using the railway bridge, and a concrete mixer was jammed between two high level cross-girders! The mixer had to be dismantled before trains could run again!

Meanwhile, I tried to plan a new road system for the town, based on the hand drawn sketch which constituted the Contract Drawings. I had no surveyors or instruments, let alone an office with a drawing board, or a table to work on, but I could do design work on the floor in the hotel bedroom. The unofficial arrangement with the State Engineer was that we produced all the drawings, but with his title block so that he could be seen to have designed the scheme! The Resident Engineer could not grasp this concept or the consequential contractual implications. The first set of drawings that I submitted were "Amendment H", as I kept adding "As Built" data! I could not imagine this happening in UK!

At last, the office building was set up and the drawing board arrived. Design could now start properly. Already the D8 bulldozer had found rock under the surface, so revisions to road levels had to be made and vertical alignments reconsidered. The State Engineer agreed with my changes and design continued. There was something thrilling about designing one day, and seeing the machines start work the next day. This was totally strange for an engineer trained in UK Local Government routines.

It became apparent that some buildings would need to be cleared to allow the full width of the proposed new roads, but the State had no mechanism or staff to undertake Compulsory Purchase. We were instructed to do this work on a reimbursement basis. I would go onto a street with a can of red paint, to put marks on buildings to be removed. I would measure the buildings, which were mostly mud or blockwork single storey, and record the name of the owner. Often all the residents would come out and try to make me decide to demolish one side of the street, rather than the other. Fights would take place, and bribes were offered. The new friendly police force was very useful at times. Once a list of demolitions had been agreed by the State, I issued Demolition Orders with a 60 day notice and painted a large red cross on all walls.

In a similar way, telegraph and electrical poles were marked for removal. This is where I came up against national regulations for NEPA, and Posts and Telegraph and Telecommunications (PTT). These regulations required that a cost estimate for the work to be agreed, the cash deposited in Lagos, and the approval and funding transmitted back to Minna. This would take a very long time, and our company had completed several other road jobs elsewhere which still had poles standing in the completed carriageway. I went to see the PTT Manager, a diminutive man who had requested a transfer away from another Taylor Woodrow road job because of the hassle of moving poles! In his office, there was a tea trolley with four telephones, of different colours. This looked most impressive, but none actually worked. He read out the national regulations to me and put the paper down on the desk. Reading upside down, I saw that "In an Emergency, such as an accident, the work should be done immediately and costs recovered afterwards". I announced that a particular pole would be having an "accident" at 9:00am the next day, and asked if his gang would be available to make the repair? Reluctantly he agreed. I had selected a pole with no wires, as a test case, merely wanting it removed and taken back to their depot. After the first pole had been removed, I departed, assuming that the gang would return to the depot. In the event, it appeared that I had been given the gang for the full day. The gang decided to remove the next eight poles, and the overhead wires. Government House lost the telephone link with the Federal Capital in Lagos! The wires were hastily replaced. This is how we proceeded from then on, with me often going direct to the foreman of the gang and taking charge of their vehicle keys to prevent them doing non-Taylor Woodrow work. Towards the end of the contract, the PTT offices conveniently burnt down together with all the records of the "emergency work" done. I was asked by PTT to provide details to re-build the records for the PTT manager.

Diverting electricity cables was slightly different. The NEPA manager was new to the area and did not trust his staff or the network. Before we went to discuss any problem on site, he would drive me to the Power Station. Here, he would shut down all the generators and put all the main fuses in his pocket, just in case someone started up a generator while he was away! Luckily, our camp had standby generators but the town supply suffered.

We moved into our new Swedish prefabricated accommodation. I helped furnish the RE's bungalows, which were in a separate fenced compound further down the hill. I instructed two labourers to carry an upright fridge-freezer to each house, expecting them to carry it out of our compound, along the main road and into the other compound using the gates. No, one man helped the other put the unit on his head. He walked down to the fence, and threw the unit over the high fence to his partner who was waiting on the other side! To finish the job, a grader was used to clean up and landscape the camp. That night it rained, and rained, and rained. All the freshly loosened soil was washed down the hill, where it fetched up against the

Resident Engineer's four bungalows. The front of the bungalows faced up hill, and, in Swedish style, the doors opened outwards. The four foot high mud bank surrounding each house prevented the doors from opening. In addition, no windows opened, a security feature, and the only openings were filled with air-conditioning units. We did not notice the figures frantically waving at us, as the bungalows were some distance away. It was some hours before a rescue was made.

State Engineer

The State Engineer, a Dane, had been a District Officer in Nigeria in Colonial times and stayed on in a similar capacity after Independence. He was a character. Pre-Independence he was sent from Sokoto to Katsina to investigate the low police morale. He found that the buildings were in a poor state of repair, as were all uniforms, and office furniture. He came up with a plan. All the prostitutes in the town were arrested and fined. The money was spent on renovations and tailors, and all income and expenditure was accounted for correctly. His superiors held an inquiry into his behaviour but had to commend the speedy solution, while deciding that his solution "was not British!" Later, at the outset of the Biafra War, he was ordered to evacuate all Europeans from the Warri area, and to bring back all the money held in the banks. Road travel was no longer an option, so he tried to commandeer a ship lying in the river. With a massive police corporal and his machine gun, he boarded a Russian freighter. In an accident, the First Mate was shot dead, but Jasper got the use of the ship. Hundreds of Europeans boarded. It was realised that food was needed. The Catholic and the Anglican Priests organised the looting of the supermarket and all sailed to Lagos. Years later, the Russian Embassy in Lagos was still trying to get the Nigerian government to accept responsibility for the dead sailor and compensate his family. Jasper had married just before we started work, and he had not had time to meet his new mother-in-law. She arrived by taxi during a drinking session at his bungalow on the hill. Jasper had a very large dog of mixed ancestry, which slept on the bed in the spare room. Mother-in-law decided not to join the drinking session and wanted to go to bed. The dog would not move. Jasper simply said "He always sleeps there" and that she could find somewhere else if she did not want to share. What a way to start married life.

Knocking down police stations

At a main junction in town, there was a need for a roundabout to help side road traffic join the dual-carriageway. On one corner was a police complex, including the town police station. I had a rough idea of where the fence line should be, but I had not surveyed or designed in detail. I hastily placed some wooden pegs and went back to arrange for the survey crew visit the spot later. No sooner than I had left, a senior Police Superintendent came to see the Project Manager and I was asked to return to the police station at 9:00am the next morning to meet the Commissioner regarding the pegs. The next morning I found that I could not park anywhere near the police station due to the large number of police vehicles, so I walked in. There were literally hundreds of police. As the sole European, I felt very alone. Standing on a high wall, part of a vehicle inspection ramp, were about ten of the largest men I have ever seen, with the sun shining between their legs directly into my eyes. This was the senior committee of the State Police, with the representatives of the Federal Police.

"What are these pegs?" asked the Commissioner in the normal aggressive Nigerian way, slapping his leg with his cane. I answered that there was a need for a roundabout under the new road scheme. "Stop right there", he said. What now, I thought. Am I to be arrested for trying to steal police land? Then he turned to the assembled senior officers and started to issue orders.

"You! Workshop Superintendent. You move all your workshop away, now"
"Signals man, get some prisoners from the gaol and take down those radio masts".
"You, Inspector, get some prisoners and demolish that building."

Then he turned to the Federal officers and asked them politely to vacate buildings and find alternative accommodation. He asked me to provide a bulldozer to make a track to allow the broken down vehicles to be removed, and to dig a hole to bury three police motorcycles. I realised that I was winning, so I timidly mentioned another possible, but not yet designed, roundabout next door to his own headquarters, and that one of the two buildings needed to be removed. More instructions were shouted and then he thanked me and said that I could go.

I was back in the office inside an hour, telling Project Manager, that I had arranged for two police stations to be demolished by the police themselves! I have often wondered if I could achieve that same success in Britain. A year later, the police realised that they had not been measured up for, or paid for, the Compulsory Purchase!

We had a fairly high turnover of staff, and the Resident Engineer also had to often get new men. I remember a new Assistant RE, who had only previously worked for a Lincolnshire Rural District Council. He lasted less than a week. On his first day, he queried a kink in a road alignment. All the residents used the slope of the valley, near the market, as the public toilet. I explained that I had placed a white wooden peg at the edge of the market area and then travelled to the other side of the valley. Once I had reached the opposite side of the valley, I had set up the Theodolite. I tried to locate the white peg in between human legs going to the toilet area. I spotted the white peg, and used it to set out the 700 metres of centreline. This involved having several labourers to keep the steel tape elevated above centuries of excreta. This was a smelly, difficult and nasty job. Only when the last peg was reached, did I travel round to the market side of the valley to check what I had set out. There I found that I had not aimed at my peg. From the evidence on the ground, I found a heap of what had been the white or pale yellow fresh substance, excreted by a Nigerian who had recently eaten maize meal. This had been my white peg. Rather than go through all the difficulty of setting out across the valley again, I simply designed a bend in the road to get over the problem. The new engineer was not impressed with my explanation until, while we stood there discussing the unhygienic habits of the population, a blind old lady found her usual toilet spot by placing her right hand on the corner of the last building then taking a known number of paces and crapped all over his shoe as we spoke! Later he was asleep in his bungalow when armed robbers took everything except the underpants that he was wearing. His fridge freezer was found in the bush a mile away. The engineer used his own money to buy an air ticket back to UK.

Once we got the quarry working, without the rifle range problem, we set up the asphalt plant. A very large area was set aside and filled with asphalt drums, ready for production. The quarry started blasting and crushing. The town graveyard was on the opposite side of the hill, and the soil was shallow over the rock. I watched one funeral, where the deceased was carried in a wheelbarrow and laid to rest only some two foot down. A particularly heavy blast would shake the ground and bodies would reappear on the surface. We had to do some rapid reburials. At the height of the dry season, a bush fire approached our stored bitumen. The local fire service helped our staff try to put out, or divert, the fire. Several hours into the battle, one of our men asked the fire chief if he would take extra care of the explosives store and the few drums of aviation fuel. That was the moment when the fire chief decided that they had worked eight hours and it was time to leave! We had to sort out the problem ourselves!

The riot

One afternoon, I was called to a row of houses that were being demolished after the formal Compulsory Purchase Notice had been served. An expat was operating the Hymac excavator which was positioned on top of the roof of a house, squashed down to ground level. The expat had the jib at full extension and the bucket teeth extended. The jib was swinging round in circles, at top speed, to keep the crowd from lynching him. In his enthusiasm, he had started on a house that still had a few more days of the 60 day notice to expire. About 300 very angry Nigerians thought that the family had been still inside the house when he flattened it and they thought that he had murdered them all! An angry Nigerian crowd can turn into a lynch mob in an instant. I have never had to talk so hard to persuade the crowd to spare us. I have no recollection of what I said. I was, frankly, terrified. I realised that the fuel would soon run out and he would become defenceless. A police sergeant and a constable arrived. I asked the police to arrest both of us, and ducked under the jib to try and talk to the operator, as the cab continued to swing round in circles. Eventually, I talked him into stopping, while the police told the crowd that we were under arrest. We were driven off to a police station nearby, where the desk sergeant recognised me, ushered us into the Inspector's office and produced mugs of tea. The arresting officers were told to go away! Later, I found that no one had been harmed, thankfully. The wrongly demolished house had been empty, but possessions were ruined. A pair of child's shoes poked out from under the roof, reminding me of what could have happened.

Railways

A remote part of the scheme involved a road crossing the railway line some distance from town. The Railways had provided a linesman to warn the survey crew of approaching trains. I happened to look up just as the linesman was frantically trying to put his whistle and his flag into his mouth at the same time. I cleared the gang off the track just in time. Dave Kilner had joined the site team and Dave was a railway enthusiast as well as a railway civil engineer. His first meeting with the Railways Area Engineer, who was seconded from the Indian State Railways, was spent discussing a particular culvert on a remote line in Assam that they both knew! Dave took over the design and build of the two road bridges over the railway. Later on, when Dave was building the bridge over the railway outside town, it was found that the only way to place the steel beams was to first unload them onto the track and then lift them again from there. An informal agreement by the Indian Area Engineer allowed this to happen; stopping trains while a lift was in progress. All the passengers would alight and crowd round the crane, offering helpful advice.

The stolen penis

There are many religions and beliefs in Nigeria, with over two hundred languages and dialects. This does lead to all sorts of misunderstandings and incidents. Annually, a rumour travels from the north, through all the market places, saying that the pagans are looking for the raw ingredients for making "ju-ju" potions. One potion in particular requires penises taken from live humans, (or so the story goes). Due to the rumours, the public are very alert, and guard against the theft of their prized possessions. When someone feels that they have been the victim of such a theft, a shout galvanizes the crowd who then chase the offender and lynch him, or anyone else who simply runs away in fear.

It was a Saturday night and the bar activity was at its height when a labourer appeared asking for Dave, to help get Dave's driver out of goal. By this time of night Dave was slightly less capable of driving than I, so I drove. We did not have much information so we decided to try each police station as we passed. At the first one I asked in my best English accent, "We are looking for our driver, Ambrose, who has had his penis stolen". "No, we don't hold prisoners here. Try further down". This was repeated at three more stations, including the State Headquarters. I was beginning to get word-perfect, (or sober). We reached the main police station and realised that we were in the correct place, because of the large angry crowd outside. We forced our way in and found Superintendent Bassey looking harassed. In a loud voice, because of the crowd, I said "We are looking for our driver, Ambrose, who has had his penis stolen". A faint shout for a remote cell confirmed that Ambrose was present. We asked to see him, and talked to him through the bars of a small cell holding forty or more Nigerians. We promised that we would do all we could and went back to talk to the Superintendent. He told us what he thought had happened and he had arrested all of them, victims, thieves, and bystanders, for their own safety, and hoped that tempers would cool over night. As we were leaving, I asked why the woman was in the cells with all the others. He replied, "She's had hers stolen as well".

Ambrose was released the next morning. Later, in Lagos, I watched a professor of medicine from the Lagos University Teaching Hospital explain on TV that penises could be stolen, but that nature lets them grow back again. It all happens in Nigeria.

Madmen

The existing roundabout in the centre of town was occupied by a madman, and my survey crews would not go near him. He was totally naked, but extremely well endowed. The expat wives had been asking the minibus driver, on the daily shopping trip, to make several laps round the existing traffic island. I needed to survey the island so as to design the new roundabout. I got all the survey teams together and we hatched a plan to do several simultaneous tasks together, so that we could watch out for each other if the madman turned nasty. The police refused to help, in case the madness was contagious. In four Landrovers, we arrived and started work. The madman walked up to me and asked, in perfect Oxford English, if he could help by holding the end of my tape measure, or in some other way! He was not mad, but just wanted his own way of life, and would be grateful if people would only leave him alone.

We concreted all the kerbing and culverts, using a fleet of small dumpers. One problem we never properly solved was that, only after filling with fresh concrete, would the Muslim operator park up and pray. Concrete tends to set in the hot sun while the operator prays! We tried to get them to pray while the dumper was empty, but had no luck. One dumper had an engine failure, but the replacement engine did not properly match the gearbox. As a result it had three reverse gears and one forward gear. This became the fastest dumper, and was steered by sitting on the steering wheel and looking over the back! To concrete the bridge abutments without a crane, Carl the Cornish Carpenter Foreman, built a walk up ramp for labourers to carry the concrete up to the top of the shutter in wheelbarrows. We had ordered the wheelbarrows but they had not arrived in time for the first pour. Headpans were purchased and concreting started. The lorry delivering the wheelbarrows arrived during the pour, and Carl got the men to change over to the barrows. As the previous concrete had been carried on the head, so were the wheelbarrows full of concrete!

Minna dinghies

Carl was an ex-ships carpenter from Falmouth. He loved sailing and wanted to take up the sport in the centre of Nigeria. The Daily Mirror newspaper was promoting sailing and had designed a small sailing dinghy, the Mirror Dinghy. Carl gave me a brochure and asked if I could produce some drawings. Using graph paper and a slide rule, I was able to work out the principal dimensions. Carl built two "Minna" dinghies, which he sailed on the dam that Costains had built for Minna. As no trees had been removed before the dam was flooded, sailing through the tops of trees added a bit of spice.

Asphalting problems

After the majority of the roads had been laid out and kerbed, the asphalting started. As soon as an area had been given the "tack coat" of sprayed bitumen, the local vehicles would try to use the area as a carpark! We would get the police to remove the vehicles, and we would have to repair the tack coat. Fuel deliveries to Minna were erratic, and filling stations would stand empty until a delivery. When the tanker was rumoured to be approaching, all the motorists in town would form a queue in eager anticipation. This happened on an area that was due to be asphalted the same day. We arrived to find some 400 cars parked on the freshly prepared road bed. We got the police to remove the cars, which they did with great difficulty and we started asphalting. When the tanker arrived, the fights broke out. The man who had been first in the original queue had lost his place and was now somewhere near the back of the queue. He angrily blamed the police. All the others were similarly jumbled up and very unhappy. On another occasion, the local taxi rank had to be cleared and the police decided that they should all operate from a new rank, some distance from the centre of town. The taxi drivers were unhappy and rioted. Shots were fired. Driving back to camp for lunch, I passed through a low cloud hanging over the road and recognised CS gas.

Opposite the State Police Headquarters, I tried to design a roundabout. Each time I drew it up and the laid the kerbs, the Project Manager would pencil in a few changes to levels and measurements. I would get the revised kerb lines rebuilt and he would change it again. A blind lady used to sit on the pavement at a junction, selling fruit. Eventually, after several changes, I told the Project Manager that I would get a signature for the latest build and that it was not going to be changed again. The blind old lady kindly signed a paper to say that she approved of the latest design, and that it was to stay! The Project Manager queried the "X", but I had several witnesses to say that the lady had signed. In 2016, the Project Manager wrote in his Christmas card that he "still keeps changing things at the last minute".

I was responsible for making sure that the town airfield was in a good state of repair for the regular visits of the new Company twin engined Cessna. I supplied the fuel drums to the aircraft, and spent time talking to the pilot while he refuelled. The Italians from a dam construction site used this airstrip to take personnel to the nearest International Airport when they resigned, or were sacked. Once, the Italian's pilot could not start the engine and asked if we could help. I arranged for an electrician and a fitter to come. Before they arrived, I was reminded of a World War 2 trick of starting engines by winding a long rope round the propeller, tying it to a jeep, and driving off fast! I suggested this to our pilot, who told the other pilot. He agreed to try the method. We found a long rope and started winding it onto the propeller. The captive Italians on the other plane where shouting and trying to get out through the windows. It was a real comic opera, and the Italians really knew how to panic. Eventually, the magneto was fixed using a screwdriver, and they left.

Toilet patrol

Eventually, the road across the valley to the market place was complete. The slopes were sown with fast growing local grass and watered. Complaints came in that the local population had resumed excreting on this new area of earth and the grass was being killed off. We needed the grass to grow, to be paid for the work. I was dispatched to ask the police for help. The Superintendent was only too pleased to help and immediately called a Constable out of the typing pool. He was ordered to go back and get his beret, belt and truncheon.

"You follow this Master. He show you dis place.
When you see someone shitting, you beat him well well!"

I took him to the site and watched him in action. He would wait until a man was fully undressed, crouched, and it was visibly evident that he was actually excreting. Only then would he pounce and beat him round the head with his truncheon. Women and children also suffered. The grass recovered.

Vultures

After the road project had been underway for a time, street lighting, electrical distribution, and telephone network contracts were let to Drake & Scull. The contractors worked with us, and the expat staff rented rooms in our camp. I was worried that the street lighting poles in the central reservation had inadequate foundations and I queried the design. The lamps were cantilevered and made perfect vulture landing pads. These birds are heavy, and the constant build-up of guano added to the problem. To check the design, the contractor had no way of estimating for the guano load. I suggested that the designer use design tables for "Snow Loads" instead!

Finding a caber

While the poles were being erected for electricity and telephones, I was handed a radio message asking if I could find a suitable lump of wood for a Scottish caber, as some people in Lagos wanted to hold a Highland Games. After checking the sizes in the Guinness Book of Records, I replied "Scots or Gaelic? " (The Gaelic caber being the longer, heavier one). "Scots, of course" was the answer, so I went off to ask the Telephone project manager if I could have a pole. I was talking to him at the roadside, near a completed length of telephone wires, when a car careered across the pavement and slammed into a telegraph pole. The two headlights were bent round to point at each other, with the radiator pushed into the engine. The pole had snapped off clean at the base, but the wires held the pole up. This was my caber, I thought. I quickly found a tipper and two carpenters. Raising the tipper body to reach the top of the pole, they cut the pole just below the cross-tree, leaving the wires intact. I told the carpenters to take the pole to our yard. The police arrived, and the driver tried to tell them that he had hit a pole, but there was no pole to be seen!

I returned to the yard, to arrange for the pole to be cut to the correct length and the broken end to be smoothed. The caber was received by Colin Bryce, a Scot, who was our company geologist working for the Well-drilling Section. The carpenters wanted to know what it was to be used for so I told them in my best Pidgin English, (which is impossible to put into writing).

"In your country, Nigeria, there are still a lot of dissident tribesmen in the North, who do not agree with the Government. They have their own culture and tribal way of doing things. They still worship in strange pagan ways. It is the same in my country. In the North, we have Scotsmen, who dress in ladies skirts. In the summer, they have festivals, where they all drink alcohol like your palm toddy, which they call "Whisky". These festivals celebrate the end of the harvest, and whole villages would gather together and drink, sing, dance, and test the strength of the young men. The music was strange, and instruments were made from local materials. The bagpipes are made by cutting off a sheep's head and pulling the meat out. Music is made by blowing down a bamboo tube shoved up the arsehole. The young men would test each other by throwing large rocks as far as they could, and by throwing trees, like the one you have just cut for me".

They looked at me and said that we were a strange race.

As work got completed, staff were moved to other contracts, and rooms became available for other contractors to hire. It seemed that, where ever we worked, the same team of Americans were putting up 800 foot high TV repeater masts. Randy and his crew from Montana had a mast to erect about 50 miles from Minna, and lived with us. One evening, none of them returned to camp. We sent someone to find out if they were in trouble and needed help. Apparently, the local tribesmen had a grievance and said that they had not been paid for the land on which the mast was being erected. The team had built about 100 foot of mast at this time. We found them all sitting in bosun's chairs at the top of the mast, in the dark. The villagers were firing arrows at them but just could not reach the men above them. The fire arrows could be seen curving up and falling away in the dark. They spent the night aloft, and things calmed down in the next couple of days.

Taylor Woodrow continued to tender for road jobs, and whichever engineer was available on a nearby site would be sent to do the site report. In UK press there had been reports of a particularly nasty outbreak of a rat-borne epidemic in West Africa. I remember finding myself sitting under a road sign reading "Ebola 1 mile". This, I found out many years later, was not the original source of the disease, which is in the Congo.

On another occasion, all the Head Office top men arrived in Minna and we flew to Maiduguri, the capital of Borno State in the far North East of Nigeria. The only accommodation we could find had a single room and a double bed. The sight of our Managing Director sleeping with a portly Quantity Surveyor will not easily be forgotten.

Hijack

The Plant Manager's wife developed a medical problem that needed urgent treatment in UK. The State Medical Officer of Health, who was our company doctor, and the Nigerian Airways doctor, both wrote letters explaining that she was not contagious and would not have medical problems flying. Armed with these letters, our Kano office secured two tickets on the British Caledonian flight leaving on the Saturday Night. I escorted the lady, and another wife, a nurse who had volunteered to travel with her, to the airport. The 350 mile trip went without a hitch and we refreshed ourselves in the company house in Kano before going to the Airport. Kano was under curfew, as gangs of armed robbers were terrorizing the town. Police and Army units were patrolling the streets and we were asked to be at the Airport before dusk. The aircraft was to depart at 2300, so there was a long wait before check-in could start. I found that British Caledonian had not agreed to carry these two passengers, because the necessary authority had not been issued from the

Gatwick headquarters. Insurance was involved, but trying to sort this out with Gatwick on a Saturday night from darkest Africa was more than I could manage. I was reluctant to let the ladies and the luggage go through Customs and Immigration, to the Departure Lounge until it was confirmed that they could board the flight. I needed to speak to the Captain, and this could only be done with the help of the Kano Station Manager. This meant passing through Immigration and Customs. Due to the curfew, armed police swarmed through the Airport. I grabbed a police corporal and told him that I was off to see the Station Manager, and that he was to stay close to me. Customs and Immigration thought that I was under police escort and let me through to the Station Manager. We had a brief radio conversation with the pilot, but he would not budge. The Station Manager agreed not to let the aircraft take off until the problem was resolved. With my policeman, I boarded the aircraft and walked onto the flight deck of the DC-10 jet. With the submachine gun visible, I persuaded the pilot that Gatwick were unlikely to respond, late on a Saturday night to his requests to allow the lady to travel, that the lady was not infectious and had a nurse in attendance, and that the rest of the passengers were growing anxious. We had marched past the front row of First Class and the machine gun had worried the passengers. Having got the pilot to reluctantly agree, my next worry was that the Customs, Immigration and Check-in staff had closed up and gone home. I was lucky enough to find them all ready to leave, but the policeman waved his weapon and they went back to their desks. I hurried the ladies and the baggage through and watched them board the flight. There was one last hiccup which caused a delay, but the policeman solved that. Although the World Health Organization had said that Smallpox had been eradicated many years before and that Inoculation Certificates were no longer needed, the painted sign requesting passengers to show the certificate for Smallpox had not been removed at this Airport. Every departing passenger was still being "fined" for failing to produce the certificate! I had to wait until dawn before it was safe to drive back to the company house. I suppose that waving a weapon on the flight deck of an airliner could be classed as a Hijack, but it was the only way to solve the problem.

There were a number of Voluntary Service Overseas teachers in the State. They worked in remote towns and villages, in very primitive conditions. On rare occasions, they had to visit the State Headquarters for Visa reasons. Some would spend the visit in our camp, and they would invite us back to their schools. I went to one school, about 200 miles away in Sokoto State, where the VSOs were gathering for a weekend party. I had the only vehicle, so I was delegated to visit the local market and help buy the goat for the feast. Four of us, including a Nigerian teacher, toured the market, looking for a likely goat. The Nigerian checked our various choices for disease, age, and price. We bargained with the "mamas" of the local tribe. They dressed solely in leather skirts, which were heavily patterned with tattoos. Their upper bodies were bare and also totally covered with matching tattoos. Having bought the goat, we bought a large bundle of firewood, on which to cook the animal. The goat and the wood were put in the back of the Landrover and we set off to return to the school. On the way, we saw a typical road accident. We were following a motorcyclist who was wearing a Hausa shirt. This shirt is about two yards wide, worn hitched up over the shoulders, and open down the side seams. He was going at some speed. We could see another motorbike approaching up the side of the embankment. At the last minute, just as they saw each other, a gust of wind

197

filled both the shirts like enormous sails. There was no way of keeping control of the bikes. To avoid running them both over, I braked hard. The goat and the firewood joined me at the front, and it was a while before the goat was happy for us to drive on. The standard punishment at this school was to send a pupil a mile to the river to fetch a gallon of water. Toilets were only flushed when absolutely necessary.

On another trip, to a different school, I had to cross a wooden bridge built many years before, with rotting decking timbers.

Across the road from our camp, there was a large girl's school. The Canadian Science teacher told me, after a year of teaching the girls, they had all failed an exam. She had been teaching "Ions" and the girls had heard "Irons".

A late addition to our contract was the provision of the main water pipe through the town. The pipe was required to be laid in a deep trench, and this meant a lot of blasting through the underlying rock. Our blasting expert, an old Africa hand, put small charges in holes drilled into the rock in the trench. To reduce the spread of rock particles after to blast, he covered the trench with lengths of old conveyor belt. Sometimes, the bits of belt were not enough to stop the odd rock landing on a nearby hut. One day he had a row with the owner of a mud hut shop that sold soft drinks, and he told this man that "If you don't do what I say, I will make the next blast put a rock through your roof". The owner dared him to do it. By accident or design, the blast sent just one rock through the centre of the roof and down into the cold drink dispenser. His reputation was made, and utmost respect was shown to him for the remainder of his time in town.

The water for the town was delivered from a dam recently built by Costains, to a large tank on the only hill. This hill also had the old colonial staff houses, where the Danish State Engineer lived. Our new water main took water from this tank and distributed it through the town. Our pipes were asbestos cement, and the townspeople realized that they could get water easily by making a hole with a pickaxe! When we came to test the new pipe system, there was a problem with the many existing valves on pipes connected to the tank. These valves had been manufactured in China, India and UK. Most screwed clockwise to close the valve, but one did not. We found out the hard way, when we thought that we had closed all the valves but succeeded in flooding the town and draining the storage tank.

Norconsult, a Norwegian Consulting firm, were hired to design the new Minna Bypass, and they liaised with me to co-ordinate junctions. While I was in Minna, the bypass project was shelved for financial reasons. They had marked out the centreline with pegs cut from nearby trees and painted them white. Black distance markings showed up clearly on the white pegs. Several years later, the project was revived and I was asked to find the route. All the pegs had grown into large bushes,

198

but the white paint could still be seen. Nigeria is extremely fertile, anything wooden only has to contact the ground and a bush grows. All my setting out pegs had been cut from trees so they often sprouted.

There were other civil engineering contracts in the State, and we would all meet at functions at each others camps. The Italians were building a dam to the north; the Irish were building roads to the east. One weekend, we hosted an "It's a Knockout" competition, with several teams from local expat teachers, the Italians and the Irish. One event was a "Frog Race", in which one jerks a cardboard cut out frog on a rope, moving it towards the finish line. The Italians did not fully understanding the rules of the games and turned up with hundreds of live frogs and they got into all the pipework of our swimming pool!!

One of the Irish supervisors from the Public Works Company had a fatal accident, caused when he dived into the shallow end of the swimming pool. In order to return his body to Ireland for burial, it was necessary for Nigerian Customs to watch the body being sealed into the casket for flight. This was arranged to be done at the Zaria Teaching Hospital, some 250 miles from Minna. The body had to be delivered to Zaria but there was no refrigerated transport available. Our Quantity Surveyor, Tony, helped out by lending the Irish company a Landrover and a chest freezer. A small petrol generator supplied the electricity to chill the body. This tall man was folded into the freezer and they set off. Frequent stops were required to run the generator. They had to stop overnight, and a careful guard was set up in case the vehicle and contents were stolen. Eventually they reached Zaria and had to wait until the body thawed sufficiently to remove it from the freezer. Thankfully, I was not in Minna when this rather unusual and abnormal duty was performed.

Lagos Head Office   1979 - 1982

When I was no longer required in Minna, I was transferred to Lagos to take over from the Contracts Engineer, covering the whole country. The job involved many different types of work, from temporary works design, assisting with estimating for tenders, building company accommodation, and visiting all the sites in the country that needed advice on engineering matters.

I was met at Lagos Airport by the incredible smell of rotting vegetation and human waste, and intense humidity. On the drive into the city, there seemed to be no end to the swirling mass of humanity. Goods and foodstuffs were sold from the pavements, forcing pedestrians onto the carriageway. The pedestrian footbridges were covered with washing drying. "Landlords" were charging rent to families to live on the bridges. I was taken to the Head Office in Abebe Village Road, which was just across the road from the Star Brewery that the company had built earlier. The Managing Director told me my duties and arranged temporary accommodation with Colin, the Geologist who had asked for the caber. I was shown round the offices and introduced to staff. The Plant Manager, who was another ex-Kenyan, took me out to his scrap heap and showed me the anvil which his staff had broken! I had thought that it was impossible to smash an anvil, but the Nigerians managed it. They could break anything.

My new house was in Apapa, a down market area. All Lagos is built on alluvial sand banks which flooded each high tide, the ground water table only inches below the surface. The frequent rains only added to the torture. The roads and building foundations frequently collapsed because the alluvial sand could not support them. The town water supply was supposed to be delivered by pipes into a ground tank at each house, but we often had to use company tankers to get water. The rain water would flood over the tank tops and deposit all manner of dirt from roads and adjacent septic tanks into the ground tanks. Cockroaches and other wildlife lived in the ground tanks. A small electric pump lifted the water, and cockroaches, to the roof tank for use. Needless to say, water was boiled many times before it was used. The buildings were covered in black mildew and fungi. The whole city was damp and stinking. Electricity from NEPA was erratic at best and we all had a diesel generator and a change-over switch. Often the NEPA linesmen would just disconnect a house and one would have to go and pay a "re-connection charge". The company had a man who seemed to do nothing else except pay these NEPA bribes. Telephones just did not exist. Cooking was done by bottled gas.

It was also very necessary to have guards for each house, in spite of the very secure bars and grills fitted to each opening. We also fitted a steel grill door to the top of the stairs. Everything was padlocked. In an emergency, one had to fumble with a large bunch of keys. To make sure that our guards were not working with the local thieves, we hired Fulani tribesmen from the far north of Nigeria. These men had an aversion to the Yoruba of the south, and they were armed with spears and machetes. Colleagues in an adjacent house returned from the Apapa Club late one night and found that the guards had captured a thief. They did not feel like involving the police that night, so they ordered that the thief be tied up until the morning. The guards must have had some resistance from the thief while he was being tied to a lamp post in the road outside, because he had lost a foot and had bled to death.

On another occasion, a Supervisor was asked to move in to a Director's house to protect it while he was on leave in England. The Supervisor woke up when a Flare Pistol was thrust up his nose. The thieves had sent a small boy in through the small bathroom window, which had no protective grill, and he had found the bunch of keys. Our man was left with a bare house and only his underpants. He was lucky to get away with his life.

There were basically only two types of car available. The Brazilian built Volkswagen Beetle, and the Peugeot 504 which was the most common taxi. There was a very high Import Duty and Tax on luxury cars, so there were very few in public ownership. I was given a new Beetle and a driver. It was essential to have a driver as he would be the one carted off to goal after an accident, if he had not already been lynched. The European usually sat on the back seat with his spare set of car keys, near the opposite door, so that he could escape while the lynch mob dealt with the driver. Mind you, at my low pay grade the Beetle only had two doors!

There are no rules for driving in Lagos. It is a free for all, and the bigger the vehicle, the safer one is. Trucks will always use the fast lane, because in an accident the driver can leap quickly over the concrete central reservation and disappear before the lynch mob gets him. Every vehicle shows multiple scars. There are traffic lights, but most of the bulbs have been stolen, so they are ignored. The average person walks in the road. Some don't make it through the day, and die. No one stops for a dead body, because one would finish up becoming responsible for the dead person's dependants for life. So the corpse lies where it fell and is slowly ground into the road surface. It becomes easier to drive over bodies, the longer one stays in the city. There are multitudes of potholes, as the constantly damp sandy road base collapses under the effect of tides and traffic. There is no way of telling the depth of a water filled pothole, so cars deviate round them, causing more collisions.

All cattle for slaughter are driven across Nigeria to the Lagos Slaughterhouse. These emaciated cattle, often with a broken leg, are driven along the dual carriageways from the Northern outskirts, to the Slaughterhouse in the South of the city. This is because no drover could afford to pay for the use of a cattle truck to carry them across the city. These cattle get confused and angry in heavy traffic, often leaping the concrete barrier into cars travelling on the other side.

I set off in my new car to visit a factory in a run down area. The driver drove into a deep pothole and we could not move. He got out and said that he would get a tow rope. What he did was find a long length of new telephone cable that was being laid, and he hacked off a length. A passing car pulled us out. A few weeks later, I went to the Ikoyi Club on a Saturday afternoon to meet other Taylor Woodrow people. When I came to leave, the Beetle was gone. It cost more to insure a car in Nigeria than the cost of the replacement. The car salesmen were in the habit of retaining a spare key and passing on the new owner details to friends in the criminal underworld. I got a lift home and a replacement soon afterwards.

An insurance assessor visited the company in Lagos and told us of another claim he had had to settle. The Italian Dam company in Minna needed a senior engineer to travel to Milan for high level technical talks with possible future client. He was flown to Lagos to board the international flight. Then things went wrong. There was no food in his company house so he went out for a meal that evening, by taxi. The taxi tried to avoid the potholes in the dark but fell into one. The engineer opened the door and fell into four foot of water liberally mixed with sewage, taking a mouthful. Helpful onlookers pulled him out, and stole his wallet, passport and air ticket. He walked back to the house and got someone to help. He was unable to fly until the missing passport and air ticket were replaced. Meanwhile he fell very ill. The meeting in Milan was postponed several times because this engineer was essential to the talks, and eventually the prospective client pulled out of the possible deal. Our assessor was dealing with an insurance policy which did not exactly specify the limits of consequential damages. The Milan company were suing for loss of profit on the aborted new contract, as well as for all the trouble in Nigeria!

Lagos is a series of sand islands, linked by elevated roads and bridges. The docks and oil refinery are in Apapa, and the more expensive property is on Victoria Island and Ikoyi. As I was living in Apapa, I joined the Apapa Club where most expats drank and ate. This was run by a fearsomely large German woman and her Nigerian husband. My superiors lived near the Ikoyi Club, which cost a lot more to join but was the place to be seen.

A typical week in Lagos was spent trying to meet officials, clients, and suppliers to sort out problems which had developed on up-country sites. As the telephone system did not work, one just kept driving round until one was lucky enough to meet someone on the list who was "on seat", meaning "in his office". They too, were moving round Lagos, trying to meet people on their lists........ Having done the business, off we went on the search for the next person. On good days, two successful visits happened. On other days, none were achieved at all. I remember one week when I met all ten people on my week's list on the Monday. Several of them were meeting people that I had wanted to catch, which made it simple. That week, I had to find some other work to do for the rest of the time.

My chief draughtsman was called Maxwell, and he was a master at avoiding work or even getting his hands dirty. One of his better excuses was to say that his house had "moved in a flood" after a heavy rain storm. Volkswagen Beetles were assembled in Brazil and shipped to Lagos in large packing cases. He had purchased a wooden packing case and he had got permission to set this up as his home in the drive of a house in Apapa. When the tide came in, it floated out of the drive and back up into another drive, blocking all the cars in the drive.

I worked with Colin designing and building the civil works for the wells that he drilled for clients. Some wells were 1,000 feet deep and water would be almost boiling when it reached the surface. A drilling supervisor thought that he would pipe this water straight into the shower in his caravan on site. He was badly scalded. Most water from deep wells in the Lagos area had a very high iron content, and arrived a bright muddy red colour. This rust had to be allowed to settle out in large ponds before further treatment. I had a small works crew and did all the

203

maintenance to our rented staff accommodation and the offices. My gang also worked on the well drilling sites.

Frequently I was sent off to remote sites by air to hopefully solve or at least advise on engineering problems or simply to deliver confidential documents. If I was very lucky, my journey was done in the company aircraft. But usually the Directors were heading off in the opposite direction! Then I had to use Nigerian Airways internal flights. This is not to be recommended. The aircraft maintenance was doubtful, the pilot skills were not of the highest standard, and the ticketing and departure procedure was appalling. Changing a ticket for a boarding pass was a scrum. The queue was ten deep, but twenty wide and often two persons high. The actual "desk" was a small letter box in a full height sheet steel screen built to protect the clerks. Once your ticket was taken, you had no idea if you would ever see a boarding pass again. It was impossible to deal safely with luggage as well as the ticket. I learnt to travel very, very, light, when travelling alone. There was a way round this scrum. A ticket tout would, for a negotiated fee, take your ticket through a side door and get the boarding pass for you. Because of "No Shows", Nigeria Airways always allocated 110% of the seats on a flight. A ticket or boarding pass was not a guarantee of a seat. Once a flight was called, there was a mad rush across the apron in blinding heat, to get on the plane. I have seen fights between two men climbing up the outside of the loading stairs! When a State Governor decides to travel, usually at very short notice, up to twenty seats are given to his party and they board early. The unlucky passengers, whose seats have been hijacked, are thrown off. One day, having got onto the apron and queued in the blinding sun by a plane, we were told that another plane was to be used. We all ran to the new plane, and the people at the back of the first queue became the first in the new queue. Those that lost their place were angry. Then we were told that the first plane was going after all, and we all rushed back again!

Once, I had to fly to Kaduna and got a tout to get the boarding pass. A policeman saw my tout in action and arrested me. I was marched into the Inspector's office. After a bit of talking we came to a sensible fee to allow me to board my flight. Outside was the constable, wanting his share of the "dash". I told him to get it from the Inspector and caught my flight. The next day, I had reached the Departure Lounge when the same constable approached me and tried to repeat the process, though he had not seen me deal with the ticket tout that time. I knew I was safe, and that it was just a "try on". "Go away, you are drunk", I said in a loud voice. The rest of the passengers cheered and the constable slunk off.

On another landing in Kaduna, the aircraft failed to avoid the badly back-filled trench across the runway. There was a terrible thump as the wheels dropped into the trench. My oxygen mask fell down. Then the shouting started. Why has the only European on the plane been given an oxygen mask? "It is a Nigerian plane in Nigeria, so Nigerians should get the mask before the visitor!!" It was only when I was, eventually, able to prove that the sticky tape holding my mask had broken, that the situation calmed down. A race-riot over a mask!!!

Nigerian Airways were trying to improve the quality of the aircraft and train Nigerian pilots. Air Tara, from Ireland, supplied Boeing 737's and training crews, and I met an Irish pilot once. The Nigerians were sent to the Boeing Flight School in Nevada. When they returned, Air Tara would not allow them to fly one of their aircraft until they had been checked out by one of their own pilots. Insurance was involved. One returned student was taken onto the Flight Deck and tested on his knowledge of the instruments. This is what my friend told me:

"What is that?"
"The fuel gauge".
"Good, how does it work"?
"It go from E to F".
"Yes, but what does that mean?"
"It go from Enough to Finish".

More training was obviously needed. Another Nigerian pilot refused to fly "because the horn wasn't working!" Nigerian drivers rely completely on the horn, ignoring brakes and steering, so how was he to tell other aircraft that he was up there?

There were other problems with the organization of the airline. Once I spent time at the airport saying goodbye to a friend travelling to Miami by Nigerian Airways, while I flew on an internal flight to Kano. We watched the food truck taking food to the aircraft and joked that they may put the food on the wrong flights. So it turned out. I had a three course meal and my friend had a can of soda and a biscuit for his 13 hour flight.

Sometimes I would be waiting patiently in an airport, hoping to get a boarding pass on a flight, when the company plane would land. I would rush across the tarmac and ask if there was a spare seat. If I was lucky, the driver who had carried me to the airport would have to find my luggage and put it on a company truck back to Lagos. I was not always so lucky, and when I failed to get a seat, the Directors would be in the Club Bar long before me that night!

Lagos Highland Games 1980

Colin introduced me to Dr Doug Edmunds, the man who had asked for the caber. Doug was a senior British Oxygen Company man and a Scottish Shot Putt Champion. Colin's brother had often competed against Doug at Highland Games. Another person I met was Jimmy Rudden, an Olympic Silver Medallist in Judo at the Tokyo Games. Jimmy was a freelance wholesale importer of building materials. He was an Arthur Daley on a grand scale. Doug and Jimmy had this idea of inviting some of the larger Highland Games competitors to Lagos and putting on a Games in December. In Scotland, the Heavies never competed against each other as they could win more prize money if they went to separate events. We wanted them to compete against each other, winner takes all. Doug had met the Minister for Sport, Youth and Culture and had his support for the idea. Jimmy could and would raise the sponsorship money, sell tickets, and generally look after the financial side. I was asked to provide practical help with equipment. Through contacts, we met the Lagos Polo Club Committee and they kindly agreed to allow us to use the club and the polo field. The Chairman was Brigadier Godfrey, in charge of the Secret Police, and another man was the Inspector General of Police. Doug contacted the "Heavies", including Geoff Capes, and also Fred Vaughan (USA) and Dave Harrington from Canada, and they all agreed to attend for a fee. Doug had also met up with an enormous Nigerian. Superintendent Chris Okonkwu was Nigeria's Olympic Shot Putter, and head of the Anti-Terrorist Unit.

Lagos Highland Games "Heavies"

Geoff Capes, Doug Edmonds, Bill Kazmier
and "Wee Dick" Martin

It was agreed that The Lagos Highland Games would be held on the first Sunday in December, 1980, and preparations commenced. My Managing Director was a Scot and allowed me to use company facilities. I had to set out the running track on the Polo pitch without using paint, and be able to remove every trace of the markings before the end of the day. Wide plastic tape secured by six inch nails did the trick. 56 lb weights and the tug of war rope were easy to find. For the "weight over the bar" I had to produce a stand and cross-bar that could be adjusted to upwards of 20 feet height. I also had to protect the polo pitch from falling weights! Manufacturers donated many old wooden doors and some mattresses. A dancing stage had to be built for the Scottish Dancing demonstration, electricity generators supplied for the cold drinks sellers and cooling the VIP Area, VIP seating and covered stands erected and a host of smaller things. In subsequent years, I was asked to produce more exotic items to be thrown around.

The event was organised as a five ring circus. There was Athletics on the track, wrestling and Tug-of-war inside the track, Scottish Dancing on the stage, and all the Heavy Events. When the 5,000 spectators, including five invited Ambassadors, finally left, it was well after dusk. Geoff Capes had been declared overall Champion.

The Heavies were with us for a whole week and various kind residents hosted them for us. As they consumed vast quantities of meat and drink, we paid the hosts to feed our boys. Companies that had provided major sponsorship money put on parties to show off the Heavies to invited friends. This meant transporting people across Lagos at night. Some of the Heavies found this daunting. On one trip I was with Capes and the others in two minibuses, when we were stopped along side each other in a traffic hold up, a "Go slow" in the local Pidgin. There was a narrow gap between the buses, and a motorcyclist drove through at speed. He hit both buses and pulled up just beyond. In true Nigerian fashion, having seen white men, he decided that they were going to pay for the damage to his machine. He revved himself up into a magnificent rant and marched towards us, yelling at the top of his voice.

Geoff Capes slowly sat upright to his full height and the man saw him. The shouting reduced suddenly to nothing and he turned and left. Geoff had not said a word!

My Managing Director hosted Jeannie Swanson the Champion Scottish Dancer. I collected her from Lagos Airport, late in the evening off her flight from London. In the car, before we set off, I asked her to remove her passport, tickets, and valuables from her pockets and handbag, and hide them under the car seats. I explained that there were several unofficial police and Army roadblocks to pass through and anything visible would be stolen. This worried her quite a bit, and what was even more worrying for her was that she knew that she could not get a return flight that night. We had trouble at two blocks, but managed to get away relatively cheaply.

Hugh reached the time when he had to transfer to a senior school. I wanted him to follow the family tradition and attend Kingswood School, in Bath. I felt that I could afford the fees on my overseas earnings and Jane agreed that he needed more stimulus than he would get at a state school. We applied to Kingswood, saying that my father and grandfather had attended the school, and that a distant relative had been a well respected headmaster. At the interview, Hugh impressed the staff and he was duly enrolled as a day boy. While I was back in Nigeria, Jane sold the Gloucester house and bought one in Bath. The surprise was that our new neighbour was none other than the same RAF pilot that had been a neighbour when we lived in Bath ten years earlier! Adrian had had postings all round the world in the intervening years, and talked about delivering supplies to the British Embassy in Saigon during the Vietnam War.

I was sent to Jos, in the cooler Highlands, to sort out the roof of a warehouse for the major supermarket chain. On this occasion, Nigerian Airways decided in mid flight not to land at Jos and dumped passengers at Kaduna. It was Saturday night and I had to meet a survey team on time in Jos, or they would return to another site. I found a taxi and eventually agreed a very inflated price for the 200 mile journey. The road was under construction and there were many rough diversions. It had also been raining and there was mud everywhere. As there were no seatbelts, I decided to try to sleep on the back seat, because someone had told me that one was less likely to be injured if you were limp when you got tossed around in an accident. I was woken when the taxi came to a halt. We had a puncture. I got out and noticed that the driver was taking off the wheel nuts by hand.

"Where be your spanner?" I asked.
He replied "A thiefman done stole it so I do by hand now!"

He changed the wheel and tightened the nuts by hand. We completed the journey at well under 30 mph, with me holding the jack handle over his head to make sure that he did not drive too fast! At Jos, I found that one column had been set lower than the others, but this had not been noticed until the roof sheets had been fixed. Having got that sorted, the company Cessna came to collect me. I had bought some punnets of strawberries which were grown near the sewage works, and some cream. The pilot and I were enjoying these, flying on autopilot back to Lagos, when the Managing Director called me up on the radio. He asked what I was doing and I told him that I was enjoying strawberries and cream at 8,000 feet. He was not amused.

Sapele

We were building a jetty and processing plant for a shrimp company at Sapele. One Saturday lunch time in Lagos, just as my soup was boiling, a driver came to the house with a message and an air ticket. I was to drop everything and get to Sapele immediately. There was just time to catch the Nigerian Airways flight to Warri, which I had never visited. Still in sandals and shorts, I managed to grab a paperback novel and my wallet. All the way to the airport I wondered if I had turned off the gas stove. Warri is the airport used by all the helicopters serving the offshore oil rigs. Because of this, it requires all passengers to carry passports. I did not have one. I was promptly taken to one side and told to wait until all the other passengers had been dealt with. The Immigration man told me to sit in his office while he dealt with another set of arrivals. He would not discuss my problem, and would not say if I was under arrest. I got bored and, realizing that I may not get another chance, went next door for a meal in the airport café. My man returned to find me missing. I watched him running up and down the runway looking for something or someone. After the meal, I wandered outside and saw that the Shrimp Company had sent a dilapidated pick-up for me. I was speaking to the driver when a heavy hand landed on my shoulder. After much discussion, the Immigration man confirmed that I was not under arrest as he did not have police powers but that I was to accompany him to the town police station. I said that was fine, but that he would have to provide the vehicle. He did not have one, and suggested the Shrimp pick-up. I sat in the middle and he got in beside me. The sun had been roasting the truck all afternoon, and hundreds of old shrimps lodged in crevices were cooking nicely. The stench was overpowering. The driver discovered that one wheel was flat and he did not have a spare. I think it was the smell that made my captor give up. He walked away after a lecture about travelling with a passport. All of this had taken several hours and my company hosts had begun to get worried. The 80 mile road from Warri to Sapele was notorious for armed robbery, kidnap and murder and they thought the worst had happened to me. Two of them drove to Warri, and finding that I was not at the Airport, and that the Shrimp Company vehicle was abandoned, they found a senior policeman. After being polite and waiting until a small boy had run off and purchased a soft drink each for his guests, he admitted that he had not seen or heard of me but suggested a visit to the Head of Prisons. After they eventually found him, there was a further long wait for soft drinks, but they drew another blank with the Prison Service. By this time we had repaired the puncture and driven to Sapele. The other two also returned, spending a worrying time discussing the radio message that they would have to send saying that I had vanished. We drank a few beers after we met up and sorted out the complete story. The problem with the piling rig was soon resolved and the Client satisfied. I managed to return through Warri without a passport.

The Managing Director asked me to build him a swimming pool in the grounds of his house. He wanted to be able to sit in his lounge and look down into the pool. Due to the very high ground water level, this proved impossible without a complete dewatering system. The MD was a canny Scot and refused to spend the extra money. I was told to dig down as far as possible and work from there. His father was staying in the house, so I had a Clerk of Works constantly checking on me. Eventually, the pool was built, but it was two steps higher than the lounge. A

Costain's man told me that he had had similar problems with the British High Commission pool. He had taken his illiterate Nigerian General Foreman to his Managing Director's house, pointed to the pool and said "Make same same at Embassy". He did, even down to the dark blue tiles showing the company logo at the bottom.

Demolition Order

In my second year in Lagos, the company decided to build three blocks of flats in Apapa to house the expatriate staff, and to be let out to others. I was sent to a friendly architect's office and "borrowed" a set of plans that had been used previously. Planning Permission was obtained and work started. When the blocks were structurally complete and the finishing works were in progress, an official Demolition Order was placed on the site "for not having been granted Planning Permission". We had official papers to prove our case, and suspected that a junior official was hoping for "dash" when he placed the notice. But how was I to prove this? I went to the Planning Office and spoke to the boss, who told me that there was no record of our application. Was he in on the fiddle as well? I decided to return very early the next morning, before the staff started work, and the cleaners let me in. I found the large, leather bound, ledger that contained the hand-written entries. The page holding our entry had been ripped out! I photographed this and left. One of our Nigerian Directors had a quiet word with someone and the Demolition Order vanished. It was normal for the Army to blow up illegal buildings, by taking out the corner columns, leaving the staircase intact. Thankfully we avoided a similar fate.

Eko Bridge joints

While the blocks of flats were being built, the company were asked to repair all the expansion joints on the Eko Bridge, which carried virtually every vehicle in Lagos every hour, or so it seemed. This elevated dual-carriageway is the main route across Lagos. It is also probably the longest continual traffic jam in the world. Heavy traffic had broken the bond between the cast metal expansion joints and the underlying concrete deck. I was asked to survey this damage and produce a report. Armed with a notepad and a tape measure, I waded into the traffic. I had to walk amongst Nigerian drivers, frustrated by traffic hold ups, to mark out pot holes and broken joints. It was the best training a matador could ever have. At each joint or hole I had to stop the traffic and measure the damage. As I bent down, the drivers behind the one that I had stopped would sound their horns and make threatening noises. At least one car was pushed forward by an impatient driver behind, who could not see me measuring the joint! Although I had arranged for police, road cones, and had men waving flags, it seemed that every Nigerian was intent on flattening me.

We analysed the report and decided that we needed a very quick setting fixative, because of the traffic problem. We air freighted a very large amount of Araldite (the two-part super glue) from Switzerland for the job. This is a material that has to be placed very soon after mixing. Because the setting time of mixed Araldite is affected by heat, the actual repair work was done at night. We developed a fast method of removing a length of metal joint, cutting a suitable new pocket, cleaning this out, mixing the Araldite with fine aggregate, suspending the metal joint and pouring the mix into the joint. We had nowhere on the bridge to store materials as there was no footpath or hard shoulder. Under each span, often on marshy ground, we set up the mixer. As soon as the joint was ready, the fresh mix was hauled up in a bucket for immediate placing. Only by placing two large lorries in the lane we were working on, could we get traffic to flow round the job. Needless to say, we worked at night, when traffic had slowed to a mere 80% of day time flow.

One night, a police car stopped a Mercedes car near where we were working. The driver was forced out and the "police" stole the car. I offered the driver a lift home. He was the Shell Oil Managing Director. On another occasion, my friend Jimmy Rudden was also stopped by the "police" so that they could steal his car. Jimmy was an Olympic Judo medallist and made short work of the thieves. One had a broken arm, and one had been thrown so hard against a rough concrete wall, that he almost stuck to it. Jimmy and I were entertained one night by a reporter from "The West African Technical Review" and some German Plant Sales representatives. Jimmy had brought his partner, Rusty Blair, a female wrestler who had fought that week in Lagos. After singing Hebridian Sea Shanties we left the hotel in convoy. Jimmy was stopped at a police check point and I heard him convince the Police that the contraband was in the car following him. They laughed and waved us both through! That sort of joke could have had very serious consequences.

I arranged for Jane and Hugh to spend the school summer holiday in Lagos with me. The company had earlier obligingly swapped me into a creekside house in Ikoyi. This was next door to the Headquarters of the Nigerian National Petroleum Company. Returning from UK leave, I arrived back from the Airport late at night to find a full scale riot outside my house. Fires had been lit and the mood was ugly. The Nigerian Press had found out that the country's oil sales income, paid into the Midland Bank in London, had been misused. The whole amount would be moved from one account to another after residing for a few days earning interest for each account holder, before eventually being credited to the NNPC. Many Government Ministers and senior politicians benefited from this. Only 4% of Nigerians are rich, exceedingly so, while the rest are grindingly poor. The poor did not like what the Press had told them. I decided not to spend the night in my own bed and found somewhere else quickly.

This new house was not really habitable, under European standards, but was a palace compared to Apapa. The garden was often under water at high tide and crabs invaded the house. All the electric conduits were full of termites and frequent power failures happened when they ate through the insulation. Jane and Hugh arrived. Hugh was just starting to climb and pulled himself up to the top of his built-in wardrobe. He opened the top cupboard above him and looked straight into the eyes of a large snake. Luckily, it was only the recently shed skin of a 10 foot monster.

It was the custom for the company to billet visitors with staff, paying the host for the food consumed. This was far more reliable than trying to find a hotel bed. Once, while Jane was there, I hosted another engineer before he flew to London. He slept in the afternoon and then we took him to the Airport. When we got back, the concrete roof beam in his room had dropped onto his bed, smashing it. He had been very lucky. The house was structurally unsound and the company moved us out. The house was taken over by the Mauritanian Embassy later.

The Irish Embassy

Jane and Hugh would spend the day at the pool in the Ikoyi Club, and I would collect them after work. Walking back one afternoon, a taxi mounted the pavement and ran deliberately and directly at Hugh. He jumped clear. For several years afterwards, every model car Hugh made was painted yellow with two thin black stripes, just like a Lagos taxi. One afternoon, Jane noticed that a roadside stall was selling Johnny Walker Black Label Whisky. We stopped, and the five year old girl told us that the Black Label was cheaper than the Red Label because "the label was dirty". We bought as much as we had cash for and went home to get more cash. On our return, we found the small crying child and a very angry mother. The prices had returned to normal. I noticed that the stall was on the lane leading to the Irish Embassy. This Embassy put on a magnificent St Patrick's Day celebration, and imported duty free alcohol throughout the year, ready for the day. Every Irish man and woman in Nigeria attended. This year, the Ambassador found that the whole of his hoard had vanished and he had to send out a message to all attending, asking them to "Bring your Own Booze". Years later, in Oman, I heard the rest of the story.

Hugh was fascinated by Nigerian TV, and watched their version of Children's Hour. The highlight was the commercial break. One Municipal announcement asked all kids to note where dead bodies lay and to get parents to notify the Council for collections to be made. The news service experimented with a new format, using two newsreaders with two cameras on alternative segments. On one day, the producer switching between cameras got a bit "out of synch" and the camera concentrated on the girl who was not talking. She extracted a large "bogey" from her nose and proceeded to stretch it.

The news often showed all the gory bits, and I was told of the public executions shown on TV. On one occasion, three armed robbers were tied to poles at the end of Bar Beach, the most popular beach, and the firing squad lined up. On the order "Fire", the two flanking robbers were killed but the central man was unharmed. "Reload and Fire". Again he was unharmed. After a third failed attempt, he was released due to "An act of God". One of the firing squad was also killed. Nigerian Radio was just as amusing. I was in a supermarket and everyone was listening to the Nigerian reporter in London describing the President's visit to meet the Queen. "The soldiers are lined up. They have red coats and animal skins on the head, and spears on the guns. The Queen arrived in a horse and cart". I tried not to laugh in case I upset the listeners. The same man reported from Nairobi and he was amazed that there was no litter in the streets, flowers were growing, and the roads freshly washed. Not at all like Lagos!

The company had a contract with Shell, and we were building oil storage tanks. I was asked to attend a meeting to help resolve a conflict. We all sat in Shell's boardroom, waiting for the Shell Managing Director to arrive. He did eventually, but was covered in excrement! He had been caught close up behind a nightsoil lorry on a steep access ramp to a flyover, when the tailboard sprang open! His resulting mood was most unhelpful in resolving the problem we had come to discuss.

Minna Christmas

We arranged for Jane and Hugh to visit Minna over Christmas, and use one of the empty bungalows. Tijani was the company's most reliable driver and he took us north. To keep Hugh amused, we played the Nigerian version of "I Spy". We counted the number of upturned and wrecked lorries and tankers in each river bed as we passed. The road was built as a normal two-way width asphalt road. However, the bridges were mostly a mere 12 foot wide and often set at an odd angle to the line of the road. No Nigerian worth his salt will let another driver beat him to a narrow bridge! Our best tally was 11 in one valley! We even witnessed an actual crash. We were being chased by an articulated lorry, and slowed to allow it to overtake. A Peugeot 504 taxi then tried to overtake the lorry, just as they both reached the bridge. The lorry's rear flicked the taxi yards out into the bush, before rolling over the side of the bridge. It was carrying bags of cement and the dust cloud took ages to settle. Some taxi passengers crawled out onto the road. Tijani advised that we did not try to help out, and drove on as soon as he could. We had a lovely and relaxing time in Minna. On our return drive, we had to pull over and stop to allow an approaching lorry to cross a bridge. A Police car had stopped some 50 feet in front of us. Tijani stopped a good distance behind the police car but accidentally eased his foot off the brake and we rolled forward about six inches. The policemen leapt out and hauled Tijani out of the car. After giving him a severe beating in front of Hugh and Jane, they demanded his papers. As he was getting them, he gave Jane his Driving Licence and asked her to hide it. Had the police got it, they would have not allowed him to move the car and return to Lagos. Eventually, a bruised and bleeding driver got back in and, after a long pause for Tijani to recover, we continued. We all felt very subdued and aware that violence is only just below the surface in Nigeria.

Another hazard when driving away from the big cities is the State Governor's convoy. A colleague was moving between sites and was held up to allow the Governor to go ahead. Our man decided to wait 30 minutes before setting off, to allow the Governor to get well ahead. On rounding a corner he suddenly found himself throwing a dust cloud over the parked convoy. The Governor had been caught short and stopped to relieve himself. The convoy escort caught up with the offender and beat him badly.

In July 1981, I was asked to visit our sister company in Maiduguri in the furthest north east of the country. They wanted a report on a road job under construction. The company plane took me to Minna for an overnight stop and I was able to fly over the completed roads in the town. There I met our newest civil engineering graduate. She was a very attractive Belfast girl who wore the shortest shorts that I have ever seen. What the local Muslims thought about that, I shudder to think. We had managed to get permission to land at Makundi, an active military airbase, for the next stop, about 50 miles from the Cement Factory site. That night I found out just how small the expat world can be. The General Manager of the Cement Factory had worked in Mombasa and had helped me make concrete blocks to anchor buoys in the harbour. The next day we drove to Makurdi and flew to Maiduguri and drove for three hours towards the Cameroon border, reaching the road site. The site bar was still under construction and we sat under the stars drinking beer. The Project Manager was a Loughborough Graduate who had worked under John Calkin in Malaysia. John was a classmate of mine, and who was on the same parachute course with me. Others there knew people that I did, from Mombasa or the TA. Sadly, the next day I found that the company plane had left for Lagos and I had to use Nigerian Airways to return home.

Lagos Highland Games 1981

The Lagos Highland Games took place again in 1981, and again I supplied all the hardware and technical help. Bill Kazmier, Guinness Book of Records holder of the Dead Lift title would be attempting to lift more than 881lbs. Doug asked me to investigate the Ministry of Sport's Olympic barbells. The bar bent when loaded with all the available weights, and we only reached 440lbs! A new set was needed.

I found a length of high tensile 32 mm diameter reinforcement bar. This had ribs along the length and the ribs needed removing. The Indians at the Nigerian Railways Workshop put the bar on the axle lathe and polished it for me. They also cut discs out of 1 inch plate, to make weights, and these totalled 1,000lbs. Avery Scales Ltd weighed each plate and marked up the discs for me. When I collected these weights, in my Beetle, I found that the brakes were useless! Driving in Nigeria is bad enough, but with no brakes and a stopping distance greater than an ocean liner, it was terrifying

The Heavies arrived a few days early, to acclimatise. My driver, Johnston, drove me to the house they were staying in and we had a few beers. As I was leaving, Johnston dropped the front wheels of the Beetle into a storm drain. I went back into the house and innocently asked if there was anyone any good at lifting. Four enormous men followed me out. Johnston had not seen them before and he started to shake. The car still had the engine running and, when the lads picked it up and threw it clear of the drain, Johnston's foot came off the clutch. Very luckily, the car shot away from the Heavies. If it had gone the other way, we may have had to cancel the Games.

That night, we took them to the Eko Hotel on the beach. There they met the crew of a large Dutch Dredger, who were celebrating the Dutch Christmas (which is fixed to the first Sunday in December). A Tug-of-War challenge was made for the Games.

Being small, I went off and purchased tickets for the buffet meal in the restaurant. When we walked in the Head Waiter attempted to try to charge us double, because my friends were large. After several refills of plates, Bill Anderson noticed that the buffet table was being cleared. He marched into the kitchen and all the buffet dishes were refilled promptly. He was an impressive size and his anger may have had something to do with the resumed service. Bill was a General Foreman and had held the Hammer Throwing title for many years.

World Record Deadlift - Bill Kazmier

Once again the Games were a success, with Capes taking the Trophy and Kazmier lifting 920lbs. This could not be a World record because he had had to use wrist straps, due to the humidity and sweat. He did, in fact, break the record the following week in Hawaii.

After many days of parties, we took the Heavies to Lagos Airport to return to UK. At the unloading bay, Capes and the others were delayed by well-wishers. Cape's luggage was still in the boot of my car when the police tow truck started to tow my car away. Capes leapt onto the truck and started banging on the roof of the cab, demanding that he wanted his luggage. When they saw the size of his fists, the police stopped and released my car. I still have memories of a screaming giant riding on the roof of the tow truck, careering round the airport.

Later, Chris Okonkwu was invited by Doug to take part in the Braemar Games in Scotland. He needed a 60 inch waist kilt. Doug got it made up from, appropriately, Black Watch Tartan. British Caledonian Airline gave him two adjoining seats by the exit, and the stewardesses looked after him well. After tossing the caber, he was introduced to Her Majesty, the Queen. Caber tossers coat their hands with "tacky", a glue-like substance used to bind the fingers together against the weight of the caber. Chris had not removed his "tacky" and the Queen was stuck to his hand! Capes had found, while in Nigeria, that a certain well known Insect Killer aerosol dissolved the "tacky". He squirted this on the Queen's hand and she was then separated from the big Nigerian.

Port Harcourt

I was sent to Port Harcourt, the scene of some of the worst fighting in the Biafran War. During this war, our night watchman had guarded all of our plant and we recovered it safely after the war, except for a single bullet hole! Port Harcourt was under curfew, due to armed robbers and the Army and the Police patrolled the streets at night. There had been recent deaths when Army patrols fired on Police at the opposite end of a bridge. A compromise had been reached, and joint patrols introduced. I was staying with another company engineer, who shared with a Shell employee. We went out for a meal together and took the Taylor Woodrow car. We got stopped by a joint police and army patrol. While the driver was showing his papers to the policeman, the American Shell man struck up a conversation with the soldier:

"Gee man, is that an AK47? Haven't seen one since I was in Vietnam! Can I have a look?"

As soon as he got hold of it, he very rapidly stripped it down to about 10 components and spread them on the bonnet of the car. The driver was told that we were free to go, so the American gathered up all the loose bits and handed them to the soldier. The look on the soldier's face was one of pure terror. How was he to reassemble the rifle? We drove away to cries of: "But Master, but Master, but Master, please help"

Another time that I visited Port Harcourt, was to collect a cheque from the State Governor, in payment for works completed many years before. Negotiations had been long and hard to get him to agree to this settlement, and I was sent to get the cheque before he changed his mind. At State Headquarters, I waved my letter of introduction and was treated royally. Eventually the Governor appeared and agreed to provide the cheque. He walked me over to the State Treasurer's building and I was introduced to the Treasurer. After comparing invoice numbers and such, a desk drawer was opened and a cheque book appeared and a cheque made out. With this in my hand, the Governor gave me a Police Escort to the Airport and they helped with the boarding pass. This was real royal treatment. I should have been more suspicious. The money was earmarked to pay for the Christmas Charter flight for bachelors to return to UK. Wimpey, Costains, and Taylor Woodrow had chartered a British Caledonian aircraft for this trip. The balance of the money went towards Christmas bonuses and salaries. The cheque bounced! The Treasurer had, carefully, used the wrong chequebook. The Christmas flight was in danger of being cancelled and I was no one's friend.

In the event, the flight went ahead. We all arrived at the Airport and cleared through to Departure. The aircraft was being prepared and the hostesses, who were on a promise of a free flight if the job was done, brought the drinks trolley off the aircraft into the Lounge. Looking out of the window, I noticed a lone Nigerian carefully carrying a food tray across the tarmac. Each time the apple fell off, he would pick it up, wipe it, and set off again and take the tray up the steps of our aircraft! He made many more journeys with a single tray each time. As British Caledonian were the principle sponsors of the Highland Games, I knew the Lagos Station Manager and went to have a word. The keys of the Catering truck, with the prepared meal trays, were in the pocket of the driver, who could not be found! My friend sorted this problem and the truck appeared which hastened the food tray loading. After much delay, we were allowed to board and the stewardesses busied themselves with getting us all more free drinks.

> "This is your Captain speaking. Do you want the good news or the bad news? The good news is that we have managed to get all the food on board. The bad news is that the truck has damaged the pressure hull, and the aircraft is grounded".

My friend, the Station Manager burst into action. Across the apron was a Nigerian Airways 747, bound for London. Grabbing some armed Federal Police, he commandeered the plane, threw off some very angry and influential Nigerians and made us change planes. We took off hours late and we were all in great danger of missing our onward connections in London. British Caledonian pulled out all stops and everyone's families were contacted. Hotels were booked for Christmas Eve in London, and onward travel arranged. This man went on to be Chairman of British

Caledonian Airlines, and left when it was taken over by BA. His attitude to customer service is sadly missed.

One evening, I met a Chief Petty Officer from HMS Endeavour, the icebreaker patrol ship en route back to UK after a long tour in the South Atlantic. The ship was moored directly opposite the Post Office Tower, and next to a stretch of highway. I took the CPO back to his ship and was invited below for a drink. While there, the Nigerian Police closed the Highway for the Presidential cavalcade to pass. My car was illegally parked, so I stayed below deck until the dust had settled. Thankfully, the car had not been removed. The next day, a fire broke out half way up the Post Office Tower. The building was a rectangle, with the tower containing lifts and stairs at one end. The other end had the fire escape. Staff above the fire level fled to the roof. HMS Endeavour sent its helicopter to rescue these trapped staff, later assisted by helicopters from the Nigerian Airforce. Later that evening, I met a Brit Post Office employee and asked how he had escaped. "I used the fire escape. It was empty, as everyone else used the main stairs". Fire practices had had no effect.

At one party I attended, there was a telephone call asking a guest to return to his home after a robbery. The thieves had stolen all the nine Rottweiler dogs that he had especially trained as guard dogs for sale. Nigerians will steal anything not bolted down.

Knee damage

The company had an asphalt overlay contract on the Lagos – Ibadan Expressway. Although the work was completed, it appeared that the company had not made as much profit as expected. Suspicion fell on the quarry and asphalt plant. It was thought that stone and asphalt was being supplied to "others" without the company receiving payment. I was sent to investigate and made the mistake of falling down the slope of the fifty foot high aggregate stockpile. My knee bent sideways. I was taken off to a company house in Ibadan and spent six days on major painkillers before I could be collected and taken for treatment. This injury went on to reoccur in Oman and Saudi Arabia, as it left a weakness in the knee ligaments. The quarry manager was later found to have sold loads to a Lebanese entrepreneur, both of whom did not realise that the gateman and the loading shovel operator were also selling materials.

After two terms at Kingswood, the school contacted us about Hugh. While he had a very high IQ level, and could discuss and talk about most subjects at adult level, he could not put any of this knowledge down on paper. Dyslexia was thought to be the problem and the school had no facilities for special teaching. We had to find a special school. It was Easter school holidays, and I was in Bath visiting a Consultant about knee operations. Somerset was a County that, at that time, did not believe in Dyslexia and had no funding or support for sufferers. However, The British Dyslexia Association Headquarters was in Bath! We made contact and discovered that they were in the same building as my knee Consultant! Hugh was tested and Dyslexia was diagnosed. Armed with this, and a list or suitable schools, we tried to find a school for him. All the staff at the schools were away on holiday, so nothing appeared to be getting sorted. I needed more time to settle this matter, and the Consultant was happy to extend my Sick Leave into term time. Eventually, we got Hugh into Grenville College in Bideford, as a boarder. This was an excellent school and fully competent to deal with Dyslexia. They taught Hugh to overcome his disability and gave him confidence. After a few terms of collecting and returning Hugh at the end of each term, Jane decided to sell the Bath house and find somewhere near the school. She would send estate agent details to me for comment. She found a delightful Grade II listed thatched cottage in Devon. Malcolm, my chief draughtsman, had one look at the photo and said "Why for you go live in grass hut, boss?" All African aspire to leave the grass hut and move into a concrete building, and he thought that it was a retrograde step for me. We did not buy that cottage, not because of Maxwell, but because there were not enough space and we could not get permission to extend the building. Jane continued to look and finally found a semi-detached house in Tintagel and the family have been in this house ever since.

Pay Day troubles

Nigerians react to rumours in a most aggressive way. The Minna Penis problem, for instance. One payday, a rumour went round our staff that the local bank had no funds. The staff got very angry and barricaded the Head Office gates and turned off the generator. About 30 angry workers demanded payment and accused the bosses of stealing their wages. I was temporarily in charge of the 150 men working at the Shell site in Apapa, and had gone to Head Office to assist in "bagging up" the wages for my lot. By noon, things were getting ugly, and the telephones no longer worked, so police help would not be available. I got my suitcase of pay packets into the car, together with three burly workmen as my guards. I was not allowed out of the gates by the mob. While I was talking to them, I remembered Isambard Kingdom Brunel. He had had difficulty with a slow paying Client, until he threatened to march his 5,000 Navvies to the Client. I told the 30 men on the gate that my 150 men would be rather upset if I was not allowed to deliver the wages, and that they would happily march up to Head Office to "discuss" the problem with the strikers. I was allowed through. Eventually, the mob realised that wages were being prepared and that the rumour was wrong.

The company had found me a new house in Awolowo Road, Ikoyi, after the creekside house collapsed. I shared this rented house with two other Taylor Woodrow men. As with all Nigerian buildings, the water pipes were galvanised and, over time, they corroded badly and flow was restricted or stopped. The pipes were concreted into the walls, so repairs were difficult. In this house we had to install a pump to force water down from the overhead tank. Gravity does not always work in Nigeria.

To combat traffic congestion, a law was passed insisting that on alternate days, only cars with a number plate ending in an odd or even number would be allowed on the roads on the alternate day. The net result was that everyone had two cars, one odd and one even. Our very small parking space now had six cars, and every day we had to solve a Rubik's Cube puzzle to get the correct number plates ready for the next day.

While I was on leave, my boss, the Contracts Director, removed our generator as his had broken down. Rank hath its privilege, I suppose. Eventually he was prevailed upon to replace our generator. The company electrician wired it up to the changeover switch and left. That night, NEPA cut the supply. The guards were asleep under the generator and Dave ran down to start the machine. He had been in bed and was naked due to the heat. The guards woke up, and seeing a naked white man, thought that he was going to rape them. The shouting woke Andy, the other resident, but not me. With the generator now working, the other two returned to bed. After some hours, NEPA restored the power. Because of the incorrect wiring done by the electrician, we now had both NEPA mains and the generator feeding into the change-over switch and there was a loud bang. My airconditioning unit caught fire and the plastic components gave out a choking smoke. In the ensuing chaos, the houseboy appeared and thought that we would all like cup of tea and filled the electric kettle, which did not boil.

Travel by box

The new Minister of Transport in 1979 was Umaro Dikko, and Taylor Woodrow wanted to get to know him, in the hope that more contracts could be won. When he was newly elected, the Contracts Director and I waited outside his office for him to arrive. Although we had been to this office before, it was the Minister's first visit to his new office. He walked round, examining shelves of books, filing cabinets, and trying the phones. He noticed a wall map, marked up with all the road contracts undertaken by his Ministry. Then he peered closely at an area in the North of the country. "That's my village, but there is no road from the main highway. Only last week, I visited and had to drive the long way round to get out". He later investigated and found that there was an immaculate paper trail showing the tendering, the award, 48 months of interim payments, and the final settlement payment. There was no road, but he did find a row of white pegs leading off the main highway..... We thought that this man was a breath of fresh air and we could trust him. When, in 1983, President Shagari was overthrown in a coup, Umaro Dikko fled to UK. There was a botched attempt by Mossad and Nigeria to kidnap him in 1984. Customs at Stansted Airport discovered his heavily drugged body in a crate marked "Diplomatic Baggage" and three Mossad and one Nigerian served several years in British gaols.

The Awolowo Road house was opposite a side road leading to the Presidential Palace. To ensure that traffic was stopped for the President, a Federal policeman lived in our garden, waiting to leap into action. To keep him sweet, he had free access to our beer. This paid off. At each end of the main road, the normal police had set up quasi-illegal road blocks, and took "tolls" off all motorists. Once I was stopped and the constable jumped in the car, took his beret off and placed it upside down by the gear lever and pointed. I explained that my money was in my house, so I drove off. When I got home, I explained to my semi-sober friendly Federal policeman that I had a problem. The problem was soon solved, with the traffic policeman being chased back to his road block!

Abuja

In Abuja, the new Federal capital, the company a contract to design and construct a section of the outer ring road. This included 4 bridges over rivers that had to be crossed by canoe. We constructed all the roads, but would not start the bridges until we had been paid for the road works. (In the event the bridges were eventually built years later by another company.) We had to survey and design the next 50km of the route and I took a young engineer out to hack our way through the dense jungle. He was much taller than me and fit. Over a week, I walked him into the ground. He thought that I was really fit but the effort to impress him nearly killed me. I gained a lot of respect when the story got round, but I secretly spent a week in bed recovering.

In addition to my duties as Chief Engineer for the country, I took over the Lagos Asphalt contracts and completed some work for the State Government and for private clients. One of these jobs was at Lagos Airport. We had to surface the apron outside the hangar containing a number of executive jets owned by the President. One of these aircraft had not been fully paid for and the Swiss owner wanted his aircraft back so he sent out two men to "maintain" it while the dispute rumbled on. These men eventually persuaded the Nigerian guards that engines had to be run, and that some flying time was needed to maintain the Certificate of Airworthiness. After many months, the aircraft was allowed out but only to taxi round the airfield. The aircraft took off. It flew low, below radar, and landed in Cotonou, Togo, the next door country. I used to talk to these men every day, and suddenly they were missing.

The country was bracing itself for yet another coup, so Taylor Woodrow, like all other companies, tried to align themselves with the possible winner of the next struggle. In addition to my job for the current President, another job was to build a palace for the Commander of the Army, while work was also being done for the leader of the opposition party.

Lagos Highland Games 1982

The third Lagos Highland Games was arranged for December, but Doug Edmunds had been paid off by his employer. Doug was in Glasgow, running his father's milk delivery business, which meant that he could keep in contact with the Heavies more easily, but that we had a more difficult task having lost his leadership in Nigeria. John recruited the Chief Accountant of the major supermarket to run our financial affairs. Kay Brown was a TA Signals captain, and very efficient. The Games ran smoothly, and the Nigerian 4 x 400 metre Commonwealth Games Gold Medal team ran for us. They were half a lap ahead of the next runners, and were barefoot on grass. The Nigerian Wrestler medallist from the same Brisbane games fought against the best that the US Marine Corps could produce. The Marines lost. The new US Marine Major had just arrived and had been watching "Roots" on TV. He was Afro-American, and really wanted to get to know his roots. "Gunny", the Gunnery Sergeant, took him in civilian clothes on foot through Lagos, to see for himself. I met him in his bar just after he got back. "Good God. Did we really come from these people? I don't believe it!" He had to be persuaded not to resign his commission immediately.

We decided to hold a mini-marathon for the expats. The Inspector-General of Police offered to patrol the route for us and asked me to show him the route. He got into my car and we were duly stopped by the illegal police road block at the other end of the road on which I lived. The corporal was insisting that I pay up, when my passenger got out and told him just what he could do with himself and to do it well before the Inspector General started to take some other, unspecified, rather unpleasant action against him. I was waved through this road block for the next few weeks.

The World's Strongest Man TV show

Doug Edmonds, by this time had returned to UK and took the format and turned it into "The Worlds Strongest Man Competition" which is still being shown annually on TV. Doug made money from selling the idea to a sports drug company, but did not realise that it would still be going some thirty or more years later. Bill Kazmier is still the Chief Judge for the show.

Hugh had taken up water-skiing and I bought a Fletcher speedboat, called "Twiggy", which I moored at Rock. We had a couple of good summers with the boat, until Hugh started working for an Outward Bound Instructor. Hugh changed to climbing and I sold the boat. Hugh's boss, Ron, had a contract taking Young Offenders on Adventure Training, climbing in local quarries, and canoeing. One offender was a wheelchair-bound arsonist, who was helped on the climbs. When it was not his turn, he made escape bids from the quarry in the wheelchair. Once Hugh looked down from the rock face and saw him stuffing rags into the fuel cap of the minibus. Another multi-offence boy took great delight in waving to policemen when Hugh was sitting next to him in the van, just so that Hugh would be associated with him.

Brief Return to Minna

The company received complaints from a contractor building new police stations in Minna, where our company was blasting water main trenches. They were alleging that we had apparently destroyed a police station under construction. I was sent to mollify the contractor and undertake repairs. The front wall had a new oversized window opening, and there was a hole in the roof slab. The contractor's labour force was in fear of their lives, as the blasting had not been finished. I looked at the whole building and took notes for my meeting with the Chief Superintendent who had lodged the complaint. I had worked with this policeman when I was in Minna before and he welcomed me with open arms. I discussed the many shortfalls in the work that I had seen, and he decided that the contractor should be dismissed and a competent company employed to finish the work. There was no mention of any blasting damage. I was loaded up with police dairies, calendars and key rings and escorted to the airport in style. The Managing Director had not expected this result, but gracefully accepted a set of police mementos.

In the early 1970s the Nigerian Government had issued Import Licences for cement as the local factories could not keep up with construction boom. Unfortunately, someone had added an extra zero to the total amount needed. This resulted in dozens of unseaworthy ships being chartered for one way trips. Many had to anchor off shore, waiting to unload, for up to a year. Others sank while waiting, and at least one was driven onto the beach. There is an ugly wreck on the beach opposite the Eko Hotel, ruining the view. The son of Sir Robert Mark, the Metropolitan Police Commissioner, was working in Nigeria and could not get his money out of the country. He realized that there were a lot of bored sailors on the ships, with foreign currency, and he arranged for working girls to visit the ships. He paid the girls in Naira and got paid in hard currency by the sailors. It was one of many schemes people had to design to get their locally paid salaries out of Nigeria. This man was an economist working for the Nigerian government and had to tour remote villages. Once he came to a wide river and took several days building a raft. He was watched by Africans on the far bank. Eventually he crossed the river and was escorted to the village chief who was sitting in state and proudly wearing his British Empire Medal. "And how is our Queen?" he was asked. Nigeria had been independent for some 15 years but the news had not reached this village!

Vultures

I made a short visit to Kano to sort out a sewer renewal contract. There I met up with Wally Burns, who I knew from our time in Nguru years ago. He had just been transferred from Sokoto to Kano by air and had all his worldly possessions in a carrier bag, including several beer bottles. Inebriated when he arrived in Kano, he did not follow the disembarking passengers but climbed on board a Jumbo ready to fly to Gatwick. Having selected a nice set in First Class, he opened a bottle of beer and settled down. It took a number of guards to remove him. Wally and I walked the site and peered down several manholes. Eventually we arrived at the manhole where Wally used to buy his "Peppered Chicken". We lifted the manhole lid and found that it was full of vulture carcases, not the chickens that he had thought that he had been eating. Wally went ballistic and chased the stallholder down the road, accusing him of trying to poison him.

Theft of a Mosque

Another trip I made was to Minna to attend a court case. Many years before, I had selected buildings for demolition and prepared all the Compulsory Purchase paperwork. I had been called as a witness because the real owner of a mosque had recently returned to find the building missing. He confronted the watchman that he had made responsible for the building. This was the man who everybody told me was the owner, and he had received the compensation. The real owner wanted his money. The defendant greeted me from the dock like an old friend and tried to tell the court that I had split the money with him. It was a nice try to avoid justice but the court believed me, thankfully.

Sokoto and Minna   1983

In 1983, during my third year in Lagos, work started to slow down. The Naira lost value and the government stopped issuing contracts. A decline set in. Staff numbers were reduced and I was sent off to be Chief Engineer on the Sokoto Hospital job in the far North. The client was not paying very promptly and we were working slowly. The Hausa tribe are polygamous, being Muslim and we had rented an upmarket Hausa home. There was a principal residence, used by the Project Manager, and four ensuite bedrooms at the other end of the courtyard for other staff

General Wushishi's Palace

After a short while in Sokoto, I was asked to be Area Manager in Minna. We still had our camp, and Mike Folkard who was at school with me in Nairobi, was building a palace for the Army Commander, General Wushishi. Mike went on leave, and I was left to deal with the Nominated Sub-Contractor for the internal furnishings and fittings. This ancient scraggy Italian crone was the bane of my life. She barely spoke English but expected me to understand, and accept, that I worked for her. Her husband worked out of their London office and was to send her containers of curtains and furniture. To meet the project deadline, she returned to UK and commandeered a Nigerian Frigate, which was on a formal visit to the Port of London, and loaded it with the containers! She expected me to read her flowery handwriting and send her radio messages to Lagos, for them to send on to UK. My radio operator could not read her writing, or understand her. The final row happened when she asked if I had sent a message. "We sent the words that we could read", I replied.

Debt collecting in Abuja

I was also meant to travel daily some 100 miles to the brand new Federal Capital, Abuja, where some Ministries had set up shop only months previously. There were few roads inside the capital, and no hotels. I was to try to get paid for various jobs that we had done for the Ministry of Communications, including the Abuja outer ring road. The bridges on this road were still missing when the company withdrew from Nigeria. In order to speak to a Minister, or even a senior staff member, there was a routine involving a lot of "dash". One first "purchased" entry to the building, then "paid" to have the relevant file produced. With the file, one could "register" with the door-keeper to the assistant to the man one wanted to see. He would issue a numbered card, and allow you to enter the room. There were about 20 other supplicants, and the numbered card was meant to indicate a place in the queue. When called, one presented the file, with Naira notes acting as bookmarks showing which pages were relevant to the current discussion. The assistant, if duly impressed, would indicate that, perhaps, he might allow you through to the top man. Another "receptionist" guarded the inner door, and he also needed persuading. Eventually one got to the boss, but on most days he had already left work by the time one had climbed through all the hoops. One just started again the next day.

One day, the Minister agreed to see me. He said that he had a cheque for me, but he could not be seen giving it to me because all the other contractors would want to know why they had not been paid. I had a thick paperback novel which I read while waiting at all the stages. The Minister wanted to read this novel. We agreed that I would swap the book for the cheque. But first I had to hide in the toilets until the office was locked up and all the other hopefuls thrown out. The lights went out, and a pipe burst. I thought that I was going to stay the night, in my soaking shoes. The

Minister found me. He got his book and I got the cheque. I never did find out how the novel ended!

Minna camp had become a centre for many expats in the area. The Italian dam building was still progressing and there were a number of English staff who visited Minna and stayed in our camp. One was the nurse that ran the site clinic, which had developed into a mini-hospital for the surrounding population. One weekend she came to Minna in a terrible state. A pregnant African woman was about to go into labour and the nurse asked for her to be watched overnight in case labour started. The Nigerian male nurse decided not to wake the nurse and to deliver the baby himself. Nigerians are powerful and heavy-handed. He pulled the baby and womb out in one piece, killing the mother. The Police and the woman's family blamed the English nurse.

The new state Government had taken on a number of Eastern European professionals. Two of the largest women I have met were Structural and Civil Engineers. There was a strong Polish contingent, still Communist. I had a local bank account for paying wages, but was not able to use it. The two signatories were not available anymore. One had died of a heart attack, playing tennis, and the other had failed to return from leave. I needed money to pay staff. I had also been instructed to maintain the wholesale beer account at the Kaduna Brewery. This meant buying beer by the articulated lorry load. As the only person resident in the camp, this would have taken a lot of drinking. By selling to the visiting expats, my source of income was guaranteed and I could pay wages. Previously, the ban on imported beers had come into effect. The company had a 40 foot container of Heineken Lager impounded on the day the ban was imposed. A year later, we managed to win a water well contract in the Port, very close to the container, and mysteriously, the container suddenly arrived in Minna. I was told to distribute the lager to the other sites and to bury the container!

Eventually, Taylor Woodrow gave up and sent me a memo saying that I "was on indefinite, unpaid, leave until the economic upturn occurs". I am still waiting for this economic upturn. The final indignity was travelling from Minna to Kano airport in the same car as the Italian female. What a journey that was.

After I left there was yet another coup in Nigeria. General Wushishi was forcibly retired from the Army and his assistant, a Brigadier, was found dead in a ditch. The opposition candidate that we had supported also disappeared. All that company effort to support three Presidential candidates and not one rose to power!

England 1983

I spent the next few months looking for work. Hundreds of CVs were sent off, thousands of telephone calls to agencies and prospective employers were made. I did attend several interviews, but it became clear that many employers were using my CV to back up tenders they were submitting. Until they were awarded the contract, there was no actual job for me. Jane and I would get up very early for the one hour drive to Exeter Station, so as to be in London for 10:00am interviews. One morning I was pulled over by a motorcycle policeman and lectured for not noticing him when I pulled out to overtake. When he allowed me to proceed, Jane noticed that I was writing something. She asked what I was doing. "I am noting his badge number so that I can get the Army to beat him up for £10". Then I realised that I was no longer in Nigeria, and all the rules had changed! The seven years in Nigeria had taken their toll.

We had bought a small Cornish cottage in Blisland from an Oil worker who was working on a rig in the Java Sea and needed cash. I made a low offer and he very promptly accepted. Our Solicitor was rather put out when we were instructed to collect the keys, at handover, from behind the bar in The Cobweb Pub, in Boscastle at 8:00pm on a Sunday. "Churchgate Cottage", Blisland, was a two bedroom stone and slate building at the church gate, on the village green. Jane ran the holiday lettings for about three years, while I was in Dhahran. One holiday couple decided not to disturb Jane when the water supply broke outside the cottage. A jet of water played on the lounge window the whole time. They filled the kettle from the public toilet nearby. Jane called the plumber that we had to check the place when we bought it. His wife said that he had been dead for two years. We eventually got the leak fixed.

At the end of his final term at boarding school, without telling his mother, he went on a parachute course. She only found out when he wrote asking for more money to pay for a second jump, because the first was mainly in cloud and he saw nothing on the way down. Jane was furious as she knew nothing about it and considered it very dangerous and the school to be irresponsible. Hugh replied "But Dad did it".

Hugh fell ill with stomach pains and our Doctor diagnosed appendicitis. Doc Young thought that the appendix might burst and that he needed to be in the operating theatre as soon as possible. We live some 60 miles from any hospital and the time it would take an ambulance to travel from Plymouth and back was too much. Doc Young telephoned the hospital and arranged for immediate surgery as soon as I could deliver Hugh by car. We were met in the car park by the surgeon and the Ward Sister. Although Hugh had had a rough time with Nigerians, he did not object to the Nigerian surgeon. What he did object to was the Ward Sister from the Children's Ward. He flatly refused to go to her ward because "You turn the lights off too early and I want to read Solzhenitsyn". He finally agreed to surgery once it was confirmed that he would be in the Male Surgery Ward.

Saudi Arabia – Dhahran   1984 - 1985

Eventually I accepted an offer from C.I.E. Consulting Engineers, who were based in Park Lane, London. The job was supervising the building of the Land Forces Facility Project, some 60 kilometres outside Dhahran in Saudi Arabia. This was a US $ 300M Army Base for a Mechanized Infantry Battalion. This consisted of 181 buildings, including ten, 10 storey tower blocks, repair shops for tanks and guided weapons, and with 43 km paved roads on a 15 sq. km. site.

I arrived on site during the fourth year of construction, and the scope of the project had changed over the years. Although a large number of buildings had been completed or nearly so, the roads had not even been started! Travelling around the site in my Chevrolet Caprice required me to have a dedicated Loading Shovel and tow rope. The site was on an area of "Sabkha", a deep deposit of waterlogged sand. All building were on large piled or raft foundations.

I reported to Ian Bell, a Quantity Surveyor, who had inherited the job of Resident Engineer after a horrific car crash on the notorious "Abqaiq Highway" had injured the previous RE. Two Saudi Project Managers from the Ministry Of Defence and Aviation (MODA) controlled our work. While the senior Saudi was on leave, the Turkish Chief draughtsman convinced the younger Saudi to promote him into the post that I was being recruited for! When I arrived, I was meant to report to the Turk! Eventually the correct seniority was sorted out, but there was open resentment from the Turk for the rest of my stay. The Turk had pointed out to the Saudis that I did not have a proper engineering degree, but only had the Loughborough Diploma. This meant that my Work Permit was in doubt. However, Loughborough decided to convert my Diploma into a BSc about this time and it turned up in the post just in time to prevent me being kicked out of Saudi Arabia.

I was in for a culture shock. On my first shopping trip, in Dhahran, I wanted to buy a radio for my villa. In Nigeria a guard lets you into the shop through the locked door. The customer is then allowed to see the empty box for the item that you wanted. A price was agreed, finally, and one paid. A receipt with four copies was made out. Three receipts and the money are passed through a small letter box in a steel sheet wall at the rear of the shop, and two receipts are returned covered in official looking rubber stamps. The third receipt is passed to the storeman for him to unlock the store and retrieve the box contents. After checking that all the contents are there, the box is hidden from sight under one's clothes and one's wallet hidden. Only then is it safe to leave the shop, which needs the guard to unlock the door, which he does in return for the final copy of the receipt. The customer then steps into the street on the lookout for bag snatchers. In Dhahran, however, it was all so normal. I found myself out in the street still putting change into my wallet in full view of passing pedestrians. I had a panic attack because I felt so vulnerable to attack by thieves. These Nigerian fears wore off and I found it a pleasure to shop in a virtually crime free country.

The permanent MODA staff accommodation had been built and furnished. I had a three bedroom villa with all the latest American equipment. One drawback was that the villas on either side were reserved for very senior Saudis visiting from Riyadh. One had been taken over by the Dhahran Chief of Police for his own (gambling) purposes, and the other was used by a Colonel Prince from MODA, who was in charge of our Project. His problem was that his wife came from Dhahran and she took the opportunity to visit relatives when he made a trip. I had not been there long when, one evening, the Prince knocked at my door asking for refuge from a house full of women next door. He produced a bottle of Chivas Regal Whisky as compensation for his sudden request. After several rounds, Jane telephoned and I took the set into the kitchen, on a very long cable, to talk to her. She did not believe that I was getting drunk with a Saudi Prince in a Muslim country and hung up.

One of the joys of Dhahran was that one could watch three different TV stations showing "Dallas" at the same time. Kuwait, Bahrein and the Saudi Aramco oil company showed different episodes so one could switch back and forward to keep up with the plot!

I needed a Saudi Driving Licence in order to travel the 60km into town. It took several months to obtain. There were two reasons. Firstly my wife had insisted that I obtain a joint English/Welsh UK licence. I was asked for a certified translation of the Welsh half, but this proved impossible to get in Saudi Arabia. Secondly, although our work address was in the Eastern Province, our Chamber of Commerce address was in Riyadh. Eventually I was able to ask the next door neighbour, the Dhahran Police Chief, to help. I still had to give a pint of blood which was taken by a female nurse after my arm was put through a hole in the wall. I visited the Driving Test Centre with a Turkish foreman from the site. He failed his actual test because "In 35 years I have never had to use reverse gear!"

I was the Deputy Resident Engineer, responsible for all materials, drawings, contractual letters, and reports, Claims assessments, and Progress reporting. For an item to be approved a manufacturers brochure was needed. These had to pass scrutiny of the Saudi authorities. The X-Ray equipment for the Clinic had a prominent photograph of the bed in use by a female patient who was suitably covered, but I had to get a brochure printed showing the bed without a patient. After a lot of fuss, the supplier managed to print a special copy of the brochure for us but had made the ultimate mistake of having it printed in Israel!!! We never got an X-Ray machine approved for the Clinic.

There was a range of moving sand dunes marching towards the Base from the North East, and we planted a major windbreak of three lines of trees to head off the sand. The trees were to be irrigated with Treated Sewage Effluent, collected from the Sewage Treatment Plant. However, the Contractor decided to deliberately mis-read the drawings, preventing the collection of effluent! There should have been an impervious layer under the sand filter beds to direct the liquid to the evaporation ponds, and onward to the irrigation system. The Contractor refused to install the impervious layer, and an angry meeting was held to discuss the matter. He would not budge. After the meeting, I asked Marwan Farouk, the contractors engineer and a Lebanese Muslim, if he knew my old college room-mate, Dany Chamoun. Dany was, at that time, leader of the Christian Militia in Beirut. I asked Marwan for his home address and suggested that I might ask Dany to pay him a visit during his next leave in war torn Lebanon. The next day, the contractor started fixing the impervious layer! What it is to have powerful friends! I had no intention of contacting Dany, but Marwan agreed with everything I suggested after that. It was not a normal contractual way of sorting out differences, but it worked.

One day we were all ordered to attend a medal ceremony at Dhahran Airbase. A Saudi fighter jet had shot down an Iranian intruder and the Saudi pilot was being honoured. An American near me in civilian clothes muttered that the pilot had "frozen" when the missile warning sounded. "If I hadn't released the rocket, I would not be here today".

The contractor denied that he had responsibility for all the telephones, apart from laying cables from offices to the exchange. I had to allocate the position of each hand set and the degree of access to local, national or international numbers, as well as two military networks of telephones. I managed this by designing a computer programme on a Sinclair ZX computer with 48k of memory!

Royal Visit

The very ornate main (and at that time, the only) gate had a concrete canopy. This had already been built but was too low to allow a broken down tank on a low-loader to reach the newly added Tank Repair facility. A new site entrance was built. At this main gate, there was still no link road to the main highway. The link road crossed a particularly swampy bit of Sabkha. Prince Sultan, The Minister of Defence and Aviation, decided to visit the project and panic set in. The contractor actually asked for advice on how to get the road built in time for the Prince to use. For the previous four years, they had blithely steamed ahead with their own preferred interpretation of the contract documents. I suggested that a bulldozer excavate the Sabkha down to 2 metres below finished surface level and large boulders be rolled in, similar to the edges of the Port Talbot Breakwater job. This was all done under water, but produced a firm embankment, and the link road was completed in time for the Royal Visit.

However, just before the Royal visit, a senior Prince was sent to see if all was ready for Prince Sultan, Minister of Defence and Aviation (later, in 2015, King). The Prince arrived the day before the Eid Holiday weekend when virtually all staff were on leave. The first thing that he noted was the architect's fancy colour scheme. The boy's school was blue and the girl's school was pink. Overnight these were painted the correct sand brown. The architect was in UK on leave, or he would (I felt) have been dragged out and shot. I was requested to produce a visit brochure for the prince in Arabic in a day, and an adjacent site also needed my help for their brochure.

Another problem with constructing in Sabkha was the very high water table. Dewatering was virtually impossible in the sandy soil. Senior officer's houses and the various Messes were to have Swimming Pools. Until these pools were built and filled with water, the empty pools (being watertight) floated on the ground water and often popped up above the ground! With my Lagos experience, I was able to show the contractor how to build a heavy mass concrete base under the pools, to work against the ground water pressure.

There were other problems on this site. Many of the Army officers had already moved into completed family houses. However, the contractor still had to repair or replace faulty or broken fittings. We received a complaint that the very expensive, US made, kitchen units were warping and falling off walls. On investigation, we discovered that the families were in the habit of killing the Friday goat in the kitchen, and then hosing down the room to remove the blood. The units had become thoroughly soaked. After replacing the damage at the contractor's expense, we told the Army to teach and train the wives and family servants in how to use modern, Western, buildings. We also used to send single electricians to house to change light bulbs. After one lad failed to return, a search party was sent out. In one particular house, all the women locked the doors and made use of the electrician as a sex slave for three days, finally kicking him out when he was thoroughly "used up". Other households started to play the same trick on defenceless staff. In Saudi, the word of a Saudi woman would carry more weight than that of a Third World National, so the lads kept quiet, rather than face a very long time in goal, or a trip to "Chop Square". From then on, a gang of at least three men were sent. One man stood in the front doorway to keep it open at all times, while the other two did the work together.

Financial difficulties

The Contractor, Pegel Arabia, was in financial difficulties. Years before, they had completed the massive National Guard complex in Riyadh but payments were still only slowly dribbling through. Then they built the International Airport at Riyadh, funding the work from the slow National Guard payments. Payments for the Airport suffered similar delays. What little surplus funds that were finally available, were used for the Dhahran contract. My employer had managed to get a six months extension to our contract in August 1984, on condition that our local Managing Director left the Kingdom that night. Eventually, in November 1984, the bubble burst. A small supplier had the Pegel Arabia Managing Director arrested at the Airport for debts. (Ironically, he was on his way to Paris to secure further funding). Other debtors joined in. Diesel supplies were cut off and we had no power to run the camp. Catering supplies stopped. The laundry contractor held onto clothes until he was paid, resulting in my villa being filled with naked expats waiting for their sole remaining set of clothes to finish washing. 700 Thai workmen, waiting for air tickets home, could not travel. The telephone microwave link was shut down, preventing us from calling for help! Things started to get ugly. The Thais had nothing to do and were starving, and they resorted to gambling. A rich Thai could buy food. Eventually a gambling debt resulted in a stabbing death. As we were on an Army Base, the Military Police were called in to find the culprit(s). A number were hauled away, some never to return. Meanwhile, the workforce tried to present grievances to the Labour Court. If two or more men travelled together in a taxi (60 Km) to the court, it was considered a "Strike" and banned under Saudi Law. The Military Police enforced this strictly. The poor Thais had no chance. Meanwhile, we organized a collection of scrap metal, which we sold to get diesel money and food.

By February 1985, our families in UK started to panic because they could no longer contact us. Luckily, the senior Pegel staff had a compound in Dhahran, and we were able to use the telephone from there. Jane contacted several UK employment agencies to see if they could find out what was happening, and where I was. I managed a final call one evening. From the telephone room, I could see into the dining room of the Pegel's Chief Accountant. The curtains were open, and I watched plates of food being placed on the dining table. This man still had access to funds, and was helpful in getting us food and some fuel for the generators. Later, I heard that he had managed to spirit his family out of Saudi that night. They had already left before the food was on the table.

The Resident Engineer got away on leave, and I was left with 12 staff. Our company discovered that they had very little chance of a payment and decided that they would close down operations. I had a Local Purchase Order pad and issued each staff member with an LPO for an air ticket to their home country. We all grabbed our tickets (and I still wonder if the Travel Agent ever got paid). Meanwhile, we could not leave until the necessary Exit/Re-Entry stamp had been placed in our Passports. We sent off the passports to our Riyadh office. Later, we discovered that there had been a police raid on a suspected gambling den, and all our staff were in goal or hospital, the Chief Clerk having jumped from a second floor window. Eventually, the passports all returned and I let staff go. My passport had not been returned. I tried to find out where it was, and stumbled across it locked in the Turk's desk drawer. I was not best pleased, but sent it off for the visa. On 1st April, I received a telex, instructing or ordering all staff to take voluntary redundancy and leave Saudi Arabia. I was only too pleased to get the order, but carefully sent in my resignation to London, timed before their telex. I got back to London, with a great sigh of relief, and eventually managed to get some arrears of salary from the company.

England (again) 1985

From May to December 1985, I was at home trying to find work. All this time I was funding the mortgages from savings. We decided to sell the holiday cottage, which we had bought during my time in Lagos, and this provided a small financial relief.

One potential employer was a large agricultural company, with plush offices in Bath. They had a promise of EU funding for an overseas aid project, and needed a road engineer. Some bright spark in Brussels had decided to donate funds to Pakistan, to convert the hashish growing Hunza valley in the North West Frontier District into a market garden, growing vegetables. A road over a high mountain pass would allow the produce to be delivered to a grateful world. Hugh's housemate, Bob, was a climber and had spent that summer walking in the very same mountains. He was terrified, at the top of a mountain pass, when he approached what would have been "my" valley, only to be stopped by a man waving a Kalashnikov rifle. This Pathan's next action surprised him even more. "You know my friend, Simon, from Llanberis?" he asked. Simon Yates was the man who cut Joe Simpson's rope in Chile, as recorded in the book and film "Touching the Void". Bob advised Hugh to tell me that the Pathans would not like any interference in the lucrative hashish market, and to refuse the job. In the event, better brains in Brussels prevailed and the scheme was cancelled.

Hugh had taken up climbing with an outdoor pursuits instructor on Bodmin Moor. A girl from the boarding school in same the town as Hugh's school agreed to meet him in a pub up on the moor during the holidays. The Instructor, Hugh, and the girl were enjoying a drink when in walked her very angry father. Sir Chay Blythe had rowed across the Atlantic and performed many other feats of seamanship. Hugh vanished into the toilets; the girl fled through the kitchens and rode off on her horse, leaving the instructor to explain.

I was getting rather desperate when The Sultan of Oman's Ministry of Defence showed interest. I was interviewed in London by Lt Col Dick Holland RE, Head of Operation and Maintenance in the Omani Ministry of Defence Engineering Division. He noted my TA Commission in the Royal Engineers, and said that virtually all the expat staff were ex-RE. I was accepted and then had to go through a very long process of recruitment by this foreign government.

Torquay Leisure Centre

While this was proceeding, I took a three month job as an Agency engineer, working for Cementation, building the Torquay Leisure Centre, now called the English Riviera Conference Centre. This was the first time that Cementation (South West) had a contract with Nominated Contractors doing part of the work and the Project Manager and his deputy had only ever worked on road schemes. The actual building had two distinct parts, one was straight forward rectangular rooms on three floors, and the other was a swimming pool complex. The staff was split on similar lines, with regular Cementation staff doing the easy bit. I had a bunch of expats with a range of skills, doing the difficult side and this led to rivalry between the sections. My General Foreman had recently returned from a Sri Lankan water project which involved using elephants for pipe laying. The setting out engineer had recently surveyed and set out oil wells across the Omani desert. One engineer had just completed several tower blocks in Kuwait. The other engineer had worked on the diamond mines in Angola. The foreman carpenter had worked in the Gulf, and had bought properties in Torquay with the proceeds. The cementation team were in awe of our experience and the difference in the output in the two sections was visible.

The Site Agent did not understand how to make claims for changes in the contract. I tried to help, but eventually the Contracts Director was sent to site to help him out.

The Client had hired a firm of Consulting Engineers as Site Supervision. I found a design problem that needed solving. When I asked the Resident Engineer to get clarification from the Client, panic set in. The RE did not want to ask, as it may reflect on his competence. Eventually, I discovered that the designer was David George, founder and owner of Module 2, a company based in Bridgend, South Wales. Dave had not only worked with me in Port Talbot, but we had also been officers in the TA together. A quick telephone call solved the problem.

On my birthday, I went into Torquay with the General Foreman and others for a drink. The lad who had been in Angola told us his stories of journeys through a war zone. Before he joined the company, he was sent on a six week Portuguese language course in Lisbon. On arrival in Angola at night he was given a car and driver to take him some 200Km to his work site. Cars were regularly searched and, leaving the airport, a soldier wanted to examine his suitcase. To do this, he put his rifle down so that he could use his torch. 150 km later, at another road block, another soldier asked why he was carrying an AK47 in the boot of the car. "My little Portuguese was not good enough to reply", he told us. The next morning, hanging from the tower crane over the whole of Torquay, was a 24 foot x 4 foot shutter with birthday greetings to me painted on it.

Eventually, I passed the Medical and the Omani authorities started processing my Visa. Until the visa was approved, flight dates could not be booked. However, I could see that I might suddenly have to drop everything and fly without warning, if the Sultanate insisted. Giving notice could have been a problem, but the day that the call came, I fell off a long ladder and twisted my right knee again. This meant that I could cancel my contract on sickness grounds. The tower crane lifted me from the depths of the shuttering and over to the ambulance. A Belgian lady doctor fully encased the leg in plaster and sent me home. Jane had got a friend to drive her to Torquay to collect me. That night, my knee continued to swell, but it was rigidly encased in plaster. Our local GP had to cut me free. By the time the swelling had receded and I could walk again, Christmas arrived. I was told that I would be flying out to Muscat on New Years Eve.

Oman - Muscat 1986 - 1987

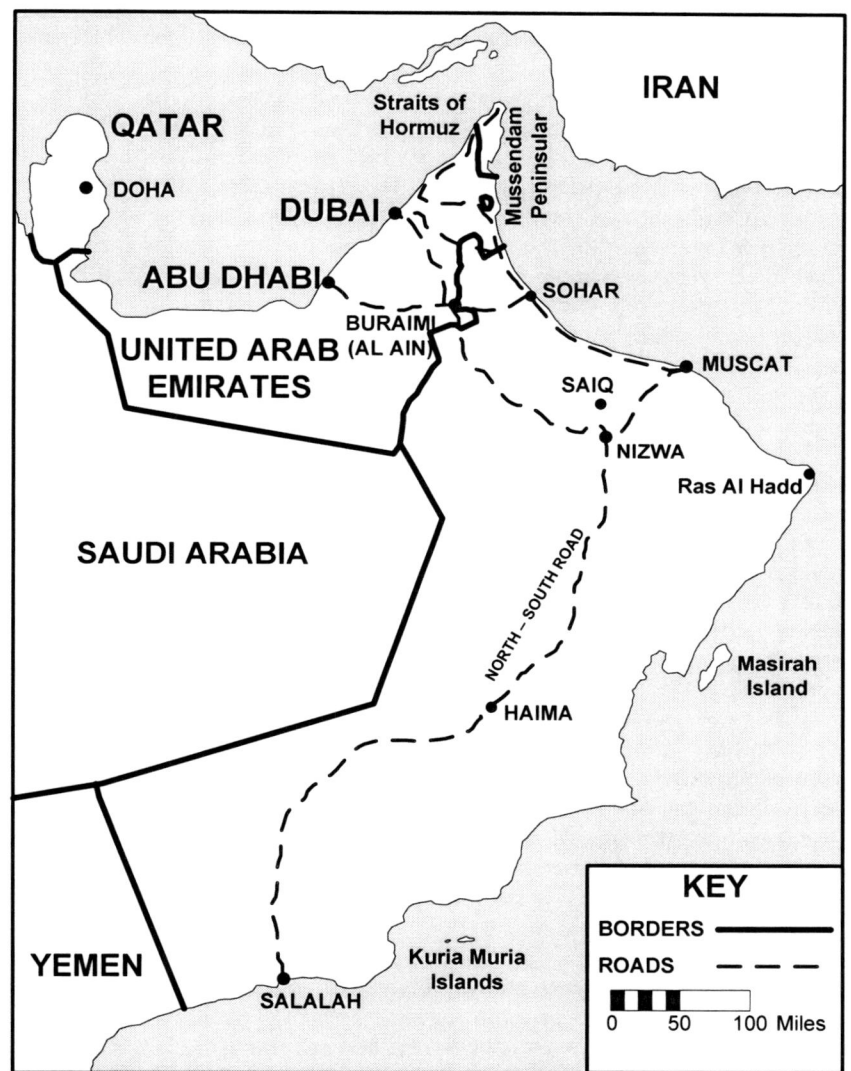

SULTANATE OF OMAN 1985 - 90

I arrived in Muscat, at Seeb International Airport, on New Years Eve. The Ministry Of Defence Engineering Division (MODED) Personnel man delivered me to the Jebel Mess in MAM Camp and I was given a room. Either side were people getting ready to attend a formal Dinner Dance in the Mess. I knew no one and decided to spend the evening recovering from the flight. The next day I met my neighbours. Mike Holliday, I discovered, was the mysterious Royal Engineer

235

Warrant Officer that I had seen in Mombasa. On the other side lived Les Painting and his wife Jacqui, who was out on a short visit. Both men were to be working with me, and they took me into the office to meet my new boss, Lt Col Dick Holland, Head of Operation and Maintenance. He introduced me to the Chief Engineer, Brigadier Bob Wheatley. I was to take over from the Senior Civil Engineer and we had about a month of handover before he finally left Oman.

The first job was to get all the necessary official Passes, a Driving Licence, and a Bank Account. After finishing with the MODED procedures, I was escorted out of the Camp to a branch of the bank used by everyone. I was given an application form, which I completed, and had to wait for a cashier to attend to me. Behind the counter there were two Omani girls chattering away and ignoring all the customers. I realised that they were talking in Swahili. I made a comment in Swahili, and they were very embarrassed and rushed to complete my application. I realised then that there were many ex-Zanzibaris living in Oman, as they had run the Slave trade on the East African coast for centuries. These "Zanzibaris" were the ruling elite of the country.

Oman is some 2,500 miles from end to end and is, in fact, three separate tracts of land. The Mussandam peninsula juts out into the Straights of Hormuz, beyond Fujirah which is part of The United Arab Emirates. Within Fujirah lies a small area of land owned by Oman, as a result of a Royal marriage dowry. This piece of land had an airstrip for which I was responsible. Then there was the main part of Oman, reaching all the way down to the Yemen border. Inland, Oman stretched out into the "Empty Quarter" of Saudi Arabia. The border with Saudi Arabia was, at that time, not marked. The boundaries in the Middle East had been drawn on maps following the Sykes-Picot Agreement after the Great War. Southern Arabia was, in the 1920s, not mapped and had no official borders. At that time, the RAF, based in Aden, supported various Political Officers in a number of Trucial States and flew regular trips to different locations. To simplify arrangements, Wing Commander Hotham instructed a draughtsman called Botham to draw a simple set of straight lines line on the map indicating the separation of Yemen and Oman, without actually allowing for tribal and geographical boundaries being considered. This line became known as the "Hotham-Botham Line".

My new responsibilities, besides giving civil engineering advice, included "owning" some 300 items of plant together with the operators and workshops, a Painting Section, a Minor Works Section for new builds under £100,000, a Materials Laboratory, a Plant Nursery, and some 30 airstrips and 2,000 kilometres of military roads. In my section I had a total of some 350 staff. MODED Oman was divided into seven areas, each with an Area Works Officer and staff reporting to Dick Holland. They had a direct labour maintenance responsibility for all military bases in their areas, including water and electricity supply and public health (sewage treatment).

My section included Les Painting, an ex-RE WO1 Soil Mechanic, who ran the Laboratory and tested runways for me. Mike "Doc" Holliday was part of an Airfield Damage Repair team, more of a think tank for emergency tasks. Richard Mitchell ran the Minor Works Section. Bill Brownlee was the Roads Superintendant, with

Workshop support from Joe Longstaff. The Painting Superintendent had a large staff of painters, and had to repaint all buildings, signs and road markings on a regular basis.

There were other Divisions within MODED. The Projects Division designed and supervised contractors undertaking new builds over £100,000. The Electricity Supply section ran power stations on bases, and exported electricity to the National Grid. The Water Section drilled water wells. A Transport Section delivered stores to outlying areas, and an Admin Section kept control of finances.

After settling in, I went on a series of inspection trips with Bill Brownlee to see some of the airstrips and other road maintenance jobs. The Fort at Buraimi, adjacent to Al Ain in UAE, was on my list. This was mentioned in a Goon Show sketch but it did actually exist. A small garrison lived in this mud and wattle fort. To reach Buraimi, out in the open desert, the road from the coast passed a Border Control point placed at very narrow pass in the mountains and 50km from the actual border. I had a Border Pass for my government vehicle and each trip was logged in. However, it made more sense to do a circular inspection trip, up the coast and through to Border Post, returning on the desert side of the mountains down to Nizwa and back to Muscat. After several trips, the authorities decided that I was exporting government vehicles (possibly for sale in UAE), as they were never recorded any return trips through the Border Post! I was eventually cleared of the charges, caused by having this Border Post some 50 miles from the actual Border.

Another long trip was to Thumrait and Salalah with my predecessor, Roger. MODED had purchased three Komatsu twin engined scrapers. Komatsu only ever made six of these machines. They were quite powerful and filled the 14 cubic metre bowl easily. The problem came with releasing the load and spreading it. The massive hydraulic rams used to push the back plate of the loaded bowl forward failed to do this. Instead, the rams ejected the rear engine off the chassis! Komatsu were prevailed upon to sort out what appeared to be a major design fault. They sent a

large team of Japanese mechanical engineers and welders to Thumrait, in an effort to beef up the rear chassis. Massive amounts of plate metal were added. Roger had obtained a Black Belt in Martial Arts following a stay in Japan. He threatened the Japanese workers, in Japanese, that he would practice his skills on them if the work was not expedited. They worked 15 hour days afterwards. Eventually, some improvement was reached, but we never attempted to fully fill a scraper bowl again. We did not trust them.

Komatsu Scraper - Dhofar - Oman

We went on to Salalah, and I found a note in the MODED Bar inviting me to the Taylor Woodrow Camp just across the road. I have seen the Bush Telegraph in action before, so I was not too surprised that my old boss from Nigeria had heard that I was visiting. I had a very pleasant evening with my old boss and I knew many of the others from Nigeria.

Thumrait and Salalah were the two MODED "Areas" in Dhofar, the southern province of Oman. The Dhofar Insurgency had recently ended, after years of battling Communist Yemen forces backed by Soviet and East German support. This war was part of Colonel Nasser's masterplan to take control, eventually, of the Persian Gulf and the oil. Nasser would then be able to offer Russia a Gulf port for the Navy and would allow world domination by the Communists. The SAS and the Oman Forces finally won, and a fragile peace was agreed, leaving Nasser's hopes in tatters. The Jebalis, (local Dhofari Arabs with their own language and almost Ethiopian looks), had agreed to give allegiance to the Sultan, but only in return for Civil Aid. MODED provided and maintained almost 2,000 Km of roads in the region. This was because the local government departments had not yet been set up to look after remote areas. Civil Aid units had built mosques, water supply points, schools, clinics, and some small power stations. However, occasionally a village would raise a complaint and they would stop the first government vehicle and take it, because "the Sultan promised to help us". Inspections and work on roads meant travelling in convoys, with armed escorts.

I was based in Muscat, in MAM Camp, the Headquarters of the Sultan's Land Forces. Each time there was a Parade attended by the Sultan, I would have to repaint all buildings, road lines and signs, replace trees and other plants. All floodlights, helicopter landing pad lights, and street lighting had to be checked, even though the Parade was in broad sunlight. Once, the square was filled with troops waiting in the sun but there was no sign of the Sultan. His car had been stopped at the Main Gate by the Corporal on Gate Duty. He had been told not to let any vehicle into camp, because the Sultan was expected. The Sultan got out, promoted the Corporal on the spot for his diligence, and proceeded to the parade.

The original Ministry of Defence building, dating from the 19th Century, was Bayt Al Falaj (Translates as "The house by the Falaj" – the Arabic water supply system). This five storey white fort was the office of the Minister of Defence. I was involved in installing a small lift to the top floor office. Due to building restraints, this had to be a very small one. Nominally a two person unit, the Defence Minister was some 20 stone and there would have been no space for an attendant. Safety considerations required that instructions in the event of failure be available for the only occupant. The manufacturer provided these in Arabic and English, and installed them without me seeing them. An angry Minister demanded that they be changed. They read "In the event of a passenger being raped in the lift...." This was meant to read "trapped in the lift". My mind tried to cope with the thought of anyone trying to rape a 70 year old very corpulent Minister in a confined space.

The Camp was run by a British Major, who had been a Guards RSM before coming to Oman. He wanted all the water courses on the Camp straightened up, so that they looked "Regimental". We told him that nature has a mind of its own, and that the task was futile. He would not listen, so we obeyed orders. A very short time later, the heavens opened and rain water found its own way across the Camp. Several brand new water courses were formed. An ammunition bunker was left cantilevered out over a 20 foot deep brand new water course. Other roads which had never previously flooded were now submerged in mud. Building foundations were exposed. We were pleased to be able to say "I told you so".

By March the weather was getting warmer. The heat and mugginess was very debilitating. 115°F and about 80% humidity leave one feeling about as strong as a lettuce leaf washed in hot water! To save electricity, the Power Station would switch off all Air-conditioning Units in our accommodation, as they were expected to be empty during the day. One of my supervisors came back from an extended trip to his Portacabin and burnt his hand on the metal bed-leg! His A.C. had been off for a week. Ramadan made drinking tea or coffee difficult from 0630 to 1200, as it could only be done out of the gaze of a Muslim.

I managed a quick trip back to UK to see Jane, and to have my knee looked at by a surgeon, having twisted it again. On my return, I found waiting three very thick envelopes full of maps, surveys, lab tests and reports for three new airstrips that had been surveyed while I was away. One was on a mountain top, which some bright RAF Loan Service Officer had thought was a good idea. I felt sure that they selected sites by throwing darts at the map. These reports were all waiting for instant answers.

Having had keyhole surgery on the knee, the Military Hospital examined the result but I failed to get Sick Leave retrospectively. Sister Candy Williams, once a GB Olympic swimmer, suggested I avoid Physiotherapy, as she knew the people concerned. My Painting Superintendent, Dave, went for Physio at the hospital, for knee problems, and his horror tales put me off. The ward was full of 'Hooray Henry' type officers with Squash injuries. Dave commented from behind a curtain that Squash was a game invented by two Physiotherapists and an Undertaker, and a very stony silence followed. Les Painting was a very fit squash player in my section. A visiting power station engineer, having nearly rebuilt most of the MAM Power Station diesel generators after servicing them, needed a game of squash. I introduced him to Les and they went off to play. Les was a bit too aggressive and managed to make his opponent run into the wall, breaking his arm. He was unable to complete the re-build of the last generator and had to fly home to UK. The head of the Electrical Division was not a happy bunny.

One night, Dick Holland came round at 11.30pm. His Majesty had complained about a road close to the border with the United Arab Emirates. It must be repaired at once! Pointless to tell him that it wasn't one of ours!! The Brigadier ADC to HM tried to get the local Fujirah Municipality to do the work, as it was their road, but we finished up doing it all. After a very severe storm, during the Khareef, a high and unstable slope had slid down and engulfed a Police Station at the border between UAE and Oman. The road was now in the sea. There was now no road link to the Mussandam Peninsula as the only interior road had also been washed away. Low cloud prevented food being delivered by air, and sea conditions prevented ships from entering the harbour at Khassab. Mussandam was running low on food and fuel. My plant supervisor reported that blasting would be required. This presented a minor Diplomatic challenge. The explosives had to be purchased in Dubai, transported across Abu Dhabi and Fujirah, for use by Omani workers, in Fujirah. Our convoy of camouflaged plant and vehicles also had to get permission to cross into Fujirah to reach the site. We completed this job and went on to rebuild the internal link road, which used the bed of the wadi. It is a good job that we did not have to cost out each task. We were a Direct Labour organization, able to respond to any emergency.

Our MODED Blaster, Mohammed, was the son of the only licensed Omani Blasting Contractor. Dick Holland and I met the father and asked why he was not employing his son, only to be told that the son was not safe with explosives. We often had small demolition jobs to do, one of which involved "agitating" the bottom of a hand-dug water well to encourage more water flow. We were tasked with one agitation job. Mohammed, our "expert", wanted to drill several holes in the dry bottom and blast the rock out. His first mistake was to use a petrol generator at the bottom of the well, to power the drill. The labourers were found unconscious because of the exhaust fumes. Before he blasted, he stuffed the well with old lorry and car tyres to stop rock pieces from destroying the village. Dick and I made sure that we were both out of Oman on leave when he was finally allowed to take the explosives out of the stores. In effect, he was building a giant mortar, and we foresaw plenty of damage. After the blast, there was considerable damage from flying lorry tires but no human injuries. The well was deepened enough for it to start collecting water again.

Exercise Saif Sareea (Swift Sword)

A big job for my section was announced in May 1986. A big Exercise, involving British Army, Navy and Airforce units, was being planned for November 1986. With two other MODED staff, I was called to the initial planning meeting in SAF Headquarters to hear what was expected of us. No one seemed able to give us detailed requirements and even the dates for the Exercise seemed to be secret! I gathered that a beach assault by 40 Commando, together with Omani tanks, would be landing on the beach. The RAF would be billeted on Masirah Island and use the runway to lift 2 Para for a drop on the Exercise area. There was a requirement for a Hercules runway, and some helipads (for HM to visit), so we started immediately on these tasks as time was short.

I knew that there would be a lot of Umpire staff, British and Omani soldiers, and visiting VIPs, all of whom would need water and toilets. No one at the meeting wanted to tell me numbers so that I could begin to plan. I was given a list the next day and started planning. In addition to the 6,000 Brits, there were also some 3,000 Omani troops involved.

I assembled a massive convoy of plant, living accommodation trailers, vehicles, and fuel tankers to send to the Exercise area, to build the new runway. The convoy was inspected by Brigadier Wheatley and approved. He had earlier stated that he did not think that I was up to the task. The convoy set off, with Bill Brownlee in command. On arrival

240

at Ras Al Hadd, they tried to set up camp, but Bill had left all the accommodation keys in Muscat! Many doors were broken that night.

This major new project required a full inspection visit by Brigadier Wheatley and his senior staff to check that all the facilities on Masirah Island were able to cope with a long stay by hundreds of RAF aircraft and personnel. I was included on the team as Dick Holland's advisor. The senior Electrical Engineer needed to look at the island Power Station, and I was told to bring my newly appointed Omani assistant (a Prince). SOAF have very strict rules about protocol. At Seeb Airport, our party threw the SOAF Ground Staff into confusion. Brigadier Wheatley insisted that I carry the files he was using to discuss the forthcoming exercise. But, as I was not a Senior Officer, I was not allowed in the VIP Lounge with the rest of the party. An exception was eventually allowed, if someone could guarantee my behavior. Then the flight was called and I was extracted from the VIP Lounge to travel out to the Boeing 737 with the rest of the lower ranks. The rest of the party boarded using the front steps and insisted that I move forward (with the files) and sit with them. There was a long delay while we waited for the member of the Royal Family to board, to sit in Seat A1. Eventually, my new Omani assistant was deferentially shown to his Royal seat!

Sometimes, MODED would provide assistance to research teams. Brigadier Wheatley asked me to fly with him to a camp in the middle of the Wahiba Sands. A husband and wife team of Entomologists were searching for bugs, and we had supplied a generator and a water tank. They had spent years looking throughout the whole of Arabia for a particularly rare species, only to have a sample try to get into their tent one night! They had a particularly fine specimen of a Chapman's Gerbil preserved in a bottle. Wheatley was holding the bottle and nearly dropped it when he was told that this animal was responsible for introducing the Black Death into Europe. There are only a sparse scattering of bushes in the Sands as there is no rainfall. These bushes gather moisture from the onshore sea breezes, and by a feat of nature transfer the moisture down to the roots.

At the end of Ramadan, all government departments closed down for a week for the Eid Celebrations. Les Painting, Mike Holliday, and I had official recces to do at Ras Al Hadd, the most easterly point on the Arabian Peninsula. This was where the Exercise was to be held, and no Army Officers had yet visited the area to do any planning! I needed to get some possible locations for umpire's camps, landing sites, helipads, and the like, sorted out before the Army arrived with maps and unworkable ideas. We packed the Land Cruiser in the evening for the trip. We had 2 Jerrycans of fuel, sand channels and spade, tow-ropes, a second spare wheel, beds and sleeping bags, 24hr Army ration packs and other minor items. We were only going away for one night! Next morning two of us were up at dawn and raring to go. Les needed breakfast, so we waited until he had finished. We set off, but Les made us go back for his sunglasses. We set off again, but Les wanted his fags out of his car. We set off again, and Les wanted to fill his 2 gallon water jug at the water cooler!!!! It took us 7 km just to get out of camp. We got to Ras Al Hadd in time for a very pleasant lunch cooked by the Brit supervisor. No cooks working during the day during Ramadan. Having bought a fish for bait, some went down to the beach to fish, Mike Holliday and I went off to do a recce for a VIP helicopter site and viewing stand about 50 km away, overlooking the beach that the Special Boat Section, the Royal Marines, and others, would be landing on in October. I took some photos of fishing dhows and turtle tracks in the sand. When we got back, the three of them had caught one fish between them, smaller than the fish they took with them to use for bait! They maintained that the turtles kept eating the bait. Turtles were around but don't come up the beach in sunlight!

At midnight we drove off to another beach to see turtles laying eggs. The turtle digs a four foot diameter hole. The beach was covered with these "Tank-traps" and, as we didn't want to disturb them, we didn't use torches. It was a good test of my recently repaired knee! We found several turtles, digging by spraying sand with the flippers, coming up the beach and returning. What also was really impressive was the sky. The Milky Way seemed to be only 100 foot above us. It was so clear and bright. The sand is phosphorescent, and it sparkled when you walked. Light pollution was non-existent.

R101 Mast - Ras Al Hadd - Oman

The next morning we all drove to the actual most Easterly point of Arabia, and found a rusting steel tower, about 50 feet high. It had a strange, but strong, circular handrail at the top. A local told us that it was a mooring tower for the Airship R101, and that they were still waiting for it to arrive. Imperial Airways had hoped to set up a route from UK to Karachi. On the maiden flight in 1930, it crashed in France, killing 48. The tower was still there sixty years later.

We prepared to head south to Thumrait and Salalah, via MAM, a 1,000km journey. The next morning we slept in until 9.00. Then we had a long cooked breakfast. After breakfast, we took ten minutes to pack, and found that the cooks had made us lunch. Ramadan was over, and they laid on the equivalent of Christmas Dinner!! We were bloated when we finally got away. After a night back in MAM Camp, on Tuesday morning we set off again, with Les under pain of death if he asked us to go back for anything. Later, we found that he had forgotten his shoes. He had to spend three days in "Hong Kong Safety Boots" (Flip-flops). The journey was long and boring. Muscat to Adam - refuel - on to Haima. After Haima, there was a sand storm driving dunes across the road. Some kind soul had placed two little road-cones at the foot of the moving dune! It took eight hours at a steady 90 mph, on a straight and level road. The three of us shared the driving. We arrived late in the afternoon arrival in Thumrait. The MODED Mess was having a "Horse race" evening by the pool side. They had laid on a "Chinese Night" and we had the meal out on the club patio, eating excellent food, from the newly promoted Indian generator mechanic and his labourer.

242

Les hoped to find some more Geodes. These are large rock crystals, hollow with the crystals growing inward. They are usually cut in half and polished for display. In the South, MODED used Geodes to mark runways, as they did not blow away. A series of panels of Geodes, 2 metres by 1 metre, painted brilliant white, marked the sides and ends of the runway. Without these panels, there is no difference between the colour of the landing strip and the surrounding desert, and pilots do need to find the runways! Since Oman, I have often stared in shop windows at fancy polished Geodes with very high price tags and wonder why I should not go back and collect a runway's worth of the stones.

Next morning early, we set off for Sarfait at the most South Western corner of Oman, and arrived at 12.30, after an uneventful ride on gravel roads that were breaking up and looking down deep ravines each side. The last 40 miles has 322 bends but it is at least on asphalt and at 4,000 feet above sea level. The road was formed by following one contour level along the side of the main wadi. The Army checked our vehicle number and allowed us into the border zone.

SARFAIT - Route down to lower level
Note heavy cloud at top

We had a sandwich and then went on the "£2 tour" with our resident expat generator mechanic. First was a drive down 800 feet to the next plateau, and we looked at some contractors work. Then on through another border post and down again to about 1800 feet above sea level, to another army border post.

We looked over the edge at the lowest army post, 1500 feet below us. It was being supplied by helicopter which was used to carry water to these remote outposts. There is an 800 foot rope ladder for emergencies for the top cliff. Once, when a soldier lost a foot in the minefield, his rescuer carried him up the rope ladder on his shoulder and saved his life. We went up to the top of a rock pinnacle by road to a Forward Observation Post and waved at the Yemeni soldiers photographing us, (actually East Germans in Yemeni service). Then we went off to look at work that Bud Spence had been doing for the local Wali in various places.

We passed an Army Landrover which had just been placed upside down in the fork of a tree, 6 foot up, and wedged well in. The Army didn't believe their driver's story. What ever he told them, it seemed impossible to do without a crane and a stuntman! By the time I got the camera out, a camel had scratched

Army Landrover in tree - Sarfait

243

himself on the tree and narrowly missed being the only injury in the accident, when it dislodged the vehicle.

Eventually, we got down to sea level at Dhalqut, where the Army wanted me to extend the runway to take a C130 Hercules. I thought that it was not possible unless we moved the whole village, the new desalination Plant, and the village burial ground. Due to scarcity of horizontal land, the burial ground has the graves very close together to conserve space, with some bodies being buried vertically. Lots of Government funded building was in progress, so there was no space for the runway. We returned and went on up the hill to a new water well site. When we had built the access road, the locals started rioting around the machines. No one had told them that we were going to dig up the only grazing in the area for the access road! The problem was all sorted out eventually. Then we went on up to 4000 foot, to the top of Darra Ridge. Here we looked at the only possible site for a Hercules airstrip. Yes, it was possible to build there, but the task required some 1,000,000 cubic yards of (mainly) rock to be moved to level the site. Even then, the planes would have to fly in over the Yemen, which was not politically advisable. I took lots of photographs for the reports, as the Military HQ boffins needed to be shown exactly what was possible and what was not. This was another case of RAF desk warriors throwing darts at a map.

Designing the Sarfait Pipeline

We spent the evening in the mess with the two MODED residents and two Army officers. One Major was an ex-Irish Guards RSM, and he had a fund of stories. He was the Station Liaison Officer, and was the only permanent officer in Sarfait. He looked after the camp and "issued" it to each incoming unit during the 6 month period of border guard duty. We spent the evening discussing ways of providing water by pipeline down the cliff to the various outposts. Up to then, people had been looking at sophisticated schemes, with all sorts of complications which cost lots of money. At the bar I came up with a very cheap, simple scheme that wouldn't cost too much and could be done mostly by the using the Army as labourers. I sketched the idea on a bar slip, which we used to record drinks for the monthly bill. I thought that the money wouldn't even have to come from the Projects Division budget, so they wouldn't be able to stop the job out of spite! There was so much jealous guarding of jobs in Projects that we all wasted time watching the manoeuvering. Years later, when the scheme was working, I met the ex-Guards Major at Seeb Airport on his way to retirement. He was still clutching my original sketch, and bought me a beer and said that I was a real engineer.

The next day was a long one. As Friday was 13th, we decided to return to Muscat on the Thursday. We left Sarfait early at 8.30am, and drove to Ayboot, a Road Construction Camp half-way back. Nick, the Supervisor, gave us coffee and we discussed his camp being moved lock, stock and barrel, to Makinat Shihan, about 100km North West, to start building another road. He should have already gone but a Gunner colonel had given him a camp site preparation job which required the filling of an artillery gun emplacement. The Brigadier had objected to the gun pit being filled, and it took a while for the argument to resolve itself. We stopped off at Thumrait for a sandwich lunch and more discussions. I had to visit two sites and meet some people before we could leave for Muscat. There were very strong headwinds all the way up the North-South Road. So strong that we ran out of petrol 12 km before the first petrol station, but thank heavens for the Jerrycans. The next leg was just the same and again we had to fill up again at the roadside. We got in at 10.30pm.

I spent the whole of the following week, including evenings, collating information and writing a summary report for Chief Engineer, Brigadier Wheatley. I was to brief him and Dick Holland on the Monday morning. Dick and I walked into the Chief's office, complete with map-board, photos, and coloured pins to lecture him. He has been in a foul mood for days, and he changing the subject and abandoned the talk. I had just spent two weeks, driven 3500 km, and spent about 15 hours overtime to prepare for this. Dick and I gave up!

I also became fed up with gardening. Due to cancellations of contracts due to be built by the Projects Directorate, my Nursery was 50,000 items overstocked and the plants were growing through the plastic bags into the ground. Hired staff had been reduced, so I couldn't re-bag plants, and I had to waste the plants.

Work on preparing for the big Exercise was proceeding nicely, but I needed to get some answers from the Army so that I could build things where they wanted them. We arranged for a helicopter trip, so that we could easily identify locations and quickly move to the next problem area. Just as I got ready, my helicopter trip to Ras al Hadd airstrip was cancelled at the last minute because half of the Army blokes who should have given me answers on the day were still away on leave. A new date was agreed for two weeks later. By this time my work was nearly finished and we were preparing to move plant away!! The Army, the Planners anyway, seem to have no concept of time.

Dick Holland held his six-monthly Area Works Officers Conference at the new Wudam Naval Base. Dick wanted suggestions as to what to do with the 50,000 spare plants in my nursery. I suggested that they set up a stall and sell them, at an average price of £2, and pocket the money! They refused to minute the suggestion! Funny bunch - wouldn't last long in Civvie Street.

After the meeting, we met on the beach for a barbeque. Other families from MAM and local Wudam staff were there to swell the numbers. The Chief Engineer and his wife were guests of honour. She was from South Shields and could in no way be described as a typical Brigadier's wife. She started talking to the Ministry's R.E. on the job, about the house he had just bought by the cemetery in South Shields. They got into dialect and the Omanis were as baffled as we were!! The Resident Engineer was a T.A. Sapper officer. After talking to the new Area Works Officer, Terry Hobbins, I discovered that Jack Nye (my father's Works Superintendent in Nairobi) had worked for Terry in the Kisumu area of Kenya.

As a further example of the "small world", another guest was Mary Coxe, who was born and brought up in Davidstow and Camelford, very close to my home in Tintagel. Her first boyfriend was the brother of Hugh Mills, who lived in Boscastle, and Hugh worked in my Section. Anyway, her 14 year old son was kicked out of his boarding school for Dyslexia, and he changed over to Grenville College, where my son, Hugh, studied!!! We spent the evening talking about the North Cornish families we knew. It is a very small world. While at Wudam, I arranged to spend a night up at Saiq, on top of the Jebel Ahkdar, with the Road Superintendent, Harry Hayward.

Saiq Plateau

The next day we travelled 100 miles north from MAM, to a road under construction by Prince Ahmed Farid's company, Desert Line. This road goes straight up to the top of the highest peak in the country. Here MODED were building a two storey radar station, complete with generators and fuel storage. From the plain we drove up to the Radar site. The top of Jebel Shams is at 10,000 feet. Frequently this peeps through the clouds as one flies into Seeb International Airport. The road is at an average slope of 1 in 5 for 25 miles. The route selection was complicated by the need to avoid all sacred Juniper bushes. At the construction camp our vehicle gave up. Not enough oxygen to keep the engine running. We changed to a specially de-rated Land Cruiser and got to the top. We passed several contractors trucks which had deliberately crashed to save dropping off the edge. Some of the drops were 2000 feet or more. At the top a gas cigarette lighter would not work, due to the lack of oxygen in the air. On the other side of the ridge the face is vertical for about 7000 feet!! There were plenty of other interesting, and very high vertical cliffs to see from the site. The rock at the top was mixed, some fossilized coral and some metamorphosed sandstone with gastro fossils. I picked up a sea shell that had been raised some 10,000 feet in a massive tectonic upheaval, millions of years ago, which had lifted the seabed to produce the Omani mountain ranges

In the July, I had an extremely busy two weeks. People had been going on leave all round me and I seemed to be holding the baby. The exercise, including the airstrip for Ras al Hadd, was the top subject, of two only, when the new British Ambassador presented his credentials to HM Sultan Qaboos!! The 80 odd VIP list included the UK Secretary of State for War, and it was rumoured, Prince Charles. The junior VIP was to be a 4 star General. I felt very conscious of my responsibilities, and wished that my bosses would take some of the load from me.

The first week involved a two day trip to Saiq. In many photo books on Oman, there are pictures of terraced gardens clinging on to the near vertical sides of deep wadis. They are twice as magnificent in real life even though they were covered with a dust haze and only a few terraces had greenery when I visited. Our road camp was up at 6000 foot. The plateau top is 7500 ft and the Army Battle School is here. We had some 45 miles of road to look after, up on the Saiq Plateau.

The little villages which survived on the vegetables grown in the precarious terraces had no electricity or water supply. One enterprising gentleman bought a small petrol generator and wired up three houses for lighting. We were called to help the Civil Police investigate a sudden death. Another Omani had decided to "borrow" electricity from this primitive lighting circuit. To make the illegal connection, he had been stripping the insulation with his teeth. The generator was supplying power at the time!

The Saiq plateau has only been conquered twice. The Persians managed it in the 10th century. Suleiman, ruler of the local Ghafiri tribe, held out against Omani rule up in remote Saiq until the British SAS captured him in 1959. The SAS mounted an attack straight up the 4,000 foot face of the massive rock outcrop. At the top is the wreck of a RAF Venom fighter which crashed when the rebel stronghold was being attacked. The pilot is buried next to it, in what is now British Soil, as the Sultan gave the acre of land to the pilot's widow in thanks for his sacrifice. Our foreman was the rebel second in command and a rocket had blasted a hole right through his stomach. He had been left out to die after the battle, but he didn't.

Suleiman's final stand was in a cave, on the inside of another cave, situated in the side of a small wadi. The wadi was only 15 foot wide opposite the cave, and it would have been suicidal to try to attack the cave mouth. Rifle fire could not have reached into the second, inner, cave. Lots of grenades were used. After this battle, the Sultan agreed that Saiq would be kept restricted to Military use, so that the locals could live a normal life without tourists. Passes were very difficult to obtain.

Costains built the high altitude Manaker Bridge on Saiq, linking two villages by road across a deep wadi. The bridge could only be built from one side and arrived in kit form for erection. The approaches, on both sides, involved a sharp right angled bend, on a steep gradient. We were asked to excavate into the hillside to ease the bends, and make the approach to the bridge deck more level. In the middle of the excavation, a villager appeared, saying that his relatives were buried on the site. He finally agreed that they did not need to be moved, on condition that we provided six feet of clearance. He agreed that we could fill over the bodies to that depth!

On our return, we stopped at Nizwa, which used to be the inland capital before Suleiman was conquered. Right next to the famous Nizwa Fort was our Mess, owned by the Army Commander. He had ordered MODED to rent it from him, so that he could get a replacement built. There was at least £30,000 worth of carved wooden doors in the building, including the back kitchen door. My Materials Section was told to do the materials testing on the General's new house for free, or else.

Eventually I got the Military to visit the Exercise area. Two helicopters with 15 Army and Air Force officers, and me, flew to Ras Al Hadd. After landing above the Marines beachhead, the uniformed lot tried to sort out a place where 80 VVVIP's could watch the dawn invasion. After an hour of incorrect grid references and many arms pointing in opposite directions, they finally decided to fix on the site which I had picked on my last visit! Then we flew to the hill alongside my airstrip job. Here the VIP's were to watch 2 Para jump! Once again, there was a long hike over jebel tops for no very good reason. The temperature was 115^0F. Eventually, the colonel decided on the site that I had selected in April! By this time there was no water left for us. On to two more sites, with the same results. I finished up with an order for 24 helipads, a mile or so of roads, and all sorts of other work. We flew back to Muscat, very tired and dehydrated.

Two days later was a special day. It is a tradition that the engineer who builds a runway flies in the first aircraft to land on it. (I think this is so that, if all does not go well, they can bury all the people concerned at same time). I said that, apart from white lines, it was ready. The Commander of the Sultan of Oman's Air Force (CSOAF), Air Vice-Marshall Erik Bennett, sent for me and we piled into his own C130 Hercules. I sat on the flight deck the whole time. The crew on the flight deck were all grey-haired majors with bags of experience. Visibility was down to 350 yards in a dawn mist, and we couldn't see the other end of the runway. I prayed that my gang wouldn't decide to take a scraper across the runway while we were landing. The landing was perfect. The only comment from the pilot was that there were no bumps. "Where are your usual bumps? It was too smooth". Erik Bennett almost never smiled and he told me to add some bumps

The enclosed cutting from "The Telegraph" gives some idea of the importance of the Airstrip at Ras al Hadd that I had been building.

Press cutting - EXERCISE SWIFT SWORD November 1986

Oman test for British 'rapid aid' forces
By DESMOND WETTERN Naval Correspondent

BRITAIN'S ability to provide "fire brigade" rapid reinforcement forces outside the NATO area will be tested in November in __the biggest show of the nation's military strength seen in the Middle East for almost 20 years__. Up to 6,000 men of all three services will take part in the Oman exercise, code-named "Saif Sareaa", along with the Sultan's own forces. The Joint Force Headquarters, responsible for planning such operations outside Nato, is to be brought to full strength and flown to Oman in RAF Hercules, VC·10 and Tristar transports.

It will be the first occasion on which the recently-acquired former Pan-Am Tristars have been used in such an exercise. But one of the nine aircraft, bought with £60 million originally allocated to converting a container ship into a Commando carrier, has been almost written off after its main spar was fractured when the plane bounced 80ft in a heavy landing at a West Country air station. Royal Marines of 40 Commando will be landed in Oman by helicopters and landing craft from the assault ship Intrepid, 12,120 tons, again the first time one of the Navy's two remaining large amphibious ships has operated East of Suez since the early 1970s. Air cover for the landing will be provided by Sea Harrier fighters from the 19,500-ton Carrier, which will be spearheading the largest force of Royal Navy ships seen in the Middle East since the 1967 Aden withdrawal. The exercise is likely to have a considerable impact on the Americans as Washington has long been critical of what is seen as the failure of NATO allies to help shoulder the peace-keeping burden outside the Alliance's geographical area.

The Defence Ministry also hopes it will raise interest in British military equipment among some Arab states where the arms market has for many years been largely dominated by the Americans and French.

End of cutting

I prepared the three VIP viewing points, above the beach landing, opposite the airstrip for the parachute attack, and at the final battle point. The last included the Sultan and his Royal Guard. HM normally requires three helipads, as his flight includes a spare helicopter, and a medical helicopter

I travelled down with an RAF Squadron Leader who had been sent to test my runway before any of his precious Hercules could be given permission to land. He knew Adrian Grafham (my next door neighbour in Bath). This bloke had brought out a portable CBR tester for testing the strength of the runway. It kept going off the top of the scale!! We thought that it was a waste of luggage space, but the RAF wanted to be sure before committing aircraft to an unknown runway.

My site caravan was full of Sultans Armed Forces British majors in the scruffiest of civilian sports gear, scoffing a breakfast fry-up, washed down with tins of beer. They were there to set out the umpire's village, with my men. Outside, was the U.K officers' delegation, who were all chinless cavalry colonels and RAF Group Captains with moustaches. The two groups wouldn't have mixed. I tried to keep them apart.

Two days later, three of us went to the School of Artillery, as guests of the Colonel, who had a list of tasks for us. Work started with breakfast at 9.00 am, which I had to pay for! This visit was to prepare for the much more important Exercise in March 1987, involving all the six Gulf States. This was to be called "Exercise Dara Al Jezeerah III".

I had to build a viewing stand for 6000 soldiers, including HM the Sultan, four landing strips, 50 km of track, and another umpire's village and hospitality area. Most of the work was in the Live Firing area of the artillery range, just across a live oil pipeline. I had to get SAF Engineers to clear the munitions out of the area first. The senior Brit in the Sultan's Engineers was an ex- Rhodesian Army Engineers Lt-Col. When clearing mines on the Mozambique border, he was known to forget that he was in a minefield, when he saw a new butterfly for his collection. This had terrified Peter Berry (the Area Works Officer in Salalah), who was actually prodding for mines when the butterfly hunter ran past him. I prayed that he concentrated when he was with us!

Another senior engineer suddenly left us. The Senior Mechanical Engineer submitted his passport for visa renewal, but it was a forged one that he had previously used when he was gun-running. His C.V. didn't show the nine years that he had spent in various jails. His wife was left trying to sell up everything, including the brand new 21 foot speed-boat costing £10,000. Everyone was asking everyone else if they were really qualified, and not just using borrowed papers! During the subsequent witch hunt, the Chief Accountant's qualification was found have been "borrowed". His professional qualification had been awarded to "F. Smith" (Frank). Our man was named Francis!

I put up the scheme for the water pipe line job at Sarfait to the powers that be, which included three high cliff faces, and said that an experienced rock climber would be required. I suggested that a contractor hire such a man for the job. Hugh, my son, would have been a good choice. However, the scheme needed funding and military approval, which did not happen while I was based in Muscat.

Before the big Exercise, I was able to get some UK leave in September, 1986. My sister Jenny had just died of pneumonia, leaving my brother-in-law Ian, and the children Fiona and Stewart. Jane had attended the funeral on my behalf, but I needed to visit the family to offer my condolences. Hugh, by now a serious and experienced climber, was a member of the Llanberis Mountain Rescue group. He was asked to use his ice-climbing skill to train Julie Tullis before her attempt to climb K2 in the Himalayas. I was sorry to hear that she had died on the climb from altitude sickness. She was one of the people that Hugh spent time enthusing about on my previous leave! It was a blow to him and all his climbing friends.

Exercise ruined

After returning from leave, I had spent two days at Ras al Hadd getting the airstrip ready by painting the edge markings and giving it a final rolling. It was finished by mid-morning on Friday, 8th August. The airstrip was ready for the big practice due to start on Sat 9th September. After lunch, I drove back to MAM, passing a convoy of Airforce ground crew and airfield defence types. I had made sure that they had enough water for the fire engine that was being delivered in the first Hercules on the Saturday.

On the Saturday afternoon, the heavens opened and it continued to rain for 3 days!!! There were 66 Airforce types sleeping on every flat surface in my caravans. The camp electrics gave up. Caravan roofs leaked, and all roads in the area were washed out. My favourite ex-Rhodesian sapper colonel got two of his three SAF Engineers Land-rovers bogged. We got them out later and towed them back for him! The hill, from where HM would watch the exercise, looked like a battleground. The bulldozer had slid off the hill in the mud. Our 6000 gallon water tanker overturned on the muddy road, and the extra water did not help. As the rain had messed up the electricity, we had no radio messages to tell of the problems, until stragglers started arriving.

Once the message about the rain damage finally got through to MAM, I took Les Painting and Dave Mayne, an Electrical Superintendant and ex-Para Sapper, down to Ras al Hadd. It took us six hours, instead of the usual four, for the 300 miles journey, due to washed out roads, and we had a puncture. When we got to camp, we all had to start in on repairs to electrics and radios. The fridges had been off over a week and a large water melon had decomposed and absorbed the snake-bite serum in one of the fridges. The melon had also managed to explode, removing fridge door and the loose fittings! We carried it out and left the wind to remove the extremely vile smell.

After 36 hours, we got all caravans back on power. Then we started to look at the roads and the runway. The runway had survived except for a deep tyre track across it. Two villages were cut off completely for road traffic. The 3 mile pass to Ras al Hadd that we had built was back down to bed-rock again, and only 8 foot wide. We had built a 30 foot wide smooth road along this pass, and all the fill material was now washed out to sea. 40 Commando and some tanks were due to use this road. Another village, on the beach, was flooded some 5 miles from the connecting wadi. My gang went back to work, replacing all the damage, which they managed to do before the start of the exercise proper in October.

On the way back to the tarmac, some 70 miles, we noted three new wadis, and found considerable damage to existing wadis and roads. The Ministry of Communications Highways people normally grade a track below surrounding ground level, as it is normally dry, just removing the soft top layer each time. Unfortunately, this makes for an excellent river bed in rainstorms!

After getting to the tarmac, we visited Sur which is the Dhow building port and watched work on a magnificent new boat. Tim Severin built the replica "Sinbad the Sailor" dhow here. Then we went on north up the coast to Qalhat, which is an old Phoenician settlement. There are still some ruins left.

In October, the Exercise Saif Sareea practice started, with only Omani based troops on site. We were at full stretch, providing water (30,000 gallons a day) and keeping the roads and airstrips working. There were 1500 vehicles pounding the roads to dust, including tank-transporters, and I spent time with the Director General of Roads, Ministry of Communication, to get his road crews to help keep the public roads (such as they were) open. I had to meet his Area Manager on site at 0900, a three hour drive from my office!! This was my second drive to Ras al Hadd in four days. A round trip is 600 miles, mostly off the tarmac. My mobile caravans were being moved out, and the Army was under canvas. This period was for us to sort out our problems before the 40 Commando and 2 Para arrived and started complaining about the lack of water! They have a habit of coming off best in such arguments! Special Boat Service and SAS should already have arrived, but no one wanted to admit that they had shown up! The Exercise Saif Sareea practice went smoothly. This was the Omani "warm-up" and was designed to sort out problems for when the Brits arrive. Our water supply excelled itself and supplied over 40,000 gallons a day. The roads stood up well, after my site meeting with the man from the Ministry of Communications. I spent three hours in his pick-up, airing my ignorance of Arabic, without an air conditioner, covered in dust, showing him the problems. He spoke no English or Swahili at all. The Arabic lessons must have paid off, because his team worked non-stop for me, including overtime and Fridays! The Airforce thanked me again for the excellent airstrip, in a meeting, when I tried to get the Army to make some decisions for the next exercise in March, (without too much success, I might add).

The boreholes that we were relying upon, and which we spent money on connecting into the system, ran dry after a day!! The wells division manager had egg all over his face! As a joke, I suggested that they put a tanker load of water down the borehole, as bait "to tempt the rest of the water to come out of hiding". This was later faithfully reported to the Director as the solution to the problem, by one of the thicker Army officers, regrettably a Brit.

Meanwhile, back at MAM, the build-up to National Day celebrations was in progress. I had to level an area of about 6 football fields for a Civilian camp. All the villagers come into town to attend the parades, dances, camel racing and other jollity. Also, HM the Sultan visited MAM camp for a Passing Out Parade. I had five days to get all the white lines on the roads in the camp, and on the parade ground re-done. My Painting Superintendent was only allowed to go on leave after he had finished!

Omanization

In the previous few months, a Study Group had been examining MODED with a view to "Omanizing" and reorganizing. The Study Group Report was released at the end of October. At this stage all we knew was that we would reduce from seven Areas to three. It sounded as though most of the Omani officers that were on the 'Hit List", were in the Admin and Finance areas. Some expat seniors would become supernumerary advisors to the Omanis that take their jobs.

The three man team that was implementing the Study Group report had to rearrange 5500 people, layoff quite a few Omanis, and get rid of 120 Officers. Their boss was Abdullah Al Harthy, a Zanzibari Omani, and who was later the Minister of Water for Oman. He had the next office to me. I saw a copy of the report summary, and my current job was not mentioned, neither were any of the tasks and functions that my section had to undertake. There were four Omani Grade 21's, senior to me, to be paid off in the shake-up. I hoped to have Jane join me for a few weeks in January 1987, but with the threat of Omanization looming, it could have been the last time for her to see Oman.

HM Sultan visited MAM Camp again on a Saturday. I repainted, again, all the white lines on the camp roads. We had done those three weeks before, but they had to be done again! I graded and rolled everything and repainted all the signboards. The floodlights on the parade ground were tested, although he came at 11.00 am!

The Exercise starts

I went down to the exercise area on the night before the official start of the Exercise. The road in was in excellent condition, all thanks to my friends in the Ministry of Communications. The water supply, at 40,000 gallons per day, was running well, with full stocks at the start. The airstrip was in prime condition and all the camp facilities working. After a look round, Les took me to the temporary Officers Mess and we dined at the next table to all the "Brass". I was surprised to see Australian, NZ, and USA officers there as observers, but this was the biggest UK Exercise for some years. We shared a table with some British officers including a Signals Major called Tarquin, who believed that the Rapid Deployment exercise was done without any preparations. After the meal, we retired to the SAF Engineers tents, supped beer, and caught baby turtles! They are confused by the lights in the tents and steer for what they think is the moon. I was kept awake by scratching noises as the turtles crossed our canvas tent floor to get at the light. We were hosts to a Captain and several men of 9 (Para) Squadron, Royal Engineers. They had come in on the night para drop, with 100lb Bergens. Only one dislocated shoulder on the drop, from 600 foot.

Next morning Les and I went up to the top of the Jebel, above the VIP stand, and sat by the mobile Radar Station which had arrived from Dubai a week before without notice. We had had to build a road to get it on top of the hill. It was a very good spot, where we could see the whole plain, including the airstrip and parachute drop zone, and we could listen to the radio traffic from the radar hut behind us.

2 PARA & 40 COMMANDO at Ex Saif Sareea

First the helicopters lifted in the VIP's from the beach landing site, to the accompaniment of noisy Harrier flights from HMS Illustrious. Then seven Hercules delivered 460 Paras in 3 minutes from first man out to last down. There were four layers of chutes below the aircraft at a time! We were sat at almost drop height. The VIP's then got into coaches, (that the Transport Regiment Colonel swore could not make the journey on my roads), and they went off for breakfast. We had another cold drink, and then watched the Hercules start to deliver the rest of the troops and equipment. The display was most impressive and showed just what British troops can achieve. The first three Hercules came in 30 seconds apart and landed in only 300 metres, turning straight into the parking apron, while the next was already landing in the dust cloud! The first had unloaded and was moving out to take off again almost before the third had come to a stop!!

C130 taking off - Ex Saif Sareea

One feature of the Hercules is that it can reverse, unlike many other aircraft, and this was very useful when the runway flooded later. Adrian Grafham told me of the time that he took a RAF Hercules to the Paris Air Show and the French Airforce deliberately parked a plane in front of him. He was parked between two hangars, and was due to be the first to take off in the morning. A "no-show" would have embarrassed the RAF and scored a few points for the French. Adrian just reversed out, with the watching Frenchmen's smiles turning to disbelief, and he flew the demonstration on schedule.

Although we had built a 2000 metre strip, the RAF took off in 350 metres, showing that over 1000 metres of runway was superfluous. While all this was going on, the VIP's returned from breakfast and tried to board their helicopters and got covered by several 100 foot high dust storms from the Hercules propellers. There was also some impressive fighter and bomber action coordinated with ground explosions to simulate attacks. RAF Tornados, RN Harriers, Omani Jaguars and old Hunters were all flying. All the RAF Hercules would climb and turn sharply on takeoff, and they passed very low over the hill with the new radar set.

253

We went to the Exercise Headquarters area to see if everything was going well and discovered that we were in danger of running out of drinking water. The first day we supplied 42,000 gallons (7,000 more than requested) and Headquarters (with 10% of the population) had consumed 12,000 gallons, or 30%. Rationing was being imposed. They wanted me to increase supply by bringing in more tankers and drivers, but I pointed out that our contract was only for 35,000 gallons a day and that water discipline was their problem.

After lunch, we checked with the Airforce colonel running the airhead, and he said that he was pleased with the strip. Everything seeming to be under control, I drove home to MAM. On the way back, the Heavens opened. I broke down between two lengths of flooded road, with a wet distributor and wet plug leads. The road is cut merely by digging away topsoil and exposing harder material at a lower level. This forms a natural sump and river bed! The road was now a 70 mile canal. Of course, this meant that water tankers would have a difficult job to get through, and that the airstrip would get too soft for flying. I drove on to Ibra, 220 km from Ras al Hadd, and tried to get messages through to my man at the exercise area, on an Army radio with only Arabic speakers present. I was unsuccessful, but I was also able to telephone (using a Satellite link), and this message did get through.

Les did a recce at 11.00 pm that night, after all the Airforce problems with the rain on the strip!! In the office, the next morning we were all trying to find out the extent of the damage, but couldn't make contact with our team at the Exercise. "No news is good news" was not acceptable to the Chief Engineer. Eventually, after hearing that an inch of water was standing on the runway, I got hold of Les on the telephone. Flying had been stopped, but only for Meteorological reasons. CSOAF himself had landed and taken off, with most of the runway under water, and had declared the strip good. The RAF was happily using the 350 metres of airstrip still above water.

The road was never blocked, and Les had managed to activate the Ministry of Communications crew for emergency work on the Friday! Much heavier rain had fallen in the Capital area, which made everyone think that the same must be happening at Ras al Hadd! Les rang to ask for a crew of fitters and spares to fix a grader. They left at 3.00 am and should have been at work by 8.00 am!

I remember the Quartermaster loading HM's red carpet on a lorry just before the rains started, as he wanted it laid out "in good time" two days before the Sultan's visit. Luckily for him, the carpet was still on the lorry, under cover, when the storm broke. HM had new Puma helicopters and the down draught from the rotors was much stronger than that of the Bell 214s of the Omani forces. We were asked to find a way of preventing dust clouds blinding the pilot in HM's helicopter. Our solution was to spread used engine oil to bind the surface. It worked well, except that the Pumas had new, light blue, fitted carpets and the oil left black boot marks.

Eventually, the weekly Arabic course came to an end. I felt that I would have to sign on again, as I still could not tell the time, and remember the rule that numbers reverse the feminine endings, is only applied up to ten. There are also the two time systems to learn. The Arabic and Swahili (dawn is 12 o'clock), and the usual

Western system. I was reminded that word suffixes are important. The retiring commanding officer who carefully rehearsed his speech of farewell in Arabic to his assembled battalion had meant to say "I salute you all", but actually said "I want to make love to you all". He had to go back with a translator and formally apologise on parade! All I had learnt was to ask a soldier his name, rank and number, and where was the enemy. This was not very useful in shops and hotels.

As part of the reorganization of MODED, it was hoped to let a contractor take over most of the existing "Direct Labour" tasks in the Operations and Maintenance Division. Two organizations were approached, each with links to strong political personalities in the Ministry of Defence. The Jordanian Army Engineers was one choice. Another choice was Desert Line Ltd, run by Prince Ahmed Farid, and was the Omani company favoured by another faction. I was delegated to answer all the technical questions to help him submit a bid. After being stopped many times at the gate, the Prince asked if he could have a Gate Pass. I had to get his vehicle details and a copy of the insurance. The insurance policy listed nine vehicles. One of the two Porches had been lent to someone, but he could not remember who! The Jaguar XK was right hand drive, and banned from use in Oman. I had to ask him which of the other seven he would designate for the Gate Pass. He could not make up his mind. I was fascinated by the 15 diamonds on the clip of his gold pen.

On MAM Camp, one of the Braithwaite elevated water tanks started to leak and an investigation was ordered. An ex-Merchant Navy mechanic decided that the only way to find the leak was to inspect the interior using Scuba gear, to look for the leak. He overheard me ridiculing the idea while we waited for Halley's Comet to fly past. He wanted a photograph of the comet and climbed a wall. To focus his shot, he stepped back and fell. He was the only person in the world, so far, to be injured by a Comet.

Jane returned to Oman with me after my Christmas leave. After a year in Muscat, I was at long last given the correct accommodation for my Pay Grade. I had been stuck in a Junior Officers bayt (Arabic for house), and now I had a living room separate from the bedroom. This was pure luxury. Jane set about turning it into a home. She also discovered Muttrah Souk, and the Gold section in particular.

I took Jane on an inspection tour of all my airstrips and camps in Northern Oman, camping in the desert on the way. We went up the coast from Muscat, to Wudam Naval base and then crossed the mountains to Buraimi. The next day, we drove down the edge of the Empty Quarter to Ibri, Nizwa and Izki back to Muscat. On another weekend, we drove south from Muscat, along the coast and camped near Tiwi. This was the limit of the coast road at that time. We sat on a small headland and watch a massive Manta Ray leaping out of the water and smashing down again. The display went on for many minutes, and eventually he must have thought that he had shaken off enough limpets and molluscs, which attach themselves to these enormous beasts. The creek at Tiwi had a 6 foot high rock face on the opposite bank, preventing us from driving on to Sur and seeing the Dhows being built. (Later, after I left Oman, Mohammed the blaster was sent to remove the obstruction and there is now a complete road all the way to Sur).

Exercise Dara Al Jezeera III

Apart from the routine tasks of my various sections, the new task was to prepare for the six Nation Gulf Cooperation Council (GCC) joint exercise called "Exercise Dara Al Jezeera III". This time, the Colonel in charge of Army Training (who had replaced the previous man, who I later met again in Riyadh) was able to give me more detailed requirements and well before the time. They required six parallel camps, with water supply and access roads, one for each country attending. A C130 Hercules landing strip was to be built near these camps for troop arrivals. On the last day of the exercise, all 6,000 troops would watch a Live Firing Demonstration on the Artillery Range. I had to supply targets and viewing stands.

Jane, I, and some of my staff toured the area and made plans. The SAF Engineers commander and the Army Signals officers were also there, inspecting the designated sites. SAF Engineers had the task of building "water points" at the different national camp sites. The colonel seemed unable to find suitable hillocks in an absolutely, to his mind, flat area of desert. It helps if the tank is elevated to make use of gravity when collecting water from the taps. Jane seemed to be able to spot them easily and told the Army Signals officers that she had found several suitable sites and that there was no problem. Later, back in MAM, an Infantry Officer was overheard commenting that the Engineer colonel had failed, and that "a MODED wife knew much more about water supply than he did". Jane was famous! The Signals people could not get a signal back to Muscat because of the high mountains between the desert plain and the coast. They had to set up several relay stations on high ground.

The site for the new airstrip was chosen, and I re-visited it in a helicopter while getting SOAF approval for the location. We noticed a camel race track only a mile away. This was about 2 miles of straight graded track, and would look very similar to the new airstrip. I was told to take a bulldozer and carve big "X"s at intervals along the track to prevent pilots from making a mistake. Later, I had to return to repair all our damage before the camel race season started. On the Range, a site was chosen for the Fire Power demonstration. Dummy airfield buildings were to be erected from scaffold tubes and canvas. The troops would sit on a long slope, and the Sultan would have a viewing stand on top of the hill. The ground weapons, and the armed Landrovers, Scimitar Reconnaissance vehicles and tanks would attack from right to left across the front of the "stands". SOAF would drop laser guided bombs on the "buildings" to start the proceedings.

An order had been given that only Omani pilots could be used during the exercise. But safety of the Sultan and the viewing troops had to be considered. It was imperative that the roof shading the Sultan's viewing position not be a rectangle in case the pilot thought that this was one of the dummy buildings. The Jaguar aircraft would approach the bomb run from behind the Sultan's stand, so this was the first "construction" that he would see. SOAF did many practice runs, while we had plant working on the site, and many a dummy bomb had dropped "early", causing not a little consternation among my plant operators. With a laser guided system, after the target is seen over the sights, there is a few seconds delay while the electronics "acquire" the target and "lock-on". The pilot has to wait until the warning signal noise changes before it is safe to press the bomb release button. The pilots were full of nerves and pressed the button early many times. (On the day, thankfully a Brit actually flew the jet, as it was assumed that no one could tell his nationality from the ground).

Jane and Maggie Thatcher

While all this preparation was proceeding, I took Jane on a tour of the road jobs in the Salalah area. We drove down the North-South road, refuelling at Haima. After a night in Thumrait, we set off to Sarfait with the Road Superintendent. We had arranged for Jane, a woman, to enter the restricted border area and arrived at the MODED Mess. The three resident British Officers joined the two MODED hosts and us visitors for a very enjoyable evening. Bud Spence, the Sarfait Roads Supervisor, showed me the work that we were doing. At one point, the local village idiot wandered over. He was a Jebali, toting an airborne version of the AK47, with its folding stock. Holding my hands, he pronounced that they were soft and obviously I had never ever done any manual work. This pleased everyone else except me, but I wasn't going to argue with him while he was armed. That evening, the Omani commander of the Regiment at Sarfait asked all the MODED team, including Jane, to his Mess for drinks. He showed Jane a photo, which had been taken just weeks before, of Maggie Thatcher standing by the Mess fireplace. Jane was told to use the same pose and another photo was taken. Photos of two very strong-willed ladies now adorn this Mess.

We returned through Thumrait, and set off back to Muscat along the North-South Road for our 1,000 km drive through the fringes of the Empty Quarter. In a mini-sand storm, I realised that an oil camp was being moved towards us along the road. To make it easy, the 30 foot long Portacabins had been loaded across the lorry beds. The road is up on a four foot high embankment, and I had to rapidly dive down off the road. Further on, after refuelling at Haima,

Oil Camp on the move - North South Road - Oman

the Land Cruiser came to a sudden stop. The bottom radiator hose had split and the engine had seized. Without the air-conditioning, life got very unpleasant very quickly. We waited for a passing vehicle to flag down. It seemed like hours later that a pick-up truck stopped for us. There were four Omani surveyors, working for the Ministry of Communications. They agreed to take us to somewhere where I could get help. This was a double cab vehicle, with enough seats for the six of us, but an argument started. I realised that they were all speaking Swahili and got the gist. Jane wanted to know what was happening. I told her that they were discussing what had to travel in the open back, the live goat or the woman. She soon settled that by leaping into the cab and throwing out the tethered goat. As we drove off, the lads realized that Jane spoke some Swahili as well, and all became friendly. One even pointed to some camels, and said "Tembo Omani (Omani Elephants)". I got them to drop us off at the camp I had set up for the GCC Exercise, where I got one of my drivers to take us into Muscat and MAM Camp. The heat and dust, while waiting for rescue, must have aggravated my sore throat because I came down with a severe dose of Pharangitis. Bed rest was indicated and a Sick Note issued. When Jane and I got back to my bayt (accommodation) from the Doctor, I found both my air-conditioner units being taken away for service. Although I had lost my voice by this time, the units were replaced very quickly.

I moved my team away from the Live Firing area and put them to maintaining the roads while the GCC troops lived in the camps. After the exercise, which as a non-Arab I could not watch, we set to tidying up the camp site. Once the troops had left, the heavens opened. Omani Army vehicles were leaving after clearing away umpires tents and equipment. One was driven by the ex-RSM Kings Troop, Royal Artillery. It was swept away at a flash flooding at a culvert and he was drowned. My convoy was last to return and the lead vehicle had the communications radio. This crossed the flood safely and came back to MAM. The rest failed to cross the flood and

camped at the roadside for five days, before unloading the plant and repairing the road so that the back-up of trapped civilian vehicles could resume interrupted journeys. Before the Ras Al Hadd Exercise, I had discovered a carefully hidden Army Regulation that said that MODED should be fed by the Army, if they were in direct support of the Army. As a consequence, my convoy had plenty of food to live on while they camped.

Flash floods are dangerous - Oman

This rain also flooded Muscat, and swept the whole of Muttrah's Gold Souk into the harbour. All the individual stalls had been built some five feet above street level because of previous storms and floods. This year the water rose even higher. There must be thousands of pounds of gold in the mud in the harbour. Jane swore that I had arranged the rain especially so that I could not take her shopping for gold.

Meanwhile, in MAM, the Omanization scheme was becoming more visible. Abdullah Al Harthy was starting to send out memos detailing changes. These he signed as "Head of Implementation Team" or HIT. He laughed when I suggested that the Brigadier grade Head of Engineering Services was his superior and should be designated "Supreme Head of Implementation Team". (I leave it to the reader to work out the abbreviation). It became clear that I was the only Brit to get a promotion out of the new organisation, in recognition for the work that I had done in the 18 months since arrival. Many others were made redundant, but those retained were the ones noted for being hardworking.

Oman – Salalah   1987 - 1990

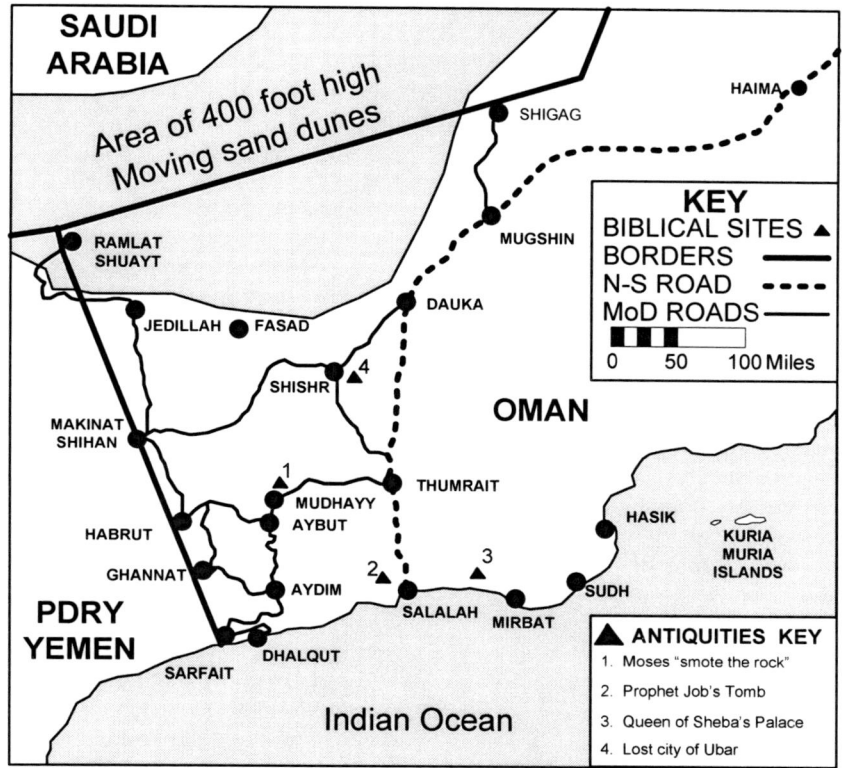

DHOFAR REGION - SULTANATE OF OMAN 1986 - 90

In June, 1987, I was transferred to Salalah to take over as the Area Works Officer until the Implementation of Omanization reorganization took place in July. I was to become the Senior Regional Officer for the new MODED Region. The previous AWO, Peter Berry, a Rhodesian Water Engineer, had been made redundant under the Implementation Plan. We spent a week on the Handover before he left.

The new Region covered the Southern part of Oman, known as Dhofar. Geologically, the whole Arabian Peninsula was tilted up from the sea bed, with the highest points in the south of the area. Water is trapped in pervious strata which dip northwards. Limestone and sedimentary rock is predominant. Geographically, and geologically, there were two areas. In the north was the southern part of the Arabian Empty Quarter, an open and flat area, with some large moving sand dunes. In the south there was a desolate, mountainous region, full of inhospitable deep wadis. This was the wilderness where Moses lived for forty years. This Biblical description does not do it justice and is quite an understatement. Two thousand foot deep gorges carved out by water and blown sand make impassable barriers for normal humans.

259

The whole area is under constant, baking, desert sun, and water is scarce. This was where I was to be responsible for building and maintaining roads used principally by the Military. One particular stretch needed constant maintenance, thanks to the efforts of an Old Testament Prophet. Just at the west end of the village of Mudayy, was said to be the rock "that Moses smote", and the spring still flows across the gravel road! Many Biblical studies seem to think that the rock was actually in Sinai or close to the Red Sea, but the Old Testament Prophet, Job, is buried in Salalah.

From the Empty Quarter in the north, the land rises to some 4,000 foot above sea level, before dropping abruptly to the sea with spectacular cliffs, leaving a narrow fertile coastal strip of land in some places. At Salalah, this fertile strip widens out to about five miles and the area was able to grow enough food to support a large part of the British Army in the Middle East in the First World War. The Queen of Sheba, 10th Century BC, had a Palace just to the east of Salalah, at Khor Ruri, and the ruins are still visible. It is made of hand cut stone blocks, which fit together with less than a millimetre of gap. This is impressive workmanship, and is thousands of years old. The Khor, or creek, was made safe each year against the Monsoon storms, by sealing the mouth with large spherical boulders, which can still be found loose on the surface in the hills above. Salalah is the home of the Frankincense Trade, and The Queen of Sheba grew rich on it. The incense was transported by camel train from Salalah, via Ubar and the Nabatean town of Petra, to the Mediterranean Sea. Ubar was the "Lost City" mentioned in ancient literature and thought to be buried for all time under the Arabian sands. It was eventually located by Sir Ranulph Fiennes at Shishr just weeks after I left Oman.

Just to the west of Salalah are several tombs, at Jebal Qara. These belong to the Old Testament Prophet Job (Ayoub in Arabic), and his followers. Job's Tomb is some 3 metres in length. Having lived and worked in the area, I now know what is meant by "the patience of Job".

Prophet Job's Tomb - Salalah

This new job meant an increase in Pay Grade and Senior Officer Status. The MOD would now treat me equivalent to Lt Colonel. I could have Jane on a permanent Married Accompanied Visa. A better car was available to me. I refused the offered Toyota Crown saloon, as it would not have stood up to the desert roads. Instead, I was given a Toyota Land Cruiser Station Wagon, after an AWO in the north had been Omanized and made redundant. Later I discovered that this vehicle had been rebuilt after an unreported serious accident. I found that, on a very bumpy road, it would fly off to the left. This was very worrying as I spent a lot of time driving out in the desert. When I reported this to my Workshop Manager, he measured the distance between front and rear hubs on each side. The difference was 4 inches. The chassis was bent. Closer examination showed that they had had trouble replacing the gearbox on the bent chassis, and had simply welded the box to the chassis. The vehicle was condemned and a new one issued to me.

Dick Holland, and his wife June, were also transferred out of Muscat to Salalah at the same time. Dick was to be the new Regional Director (South) and my boss.

My predecessor's office was equipped with brand new metal furniture, following a fight with his Plant Superintendent. The Plant man was a short, wiry, and alcoholic, Omani. He used to drink perfume for the alcohol content, which made his breath sweet. He had an argument with Peter, and literally used Peter to smash up the furniture. He was as good as gold while I knew him, but there was a story of him picking up Brigadier Wheatley by the collar and sitting him on the roof of his car, to "discuss his promotion". Soon after my arrival, he brought the whole of Salalah to a halt by parking at right angles to the kerb in the town center, blocking the whole road. The Police hauled him away, as he was drunk. When the Magistrate was about to sentence him to a long period in prison, his wife marched up to the Magistrate and made an impassioned plea for clemency. He was sent down, which allowed me to have him discharged. Having a criminal record was the only way I could dismiss an Omani, and I had the trial papers giving his wife's plea.

Once Peter had left, after several heavy parties with ex-Rhodesian Special Forces officers working for the Sultan. My new steward, Vymal, was Sri Lankan. He was young, enthusiastic, clean and tidy, but not at all kitchen trained. Electric coffee percolators do not like deep immersion in water! He folded a mean table napkin for dinner parties and practiced every day on the ends of the toilet rolls.

Graham Solly was my District Superintendent for Salalah, and he continued the introduction visits to useful places, such as the laundry and Garrison Video library. Graham was the last expat still on site in Dubai when Laings completed the Deira Tower, virtually the first high rise building in what was then only a fishing port many years before. His job was to clear the site of the contractor's equipment, and he went home on leave during this process. He was badly injured in a car crash in UK, so Laings sent out a young engineer to cover for him. The Emir sent for this engineer to ask for some engineering advice, and eventually this man became the Emir's Advisor on all construction matters. He became very rich, and even now Laings Directors have to ask his permission to visit Dubai for work. Graham kept saying "If only....."

Dick Holland and I were introduced to the CO of the Salalah Air Force Base, Wing Commander Kerry Drew, which resulted in us becoming members of the SOAF Officers Mess and the video library. Kerry's wife was German, and he said that he only married her because she had a Swastika on her Birth Certificate. The Station Admin Officer was Squadron Leader Mike Moore, who also found work in Riyadh with me later.

June to September was Khareef time in Salalah. During the Monsoon season, each year, the Salalah plain is blanketed in fog and mist caused by the onshore moist air from the Indian Ocean being unable to move northwards over the cliff tops. This wind is prevented from going further inland and climbing up over the Jebels surrounding Salalah by the hot desert winds coming South from the Empty Quarter. The result is that the moist air sits over the plain. Everywhere is damp. Mould grows on all non-moving surfaces. It is much cooler than the rest of the Arabian

Peninsula. Arab tourists from other Gulf States, and northern based Omanis, visit Salalah to get some relief from the desert heat.

That year, Graham had just finished installing lots of expensive new air conditioning units in the Commanding General's villa in Salalah. During the Khareef, the General was actually living in a tent behind Salalah because that had been his family tradition for many years. We had supplied his tents with generators and water supply. I went to ask if there was anything else needed for his villa. He was sitting outside in the drizzle, trying to read a sodden newspaper. I asked myself why we had bothered to install air conditioning, but one cannot argue with tradition.

In July, the new organisation came into existence. Dick's job was to weld the two Areas into one Region. The region had a staff of some 1200, and some 300 contractors. The two old Areas became one entity, or that is what should have happened. Old habits die hard, and Thumrait (under Peter Rogers, previously AWO Thumrait and now just a District Superintendent) refused to acknowledge our authority. Peter still dealt direct with his cronies in Muscat. Peter was, on paper, responsible for all plumbing, electrical, painting and building repairs all along the borders with Yemen and Saudi Arabia. However, he limited his staff to Thumrait Airbase and the adjacent Army camp, home to the Western Frontier Regiment. It was like operating a wheel with two hubs! As there were some 65 "locations", and Peter was effectively looking after only 5 of these, the workload was uneven.

Shortly before I arrived in Salalah, two MODED Plumbers had been called to a problem at Jedillah. At that time there was no formal road north to Jedillah from Makinat Shihan. A route had been marked by "burmails. (A burmail is an empty 40 gallon oil drum. The name originates from when the Burmah Oil Company operated in Oman). This lead to many sets of wheel marks over a kilometre width, as drivers tried to avoid patches of soft sand. Our two plumbers were not skilled desert drivers, and lost sight of the line of burmails, which is easy to do in the heat haze. They veered off and got lost. When they had not arrived at the task, the alarm was raised and a massive search started. A Baluchi Warrant Officer managed to follow tracks, and came upon a bit of fresh orange peel. He found them and rescued them. The Baluchi had been hauled off his flight home on leave to do the search, and we were extremely grateful.

My Omani Electrical Supervisor went absent one morning, because the Queen Mother had sent for him! He has known her family for generations, and she only wanted to give him some Eid presents. He got a Silver Rolex "Oyster", with the Sultanic crest on the face picked out in diamonds. He also got 1000 Rials cash (£2,000), and 500 Rials (£1,000) worth of very fancy Shamags, the Omani headdress. He was disappointed because the previous year he got a car and a gold Rolex! There is no pleasing some people!

The Civil Engineering Supervisor, Suhail, was a very active and hardworking Dhofari. In his youth, he had hitched a ride on a dhow and travelled to Dubai to find work as a carpenter. His favourite responsibility was the care and maintenance of the Martyrs Cemetery. This military cemetery had a special section for soldiers killed in conflict (the rest was for military personnel who had died from illness or

Martyrs Cemetery - Suhail and Jane

natural causes). Suhail guarded the special area and would not allow road accident victims into "his" Martyrs section.

One day, Suhail took me to another military grave that he maintained. In the 1920s, an RAF aircraft was transporting gold and Maria Theresa silver coins to the then Sultan of Oman. The aircraft crashed and some crew died immediately. The pilot was alive but trapped in the wreckage. Some Omanis arrived and looted the aircraft and made off into the desert. The pilot was able to take photos of the gang before he died, and the film was found later and used to arrest the thieves. The crew were buried at the crash site some 10 miles west of Raysut.

I needed a barber badly. I was told where to go but wasn't told the name. I had my first Salalah haircut at Ali Baba's. I found that Salalah, unlike Muscat, is a very small and friendly village. In MAM I still knew very few people after a year. In Salalah, everyone knew everyone else and they all helped and co-operated as much as they could. The overwhelming bureaucracy and armies of head office wallahs were over 1,000 km away. I found that I was able to actually follow the Royal Engineer code to "Help the Army to live, to move, and to fight". Captain Neil Ross was the Quartermaster of the Southern Oman Regiment, (Kateebah Junoob or KJ), based in Salalah. Neil had worked for King Idris of Libya, and had trained the Palace Guard, which was commanded by a young Captain Muammar al-Gaddafi. Neil had qualified as a plant operator in the Army and we often loaned him plant to do maintenance work on his camp.

I managed to get leave agreed for mid July and flew home to Jane, who was to meet me at Plymouth Airport. Before I could do that, I had to return to Muscat to close my bank account and inform Personnel of my new Salalah account. I flew both ways as a privileged Senior Officer for the first time. On my return from leave a typical Salalah weekend evolved. I had travelled back with Col Ravi, the CO of the Military Hospital in Salalah, and we met again at the Garrison Mess barbeque on the Thursday evening. As that party broke up, we were escorted to the Garrison WO & Sgts Mess and continued the party. A games evening was in progress and Balfour Beatty's team included Tom Oliver, an ex- Taylor Woodrow Nigeria engineer and his wife. Tom had stayed in my house in Lagos the night that the concrete beam fell across his bed. Although I left relatively early, some stayed up to hear the UK Election Results. The next day, Colonel Ravi invited me and several of my staff to a Farewell Party for the Manager of the British Bank, held at the Holiday Inn. The head of CID, an ex- Suffolk Police Superintendent, and others were there. About 50 people of all races attended.

While touring roads near Thumrait, I received a radio message asking me to send Bud Spence home. He was the Sarfait Road foreman. His daughter had just died in a free fall parachute accident. That week I also lost a painter was killed in a car accident, while he was travelling to visit his son in hospital after a car accident.

Driving in Dhofar is very dangerous and I lost six staff killed in road accidents during my time. One Pakistani carpenter had been involved as a passenger in two fatal accidents and asked for an immediate discharge. His nerve had failed.

MODED Headquarters believed in bulk buying of spare parts, usually from the lowest bidder, and this resulted in inferior items. In particular, the shower and basin taps were definitely not "soldier-proof". I frequently had to send plumbers on 300 mile round trips to replace shower taps wrenched off by soldiers. After I lost two plumbers, killed in vehicle accidents on separate trips, I asked if I could buy suitable heavy duty replacements and not use the bulk buy items. Permission was refused until I pointed the relatives of the dead men towards the Chief Buyer so that they could collect Blood Money from him.

Wadi Atholl - Dhofar - Oman

While I had responsibility for some 2,000 km of desert roads, the Dhofar Municipality were building many roads in the more populated areas. I accepted the invitation from Balfour Beatty to visit their road job. For the last 15 years, the only way to reach Sarfait from Salalah, both on the coast, was to drive 80 km inland to Thumrait, and then go west. This new road would remove some 140 km from the journey. The road climbed up some 2,000 feet onto a ridge, then dropped into a vast wadi, at almost sea level. At the other side of the wadi was a near vertical rock face. The road was planned to ascend the face in 13 hair pin bends. Blasting and excavation at several levels was in progress. Spoil was carried by dump trucks and tipped down a 700 foot face. Eight dump trucks had missed the "stop log", and rolled to the bottom. One driver had got to the bottom, unhurt, but slammed the cab door on a finger as he got out! Rock bolting and concrete spraying, as I had done in Dover, protected the new faces from erosion. Until the main route was complete, site access was by very steep and narrow tracks, with loose and powdery surfaces, that no self-respecting mountain goat would tackle. The Jebalis tried to use this new but unfinished route in their tattered old Toyota pick-up trucks, and several had been "written off". Often the morning sea mist would make driving conditions on the site tracks treacherous, and a lorry carrying many labourers to work slid off the track and rolled into a wadi, with some 30 killed.

Hugh, now 18 years old, said that he would like to visit Oman. There was plenty of brand new rock climbing to be explored, as the southern Dhofar cliff faces had been "out of bounds" since the Dhofar War. After the usual Middle East problems of getting a visa for him, his trip was arranged for October 1987. Jane decided not to accompany him, but travel later. This was the first holiday that Hugh had spent with me alone and was to be our "bonding time".

I went on leave at the end of July, returning mid August. Hugh came down from Wales and we made preparations for his trip out to Oman. One rainy Saturday, Roger and Jill Flory, our neighbours from Gloucester, called in during their holiday in Cornwall. Roger, now a successful factory owner, was driving his Lamborghini. Jane insisted in sitting in it and taking Roger the long way round to the pub meal. As it was raining, no one in the village saw her! She was most upset.

On arrival back at Seeb Airport, there was no problem at Immigration, and Customs was a formality. The regular Saturday Buffet was on, and Dave Mayne was in from Shafa and Bill Rudd up from Ibra, to share a table with Les, Mike and I. I was quickly brought up to date on the news and rumours. Louise Painting, Les Painting's daughter, would probably be visiting later in October and at roughly the same time as Hugh. I met Hamid Mahrouky, Wheatley's Omani deputy, who explained that my pending promotion and pay problem was all part of a much bigger MOD problem

Next morning, we got to the airport early and checked in. I discovered an upstairs lounge for Senior Officers and VIP's. The plushest leather suites and fittings I have seen in years. I spent 30 minutes in the lounge before boarding. I was the only Senior Officer on the flight and had my own bus to the front steps of the plane. My desk was piled high with files, plans, and notes to be read before I could start work. Graham Solly, my stand-in, flew out of Salalah on the same SOAF plane that I arrived on, and we were kept apart by the security system, so I did not get a "hand-over" talk. All the first day was spent trying to sort out in which order I had to tackle the paper mountain.

On the Monday, a German engineer had to be met and sent on to look at some Power Station problems in Thumrait. He wasn't on the early flight that I met, but was on a special, extra, flight which had been arranged to cope with the holiday rush, but it arrived early. He had tried to get a taxi to a P.O. Box number address, which did not help. After I caught up with him, Dick and I gave him lunch and transport to Thumrait. After a meeting on Tuesday morning, I drove Dick to Thumrait to see the German and the problem. The Khareef has really arrived. Thick fog, low cloud, rain or drizzle, combined with spilt oils and camel droppings made the hill climb part of the road into a skidpan! I watched a Jebali jeep overtake a truck and go into a skid. They were both coming down towards us. He missed us and managed to correct the skid. On the way back, the fog was dense and we were overtaken on both sides while following lorries down the hill. There are many new scrape marks on the concrete walls. The previous week, one of our vehicles had been forced to stop on the hill but it was so slippery that the vehicle just slid backwards over the edge. Later, when the Khareef lifted we recovered the vehicle from the 1000 foot ravine. There were no injuries!

The next day, I got up at 4.30am and again drove to Thumrait through even worse visibility. I arrived in good time to catch the weekly air delivery of frozen food to the outstations on the north and west borders. Ian Scott and I were going to look at the road construction work and got a lift on the SOAF Skyvan. This is a very good description of the smallest, noisiest, slowest plane that SOAF use. On the flight was the New Zealand climber that I had mentioned to Hugh. There was no chance to talk because of the noise. We looked at our road crew's work and the temporary camp, in the 50 minutes allowed and flew back to Thumrait via two other outposts. I finally got back to Salalah in the middle of the afternoon.

The steward was going on a month's leave in September. To save weight for Jane, I had brought some of her dresses with me when I returned from leave and they were a little distressed. He had learnt to use the steam iron and the dresses had been pressed and hanging up ready for her visit. I had taken a risk, as he could have ruined them all. I finally received Hugh's No Objection Certificate from Muscat. I sent a copy of the NOC, together with a copy of the air ticket and flight details to Hugh, so that he knew when he was flying.

In August, a friend from Muscat was posted to Salalah. He was the SAF Engineers Captain that I worked with on the Exercises. I got on well with Steve in spite of his boss, the colonel. We had a sandwich at the Airforce Mess and agreed to help each other. Dick Holland has been asked by the Brigadier to keep an eye on SAFE, as the Omani major was not coping.

All the Omani Army units in Dhofar are commanded by a Brigadier. I was invited to a "Brigadier's Lunch" in Thumrait, during his inspection tour on a Thursday. I returned to Salalah to attend the afternoon farewell bash for "Sid the Horse". He was the ex-Metropolitan Mounted policeman in charge of the Royal Stables. He was joining the Traffic Police of a northern UK county, and was presented with a dashboard incense burner that he could plug into the patrol car's cigarette lighter socket! In the evening I was a guest of Colonel Ali Abdullah of The Frontier Force, an Infantry regiment of Baluchi soldiers with British officers. Ian and Sabina Scott came down on the Saturday. We dropped Sabina in my house, with a steward and some videos while we went to work. Sabina apologised for screaming when, during the murder scene in the horror film, the steward padded in barefoot on soft carpet to ask if she wanted a coffee!! The next week was a short one. The Muslim New Year gave us two days off. I was on duty for the first day. A fitter demolished a roundabout at 6.30am and the municipality decided not to charge damages if I got my lot to repair the damage

The next day, Friday, I took Steve and his nurse girlfriend, Maja (Latvian for May), to see the Balfour road again. I had just had a new, more powerful, HF radio fitted to the Land Cruiser for communication. We were going up the steepest hill on Balfour's site when the engine cut out and I lost power to the brakes and steering. I jammed my foot on the brakes and ordered the others out of the vehicle. They found great difficulty standing on the steep slope, on a surface made of about six inches of talc-like dust. There was only about two foot of road each side before the near vertical drops. Steve looked down and could hardly make out a bulldozer working some 700 feet below his feet. I sat for hours, getting cramp in my leg, keeping the brakes locked. Steve went off and found a tracked machine with some tow chains. After being rescued by the contractor, we found that the radio mechanic had earthed the radio through the starter and left a long dangling wire, which swung against the engine when the vehicle was on a very steep slope, and this shorted out the electrical system. We got started again and went on 40km to the camp at the other end. There

266

I met Vic Armstrong, who had had the next door room in Minna! We swapped names and reminisced over a beer or two. He was leaving Oman that day so I was lucky to have met up with him. On the way back down the hill, the engine stopped again, at the top of the steepest bit. I steered into the side and had to sit with my foot on the brake while the others found a tracked machine to tow me out again and lower me down the hill. While we were waiting, a Jebali tried to overtake. The road was only ten foot wide, with very long drops both sides, and I was blocking most of the width!

One Tuesday morning, Dick and I, with the Omani MoD Public Relations Officer (a Navy Commander), drove via Thumrait, to Sarfait. It took four hours from Salalah to Sarfait. Dick and I had an early sandwich and set off to walk the proposed pipeline route. I had got him interested in my pet project while we were both in Muscat, but now we were both now actually responsible for water supply in this area.

Firstly, we drove down through the clouds (a drop of 800 feet) to the army post at the start point. There, we were given two soldiers as escorts, as we had to follow the line of the actual barbed wire fence of the Border. The escorts were also there to make sure that we did not stray into the minefields. The first 200 feet of vertical face was down aluminium ladders loosely tied to the rock at odd angles. There were some loose ropes to help one scramble along the ledges between ladders. In dry weather, that is probably sufficient! At the time we went, the area had been soaked by two months of rain and visibility was 10 feet in the low cloud. There was thick jungle where normally there is dried grass! After that, the slope changed to a mud slide about 45 degree or steeper. Loose ropes with knots helped us avoid occasional rock outcrops.

SARFAIT PIPELINE ROUTE

A mile of that and we were both mud from head to toe. Somehow our escort remained clean. Then we reached an army post where one of the supply tanks would be fitted. After a rest, we slid down the other 2 mile length. This time we were below the cloud and could look down, some six hundred feet, onto the tree tops that we would have to walk through later. All the way we were trying not to fall on the rusty barbed wire fence that is the border! After a long rest at the bottom, we went back up the hill. In all, we had descended some 3,800 feet to the lowest outpost. It was two hours of sheer hell and it confirmed that I was not fit. Even Dick was panting. After frequent stops, even the soldier escorts were worried that they might have to carry me! I made it up on my own, but only just. The dye from my trainer's left me with permanently blue feet. The socks were thrown out. The trousers had four washings to remove mud, before being clean enough for laundry. My legs were all atremble and I slept like a log that night.

When we drove back to Salalah next morning, we arrived in time to find that the Sultan had ordered the cleaning of a kilometre square walled area to be completed by dusk. He flew over in a helicopter while we were working, and we did finish in time for the Brigadier's inspection. I got the Brigadier's permission for Hugh to help at Sarfait with the pipeline job. While Dick and I were clearing the area, HM had ordered two buildings to be demolished. A year previously, our Projects Directorate had arranged for contractors to build a POL Point for the issue of fuel, oils and lubricants to all military vehicles in Salalah. This was sited inside UAG Camp. Underground tanks, large areas of concrete hard standing and access roads had been built, all overlooked by the buildings, which contained all the electrical components to run the pumps. Apparently the glare from the galvanized steel roof had upset HM. The buildings were nearly demolished when we arrived. Having made sure that the electrical supply had been isolated, we left the gang to complete the task. The next day was the start of a major Brigade Exercise, and long lines of vehicles arrived to collect fuel........

The following week I had to meet the Brigadier at a camp, for their Annual Inspection, which went off well but left me shattered. I had given orders to my gang for a large area of this camp to be cleaned of rubbish only. I got a call to say that the Palace Office had told the Brigadier that my people had dug up a tree that the Sultan had planted! The Brit major and I spent the afternoon cutting up and burying the evidence! So far, the Sultan has not noticed!

Since 1975, the end of the Dhofar War, the border with Yemen has been guarded to prevent further incursions by Yemenis. On the pipeline route, there were six machine gun posts along this portion of the border, below Sarfait, and this was known as the Nizwa Line. The most prominent feature was called Capstan, the code name used during the Dhofar War. Regular helicopter flights three times a week were required to keep the troops supplied with water, food, and ammunition. As the helicopters are based in Salalah, a considerable number of flying hours had been used over the previous twelve years. So much so, that RAF and Army Loan Service pilots were being sent out on two year attachments to SOAF to gain desert experience. I had designed and costed the project two years before while based in Muscat, and had convinced Brigadier Wheatley that the cost was equivalent to just two weeks of helicopter operation costs. Why had no one thought of this cost saving earlier? However, I managed to convince the Omani Squadron Commander that he should lend me some helicopters to build the pipeline. It probably helped that we both spoke Swahili. I then flew up to MAM to sort out pipeline materials with Mike Holliday and Les. We needed some Glass Reinforced Plastic square tanks. Amiantit

Ltd, agreed to make these with helicopter lifting points and in approved Omani camouflage colours! We purchased a black, UV resistant, 50mm bore plastic pipe and fittings, for the main pipe run. This would be light to handle and easy to fix to rock faces. All items had to suit being delivered by helicopter.

Dick Holland went on leave in September for 30 days. I was left in charge. The first two weeks were normal enough. We had just started a major new road building project. The military road was being extended from Jedillah in the North West all the way to a new Border Post at Ramlat Shuayt, tucked into the corner next to the Yemeni/Saudi Border. This would complete the 170 mile road from the major army base at Makinat Shihan. The last leg of this road had to swing a long way West to get round the ends of 300 foot high moving sand dunes! I hitched a lift with SOAF on the weekly replenishment flight to Ramlat Shuayt, from Thumrait, to see the work in progress. Capt Blackwell of WFR came to visit his troops. When it was time to depart, I looked for the Captain. The pilot told me that he was walking back! It was 376 km by road, but he would be going in a straight line across the hot flat open desert. He was, after all, ex-SAS.

In October 1987, I went to Muscat and met Hugh off his flight from Heathrow. We stayed in MAM for one night, and I showed him a bit of Muscat before we retired. Although we were treated like royalty by SOAF, Hugh did not notice. He slept the whole way to Salalah, not even waking when we landed at Thumrait. He was shattered when he got to Salalah. He went to bed at 7.00pm and didn't surface until very late the next morning. It was a special honour when some Omani officers came to the Mess to greet Hugh but he failed to wake up!! The next day, Wednesday, after work, I took him round Salalah shops and had a drink in the Mess before the meal. My supervisors invited Hugh to go out fishing in the Navy launch on the Thursday afternoon. My steward was told to leave Hugh sleep in the mornings after I had gone to work, but to give him a mug of coffee when he woke. The first morning coffee mug was thrust into Hugh's hand while he was actually in the shower.

I had hoped that Dick Holland would have been back in time to fix up the budget, but he has been delayed in U.K, so Thursday was a good opportunity to get on with the job while Hugh fished. He thoroughly enjoyed his time, which started at an Army Mess overlooking the Royal Yatch. On Friday, I again spent time on the budget, and then took Hugh on a visit to my office, to show him around.

War with the Yemen

On Saturday, 10 October, 1987, I had to visit the Frontier Force at Raysut, to discuss some work wanted by the CO. The Quartermaster, Major Wally Hammond (ex Airborne Military Police) and I were called into the Communications Centre in Regimental Headquarters to listen to radio traffic from an outpost. We had been told that two serious border incursions had taken place the day before and Omani forces had been pushed back by the Yemenis. The first incident was a civilian vehicle which came across the border and an Omani vehicle chased it back to Yemen, but they ran into an ambush of seven armed Land Cruisers from Yemen. One of ours was killed and one was missing. The radio conversation we listened to was from a small patrol, further up, near our new road works, but some ten miles in from the border. 13 vehicles were attacking a section observation post of 8 men. The last radio message was "We have run out of ammunition." I could hear the sound of incoming rifle and machine gun fire. Then there was silence.......

We immediately told our road gang by radio to cease work and retire back to camp. At that time they were the closest Omani people to the border, only a mile away. Even the Army was some ten miles further from the border. Later, SOAF jets rocketed some Yemeni vehicles and our ground forces went to collect information. They found our missing vehicle from the first incident.

I went to Brigade HQ, at their request, and but they did not have time to see me. Panic had set in. Sunday was also filled with incidents, sightings and reinforcements from Salalah moving up to the border. We were restricted to moving under escort in the forward areas, and were given permission reluctantly. Hugh was walking round saying that this was what he wanted, "a holiday with a difference". We started checking all our fuel tanks, water supplies, roads, plant, generators, and all other things that could be required. Meanwhile, the Army in Thumrait and our lot are co-operating excellently. In Salalah, I could not get anyone to tell me what was going on, what they wanted, or even to listen to our route reports, airfield reports, fuel states and so on. While I was in Thumrait, the Commanding Officer of the Sultan's Armoured Regiment reported to me, a civilian, and asked me for orders. We supplied him with maps and loaned him guides in white pick-ups to lead his camouflaged Scorpion Armoured Cars to the Border. Thumrait were organising fuel and water to in-coming reinforcements, setting up kitchens, water bowser points, lending JCBs and Excavators to dig trenches. During all this time there was no call from Brigade to me.

Two days later, on the Monday, we finally managed to arrange an escort for our 27 men at the road camp, and got them safely to the main border camp, 100 km south at Makinat Shihan. We had told them to camouflage the white vehicles by wetting them with diesel and throwing sand over them. It seemed to work and they returned safely. At Makinat Shihan, our men helped out digging slit trenches. One plant operator, who was hired in for the road job, he said that it was beneath his dignity to use a shovel and pick. "OK, so stand up and get shot at, then". He started digging immediately.

I was asked to meet Brigadier Wheatley on the Monday in Thumrait. He had gone "overboard" on this. It was his last war and he was going to get fully involved, even if it totally destroyed us, our purpose, and capability. He ordered lots of people down from MAM, lots of equipment from the North and up from Salalah. I was told that I wasn't pushing the Brigade hard enough into accepting our offers of help. Other staff were ordered to get out of Salalah and work in Thumrait, where they were away from communications, stores, workshops, etc.

Ron Doyle, Wheatley's Assistant, left MAM at midnight on Sunday night and drove down with his wife. Ron was to be the MODED Liaison officer with Brigade, as Wheatley appeared to think that I was not able to communicate with Brigade. Ron was told firmly that he was not wanted by Brigade, and they had telexed their objection to his arrival. Ron found himself between a rock and a hard place and didn't know what to do!!

Late on the Monday night, MODED were tasked by HQ SOLF to provide a C130 Hercules airstrip in a day. I got the request at midnight and asked for permission to move plant before first light, which was refused. It had taken 8 months at Ras al Hadd to build a runway. Here we had a whole day! As luck would have it, Ian Scott and I had realigned a road and extended an airstrip fairly near where they wanted, but we hadn't told anyone so we were able to pull this "out of the hat". The next day I told Wheatley that the airstrip is available and he sounded happy. We all kept our fingers crossed that some other Planner in SOAF wouldn't want another instant runway.

Our troops were guarding my people in Makinat Shihan camp. During the night, unbeknown to us, the troops pulled back to safety in the middle of the night and left my lot sleeping happily. They came back the next morning! At another place, the Brigadier ordered the Claymore mines to be disarmed "in case the Yemenis come"! I thought that a minefield was meant to stop the enemy!

At Sarfait, blackouts were ordered and we complied by simply turning off our generators, but the troops didn't, and the frontline was lit up light Blackpool seafront! The Airforce refused to supply water to the Army.

We were ordered to improve a road through a minefield between Habrut and Ghannat, and we insisted that the Army Engineers check for mines first, as there had been a mine fatality the previous year on this route. They arrived without batteries for their mine detectors! The army discovered that the new fancy plastic lightweight rifle cannot even break the windscreen of a Yemeni jeep! The new 0.556 ammunition was not as powerful as the old NATO standard 0.762. The second air strike against 13 Yemeni vehicles killed 9, including the Yemeni Army Chief of Staff, and one of ours, who was a prisoner. Twenty five were wounded. Immediately after this, diplomatic visits to the Sultan were made and the whole situation cooled down.

Being on call, by radio and telephone for 24 hours a day was exhausting. Hugh would sit by the instruments while I had a shower, or dozed. A water supply problem call came at 3:00am and had to be sorted. I tried to sleep between calls, but it was not always possible. Hugh swam and read. It must have been boring for him, not being able to get out and about. We have had some good long chats, and he met some ex-SAS officers one evening.

Hugh wanted to know about the climbs in Sarfait, as these looked exciting to him. It was pointed out that each cliff face had a level area at the top or bottom, strewn with mines, making the "walk-in" to a climb a bit dangerous. Hugh looked at this hardened major and innocently asked "But what 'bang by' dates do these mines have?"

Cutting taken from "The Sunday Observer ", dated 25/10/87.
BRITISH IN CLASHES ON OMAN BORDER

Nigel Hawkes Diplomatic Editor

British soldiers have been involved in a series of fierce and unreported clashes in the border region between Oman and South Yemen during the past month. In what one participant described as "a small war", a Yemeni combat team was destroyed and most of the Omani army mobilised on the border before negotiations ended hostilities. In one clash, at least eight Yemenis were killed and more taken captive. British officers who serve with the Omani defence forces as advisers were involved in these clashes, though none is thought to have been killed or injured." Other foreign nationals, including former British Army officers who serve as contract officers with the Sultan of Oman's forces, were also involved.

Both Oman and South Yemen are said to be embarrassed by the clashes, and are claiming that the conflict "an accident". A different account comes from an observer on the spot who claimed that a large Yemeni patrol launched an assault on Omani positions on the Omani side of the border. Official British sources confirm that the battles took place, but say that only a "smallish" number of South Yemeni troops were involved. They are said to have crossed the border, which is unmarked and disputed by both sides, and set up observation camps inside territory.

For some two months: according to this account, the Omani forces kept the Yemeni positions under observation until the Omani Defence Minister lost patience. He ordered the Omani troops to slip behind the posts and surround them, then destroy them. Sources in Oman suggest, however, that operations were neither as well organized, nor as quick as this. They say that the Omani command structure was incompetent, the supply of weapons to the front was inadequate and that orders were constantly changed.

Three contract officers resigned in disgust at this display of military incompetence. In spite of the problems, however, the Omanis seem to have got the better of the battle. The clashes have come as somewhat of a surprise because it had been thought that Oman and South Yemen had settled their long-standing differences. These date from the time when South Yemen harboured Dhofari rebels attempting to overthrow the Sultan of Oman. According to Omani sources, the war broke out while the Yemeni Minister of Justice was in Oman for talks. He was able to talk to the Sultan directly, and peace was declared.

Some sources believe that the trigger for the clashes appointment of Maltassan bin Hamoud as Minister of Defence (a job which Sultan Qaboos used to do himself) and the appointment of a new Omani Chief of Staff. Whatever the reason, neither side has seen fit to make any official announcements about the clashes. Although battle took place on 9 October, more than two weeks ago, no reports of it have appeared.

End of cutting

The three contract officers, from the Western Frontier Regiment had refused to obey their Commanding Officer. They had objected to being given what they considered suicidal orders. They were given 24 hours to leave Oman, or be shot as traitors. The two New Zealanders and a Canadian left Oman safely, although I was involved in getting a wife away to Muscat. Later, other expat officers told me that they agreed with the sacked officers and that the Omani colonel was incompetent.

On 24 October, it was reported that South Yemen's Justice & Endowments Minister Abdol-Wasei Abdel-Salam visited Oman to deliver a message from President al-Attas to Sultan Qaboos. His visit was part of efforts to prevent any negative repercussions from Oman's killing of eight South Yemenis.

Troop reinforcements returned to barracks, tension was much reduced, but we were then involved in making improvements caused by the lessons learned from this conflict. We returned to the road works that the Yemenis had surrounded. There was some £1.5M worth of machines "lost" to us for two weeks. All had to be checked for booby traps before work could restart. As the road progressed, it had to divert round the south westerly tips of moving sand dunes, some 300 feet high. The route was well to the west of the Hotham-Botham Line and brought the road very close to the unmarked border. At one point, the bulldozers had to reverse into Yemeni territory to work. Permission was granted after Diplomatic talks, involving both Foreign Ministers. Once again, I was involved in working outside the official country borders.

Three new military outposts had been set up between Habrut and Ghannat, and we were asked to bring them up to standard. Firstly, roads had to be cut in rock to reach these new sites. When we finally reached the top of the ridge with the bulldozer, we made the operator turn a slow full circle, so that the Yemeni East German Advisors could see that there was no gun mounted on the machine, and that the bulldozer would not pose a threat. Shower blocks, septic tanks, soakaways, kitchens, barrack blocks and Mosques were required.

SAF Engineers were tasked with most of the work, which we supervised. We put in elevated fuel tanks on an earth ramp, to allow gravity filling of vehicles, and built generator stations. We would not let the generators be connected to buildings until we tested the SAFE wiring. This turned out to be a wise move. Between any two junction boxes, a bundle of the same coloured wires was used. These connected to another bunch of a different colour leading to the next junction box. It had to be rewired correctly by us. There were long discussions with the Brigade religious people about the correct colours and patterns for camouflaging the mosques. Camouflaging mosques was not part of my college course, and I was unable to research this. The colour scheme had to be signed off by the Head of Religious Affairs in the MOD.

Eventually, all calmed down and normal life resumed. I took Hugh down to Sarfait for the pipeline job with Tariq Al Hinai, a young Omani Mechanical Engineer, who had been tasked to be the Project Manager. Tariq's father was Oman's senior diplomat, and his mother was Swedish. Hugh took Tariq aside and talked him through safety procedures and knots and lashings, and they got on well together. There was one humourous moment when the three of us were stopped at a military check point. Hugh and I had beards, but the guard was heard talking on the field telephone about two MODED men and a woman. Tariq was most upset and explained forcefully in Arabic to the guard that he was male. Hugh had spent the previous year assessing groups of UK middle management sent on outward bound courses. He said that he thought that Tariq would do very well on the task. We also found that my VHF Radio, with a normal range of about 15 kilometres, could reach Salalah from Sarfait, from one position. Across the sea, in the coastline curve, was a "line of sight" of some 120 kilometres. That solved the problem of Tariq contacting me as work progressed.

Hugh was really impressed with the countryside, especially the Jebels and the cliffs at Sarfait. "There's 200 years worth of new climbing routes here." Sadly, Oman has not yet allowed climbers into the restricted military areas yet. Hugh and I crossed swords and begged to differ on the new Balfour Beatty road. I thought that it is a great feat of engineering but Hugh felt that it was a desecration of nature and that I should have stopped it. He thought that all engineers should be burnt at the stake! He could not accept that we work for clients, often politicians or rulers, who have more pressing reasons for requiring the jobs that overrule mere environmental considerations. I felt that I had boobed by defending my profession. This had been the first time that Hugh and I had spent time together. Apart from the above disagreement, we got on well. He was like me and we sat and read together, chose videos, and had the odd drink in the mess. He definitely did not like drinking at lunchtime, as I proved one Friday! The rest of the day was a washout. We found the Salalah Gold Souk and he was very interested. The Khunjar is the ceremonial dagger worn with National dress, and one could be made in the shop for you! We did not enquire the price. The steward, Vymal, returned from leave in Sri Lanka and gave me a Sapphire and a Topaz. Ian Scott later introduced me to his foreman's cousin, who is a goldsmith here, so when Jane arrived later, we had the stones set in rings.

At the end of Hugh's stay, we flew up to MAM on a Thursday, and ate in the Jebel Mess with the whole crowd, as Mike Holliday was going out on leave. Les was due to meet his daughter, Louise, off her flight at 0900 hours on Friday. At 1130, after we had had a Jebel breakfast, Les and Louise took us down to the SAF Beach Club for a swim and a bit of wind surfing. Hugh and Les surfed until Louise was attacked by a jellyfish. Les rushed her to the army hospital after dosing the leg with vinegar. We put away the windsurfer for him and grabbed two hours in Muttrah Souk. Hugh bought more Shamags, blankets and some antique brass from Jane's favourite shop. We got him a shawarma or "camel banjo" as Les called it, roasted lamb and chicken presented in a wrap. We were due to meet for a "sizzler steak" and the film. Louise was so drugged, that she was taken home after the first reel. Louise still has the jelly fish scar on her leg to this day.

Hugh showered, changed and broke the zip on his grip, getting ready for his flight. I raided a nearby house and stole a washing line, leaving two pairs of underpants on a convenient fence. Hugh was in a blind panic and covered in sweat, but got the grip roped up. Eventually, I got Hugh on his flight to London. His last words were "Great holiday, Dad, but next time don't have another war". I think, on the whole, Hugh enjoyed his stay.

Medevac from Communist Bulgaria

Jane's niece, Fiona, had a problem travelling back from Turkey. Fiona had survived on about half of a kidney since she was a child, and, due to recent advances in medicine, had been able to travel to visit her husband's family in Turkey. Driving back through Bulgaria, Pepe, her Turkish husband, had been turned back at the border. Fiona and her young son Enis went on. Fiona developed a serious complication, requiring a medical evacuation by air. She was behind the Iron Curtain, at a weekend. A kidney transplant was urgently needed. Her brother was in Dhaka, Bangladesh, with ODA, now DfID. Jane was in UK, and was asked to get hold of Christopher. The switchboard girl in the Foreign Office was "not one of the most intelligent". "Bangladesh? Which country is that in, then?" We heard later that she had been fired after Jane complained. Meanwhile, the Bulgarian communist authorities had become loath to open a military airfield, at night, for the evacuation flight. Jane found a retired Ambassador in Tintagel, who helped. At the same time, she asked me to contact the Air Attaché in Muscat to see if he could get his opposite number in Bulgaria to help. It was all very complicated but the plane landed in the dead of night and Fiona made a full recovery without needing a transplant from Christopher at that time. She has since had a successful transplant.

Brigadier Wheatley retired in December 1987. Before that, he toured the South with his wife to say goodbye. Dick Holland and I escorted Wheatley by aircraft to a number of outstations. Ian Scott was expected to be at the road camp, but he was "working to rule" and wasn't going to have his hand shaken. Apparently some Pakistani clerk had refused to pay his leave airfare from Berlin to Muscat, because he had found a cheaper flight via Bombay which took three days extra days.

Dick Holland wrenched his back and was in agony. After a week, he agreed to see a doctor and was sent to bed for a week. Once again, I was carrying the can.

Sarfait Pipeline

Tariq had started the pipeline job. We had arranged with SOAF to have the use of a helicopter for a week, to fly the materials down to various sites along the pipeline. Nets were used for cement and aggregate bags, water containers and other small items. The 100 metre rolls of plastic pipe were distributed along the route.

We hired about 40 Indian labourers and took them to Sarfait. Tariq and I wanted to sort out which labourers were not afraid of heights so we immediately set off with the new gang to walk the route. I led, and Tariq was at the back collecting stragglers and casualties. We had a few hesitations when they reached the poorly tied aluminium ladders but got past that hurdle.

Ladders - Sarfait Pipeline Route

On the second stage was the 1500 foot drop. I got to the bottom, but Tariq did not appear. Had he fallen, and no one noticed? A labourer said that Tariq had told them to wait for him at the bottom. He did eventually appear. About 400 feet down, a labourer had lost a "flip-flop". Tariq had watched it float down until it vanished through the tree canopy. He climbed down and with great difficulty, he found the shoe. Tariq met up with the labourer, who was waiting with me. "Here is your shoe". "Thanks, but when I lost it, I threw the other one away, so this one is no use now". Tariq was too tired to throttle the labourer, but I think that he wanted to.

HELICOPTER LOADS - SARFAIT PIPELINE

I was impressed, because I could not imagine someone normally taking that degree of effort and risk. Tariq proved to be an excellent choice for the task. He coordinated the use of helicopters to deliver the large rolls of plastic pipe, the GRP storage tanks, and bags of cement and aggregate for the bases.

HELICOPTER DELIVERY - SARFAIT PIPELINE

We needed the large number of labourers to handle the 30 metre pipe rolls, which did not easily uncoil. These were laid out in the sun, on the route, and were allowed to straighten out gradually in the heat.

In a week, he laid and jointed the full length. The tank bases were cast and the tanks were connected to the pipes. The troops watched and waited for the water to start flowing.

PIPELAYING NEAR BUNKERS

TARIQ AT TYPICAL TANK - SARFAIT

276

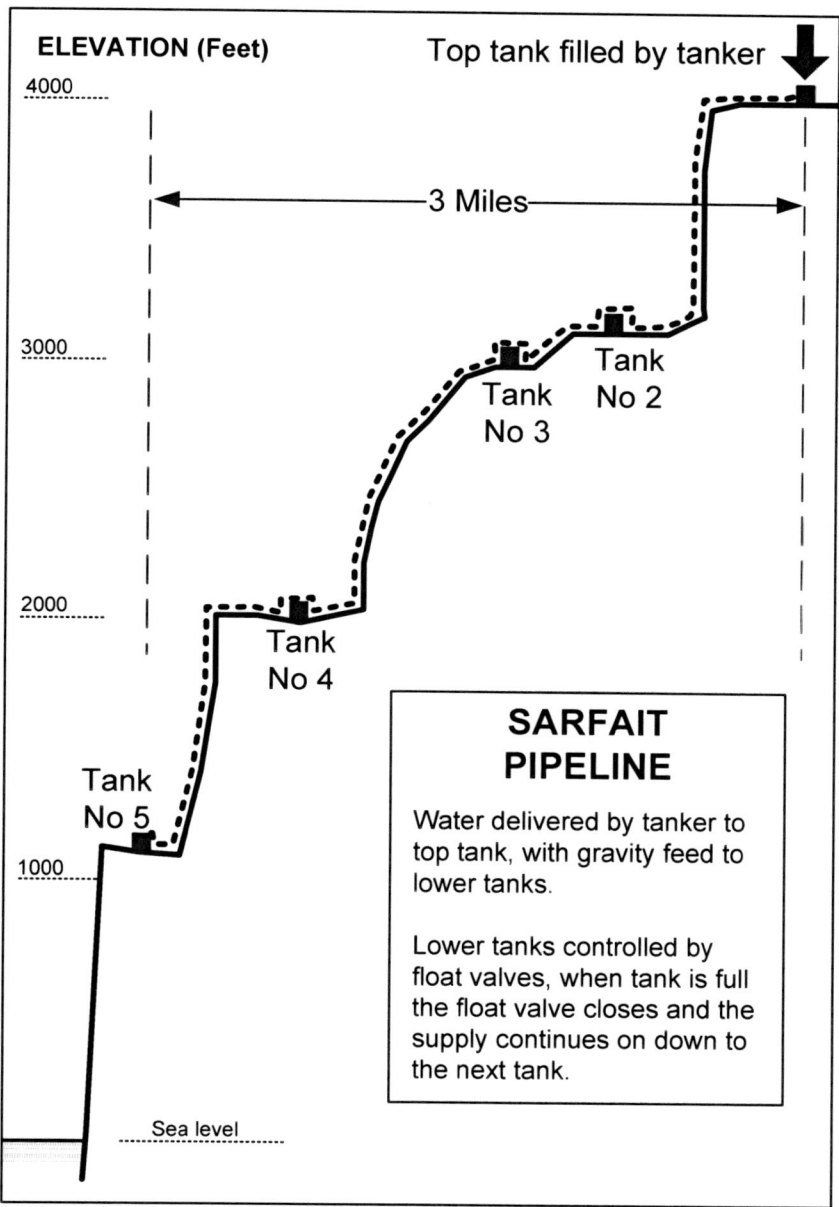

ELEVATION (Feet)

Top tank filled by tanker

4000

3 Miles

3000

Tank No 2

Tank No 3

2000

Tank No 4

Tank No 5

1000

SARFAIT PIPELINE

Water delivered by tanker to top tank, with gravity feed to lower tanks.

Lower tanks controlled by float valves, when tank is full the float valve closes and the supply continues on down to the next tank.

Sea level

On one inspection visit, I was following the pipe route when a burst of heavy machine gun fire made me dive for cover. The pipe was placed next to the barbed wire border fence, and the machine gun was some distance behind the line. It had fired over my head, but the noise was terrifying. I had become entangled in old and rusty barbed wire and had a number of cuts on my hands, which bled copiously. The wounds were superficial. On investigation, it turned out that the gunner had noticed

277

an Omani fisherman was drifting into Yemeni water, and had fired a warning burst to wake him up. The result was a return of fire from the Yemeni side of the border!

This incident was reported to Headquarters in Muscat and a high level team of military experts was dispatched to discuss the erection of a suitable "Border Marker" for fisherman. I would have to manufacture and build the "day-glow" orange tower. The Omani Navy sailed off to survey the cliffs and decide the best position.

Navigation was not a strong point, apparently, as the Army stood on the cliff and watched the Navy survey vessel stray into Yemeni waters and get fired on by the Yemeni forces! Eventually no one could decide if it should be erected on the actual border line, or a distance before the line. The actual line would need Diplomatic discussions with Yemen, while placing the marker at, say a 2 mile warning distance was, it was felt, an invitation for Yemen to think that Oman was conceding territory. In the end, nothing was built.

The first sections of the pipeline were commissioned by the filling of the top tank and turning on the valve. We were thanked by the troops, who had had years of uncertain water supply. The only adverse comment was from the lowest position, who complained that there was insufficient pressure for a shower!

Tariq did a very good job on the pipeline. This was the job that the SAF Engineers colonel had said was too difficult for his men when I first proposed it as a training exercise! This same man turned down some road works on the grounds that "his plant is fully committed to road maintenance on the border". I wrote to ask him which roads I no longer have to look after, now that he is doing them. I did not get a reply!

In order that the project would be successful, I had ordered spare tanks, pipes and fittings for repairs and replacements. It was agreed that some of the surplus, keeping enough for future maintenance, would be used to complete the whole route from the main Army location at Sarfait, down the first vertical 800 feet drop. Water tankers could reach this new top tank more easily and safely than the tank lower down. The Army water tanker had crashed trying to deliver to the lower tank, killing the driver.

I received a job offer building logging roads in Indonesia. Trevor Henry, Brigade Intelligence Major, offered to go with me as he loved the people. Later, in Camelford Library, I found a book on the Borneo Campaign and Trooper Henry, SAS, was listed. In retrospect, I realised that the logging was a crime against nature and I am pleased that I had nothing further to do with it.

In November, Sultan Qaboos caved in to the financial problem that all expats were suffering. He decreed that all MOD expats would benefit from a fixed Rial/Pound exchange rate. I had tried to get out of Oman, and into a better paid job but interviews and leaves never seemed to coincide.

Dick Holland returned from leave and, shortly afterwards, wrenched his back again. He spent a week in bed and I took over again. He went to MAM for traction, to release a trapped nerve in his back. The nurse strapped him to a mechanical traction table, but was too shy to ask him to completely strip off. The lower strap was fixed over his trousers. She switched the machine on and left the room. By the time she came back, Dick's trousers were round his ankles, pulled off by the straps. She screamed and fled, looking for a man to help her cover Dick's embarrassment. Meanwhile, for the whole time, Dick was being jerked and stretched by an uncontrolled machine which he could not stop! Muslim nurses do have some drawbacks! Dick, by the way, seemed much better for the experience!

December 1987 was a comparatively quiet month, before I went home on leave. One Thursday evening, I was enjoying the company in the Officers Mess at the Frontier Force when the telephone rang. My operations room had traced me, and wanted me to call Hamid Mahruky, the new Head of MODED immediately. I listened to his orders. He had just returned from meeting senior Army Officers and wanted me to immediately mobilize my complete earthworks team to make a new road at Sarfait. The only existing road there snaked along the top of a very narrow ridge, under full time observation by Yemeni forces. I was to find a new route in dead ground behind this ridge, out of sight. I gave orders for the plant and workforce to start moving that night. Hamid made me understand that a new threat from Yemen had been issued. My work was to be secret and kept out of sight of the Yemenis. At dawn on the Friday morning, the equivalent of a UK Sunday, I was at the check point outside Sarfait with a column of plant. It was a two hour drive. The Army knew nothing of my task. I put the plant to work starting a ramp off the road and down into the deep wadi, while I went to speak to the Commanding Officer. The CO was in Muscat, so I woke the Training Major, a Brit, who was confused by what I told him. We had breakfast while he queried the task with his Headquarters. We made some progress in the initial few hundred metres and set about walking the route from the other end. It became apparent that considerable blasting would be required. This would be difficult to keep secret, so I asked Hamid what I was to do. I was told to demobilize immediately and not to refer to the task again. It appeared that he had decided on the job without an official request or permission!

After a short leave in UK, mainly attending job interviews in the weeks before and after Christmas, I returned to Salalah. I spent time touring Dhofar and looking at camps and roads. On one trip I drove 1050 km in four days, visiting border posts and looking at our roads. I took a second vehicle with Ian Scott, Paul Lawrence Water Engineer, and Terry Bell a Well Driller. Terry was ex Taylor Woodrow Nigeria and had drilled the Guinness brewery borehole in Lagos. He has just arrived and was being shown all the boreholes we look after. We met two Brit SNCO's training some SAF Engineers. They complained that their men would not work. They christened the Omani officer "Lt Ali bin Scargill", as he sided with his men. Just over the hill from the parked SAFE machines, infantry soldiers were having to dig trenches by hand in rock. The Baluchi soldiers were not complaining!

I finally got to the bottom of why SAFE were "committed" to work in the South. They had been tasked with constructing a new airstrip at Mugshin, near the North-South road. The surveyor had set up profile boards to control the fill. The new runway was to be slightly above surrounding ground level, to prevent rain damage. The profile boards were designed to be used with a 1 metre high "traveller" (or sighting board). This would have meant the finished level would have been 1 metre below the profile boards. SAFE had placed fill up to the level of the boards, requiring an extra year's work, and leaving a steep drop at the sides of the new runway! No wonder I had not been told about this. Needless to say, SOAF refused to use the new, delayed, and dangerous, airstrip.

Although it was only February, and outside the Monsoon season, dark black rain clouds and rain all indicated that the 1983 floods may be back! We prepared emergency schemes, as roads would be washed out and fuel and water supplies disrupted. Also, the Yemenis moved into our territory at Sarfait, again. Ramadan was due.

Social life continued. I watched a very competent tap-dance, given by a male nurse, on four coffee tables pushed together, in the Garrison British Sergeants Mess. All to music played by the ex-Pipe Major Scots Guards.

The Cookhouse misunderstanding

The Artillery Regiment camp needed some upgrading. The smell of rotting vegetables in the Cookhouse was overpowering. I decided that they needed an air conditioner to be installed in the vegetable store to prevent further loss of food and one was installed. In my monthly report to Muscat HQ, I mentioned this and the report was duly translated into Arabic. I heard nothing more until the "Wrath of God from on high" came down to me. In Arabic, the word "Cookhouse" (Army talk for the Other Ranks Dining Hall and kitchen) had been translated as "Cook's accommodation". At that time, all Other Ranks in the Omani Armed Services were not entitled to air conditioning. My action and report had opened the way for this to be changed; so it was thought by those affected. It was estimated that two power stations, extensions to the National Grid and vast quantities of building work would be required, and it was all my fault. People at the highest level were not amused. I was asked to explain myself. Only after sending copies of my English report and the Arabic error, was I able to convince the Oman Government that I was not to blame and that a simple translation error had caused the problem. With the large quantity of documents that required translating, one cannot cross-check everything.

Salalah Golf Club

Jane flew out to join me in March 1988. About this time, HM Sultan Qaboos decided that the Royal Salalah Golf Club could no longer use his Flamingo Wildlife Park as a golf course. Perhaps birds were being distressed by golf balls? I was asked to find a suitable area and build a nine hole course. There was a patch on the edge of the Salalah Airbase, used for years to tip builders rubble. Golfers started to use this land, but balls were hitting twisted rebar 15 feet up in the air and balls were being redirected. I put the road team plant to work and produced a course. As in all Arabia, the "greens" were as brown as the surrounding desert. After the plant had returned to road maintenance duty, complaints came in. There was no "rough". Balls would roll for many yards on the beautifully rolled and compacted ground.

After all, that kind of surface was what my men were trained to provide! We returned and roughened the ground, adding a bunker or two and a ditch. Everyone was happy and Jane and I were invited to play in the inaugural tournament. Neither of us had played before. We were partnered by the Station Commander Kerry Drew, Club Captain, and his wife, Uta. I won a T-shirt for the most strikes to get off the tee. Jane won hers for the longest drive by a lady. Unfortunately, it went off at right angles to the course! Later, a club house was required. Two Portacabins were given to the Club by the local manager of Shell Oil, the Club Chairman. These needed electricity. I decided that the adjacent ammunition bunkers needed security lighting and an additional budget was successfully requested for this vital security work. I provided a short extension cable to supply power to the Club House.

Hugh found that he needed some cash and applied for jobs. He had listened to engineers talk about materials and testing over the years. He was successful in being given a job as Materials Engineer on the building of the A55 along the coast of North Wales. After being given a saloon car and his laboratory, he had to "come clean" to the Project Manager that it was only because he knew some technical words that he had passed the interview with the HR department of an internationally renowned company. I wonder just how many other inappropriate appointments they made.

I flew home with Jane at the end of her visit in April, and returned in May. I had a Civil Service interview for the job of Director of Public Works on the island of St Helena in the South Atlantic. This rocky outcrop had a population of about 5,000 and no airstrip. A ship visited at intervals on the route from Cape Town to UK. Most of the islanders were called Thomas, and were descendants from the man in charge of the coaling station run by the Royal Navy 150 years ago. Many children were born out of wedlock, referred to as "others", and these became officially part of the family on marriage. All the young men left the island to get jobs on Ascension Island or further afield. I was to be the third most senior man on the island, after the Governor and the Treasurer. I was selected for the post, but Oman had finally promoted me and given me the pay rise, so I turned the job down.

Arriving at Salalah, Dick Holland met me and told me that there was still no replacement chosen for him when he left. The latest idea is a meeting of four Grade 23 Colonel level Omanis to decide which one should come on a one year rotation basis! This would also mean that they are away from their own jobs and families for that year! Eventually, it was agreed that Mohammed Noor Sharif Al Bakhry would be my new boss. He was a Zanzibari Omani, schooled in a Church Missionary School in Tanganyika and who later was a tutor at Mombasa Polytechnic. He was deeply religious but was not an aggressive Islamist. He was known never to make a decision or sign an awkward letter. I liked him and we got on well together, often speaking in Swahili, although his English was excellent.

In order to finally complete the promotion process, I was required to go for a medical examination. It was Ramadan, and Omanis were in a bad mood due to lack of sleep. Unfortunately, I was wearing underpants that Jane had bought in UK while I was on leave. The Doctor noticed that the label showed that the garment was made in Israel. I had to assure everyone that I was not, in fact, an Israeli spy. Oman is very touchy on this subject, and the official Armed Forces Diary contains a map of the Middle East omitting Israel. The blue Mediterranean Sea extends eastwards to the Jordan Border!

At the end of May, we saw Dick Holland off at Salalah SOAF air terminal. Mohammed Noor and several Omani officers made certain that he caught the flight. On the Thursday I hosted an Omani style Barbeque in the evening. We had the whole place lit with flashing coloured lights, more than His Excellency the Under Secretary had on his visit, and a full Omani band! Apart from the Brigadier, all the Commanding Officers and the Chief of Police came. As I hate public speaking, I had several gins before becoming Master of Ceremonies and presenting Dick with a silver Khunjar. I was able to get a free presentation box from the Palace, and to get a silver plate engraved (at a cost of 2 gallons of paint) and the whole thing looked very good. Dick, in return, gave the Mess a framed photo of Elizabeth II walking with Sultan Qaboos in Muscat, which went down very well with the Omanis. We completed the evening with all of us, in turn, dancing duets of the Omani Dagger Dance, including waving a naked Khunjar at each other! All except the Matron of the Military Hospital, who felt that her being the sole lady guest might upset the Omanis, although they asked her to join in

Mohammed Noor was now in charge, and Dick had formally handed over to him. One of the results of the change of Regional Director was that Dick's old steward did not want to work for an Omani. I took Bakker, a senior Pakistani, into my house, and transferred my young steward to the Officers Mess, where he could earn more overtime pay. Mohammed seemed happy with the other lad we got him.

After Dick left, I went to Sarfait for two nights, to organize the extension to Tariq's water pipeline. That week there was a Border incident, involving one of my new Omani MODED drivers taking a brand new vehicle across the Yemen border. He had delivered a group of tradesmen to work on the Army camp at Habrut. The driver found an Army tent to sleep in while the men worked. The Army threw him out of the tent, so he drove off in a huff across the border. At the other side of the border is a white "Beau Geste" fort that used to belong to Oman. He was arrested, and our new vehicle impounded. The Brigade duty officer called me all sorts of names for employing traitors and would I please bring the man's file. I did, and the duty officer realised that the offender was his cousin. I then went on about the type of people from that tribe! His face was red. We got him back, with the vehicle, that same day.

Kuria Muria islands

On another day, Kerry Drew, SOAF Station Commander asked me to fly with him to the Kuria Muria Islands on the weekly food and passenger run. The SOAF Doctor, complete with a large medical kit, came to take care of the islanders. The islands have a population of about 120, but recently Tuberculosis had killed off all but three of the women, and only one was of breeding age. Following an earlier petition, the Sultan had given some gold to the Wali to go and buy brides from the mainland. However, the nearest mainlanders had been enemies for centuries and were not too happy about selling their women. They raised the price once they knew that there was gold available.

The Wali of Kuria Muria Islands
with Kerry Drew (CO Salalah) and SOAF Doctor

We were met by the Wali and his two Askaris, who were carrying a large chest full of gold. Kerry was asked to fly the Wali and the chest to London in the Skyvan to buy more brides. Regretfully he had to refuse, although I offered to carry the gold and the doctor wanted to help in the selection of the ladies. Kerry regretfully explained that the Skyvan did not have the range!!

While inspecting the runway, I saw Skipfish in the rock pools. These skip along dry rocks to the next pool if the tide goes out. One had a stand-up fight with a big crab and chased it off, while on dry land! We did not see any whales, which was unusual apparently. Then we flew to a coastal village that has no land access. The runway has three sets of white edge markers, not two, to catch the unwary pilot. A wadi flows along between two of the lines, but the pilot cannot see which pair to use until too late. I was asked to try to "rub out" the wrong set of lines! The rest of the flight back to Salalah was along the coast at 100ft, and the crystal-clear water allowed all the coral and fish to be seen. On another occasion, I was requested to send a road gang to a remote airstrip in the north-east of my area to prepare an airstrip. The Sultan was re-introducing Oryx into the wild and the first animals were to be delivered by Skyvan.

In June 1988, I spent a lot of time travelling around the Region. At least one long journey each week since Mohammed arrived. For the first month, he did not move outside his office, even to meet senior Army commanders and other regional dignitaries. Even Brigade Headquarters were asking when he would visit the Commander. During a visit to Sarfait, I was invited to the Officers Mess for a party. The regiments were changing and this was the joint Welcome and Goodbye party. I had worked with the incoming Lt. Col. when he was a Staff Officer (Major) in Brigade Headquarters, Salalah, during the previous year.

Early the next morning I took Mohammed Nawaz, a newly appointed Pakistani foreman, down to the pipeline job and explained what was wanted. He had recently been transferred out of the Projects Directorate, where he was the Civil Supervisor who had stirred up trouble for our Thumrait District Superintendant the previous year. I casually asked a question about a length of pipe that Tariq had put in, and he ordered a Foreman to go down and find the answer. I got on my high horse and said that he should know intimately all of his area of responsibility before attempting to give orders about work. I then took him down the ladders out of spite. Then I found another job he knew nothing about and walked him a mile through the bush to a new outpost on the border. He was very tired when we got back to the Mess for breakfast, although I had carefully timed it to be too late for food. We went straight off to the water treatment plant 30 Km away and only left at 2.00 pm. when the work was done. He finally got a late lunch. He disappeared back to Aydim in the afternoon, without a word! The Foreman was very grateful that I had taken him down a peg! This foreman had worked for Taylor Woodrow in Dubai, and remembered Dave Kilner and Jim Sample and others. He could not stand the ex-Projects Supervisor.

When I got back, I took Mohammed Noor to all the little Jebel camps on the jebel above Salalah. It was a gentle introduction for him to the area and the scale of our work. Graham Solly, the Salalah Civil Superintendent, was responsible for this area and he came on the visit. The full visit takes 5 hours. The new regiment was already in and the cleanliness/hygiene standards had dropped below the high standards set by our friends in the Frontier Force (FF), the previous occupants. Les Painting, down on a visit from Muscat, and Ian Scott joined me for a working breakfast at FF the next morning, and I mentioned to the FF Quartermaster, my visit to the Jebel camps.

One night, I was "Duty Driver" for Mohammed Noor when we went as guests to the Artillery Goodbye party. Each year one of the two Artillery Regiments does a tour in Dhofar, in rotation. We had to join in the Omani dancing, but with old stainless steel table knives instead of Khunjars!! Even the waiter looked ashamed when he brought the kitchen knives in on a red plastic tray! Mohammed Noor was introduced to an English young lady, who was teaching English in Salalah and she was proud of her knowledge of English Literature. He kept dropping quotations, which she had never heard of. Mohammed complained of the drop in standards in UK education. Mohammed had studied at a Church Missionary School in Tanganyika. A few weeks later, the main door of this Mess was jammed shut with many officers trapped inside the building. The new Colonel had bought an Arabic door and frame from the Souk and had his officers install it. No lintel was used, so the weight of the roof pressed on the door frame. It cost us more to repair the building than the cost of inserting the door. If the Commanding Officer had asked us, we would have done the job professionally, and without charge. He did not know this, as staff in the other MODED regions were not so helpful. Shortly after this, he got married and, driving away from the wedding, died under an articulated lorry.

Visit of the French Navy

I had an invitation to a party given by the Omani Navy to host 30 French Naval Officers off the "Meuse", a fleet refuelling ship. This was held at the Frontier Force Officers Mess, the nearest Mess to Port Raysut. My French was the best in the room, all six words!! Wally, the Quartermaster, got his Baluchi officers, who have little English and no French, trained to ask the way from Waterloo Station to Trafalgar Square, via Agincourt and Crecy! Wally proudly wore his St Cyr French Parachute Badge. The majority of the officers were elderly French Merchant Marine types, while the Captain was a young Super Entenard fighter pilot. The French Navy insists that, to gain promotion to Lt Colonel, an officer has to command a ship for a year. He had to spend his year in the Indian Ocean delivering food and oil to the rest of the Navy, without doing any flying. He was bored and needed more lively company. After the formal party, he escorted his older officers back to the ship. He then filled a rucksack with champagne bottles and came back to the party. He spotted a clock on the Mess wall which went backwards, and he asked for it. He intended to give it to his Navigation Officer, to help speed up his calculations. I suggested that I take two of his officers on my inspection trip to a border outpost the next day. At dawn the next morning, I collected two French Officers and put them in the Land Cruiser with my Omani Army guard and trundled off to Ghannat. They were impressed with the arid desert and the geology in the jebel, and wadis that we passed through. The Baluchi lunch was not quite up to French Five Star standard, but they seemed to enjoy sitting cross-legged and chewing on old mutton. In return, they gave me a pewter ashtray inscribed with the ships crest.

Near Ghannat, the Army established a new presence at two locations in land disputed in the recent border clash with the Yemen. I was asked to meet the Quartermaster, the SAF Engineers officer, and the local Army Commander, to discuss what further work that they required. I went with Ian Scott and we started the visit by staying overnight at Aydim, with the MODED officer, a Pakistani, and had Indian food. The bedroom block had been built on steeply sloping ground, so to save a lot of levelling of the site, the baths were all "sunken". When it was first reported to Brigadier Wheatley, before my time, he promptly sacked the man responsible for this frivolous waste of money. In fact he had actually saved money. The next day we drove on to Ghannat and met Captain Boswell. His father was General Boswell, Governor of Jersey, who was visiting his son the following month. Lots of access tracks, generators, water tanks and septic tanks were discussed and a plan was agreed with the Army.

Ian Scott finally got his promotion to Roads Superintendent confirmed. Previously Rashid, an Omani, had held the post, but had been sent back north for medical reasons. As at the major Exercises in the North, I had managed to secure Army Rations for the road crews building new roads to new Army locations. Rashid had hoarded and stockpiled four months worth of "surplus" rations for 50 men and had been selling them in the north. The crew had been kept on short supply for him to build up the stock. This was discovered by Ian and sorted out. Camp food returned to a normal healthy diet for the crews. One sleeping caravan had been gutted to store the surplus food. I had only borrowed it from the north. I had to completely refurbish it before I could return it. I caught up with Ian a few days after he had found the food stockpile, on the new road we were building to Mugshin. That was a 500 mile drive in temperatures up to 55^0C, and the air-conditioning in my Land Cruiser had failed. Months later, Rashid died from complications when his stomach ulcer burst.

The next week, I arranged for a helicopter fly myself and some Army officers to the new camp being built at Mugshin on the Saudi Border, and especially to check and agree the route of the new access road. SOAF asked me to pre-position aviation fuel for the trip at refuelling points for the flight. On this flight was the Firqat Major commanding the troops at the border, SAF Engineers officers, and the Brigade Major. I was the senior MOD officer on the flight. We were not allowed to take off by the Ground Staff until I had surrendered my Swiss Army penknife. All the other officers were armed including the helicopter crew, but it was feared that I might hi-jack the aircraft! Although I had ordered the flight, the knife had to go into a strong box and wait for my return. "Rules is rules" was the motto to obey! While at Mugshin, a C130 Hercules landed on our airstrip without warning. The Army tried to contact it by radio and failed, so a vehicle was sent off to speak to the pilot. While approaching the C130, the Army saw the door open and two fighting bodies fall out.

One lay on the ground while the other climbed back into the aircraft, which promptly took off. The C130 was a Saudi Airforce plane and the severely wounded Saudi officer was quietly bundled away before a diplomatic incident developed. Mugshin was known for the extremes of weather. The walls of the buildings were nearing completion and the Army platoon were in tents, when a hailstorm wrecked the camp. The radio mast was blown down, and a new 6,000 gallon fibreglass water tank was blown a kilometre away. Hailstones the size of cricket balls were heaped up against the walls that were still standing and the temperature had dropped to freezing. To get help, the Army had to drive 80 miles to find a working telephone. We sent up food, blankets, generators, water, and a repair crew.

June 1988 saw Margaret Thatcher visit Oman again. I had to make sure that roads were passable, generators worked, and water supplies were in good order. For security reasons, I was not told where she might visit, so the whole region had to be checked out. Roads were closed for her cavalcade, but as it was raining heavily, there were only a few homeless sub-continent workers on the streets to wave to her. She did include a visit to Sarfait, where she viewed the PDRY troops and the East German and Russian advisers staring back at her through telescopes.

This was the first full month under my new boss, Mohammed Noor. He drove everyone crazy with his very careful and thorough examination of all papers that got anywhere near his desk. At one point it took me a day to sort out the three week old papers in his "In Tray". His slowness meant that I spent endless extra hours trying to keep things moving. He went on leave at the end of July, leaving me to sort out the backlog, but with most of the other staff also on leave at the same time.

We got a new Phillipino Electrical and Mechanical Engineer, so I took him and Mohammed Noor on a trip to the border. We went along the new Balfour Beatty road, which was under construction, through Wadi Atholl. This included a 2000 foot climb up through the partially blasted wadi wall. Both passengers were most impressed, even speechless. Mohammed kept stopping for prayers, and the Phillipino kept smoking and I hate cigarette smoke. Eventually we arrived at Ghannat, to be met by the Captain. The Phillipino was most impressed by this young officer. I found out later that, only being used to US rank badges, he thought that he was a General. We got back to Salalah at 8:00pm, tired and thirsty, only to find the roads sealed off for the return of the Sultan to his Summer Palace.

Mohammed asked me to go with him to a meeting with four other Ministries, to sort out an action plan for some undisclosed matter. This was held "on site", at an unmarked patch of desert. Mohammed was asked for a copy of "the letter" which the other Ministries had been assured that he would bring to the meeting. The letter would explain everything. He denied all knowledge of the letter. Later I found it in the infamous "In Tray". Finally, the Brigadier sent for Mohammed, as Mohammed was not keeping the Brigadier informed. I was asked to be present by the Brigadier, who berated Mohammed very gently, in the Arabic way.

About this time I received a replacement for one of the Roads Supervisors, which was really a muckshifter foreman's job. He was a Phillipino with 7 years experience as Principal Resident Engineer in Nigeria, two years road design in China and a tour

286

in Sri Lanka. His was the one C.V. that I said was far too over qualified for the kind of work needed. The MODED Acting Chief Engineer recruited him in Manila, in spite of my comment. He could not grasp what kind of work he was to do. He was horrified at being sent 200 miles into the desert and being the only officer. At the interview in Manila, he had asked if he could take his girlfriend there and play tennis. The troops would have made short work of the girl, before he was fired for un-Islamic acts with an unmarried lady. Getting his tennis balls back from the Yemen would lend a whole new meaning to the words "International Match". We had to search for a cook familiar with Chinese cooking, so that some Pilipino food could be given to him. Ian nearly strangled the new cook during his first few days. Nel Santos proved to be very competent.

We had a week's holiday for Oman Renaissance Day, 20 years after Sultan Qaboos succeeded his father in a virtuously bloodless coup, aided by the SAS. We all got a Medal commemorating this anniversary. I was sitting with Mohammed when my radio bleeped. It was Graham asking me to "urgently join him to sort out a problem with the air conditioning in Building 97", so Mohammed reluctantly allowed me to go. This building was the Brigade Officers Mess and the week long party had started. That afternoon, Graham and the Head of the Omani Police CID spent the afternoon in my villa before going on to another party. The next day my staff organized a party in my house with a live band. I only wished that they had told me first. On another day, the Thumrait staff came to our Mess for a Barbeque, but the band failed to turn up. Some of us went to a party at the British Warrant Officers and Sergeants Mess at Brigade Headquarters. Three Germans had just completed a contract to add 10 tons of gold leaf to the Salalah Palace. "Hilda, the Guilder", was the life and soul of the party, and excellent on the keyboard. She showed us photos of all her work. The Palace was really ornate and attractive. Music was provided by the same live band, augmented by Army pipers and drummers. The Germans tried the "Doodlesack" (Bagpipes), but failed to produce a tune.

Eventually, I found that I could cope with Mohammed's work in three hours a day, on top of my own duties. It seemed better when he was away. The Khareef was starting up again. Patches of green shoots were appearing all over the desert. It was strange and exciting to see the almost miraculous change from inhospitable and hostile sand, to lush and green pasture after the merest hint of moisture.

My opposite number, Peter Clements, the new SRO Central, arrived to visit Salalah. He told me that he had been the Director of Works on St Helena for 12 years, and had been waiting for me to take over from him! He told me that the job was difficult in that the Governor and the Treasurer were not on speaking terms. When his father died, the boat had just sailed, and it took him 2 months to get home! I said that as I had aged parents, that was why I had refused the job. What a small world! They were shortly followed by the Walkers, my other opposite number SRO North. We all had drinks in my lounge for the rest of the afternoon. Maurice Walker does look like me, except that his beard has given him the nick-name "Garden Gnome". They spent a number of years in Lagos, and we reminisced. His Irish wife had worked in the Irish Embassy in Lagos, up the track from where Jane had bought the Black Label Whisky near the Ikoyi Club. She told us that that was the stall was where the Ambassador had to buy back the booze stolen from the Embassy!! The stallholder was the wife of the Embassy Driver. It was good to hear the rest of the story started years ago in Lagos. It was good to have my two opposite numbers together and to discuss working restraints in each region. It appears that I was the only true second-in-command, the others were merely allowed run a small area, and are discouraged from trying to help their Director. They just kept their heads down and obeyed the last order, however stupid.

As it was Eid, we all travelled over to the Frontier Force Mess and had a patio barbeque outside Wally's bayt with Dermot, Wally, Jill, Ron, on the Thursday evening. Dermot Fulton was a Scottish infantry officer sent to Oman to recover from a terrible incident in Northern Ireland in which two plain clothed soldiers were lynched at an IRA funeral and he had commanded the troops attempting their rescue. Ron was the Canadian Training Major in the Frontier Force and Gill was the Matron at the Military Hospital. The next morning I woke up an hour before the Mayne's arrived at noon from Muscat. We all ate in the Mess that night. We just ordered by phone and wandered over. This much more civilized than arrangements at Wudam or MAM, and compliments were paid. On the Saturday, we were up early and went through the back streets of Salalah to Job's Tomb (Ayub, in Arabic). On the way, we met Graham and his guests from Muscat, and two of my staff, Les Wornham and Alex Duncan. I took my guests along the Jebel to the Thumrait road, and collected real Frankincense gum off a tree. Then we continued across the main Thumrait road, past Zeak, on down to Ayn Arzat Springs and the Queen Mother's Garden, finishing with another Mess meal.

The next day, Sunday, was much longer. We travelled up the new Balfour Beatty road and into Aydim camp. Dave's District Supervisor had just been transferred there and we called to see him. We had coffee and sandwiches, and then we drove to see the blow holes where the sea has broken through the base of the cliffs. We stopped for tea at Wally's bayt in the FF Camp. Colonel Ali had ordered his bar open on the First day of Eid, and Wally and Dermot were suffering. Colonel Ali had laid on a Patio Party and we were all invited.

Monday was a late start, but we went shopping in a virtually shut town! Jill had told Elsie Mayne where to buy Myrrh, to link up with the Frankincense. The stall was closed, so we tried all the others that were open. Eventually we got the Myrrh just next to where we had parked. Elsie then dragged Dave and I round the dress materials shops! She got something in the end. They took me to the Holiday Inn Coffee Shop in the evening. On Tuesday we travelled eastwards along the coast to Taqah, Medinat al Haq on the jebel above Taqah, Queen of Sheba's palace, and then on to Mirbat to see the Fort. It is famous for the battle in 1972 where nine SAS soldiers took on 500 Yemeni communist enemy and won. At least two Victoria Crosses should have been awarded for this action but Britain was not officially at war. This turned the tide of the war and defeated Colonel Nasser's plan for dominating the Arabian Gulf. From Mirbat, we went straight up the jebel, and reached Tawi Attair from the east. On the way down to the plain, we turned into Wadi Darbat, to see the bathing camels. During the Dhofar War, several Omani and British officers died in an ambush here. That night in our Mess, there was an Omani Night complete with live music and stuffed goat barbeque.

On Wednesday, the Walkers and Clements drove north and the Mayne's went shopping on their own. I was on duty and stayed by the phone. That night, at FF, I hosted a patio meal for the Mayne's, Jill and Ron, and Wally. FF did me proud and we only left because the Mayne's wanted to be up at 5.00 am to drive north. I got a duty call during the evening. At Thumrait, one of our pick-ups had tried to chase a camel out of the sewage lagoons and had rolled into the sewage. The vehicle had been pulled out and first aid given. I said that I needed a statement from the only other witness, to use on the file, and that they were to interview the camel.

After the Mayne's drove off on Thursday morning, I went back to bed for a bit, only to be woken by the door bell. Dave Williams, previously my Accountant, came to call. He had a new job with Airworks Ltd in Salalah. The Royal Fleet Auxiliary would not have him as he hadn't held a U.K. address in 20 years. His new job was a tenth of the MODED work load, and he had 2 Brits and 4 Indians to help him. The pay is only £14,000, but it is money coming in. While he was away, he had two visits to Thai hospitals without insurance cover, for Appendicitis and torn muscles, using up all his cash

Saharan trip

My son, Hugh, had bought a clapped out ex-Dutch Army VW Kombi. He and his friend Andy from school days drove off to visit Tamanrassat and the climb the Haggar Mountains in southern Sahara. By the time they had reached Tamanrassat, they had worn out the clutch in the soft sand. A frantic message reached Jane, asking for a replacement clutch to be sent. Jane contacted Andy's mother in London, who was able to get the parts. She packed the parcel with food items to protect the parts. Jane was telling me about all this on the telephone, when I noticed that the local newspaper was announcing that Algeria had placed an immediate ban on the import of vehicle spares and food. Needless to say, the parcel arrived safely. In the intervening week, Hugh and Andy got a taxi to take them 180 km out to the Haggar region. They had a good week climbing, and then they realized that there are no passing taxis to be found in the desert. They had to walk back to Tamanrassat, all 180 km. I had previously given Hugh some Omani Army desert boots obtained from the FF Quartermaster. After this epic walk, he asked me to tell Wally that the boots were not fit for purpose. By this time, both mothers were nervous wrecks and were calling each other daily for news. They arrived back safely, and then Andy disclosed that, as he had not got a driving license, he really ought to take some lessons. All that distance, with only one qualified driver! No wonder the mothers were worried.

In April 1989, Jane had come to Salalah for a visit. After taking her on tours of the area and various military camps, she settled down to increasing her wardrobe. There are many dress material shops in Salalah, and a number of tailors. The routine is to buy material and then go to a tailor with a dress, for instance, and ask him to make "Same same". Some tailors are better than other at making copies. After a period of trial and error, and some wastage, one finally found a competent tailor. She also set about making my bayt into a home. I was forced into getting the three-piece suite recovered and buying new curtains. One day she noticed that my next door neighbour's kitchen units were being removed and telephoned me. This was her excuse to get me to replace our kitchen units. I checked with Suhail, the Civil

Supervisor, who said that the units were only out to discover the source of a vile smell (which turned out to be a dead cat under a unit). My neighbour was the Omani Navy Lt Colonel responsible for liaison with the Civil Authorities. Jane did not like the way that he used the fixed washing line posts for hanging his freshly killed goats when they were being butchered. Our lounge windows overlooked his rear garden.

One quiet Thursday afternoon, I was called by the Radio Room operator. There was a serious accident at the mobile road camp. An Omani had walked in looking for a job as a watchman, and had fallen asleep in the shade of one of the accommodation trailers. The road crew returned after work, and the vehicle had driven over his head. I mobilised the SOAF helicopter medical team, and the Army doctor from the nearest camp. The man was pronounced dead. The problem of prosecution and "Blood Money" compensation loomed up. Eventually, it was found that the man had been kicked out of his community and that no one was interested in pursuing any claim. He had previously tried to get us to give him a job as a watchman, but this time he had failed the trade test.

HMS Brilliant, a frigate, came into Port Raysut for a short visit. She later appeared in a 1990 BBC TV documentary. The Captain hosted a party onboard for the Sultan's Army, Navy and Airforce Officers, to which Jane and I were invited. The Royal Marines Band played on the quayside. It was all very impressive. They sailed on to Kenya for exercises. Shortly before arriving, the helicopter was sent ashore with people to liaise with the port authorities in Mombasa. It crashed, killing all nine aboard, some of whom I must have spoken to during my visit to the ship. The sliding door had come off the runners and hit the tail rotor.

After my 1989 Christmas leave, Jane came out for another long visit, returning to UK in March 1990. She had spent a lot more time with "Mr Same Same", the tailor, and filled a number of suitcases. I stayed in Muscat after seeing Jane onto the UK flight. Brigadier Wheatley had organized a Dinner for all serving and ex-Royal Engineer officers in Oman. The dinner went off well. The only other TA officer was the Vice Consul at the Embassy. We had met at the TA Annual Camp in Lancaster the week after Jane and I got married. The air-conditioning broke down and the Jebel Mess could not find any MODED people, as they were all at the Dinner.

The next morning I was at Amiantit Ltd by 8:00am, to get details of the dome for the "Martyrs" Cemetery job. The new mosque was to have a fibreglass dome, and I wanted the measurements to design and build the supporting concrete. That night, I went to the Clements party in the evening. It was the usual collection of Admirals and senior officers. I met Mary Walker, who had previously been in Lagos. She lives in MAM while her husband works away in Shafa all week. She has two small girls and had been promised that schooling would be available in Shafa, but it was not to be.

I got back to Salalah to discover that Hamid Mahruky had asked Mohammed why I was in MAM. Mohammed reminded him that he had already given permission. Apart from lots of work, we had the long awaited trip to the Border, where the Brigadier investigated the extent of the work that we thought Peter

290

Rogers' staff should have been responsible for, but that my staff had had to cover. This followed Wally's visit to MODED in Salalah and his further talks to Brigade about the lack of support that his Regiment was getting from Peter in Thumrait. Peter was forced to agree to station a Supervisor at the Border, and to some other changes. The meeting between Peter, Mohammed, and me, wasn't easy. Peter thought that we wanted the Salalah Superintendent, Graham, to take over some of his area, but this was not the intention. Some of Wally's ideas needed curbing as well. It was a difficult meeting all round, but it exposed Peter's lack of acceptance of the new organisation, and with him having to report to me.

Lots of officers came down for The Great Dhofar Road Race, which is a marathon length road race from the top of the jebel, down to the plain of Salalah. As usual, a Canadian lady diplomat won the women's prize. I seem to remember that the men's trophy going to a civilian, rather than one of the supposedly supremely fit ex-SAS types. The Brigade Mess was packed. Col Ravi, the CO of the Hospital, and his wife, Gauri, were invited. A brass plate had been fixed to the mess bar, in the corner, saying "Ravi also sat here". Later that afternoon, the Annual Raft race was held along a course set out in the sea next to the Holiday Inn beach. The Royal Oman Police team won the Raft Race, as expected. For some reason, best known to the hotel management, I was asked to present the prizes.

In April, 1990, Owen Jones, the Public Health Engineer, came back clutching his resignation letter. He wanted to leave in three weeks, so that he could start a new job in Manchester. At that time, there was plenty of work around with Councils trying to get the water and sewage up to EU standards. This was a real blow. There was no one else in MODED that can do Owen's job and an apparent end to all our schemes to improve health in the south. In addition, Ian Henderson was having Farewell parties. He would leave in May. As morale dropped, following Omanization, more and more ex-pat engineers decided to move away from Oman. Those that stayed had to shoulder more work. This resulted in a lowering of standards of service to our client, the Armed Forces. Individuals became more stressed out, and even more tried to leave. Mike Young, the MODED Chief Electrical Engineer, came down and stayed with me for a night, while he did the final interview on Sheik Hosnain, the new Power Station Manager on Thumrait Airbase. The previous Supervisor, an expat, had been fired after exposing himself to the Adjutant of the Western Frontier Regiment. His replacement did not settle down and had not produced any work. Sheik Hosnain was sent home at the end of the month, having failed his probationary period. With Deryck Robinson, Mechanical Supervisor, this was four senior staff lost in a month. Just like early 1989, when the Sultan had to step in and fix the exchange rate to stop the exodus.

I met Ron, Training Major and Second in Command of FF, in Raysut, while he waited for Colonel Ali to come back from the border. Ron spent a lot of his leave arranging for his fiancée's Immigration into Canada and not too much time on his career assessment interviews. They had arranged with the Vice-Consul, Chris Ling TD, (he was the only other ex-TAVR Sapper in Oman), to get married in July, just before Jill left Oman. She had got her Midwifery ticket and had job offers in Canada. Ron was programmed to leave in November, after National Day.

I spent two days in Sarfait. I had to get out of the office, because Ramadhan was driving everyone mad. I had arranged to meet Roads Supervisor Nel Santos there, but he was in the Isolation Ward of UAG hospital with an infectious skin fungus. I had not seen the work that he was doing in Sarfait and I was quite impressed. The Brigadier asked me to meet him at Habrut Camp, on the Border, to see what improvements had taken place since our attempt to resolve the Peter Rogers problem. I was asked to make sure that Peter Rogers arrived as well. I travelled with Wally, John Evans, the Brigade Mechanical Officer, and Major Cowley, the Army Catering Advisor, known as "The Silver Sausage". As it was Ramadan, we took a picnic, which was provided by Wally - as Cowley was not allowed to forget a previous trip when he forgot to arrange the promised food!! The result of the meeting between Peter and the Brigadier was that Peter was transferred to Muscat, to write reports until he resigned. This allowed me to take full control of all staff in the Region.

At the same time, Health & Safety arrived in the south. The Safety Officer arrived to be sent off with a driver to visit all the border locations for three days. His inspection produced no adverse comments. I think that the vastness of the area, and the strange food and beds awed him. Mohammed got back from his leave looking sick and was swigging bottles of potions. There was a bug in the local Jebali cattle which was giving cause for concern. Fresh meat gave people aching joints and skin sensitivity, together with other internal effects, but apparently frozen meat was acceptable.

Once a year, the Sultan drove from Muscat to Salalah, taking a different route each time. His convoy of 100 or so vehicles included a complete field hospital. At every village stop, he held an outdoor Majlis, where anyone could present a petition and discuss problems with the Ruler. The sick and injured were treated in the travelling hospital, and patients were often flown out to a main hospital. The Sultan would inspect the places that he passed through and instruct changes and improvements. He would also follow up these instructions personally and woe betide anyone who had ignored him. A shopkeeper in Salalah had a badly spelt shop sign which had offended, and the Sultan ordered it removed and corrected. It was not done and, on the next visit, the Sultan ordered a new shop sign saying "This man is bananas" be installed and for it to remain in place for several years. When the convoy entered my area, I had to make sure that all airstrips and helipads were in perfect condition, and all roads properly graded and prepared.

The Sultan had spent two years studying Town Planning in UK, and wanted Oman to have the best that it could afford. Instead of splashing out on one or two showpiece projects, each village got a school, a mosque, a clinic, and a water supply as a minimum. This improved the lives of Omanis over the whole country. One day workers started arriving late for work. The Education Ministry had removed all school buses, due to budget problems. My workers had to hire taxis to take children to school, taking time away from work. The angry mutterings were heard in the Palace in Salalah. In the early hours, the Sultan walked out of his Palace, commandeered a taxi and changed clothes with the driver. While the driver was entertained by Palace flunkies, the Sultan drove round the town, listening to the complaints made by his passengers. By noon, the school buses were back at work. He took a personal interest in his subjects and I admired him for this.

Our Mess often was required to host expat sub-contractors to the MOD. One lot provided the target drones used to train anti-aircraft gunners. Oman had arranged for them to help train the Navy gunners, and the ships duly arrived in Salalah's Port Raysut. The Sultan had many hours of TV film showing his forces in action, and had arranged for this target practice to be filmed as a live broadcast. As the drones cost £50,000 each, only two had been ordered. They were controlled by radio. Our Mess guests arrived back from the demonstration rather earlier than expected. Apparently, the TV rebroadcast frequency was similar the drone control frequency and both drones crashed as soon as filming started.

Following the successful installation of the Sarfait pipeline, further improvements to the Sarfait Water Supply system were made. Although the Ministry of Water had built the Desalination Plant on the beach at Dhalqut, they had no one to run the plant or sort out engineering problems. We took over this unit, as we were the major user of the water. We improved the 30 km road from the high jebel down to the beach, and purchased Mercedes Water Tankers, with very low range gearboxes. The gradients and bends required these special vehicles, as drivers had been killed previously. Mercedes instructors trained our drivers to cope with heavy loads on these difficult roads. While we were blasting the hillside above Dhalqut to improve the road for the tanker, we nearly knocked a SOAF Medevac flight out of the sky. It had been called to an emergency and we had not been informed of this unplanned flight. The plane landed among a shower of rocks and dust but was not damaged.

UNESCO Water collection Study

The United Nations decided to study rainwater harvesting from the onshore monsoon winds during the "Khareef" season. For three months, June to September, the southern Omani coast is blanketed with low cloud and drizzle caused by the onshore winds being prevented from moving north to the interior of the Arabian Peninsula. The first obstruction is high ground, at 1500 metres, immediately beyond the coastal plain, and the second being the prevailing hot, dry, winds flowing south from the Empty Quarter. The high level warm wind holds the damp onshore wind over the coastal plain, causing the release of rain. The result is a well watered and fertile coastal strip. The United Nations hired the University of Santiago, Chile, to do the investigation. I was asked to provide the practical help and assistance. Chile already harvested rain from the South Pacific Humboldt Current, where weather and land shapes were similar to southern Oman.

At the top of the cliffs, I erected a series of collection nets, supported on metal tubular poles, and with a collection trough under the nets. The mist had pass through holes in the cloth and for it to condense on the material around each hole. Too large a hole and the moisture passed straight through and did not

UNESCO FOG WATER COLLECTION
Note misty conditions

condense. Too small a hole and the net worked like a sail as the wind tried to overcome the obstruction. The netting was the same as that used by market gardens to shade plants from the sun. It is woven in a range of hole sizes. We tested several nets and found that a net with about a 70% opening to material ratio produced about 1 litre of water per square metre of cloth in 24 hours. Getting accurate measurements was difficult because the local herdsmen drove their cattle to this "free" water, so we had to get Army guards to prevent theft before we took measurements. The Canadian UN scientist was assisted by a young and glamorous lady professor and a post-grad student from Chile.

Another water supply problem was more serious. All borehole wells extracted fossil water, which is irreplaceable water trapped in rock strata. The whole Arabian Peninsula is basically a tilted plain, with a high edge in the south, dipping northwards. Thumrait Airbase was supplied by a number of boreholes, and the more southerly holes started to dry out. On examining the geological strata, this showed that the only way to ensure a supply of water was to drill more holes, further north. The nearest test well that found water was some 100 km north of the Airbase, and was deeper than the Thumrait wells. After costing the work required for the new well field, and the necessary supporting infrastructure, roads, and (essential to a military mind) the defence of the new site, it was almost cheaper to move the Airbase to the water, than the water to the Airbase.

Another Border incident

The new road to Jedillah and Ramlat Shuayt also needed wells to be drilled for the new camps. Water was found at Jedillah and the camp was provided with a supply. However, the local camels can smell water from 50 km. The Army camp was invaded, and we had to put a drinking trough about 1 km away from the camp. Camel owners and the Army were happy with the new arrangement, even knowing that some of the camels were from the Yemen. The float valve, controlling the water level in the trough was exactly the same as a standard W.C. ball valve. One day, the cover came off the ball valve chamber. Camels saw the bright orange plastic ball and were spooked. The herd fled across the border and had to be found and returned. This caused a Diplomatic Incident, much discussed between Foreign Ministers of both countries. I was unaware of the problem until I was summoned by Higher Command to explain. We had only just ended a previous war with the Yemen, and I was now accused of trying to start another! A plumber was sent off 450 km with a tin of black paint and he hid all traces of the nasty orange colour before replacing the tank cover. Honour and satisfaction was restored.

On another trip to check on road maintenance progress, we stopped off at an old Army camp which had had the Dhofar War code name of Coke Oven. After the war ended, the camp was removed, leaving some concrete bases. When we arrived, over ten years later, one slab was immaculate. The sand had been freshly swept off it, and the steel holding down bolts had been freshly polished and oiled. No one was in sight. As we snacked, two Omanis appeared, a father and son. It appeared that, when the camp generator was removed, they had been promised that it would be returned later. They had been keeping the slab ready for this day. It also appeared that they were still on some unknown Army pay list and were being paid to look after this slab. There was no intention of ever returning the camp to this location but someone had forgotten to cancel the caretaking arrangement.

Knocking down Brigade Headquarters

Meanwhile, in Salalah the infrastructure was showing signs of decay. A number of buildings had been built during the Dhofar War by the military, while under shellfire from the surrounding jebel hilltops. Concrete sand was, unfortunately, only available from the beach. In time, the sea salt decomposes the concrete and accelerates the rusting of the reinforcement. The Brigade Headquarters building, including the Airforce Commander's offices, was the only two storey building from that era. It was 15 years old, and cracks were appearing in columns. Although the concrete roof slab was only 100mm thick, many signals masts had been erected on the roof, with bolts drilled through the slab. Rain water ran down these holes and encouraged the reinforcement to rust. The sideways wind forces on the masts had also twisted the slab, opening up more cracks. The Brigade Commander's office had been enlarged by removing a load bearing wall, which had supported the roof slab! To hide the spalling of concrete from the ceiling, someone had fitted a suspended ceiling. An electrician working on lights above the ceiling in the BC's office was knocked unconscious by spalling concrete. After rescuing the electrician, I decided that the building was unsafe. I ordered the Brigade HQ and the Airforce out of the building, putting in a forest of props for their safety, and we transformed the old Umm Al Gwariff Fort into the new Brigade Headquarters. My superiors told me that I had caused more damage to the Brigade than the recent Yemeni actions, but they reluctantly accepted my decision and found funds to rebuild the condemned building. When demolition started, one single sledgehammer blow on one end of the roof slab resulted in the collapse of the opposite half of the building.

At the Salalah Airforce Officers Mess, there was a remnant of the Dhofar War. An air portable mortuary had been delivered in 1971 and had been later incorporated into the kitchen as a freezer room. This had deteriorated so much that it was beyond economic repair. I obtained a new freezer room and had it installed. The Base Commander, Kerry Drew, invited Jane and I to a formal Mess Dinner to celebrate the kitchen upgrade. When the main course was about to be served, a piper marched in, followed by a waiter bearing an enormous silver salver with a domed cover. This salver was placed in front of me, as chief guest, and Kerry made a speech. He said that I was being honoured for providing the new freezer room and that I was to have first cuts from the arm that they had found when the old mortuary unit was defrosted. Jane and I looked aghast at the salver, and so did a number of others who were not in on the joke. The salver was empty!

On previous visits to the SAF Engineers headquarters, I had seen a bitumen spray tanker parked in their compound. This had never been used, and there was plenty of work all over the country that it could have done. It took about a year to get this tanker transferred from the Army to the Engineering Directorate, after I had made many representations. SAFE did not want to admit that they did not know what it could do or that they did not know how to operate it. Eventually it arrived in the South and we started surface dressing some of the 2,000 km of roads we maintained.

Sultan's Special Forces

On occasions, the Commander of the Sultan's Special Forces (SSF) would invite me to his headquarters at Zeak. Colonel Keith Farnes had commanded the TA SAS at White City during the time of the Iranian Embassy siege. I provided plant to maintain and improve roads, tracks, ranges and helipads for SSF. Once, after a long lunch in the Garrison Officers Mess, Keith and a group of his officers, in full camouflage uniform wanted to prolong the drinking session after the bar closed. Keith had his red tab collar badges and I telephoned the Warrant Officers Mess to get them an invitation, saying that I had a "bunch of clowns in fancy dress" with me.

Keith was replaced by another commander later. The new man had served in the Foreign Legion as an airborne sergeant. His unit had mutinied in Algeria against General De Gaulle and had been sent to fight, as a punishment, at Dien Bien Phu during the First Indochina War in Vietnam. He survived that and joined the Royal Artillery as a Gunner and rose to the rank of Colonel. He was a very tough individual. He married a much younger and very attractive French lady. Attendance at SSF parties was fraught with danger as one could not help admiring the wife, but had to avoid being caught looking at her.

One day, sitting in my office, an important visitor was announced. The Commander of the Palace Guard in Salalah wanted our help with some project. This major had lost a leg in the Dhofar War. While leading an attack, his infantry unit ran into a minefield. He heard a "click" as the plunger of the detonator went down and immediately stood still. He commanded the rest of the battle while keeping pressure on the mine plunger, until he won the skirmish some hours later, before thinking about saving himself. He then carefully arranged for a Medevac helicopter, several stretcher bearers with stretchers, and a doctor. When all was in place, he threw himself backwards. The blast damaged his leg. The Sultan gave him the highest gallantry award. This officer was from the Frontier Force, and was also at the last battle of the Dhofar War at Sherashiti. The door from the Wali's house in Sherashiti is now the centrepiece of the FF Mess, and the Major's portrait is in pride of place above it.

Round the world solo yachtsman

While I was in Muscat, I had seen a large yacht up on blocks behind our Mess. At odd intervals, some work was being done. One day it was loaded onto a low-loader and taken away. In Salalah, years later, I was invited to a private breakfast at the Frontier Force Mess. This was to meet an ex-RSM who had just completed a solo round the world trip. He wanted a very small gathering as he was no longer used to meeting people after more than a year at sea! He looked thin and underfed, which he explained away. There was only so much storage onboard and there was a difficult balance between cigarettes and food. He spoke about his scariest moment, in the South Pacific Ocean, many miles from help, when he was trying to fix a broken rope in a storm. With the boat at a steep angle, he looked down and realised that he had both ends of his safety harness in his hand and the he was not clipped onto the boat.

Selling alcohol to the enemy during a war

During the war with the Yemen, something else was going on that was not so savoury. Reports had been coming in to the Police and Military Security that one of my vehicles was selling Whisky to Yemenis. Trading with the enemy was bad enough but both countries were Muslim and banned all alcohol. I had asked my Roads Superintendent to meet me one morning. He failed to arrive, but telephoned me from Berlin, saying that he had heard of the alcohol investigation looming up and had fled. As the officer responsible for all alcohol used by MODED in the Region, I immediately did a full stock check on all the MODED Messes, and could find no signs of missing stock. I reported the disappearance of the Superintendent and arranged for his vehicle to be recovered from the airport in Muscat. Thereafter, I had the MOD Special Investigation Branch (SIB) and the local CID crawling all over me and all of our affairs. Eventually, it was found that the Indian clerks at the wholesale company had used our account to hide the removal of stock, thus implicating us. We were officially said to be innocent but that did not explain my Road Superintendant's sudden departure. He must have had some knowledge of the arrangement. He may even have transported the whisky, as he roamed far and wide along the border as part of his duties. It did not do my reputation much good. It was a very uncomfortable few months.

Hunter Fighter crash

Following the Yemen War, the Airforce in Thumrait realised that their radar system would not have warned them of approaching MIG fighter bombers until it was too late. The radar set was placed next to the runway, and was "blinded" by high jebel peaks to the southwest where the attack would come from. I suggested that the radar set, a trailer mounted unit, be towed up to the top of a suitable jebel and put to work guarding the base. SOAF officers said that it could not be done, most were ex RAF desk warriors, but agreed that the move was needed. I pointed out that several other radars in the north of Oman were on hill tops, but they professed not to know this!

I selected a jebel and we built a road to the top, levelling out a wide area for the radar, the control cabin and the fuel tank. The full SOAF Inspection team insisted on approving the earthworks before allowing their precious radar to move from the safety of the airbase. They came, they saw, and they were amazed. I was graciously allowed to tow the radar units up the hill and assemble the system. A final inspection was due on a Saturday, at the start of the week. On the previous Thursday, I visited the site to see if all was ready for the "Royal" visit. Whilst at the top, a Hunter jet fighter got into difficulties and the pilots bailed out. The aircraft thumped into the jebel, crashing on the road half way up to the top. The jet was fully fuelled and armed. We could not get down until everything was safe from the fire and the exploding ammunition, and I had the prospect of spending the rest of the weekend on the top of the hill. Eventually the two pilots were found and collected safely, and the fires died down. It was dark when I was able to start my 80 mile drive home. The inspection was a success.

Flying in Dhofar

The three years in Salalah involved almost weekly helicopter or light aircraft trips to outstations. Not all flights were incident free. The SOAF "Defender" is a Britten Norman Islander. This twin engined eight seater was ideal for short desert runways and was used to ferry personnel, food, and spares. Salalah had one Omani pilot who could only navigate by following roads. The desert road is made from the desert materials and is exactly the same colour as the surrounding desert. In strong sun glare, it can be difficult to see roads or runways! On journeys with this pilot, we all made great attempts not to interfere with his concentration. On another trip, with a generator mechanic, we had a medical problem. This ex-Merchant Navy mechanic had short legs and could only get out by sitting and sliding his legs out of the door. On landing, we all got out and walked away to our various duties, and then a scream came from behind. The mechanic was half out of the door, with a cargo hook through his scrotum holding his weight. His legs did not reach the ground!

Another aircraft was the Short SC7 Skyvan. This was a slow cargo workhorse, with access to the rear through a roll-up garage door. Everything rattled. Bill

SKYVAN - Load bay

McGillivary was an ex-Phantom jet fighter pilot and was used to having tremendous power at his command. He once flew me directly at a cliff face, hoping that the Skyvan would eventually have enough power to climb over the top of the cliff. There was a point where even Bill though that he may have misjudged the situation.

Approaching Sarfait by air was tricky. Due to the onshore winds competing with the prevailing winds in the opposite direction, there were three windsocks to check on the approach over the deep valleys. Invariably, they would point in three different directions. Just before the start of the runway, one crossed a deep wadi, which had for most of the time a strong updraft. Some time before, my staff had had to paint a large horizontal line about 20 feet below the top of the wadi face. Pilots aimed at this and prayed that the updraft would gently waft them up and onto the runway. There were days when the uplift did not happen and there were three wrecks on the wadi face! This runway had 2000 foot drops on three sides, and was carved into an unforgiving cliff on the other side. The runway was some 300 foot short of the recommended length, and sloped upwards towards Yemen. On taking off, the aircraft had to bank sharply to avoid flying over Yemeni territory just across the wadi. Although normally bathed in intense sunshine, a mist cloud can form in an instant and the runway can vanish from sight. After my first fixed wing visit to Sarfait, I only ever travelled there by helicopter or by road! After a visit by the Sultan, by helicopter, where I had sprayed old engine oil to reduce flying dust on the helipad, complaints from the Palace came down from on high. Oil had ruined the plush carpets in the helicopter. Therefore a hard surfaced helipad was needed. As this instruction got passed down the line to me, the requirement grew like Topsy to include hard surfaces to all landing sites in

Sarfait, including the runway! Pilots thought that surfacing the runway was a bad idea, as it would induce skids in wet weather. The existing open crushed rock surface drained in wet weather and provided skid resistance. Open mutiny by pilots, who feared for their lives, finally persuaded lower grade Palace officials to admit that they had increased the minimum requirement, to please his Majesty.

Pilot fatigue, in the heat, was a problem. Flying back to Salalah in a helicopter once, I noticed that the wadi walls were rising as we flew on. I looked through to the pilot, and saw that his helmet was resting on his shoulder. I told the Loadmaster, who screamed something in Arabic into his microphone and the pilot woke up! Most flights were on known routes to known destinations.

When I had to escort the Government Chief Hydrogeologist, searching for new water sources, we went right off the beaten track. This man was from USA, and that country had a poor reputation with most Muslims. He learnt to avoid trouble, when they heard him speak, by saying that he was from the "Southern Province of Canada". On these trips we would be issued with smoke flares and would hope and pray that the returning helicopter could find us.

My last trip was up the border, to look at road building work. A new Loan Service RAF pilot had arrived and he was being shown the area by an old hand. They had a lot of RAF things in common and had a great conversation on the intercom system, to which I was listening. We visited Ghannat and Habrut and returned to Salalah. On arriving in Salalah, I offered the two pilots a drink in my Mess to thank them. An hour or so later a very agitated Omani Airforce officer burst in, asking us for our report on the bullet holes in the helicopter. We had not felt a thing and there had been no interference with any controls. Apparently we had flown over a wedding party, who were firing wildly into the air, in celebration.

The Brigadier decided that a new road route into Sarfait was required, to avoid passing along a very narrow section on a ridge in full view of the enemy. I met my Road Superintendent, Nel Santos, near Sherashiti where the helicopter carrying the Brigadier was to land. After studying the map, we set off on a 26 km walk across rough terrain. We started at about 4000 ft above sea level and continued dropping down, valley after ridge after valley, until reaching a point in the main wadi, some 10 km from Sarfait and at about 2000 ft above sea level. Nel had worn his steel toecap safety boots and every downhill step had forced the toecap onto the tops of his toes. At this point he decided to tell us that he could walk no further. I was asked to stay with him, while the Army party went on and arrange for the helicopter to collect us. Eventually, with night falling, the helicopter arrived and winched us both out of the wadi. Nel was taken to the sick bay for treatment. The Army party had left in road vehicles and my Landcruiser was still at the start of the walk. The helicopter pilot agreed to try and find the vehicle in the dark. It was parked miles off the main road. We found the vehicle and I finally got back very late at night.

The Airforce had a peculiar command structure and new security passes had to be issued. The Airforce security guards were not under the Base Commander, but reported to Airforce Headquarters. A Maximum Alert exercise for Thumrait Airbase was ordered. Combat Air Patrols had to be flown over the base. I was in a queue at the main gate, behind two pilots in full "G-Suits", who were meant to be airborne. None of us had the new passes, and we were prevented from entering the base! A request for maintenance on the sand runway came in. This was the longest sand runway in the Middle East, and needed regular grading and rolling. Without the new passes, we could not get the plant into the base. What the Air Police did not know was that the fence did not go the whole way round the base, and the boundary was wide open on the north and west sides! The plant went in and did the job. The problem then arose when the plant convoy tried to leave the base though the normal gate! Eventually, sense prevailed and normal working resumed.

While visiting Thumrait one Thursday (which is like Saturday elsewhere), I watched two jets take off. This, on a Thursday, was unusual, so I parked up on the perimeter track near the end of the runway and watched. I have never before or since seen such a display of aerobatics. Two Jaguars tried to outshine each other, racing low along the runway and climbing slightly to get over the roof of my Landcruiser. It lasted about 40 minutes. Later I heard that the two pilots had had words in the bar about each other's skills or lack thereof and a challenge was given. One was ex-Red Arrows, the other ex-Chief Flying Instructor at RAF Cranwell, both "Contract Officers" or as Jane would have called them, mercenaries. These jet pilots, out in the desert, often got bored. Playing "chicken" on the main road was fun. Flying straight at an oncoming vehicle, with the aircraft headlight on, was a favourite. There was a photo in the vehicle workshop of a pick-up with a groove in the roof caused by a Jaguar nose wheel! Another pilot had his family out for a visit and took them to a picnic site, on one of the viewing stands built for the Sultan on a bombing range. This elevated site had a metal hand rail to stop people falling down a cliff. The pilot flew his Jaguar, to show off to his family, and got a bit too close to the viewing stand. He landed with a length of handrail stuck in his wing! We were asked to remove some serious grooves cut into the main runway because, one weekend, an officer was showing his wife how to drive the new fire engine, when she rolled it many times.

Gulf War 1

Towards the end of 1990, the first Gulf War preparations started. In August, squadrons of RAF and USAF fighters and bombers started to transit through Thumrait and Salalah, en route to Saudi Arabia. We provided levelled areas for new tented cities, parking areas for dozens of aircraft, generators and electrical systems, water and sewage systems, and any other item demanded. The USAF Field Hospital was set up in a hangar, and I was asked to produce 100 foot length of lead sheet to make a wall round the X-Ray room. There was no lead in Southern Oman to be had, so other safety precautions were needed. The CO of the USAF Hospital was a Paediatrician, and his deputy was a Psychiatrist. I felt that this combination was the perfect choice to match the US personnel that I met! The Hospital Matron was a Jane Fonda look alike. These three visited my villa in Salalah on one of their free days. On another day, a frantic telephone call came from a supplies officer. He was having to pay demurrage on a ship in Port Raysuit because he had nowhere to dump 3,000 tonnes of bombs. Could I help? We cleared a large area in the desert a few miles from the Thumrait Airbase and trucks delivered the bombs. No fencing or guard posts were asked for or provided. The US delivered material in a fleet of

300

Lockheed C-5 Galaxy aircraft, one of the largest freight aircraft in the world. The tail fins stood many feet higher than any building on the base! When the first one arrived, we all rushed over to gawp at it. A diminutive female Lt Colonel stepped off the plane, unholstered her Colt 45, and declared that her all-girl crew were "off-limits". The sand runway was converted into a parking lot for C130 Hercules planes. On one day I counted 29 aircraft parked on this runway.

The USAF "Top Guns" spent time bragging that, having flown in Nevada, they knew all about desert flying. The two SOAF pilots that had given me the demonstration decided that they needed a bit more instruction. F15 Eagles are much faster than the SOAF Jaguars, but the first casualty of the Gulf War was an F15 pilot who was outflown by a slower aircraft. I had to send a generator and water to the guards at the crash site. Later on, another F15 tried to fly under a camel. Once again, a generator and water went to the site, while waiting for the Accident Investigation Board to arrive. When they arrived, they asked what had become of the camel, as they could not confirm that it was part of the accident without seeing evidence. The guards had eaten it while waiting for the AIB.

My Regional Director, Mohammed Noor, had been replaced by Mohammed Al Baluch. My new boss had started life as a tyre fitter and was unsophisticated. He was keen on reducing costs and some of his edicts were questionable. Electricians did not need a mate to hold the ladder when changing street light bulbs. I was ordered to cancel the hire contract for the only welder skilled enough to make exhaust pipes. We had some 300 different shapes in the vehicle and plant fleets. Simultaneously, he banned the purchase of exhaust pipes because we could make our own! Life got increasingly more difficult, especially when he found Colonels coming to my office rather than to him. He fell out with the Brigadier when he refused some of the Army requests.

For three years, I had been trying to get an earthworks Foreman the correct pay and grade for the excellent job that he had been doing. He was still being paid as a plumber's assistant. Every attempt failed, no matter how high the senior officer was who endorsed the application. The Head of Engineering even failed to get the Head of Personnel to grant the promotion. On investigation, I found that the Head of Personnel (a Lt Col) was being controlled by a civilian Pakistani Chief Clerk. This clerk was from Sind province, near Karachi, and hated anyone from the North West Frontier of Pakistan. This was why there was never any promotion for my deserving foreman. In my last year, I exposed the clerk to all and sundry, hoping for his rapid replacement. He held onto his post and his boss the Lt Colonel was transferred. I had made a powerful enemy of this clerk. Once a year, my ongoing employment contract had to be ratified by the Palace, and I had submitted my papers some eight months before the anniversary, as requested. Nothing was heard and I assumed that renewal was proceeding normally. Just before arranging my annual leave over Christmas, I checked to see if renewal was happening. The Palace had not received the papers, and time was running out. It appeared that the personnel clerk had "lost" my application. I went on leave and told the Head of Engineering that I would not be allowed back into Oman without a visa based on a renewed contract. Many frantic calls were made to rectify the situation and to persuade me to return without a visa. In December 1990, Oman gave up the struggle to get me a visa and the Chief

Clerk had me "Administratively dismissed" for failing to return from leave. He had won, and I was now officially made "Persona Non Grata" in Oman. Never underestimate the Pakistani Mafia.

The five years in Oman were the best years of my life. I had had a great job, in a very professional military organisation, with freedom to do the best I could for the armed forces with my 1500 staff. The country was fascinating and gave me real challenges unrivalled elsewhere in my career.

England (again)   1991

During the build up to the start of the first Gulf War, I attended a small number of job interviews and secured a job with W. S. Atkins in Dhahran, Saudi Arabia. I foolishly told other possible employers that I had a job. I was due to fly to Dhahran and was all packed to go, when the war started. My flight into the war zone was to be on the first night of the war, and was cancelled by BA. Atkins told me to sit tight until they called me. The weeks went past, and still no call.

My interviewer was David Coppin, and I spoke to him weekly. He had been an Infantry Officer in Kenya during Mau Mau times. He resigned and joined the Kings African Rifles and served in East Africa for a number of years. Later he served with the Trucial Oman Scouts in Dubai, before joining the Sultan of Oman's Army. He had almost a parallel existence to me and we became friends. I later found out that, in spite of him fighting under four flags, he was awarded the George Medal as a civilian. He had, by himself, disarmed and arrested two armed robbers outside a Barclays Bank in London, using a piece of wood from a rubbish skip! David had earlier asked if I could recommend any Materials engineers for the work in Saudi Arabia and I told him of Les Painting. Les was working for Atkins in Saudi when I arrived. Eventually Atkins told me that, due to the war, the Saudi Government was unable to proceed with the work that I was recruited for. The site of the work was now covered with a huge, but temporary, US Army and Airforce Camp. I got a payment to cover the standby time, and started searching again for work. The Gulf War had disrupted plans in many countries, and funding for schemes had dried up. Work in UK, for my background, seemed non-existent.

After eight months unemployment, Pell Frischmann offered me a job in Riyadh, on the Al Yamamah Project. I was to start in September 1991, subject to the usual Saudi Visa requirements being satisfied. This long period of unemployment used up all our savings and I had to remortgage the house to survive.

After being approved by the Saudi authorities, I had to attend an Induction Course at BAe Warton Aerodrome, Lytham St Annes, Lancashire. This week long course was to teach me how to behave with Arabs, and the cultural differences between our two nations. Unfortunately, having some seven years recent experience of working in the region, I found that the course had little or no relevance, and was aimed at first time expats. I was able to take Jane to Lytham with me and we saw a bit of Lancashire. I also met another Pell Frischmann recruit, Mike Mead, who was to share my office for several years. Mike was an electrical engineer who had recently returned from Kuwait, after being released from being a hostage of Saddam Hussein. Although he had resigned from his job, he had stayed an extra week to claim his correct final settlement pay and to ship his car and goods home. Saddam invaded and Mike finished up in the Embassy, wearing the Ambassador's dressing gown, and losing all his possessions to Iraqi looters.

Saudi Arabia – Riyadh   1991 - 2004

On the eve of my Birthday, 26 September 1991, I arrived in Riyadh late in the evening, after a pleasant flight direct from Heathrow, and was met by the British Aerospace personnel officer. There were four of us on the flight, and we were all driven to the Bachelor Accommodation. In the morning, we were all taken by minibus to BAe Headquarters to be issued with passes, to open bank accounts, and to obtain driving licences. I was issued with a car and then taken to meet my new Saudi boss in the Al Yamamah Project Office, on the top floor of a large office block in central Riyadh.

The Al Yamamah Project Office (AYPO) was responsible to the Saudi Government for the administration of the whole Project. The Government to Government Agreement between the United Kingdom and the Kingdom of Saudi Arabia was covered by a Memorandum of Understanding signed by Margaret Thatcher and Prince Sultan, then Deputy Prime Minister. The United Kingdom was to supply aircraft and support services through BAe, whilst being supervised by the UK Ministry of Defence. A strong British military and civilian team was in place to oversee the project, which was Britain's largest ever export contract.

It had been realised by the Saudi side that they had no qualified engineering staff to control and supervise all the necessary construction work required. Pell Frischmann, operating overseas as Conseco International, negotiated a management contract for this supervision. A Conseco Technical Director, Gordon Fletcher, was in Riyadh, and Mike Mead and I were to join his team. We all reported to Eng Mohammed Saad Al Moammer, Head of Engineering for the Al Yamamah Project. He, in turn, reported to the Airforce General in charge of the Al Yamamah Project, and he in turn to Prince Sultan. Eng Mohammed was a USA trained Engineer and Architect, with superb commercial skills, and was a pleasure to work for over many years.

BAe Riyadh was a culture shock for me, because I had spent years in grotty overseas accommodation, on low contractors pay. The Bachelor accommodation had marble floors, black jacketed Indian waiters giving silver service in the restaurant, a room with plenty of space for the king sized bed. Laundry and food was supplied free of charge. I quickly accepted the improved situation. Newly arrived staff on married status contracts had to serve out three months probation before wives could join them.

The Project had been running for a number of years before my arrival, so I was told to first read all the files to get a picture. We were required to analyse and criticize all schemes proposed by BAe and provide support for Eng Mohammed in his negotiations. Gordon was a Fellow of the Institution of Mechanical Engineers, who had been in charge of replacing all the HVAC (Heating Ventilation and Air-conditioning) plant in the Bank of England building. Mike had put the Institution of Electrical Engineering Regulations into Kuwaiti Law and Kuwaiti Standards. (The Arabic translation for requiring a 2 metre distance between kitchen taps and any electrical outlet was translated as "No outlets within 2 metres of a kitchen".)

I was the Civil Engineering part of the set up. Also in the office was an Architect who had worked on many buildings on many Saudi Airbases. He was married to an Iraqi dissident, and had converted to Islam. During the first Gulf War he had been sent to the basement archives in Airforce Headquarters to retrieve some drawings. Security was tighter than normal, and his link with Iraq was discovered. He was banned from looking at the drawings until he pointed out that his signature was on each drawing. Down at Khamis Mushayt Airbase, Keith Barrow was our eyes on the ground where considerable construction was in progress. This was a total of five engineers to control some £1Billion worth of construction work at that time. The total value was to quadruple in following years. The Memorandum of Understanding was supported by Letters of Offer and Agreement. These LOAs detailed what the UK would provide, and what Saudi Arabia would pay for. Separate LOAs covered Aircraft, Weapons, Maintenance Support, Training, and Construction. Our initial responsibility was for all works covered by the Construction LOA, but many more LOAs were added to our workload in later years, including Minesweepers for the Navy, and work on new airbases.

While waiting for my probationary period to end, I spent my evenings driving around Riyadh to get the feel of the place. The great majority of the city was laid out on a one kilometre grid of major roads. This was the idea of the Australian woman Town Planner then in charge. Her idea was for the centre of each "village square" to have shops, schools, library, mosques and other public buildings, thus encouraging building of a community. The main highways were wide, and were three lane dual carriageways, with two lane side service roads on each side. Crossing a main road on foot felt like an expedition. Her idea of building communities fell down, however, because the Municipality passed a Bylaw allowing shops to spring up on the service roads to the main highways, to catch passing trade. The "village square" community centres became abandoned.

My only traffic accident in Saudi Arabia happened in my first week. The steep ramp up to a bridge over the Expressway meant a handbrake start. I was new to the car and rolled back into a bus, removing its front bumper. The Phillipino bus driver, fearing for his job, insisted that I follow him to his depot to explain the damage. On arrival, I telephoned the company "Mr Fixit", who sorted out traffic accidents. While the bus company workshop assessed the cost of the damage, I was asked to sit in the Foreman's office. The Foreman locked the door and opened the safe. He brought out a huge bundle of handcuffs and asked me what size I took, as I had to remain until the repairs were paid for. It turned out, eventually, that he was joking and the handcuffs were there to help transfer prisoners between jails. Mr Fixit arrived and sorted the problem, to my relief.

Towards the end of the first three months, I started the process of getting Jane's Visa and getting BAe to allocate a villa on a compound. All expats in BAe, and most larger companies, had their staff housed in walled compounds with from six to eighty houses, which were rented from Saudi Landlords. Foreigners could not own Saudi land. I was allocated a house in a six villa compound very close to the Ministry of the Interior Headquarters, and only a few yards from one of the main cross-roads in the city. As my job in Saudi included building inspection, I looked at the villa and made a list of defects needing to be rectified before it was fit for human habitation. BAe considered I was a "new boy" and a "sub-contractor", and that I had "no knowledge of building inspection". I was sent to the back of the queue for the work. BAe quickly found out that they had made a mistake, and they suffered during the next thirteen years of inspections which were much more rigorous than they expected.

The end of the probation period coincided with Christmas, so I went on leave to collect Jane. On our return, I felt it easier to spend the first night in my bachelor room and give Jane a taste of five star living. My colleagues, Mike and Colin, a senior bean-counter, normally ate with me at the same time and table, so my habits were well known to the waiters. Jane had been nagging me about weight loss, without success. I had a fondness for custard and the waiters quickly got to know that I would have it with almost every dish, if allowed. That evening, I introduced Jane to the others and we ordered the meal. When the sweet arrived, the Head Waiter and another arrived carrying a two gallon jug of custard, "Especially for you, Sir". Jane's face was a picture. Mike and Colin admitted the joke.

As soon as we moved into the new villa, now fit for use, Jane had to shop for food. The Abaya that I had bought for her in the Souk for her was the wrong type. A man can never buy the correct garment for a woman, but choosing an Abaya is impossible. Luckily, Ann Fletcher, my boss's wife, had offered to take Jane under her wing. Ann soon sorted the correct Abaya and told her where and what to shop. Ann was a jolly, plump, short lady in late middle age. In my imagination, she was a typical Women's Institute member. We all had an Indian house servant supplied by BAe. Ann had had an experienced man, who was promoted away, and he arranged for his nephew to come as his replacement, knowing that Ann would help train him. Reasonably skilled in most things, he was hesitant in using English. The older man asked Ann to spend time in the same room with the lad, to talk to him to give him confidence, and hoped that he would speak. One day, while ironing behind Ann, he spoke his first English words: "Madam. Do you break-dance?" he enquired. The thought of Ann break-dancing broke the ice. Later, Ann walked to her nearest shop, and on her return journey she was harassed by the Mutawween, the Religious Police. The large estate car, with a powerful public address system, followed her all the way home with about six men screaming at her. They demanded, by loud hailer, that she "cover her hair", but Ann had no scarf with her. They kept up the shouting all the way to her gate. She got in and collapsed in tears. The new young house servant tried to console her. "Madam. Not to worry. The law about covering your head is not for you. It is only for the young and beautiful". For Ann, this was the last straw. She was not amused. However, she recovered to relate the story later.

It was an offence for women to show any hair, and to have coloured hand and toe-nails. Jane, when shopping, could "tune out" the Mutawwa when they spoke to her. Friends would often tell me of an angry Saudi tapping his camel-cane and yelling at Jane who ignored the noise. It worried Jane's friends. It frustrated the Mutawween and I feared that she would be dragged off to explain herself. She did use coloured nail varnish, after all. A woman arrested had to be collected by her "responsible male". As the Mutawween confiscated mobile phones and denied the use of the telephone, a worried husband could not find where his wife was being held. It could take days to locate, and release one's wife. Wives quickly learnt how to behave in public, for fear of a night in the cells.

Colin, the Financial Manager on the Al Yamamah team working in the office next door, also brought out his wife and two small girls about the same time. She did not like Riyadh and demanded that she return to UK. Colin, in an attempt to bribe the girls to convince the mother to stay, bought a Siamese kitten. This move did not work. The family went back to Britain and we got Charlie, the cat. Charlie was our companion for the next nineteen years. Colin lived next door to the Company Doctor, Dai James. Dai had worked previously in Libya, where he had extended his contract "because his new house had an alcohol still concreted into the staircase". One of the problems of working in a Muslim country is the availability of alcohol. Dai had been a Locum GP in Gloucester, and had the murderer Frederick West and his family on his list.

In theory, we had to visit Airbases to inspect building work and attend meetings on proposals for new work. Normally, site visits reveal problems sometimes omitted from drawings, and discussions with actual users are vital to getting a product that is workable. In practice, it was difficult to get visits arranged away from Riyadh. So we operated with minimal information, inaccurate drawings, poorly translated documents, and no overall feel for the site of the works. It was like being a surgeon in a darkened room, trying to operate on a patient in the next room by remote control, while wearing ear plugs and an eye mask. We tried to overcome the communication problem by asking a barrage of detailed questions, not always getting answers successfully. One main stumbling block was that any deviation from the plan that BAe had put forward meant an imagined possible loss of profit by BAe and a delay in starting the works. As we looked after some 3000 buildings over seven airbases in the thirteen years, life was not easy. While some facilities were purpose made new builds, a lot were "work–arounds" where adaptations to existing buildings were needed for a new use. Inserting specialized technical military equipment into any scheme, without specialist knowledge of RAF current practice and procedure often gave rise to difficulties. The UKMoD team of RAF experts worked closely with BAe, but not with us. We would only get queries after the RSAF user had a problem!

Up to 1999, although I had an "All Bases Pass", I only managed to visit Airbases in Taif and Riyadh, in all that time. Later, I managed one visit to the Navy Base at Jubail. The other AYPO staff were no more successful. BAe and the Royal Saudi Airforce seemed to conspire to restrict our movements, and our effectiveness. We had to limit ourselves to restricting the more blatant excesses, where possible. All we could do was inform Eng Mohammed and hope that he could influence the Al Yamamah Project Officer (AYPO), Major General Prince Turki bin Nasser Al Saud (known as TBN).

In 1991, the resumption of normal Al Yamamah work replaced the emergency works done in support of the Gulf War. Lessons learned from the Gulf War changed requirements and equipment. Earlier designs had to be modified to cope with new ideas for the deployment of Air Squadrons. Frequently this meant reassessing the total electrical load required for an airbase, and upgrading the incoming supply.

Similarly, water and sewage upgrades sometimes were required. The costs of these vital considerations were not always included by BAe, and this caused friction. As we progressed, BAe started to realise that we actually could help the project, and we started to act more as a team. This combined approach was developed to include civils sub-contractors, sub-contract design consultants, and specialist equipment suppliers. The end result was that, in the thirteen years I was there, only one "Contractual Letter" needed to be sent. This was remarkable, as a UK litigious culture would have led to a Claims Assessor "feeding frenzy". There were some BAe Managers, fresh from UK, who had the Claims Culture firmly fixed in their minds, but Eng Mohammed was able to train them into the Al Yamamah teamwork method.

Jane and I were able to spend a long weekend in Jeddah, at the Red Sea Hotel, during Ramadan that first year. Michael Palin stayed there when he filmed one of his round the world trips. Much better hotels have been built since, but that was about the best at the time. We wandered around the old town and the old Souk. This was a complicated maze of old alleyways and mud-brick buildings. I realised that my gut feeling for turning down the job with A. G. Streeter, to rebuild the sewer system, had been a very wise move. No wonder that they went bust after attempting this job.

Heart attack

We got to know our compound neighbours and several parties were held, round the shared pool. On Thursday 7th May, 1992, we had a party and I spent the evening talking to an enormous Irishman. Captain Dennis Grey had been Marine Superintendent of the Irish Lights, the equivalent of the UK Trinity House. His only regret in life was that he had not been as large as his father and grandfather, who had both played Rugby for Ireland. About dawn the next morning, I woke with pains in my chest and arm. Sheila, a neighbour's wife, had been a Hospital Sister and immediately diagnosed a heart attack. The company ambulance came and took me off to a hospital. As the stretcher went out past the pool, Dennis raised his glass from a lounger and wished me luck. As it was a Friday morning, all the city's drivers were attending mosques, so the road was clear. Any other day, the journey could have taken over an hour. The A&E doctor pumped me full of drugs and stabilized me. I was transferred to the Intensive Care Unit. Jane, as a woman, was ignored and not told anything. She could only travel to visit me with a male relative, which we did not have in Saudi Arabia! Eventually, my boss Gordon was accepted as the "male relative". Sheila could read my charts and suggest treatments, but she was also totally ignored by the Muslim male doctors.

At this time, BAe launched an attack on the Pell Frischmann presence. If we could be removed, they would be free to manipulate the contract as they wished. Now they had a chance to insist on my dismissal on medical grounds. I spent the next two weeks, in ICU and in the High Dependency Unit, fighting for my job. I had to enlist the Heart Consultant to my defence, as he was trying to reduce my high blood pressure, caused by this extra stress. Senior Pell Frischmann partners visited Riyadh to defend the contract. While in bed in hospital, they asked me to write a proposal to take over the full Operation and Maintenance of Airforce bases, based on my Omani experience. What a way to recuperate.

Eventually, BAe were frustrated and I was allowed to stay. After a slow recovery back in the villa, and then some part-time work, I was considered fit enough to return to UK for an Angiogram. In August, I had an Angiogram in London, and took the results to a Heart Consultant in Plymouth, who has looked after me ever since. I queried why, with the abundance of modern equipment, this procedure had not been available in Riyadh. The reason given was that General HRH Turki bin Nasser, my superior, had had a heart attack on the same day as me. After he found himself a captive audience to all sorts of Saudi petitioners while stuck in hospital, he ordered an Airforce medical team to take him, and their Angiogram equipment, to a USA clinic so that he could have some peace!

I returned to routine work, through to and including my first Christmas spent in Riyadh. The Saudis insisted that we only had Saudi religious holidays. We also had to provide "cover" for when they were absent for Muslim festivals, so we seemed never to have time off. The weather was totally unseasonable. It was cold and with prolonged rainy, thundery periods. We tried to find a suitable "Artificial Evergreen Seasonal Tree", as they have to be called in advertisements; to decorate the villa, but the Mutawwa (Religious Police) had managed to intervene with the usual ruthless, but mindless, efficiency. We all finished work on the Wednesday and that night we had arranged a "Safari Dinner" on the compound. As it started at our house, I supplied two gallons of Mulled Wine. This effectively "nobbled" the wives who were trying to prepare all the subsequent courses at all the different houses! The cheese and biscuits were served, eventually, at 2.30 a.m. An Irish friend managed to find a Leg of Pork for a Christmas Dinner the following day. On the Friday (Christmas Eve), 24 of us met for a Seasonal Lunch in the Intercontinental Hotel. This included George Doublesin, the outgoing Maltese Ambassador, and his family. He was waiting for Col. Gadhafi to approve his appointment to Libya. As it was Saturday, several guests had to return to work for the rest of the day. We all met up again at our house for an informal barbeque.

We were guests at the Maltese Embassy on several occasions. George was a good host and liked to return hospitality after we asked him to our parties. At one of his parties a Dubai diplomat told us that all GCC (Arabian Gulf) diplomats posted to Riyadh are given "Hardship Allowance", because of the Fundamentalists, and were allowed frequent trips back to the Gulf States. An Omani diplomat there knew several people that I had met in Oman, and we often met in Riyadh. All of them could not stand the Mutawween. One weekend, several friends, including "Malta George" and family went on a trip to the Red Sands south of Riyadh. These sand dunes are a different colour to the rest of the country and are quite impressive. After a picnic, in the dusk, we travelled in convoy back to Riyadh at night. George had a new car and he was not too familiar with it. At a junction, he ran into the back of a Land Rover driven by David Coppin. I was immediately behind George. In the headlights, we ran to rescue George and family. The daughter had damaged ribs, while his wife had slight head injuries. We had to wait until the Police arrived and dealt with the situation. George had Diplomatic status, but this cut no ice. All the injured had to be taken by police ambulance to the hospital that dealt with all police cases. We had to get the vehicles back to Riyadh and find the hospital, which we managed by about 3:00am. The police doctor examined all his cases together in a large room with no privacy. Mrs Doublesin and her daughter had to strip off in front of manacled prisoners, in spite of them claiming Diplomatic immunity. We were shocked, as normally women are kept separate from men and are dealt with only by females.

In January 1993, Jane and I visited Istanbul and Hugh flew out to share the holiday with us. The BAe leave travel allowance was easily converted to cheap tickets and hotels. Our Travel Agent linked us up with a young Turkish travel agent, who took to Hugh and introduced him to a local radio station DJ. I am not sure whether Hugh actually broadcast, but he did spend a lot of time in the studio. There was a lot of frozen slush and fresh snow everywhere, and it was cold. After Riyadh, this was a shock as we did not have the correct clothes.

Institution of Civil Engineers (Illegal organisation)

About this time, I started to meet some of the other professional civil engineers linked to the Al Yamamah Project, in spite of being "warned off" by my boss. Gordon thought that the best way to combat BAe was to remain aloof and professional. I thought that it was better to gain their confidence and act in a friendly manner, and I was proved correct. A group of BAe, Scott Wilson, Taylor Woodrow, Alexander Gibbs and W. S. Atkins engineers, all working on the Project, would meet informally once a month to hear a talk on some engineering problem. This was done in the Project Headquarters building. Under Saudi Law, any public gathering over about five people needed permission, so we met behind doors guarded by the RSAF Air Police. Effectively, we were an illegal organisation. There were about 20 engineers on the list, and the secretary had just been made redundant. I offered to take over his duties. Over the next twelve years, I raised the profile of the group and it became the Institution of Civil Engineers Local Association in Saudi Arabia (ICE LA). This gave us formal recognition from UK and access to grant funding. We expanded to include engineers not connected to the Project, and to have visiting speakers from UK and USA.

I spoke to the Saudi Engineering Committee about affiliation and co-operation. The SEC said that they were still unrecognized by the King, although a draft Royal Decree (Act of Parliament equivalent) had been submitted. Until the Decree had been granted, they, too, were only informal and, therefore, could not be seen to support a non-Saudi group. One member of the SEC helpfully pointed out that the various secret police forces were infiltrating every kind of group, and people could "disappear" if they posed a perceived threat to the Kingdom. As he put it, "There is invisible line drawn in the sand, which only we Saudis can see, and if you cross it there will be trouble. The line is moved daily". So I was, in effect, running an illegal organisation in an unfriendly country. I was duly warned.

UK and USA Engineers were being asked to demonstrate that they had undertaken a minimum amount of "Continued Professional Development (CPD)" training each year and this CPD element is examined when engineers wanted to progress through the grades of membership. There were very few opportunities available in Saudi Arabia for CPD, so we filled a need.

Taif

The AYPO was asked if money could be found to repair some buildings on Taif Airbase, which were not connected in any way with the core BAe project. I was dispatched with Bill Donald, a BAe architect, to examine the problem. The radar equipment, in a bomb-proof bunker, was covered with plastic sheets to prevent water damage from the rain pouring through the three foot thick concrete roof. The roof had been waterproofed, using Dow Chemicals "Hypalon" sheeting. Over a period of some 10 years, extremes of temperature, combined with ultraviolet degradation, had destroyed the Hypalon. The roof needed a new waterproof cover. While standing on the roof, I noticed that the same specification had been used on 90% of the Airbase buildings; all constructed at the same time by US contractors. Much money was needed to make repairs.

Bill Donald and his wife, Phyl, became very good friends with Jane and me and we still communicate and visit regularly. Bill talked about his time building hospitals in Baghdad and then watching the USA bomb them to pieces in the first Gulf War.

Keith Barrow, our man in Khamis Mushayt, reported that the new multi-screen radar display units had melted and no longer worked. UKMoD staff had signed off the BAe installation of the Aircraft Early Warning Ground Station electronics, which displayed the AWAC signal to controllers in a bunker. All this was very expensive. The RSAF were now in charge of the bunker, and had been fully trained in care of the equipment, especially the need for continued air conditioning to prevent the plasma screens from overheating. However, the RSAF decided that the equipment should not have failed within weeks of being handed over, and wanted a full replacement at BAe's expense. On investigation, it was discovered that the very essential air conditioning equipment required to cool the plasma screens had been switched off for some time. The Airforce policemen finally admitted that they could not sleep, while on guard, with noise of the fans. They had enjoyed peaceful nights with the bunker doors wedged open and the fans switched off. After the replacement equipment was installed, a period of re-education started.

In August 1993, Jane and I converted our leave tickets into a tour of Jordan. Once again, the Riyadh travel agent linked up with a Tour Operator in Amman, and we stayed in The Intercontinental Hotel. Had we known that August is the peak month for weddings, we would not have travelled. The hotel ran at least four concurrent weddings every day. Bagpipes played continually, corridors were full of noisy guests. Doves were released from cages suspended over the swimming pool, and repeatedly collected back for the next release. They were too tired, in the heat, to fly far. We toured the sights at Jeraish, Dead Sea, various Roman cities and Amman. An American couple were looking at a large floor mosaic in Jeraish. He turned to his wife and said "Gee, honey, that must have been some picture before they broke it". We drove to Petra and explored Petra and the little known "Little Petra" which is totally unspoilt. We talked to the gate guard for Little Petra in

Arabic, while he tried to get some excitable Italian tourists to climb into the only available transport that he could arrange after a breakdown. They did not want to travel in a rickety windowless van supplied by the Petra Laundry Company. Jordan makes an acceptable wine as judged by a Saudi resident, and the label states that it is bottled in The Holy Land. King Feisal had just declared that he was no longer the King of Saudi Arabia, but wished to be called the Custodian of the Two Holy Mosques. I asked if Jordan had had any success selling wine bottled in the Holy Land to the Holy country next door, and they laughed.

Jane had found a job teaching English to Saudi Princes and Princesses. All the students were part of the family of Prince Salman, the Governor of Riyadh, who became King in 2015. He was the eldest of the sons of King Saud, and was the "enforcer" in the Royal Family. When Jane asked me to write in Arabic my telephone numbers for the Palace to use, I used a letterhead with Prince Sultan's name. This helped her get the job, and on her first day I delivered her to the Palace. I wanted to know where she was, in case she did not return. After she had been met, a figure approached my car. It was Prince Salman, wanting to "inspect" me. Whilst the Princesses were delightful to teach, the Princes were difficult. Taking orders and instruction from an infidel, and a woman, was just not acceptable. Jane said that she used to pick up the four year old Prince and tuck him under her arm, and sing lullabies to him. "La la la la" – the Arabic for "No no no no". Another trick that he tried, whenever he had a paddy, was to stomp off and pull out his Prayer Rug and start praying.

In 1995, another 48 Tornado fighter aircraft were due to arrive and more building work was required. This included the Tornado Geographic Support Facility (TGSF) in Riyadh. This was a new large two-storey building with a large quantity of map-making equipment. A "moving map display" is provided in the cockpit of the Tornado (similar to the GPS system used in cars), and a facility for making the maps was required. The Saudi Army provides all the mapping in the Kingdom, and they are ferociously security conscious. The Army Major Project Manager was a serious pain in the proverbial and cause of endless delays. Eventually BAe came up with a cunning plan. Knowing that there was only about 18 months work left, they arranged for him to take a three year MSc course at Nottingham University. His deputy, a Captain, was not allowed to make any decisions and telephoned the Major daily from UK. The build dragged on for years, and the Major returned before completion. I never achieved a Handover Certificate for the TGSF, and BAe could not be paid for this building without one!

Meanwhile, back in Riyadh, work on the Air Academy on Riyadh Airbase was progressing. This Base is in the centre of Riyadh, and Saudi student pilots skim low over the city rooftops. The Mayor of Riyadh and many others had tried to get the flying training and the Academy moved away from the city for safety reasons. As the Base was also the home of the Royal Flight, there was stiff resistance from the Airforce. The new Academy Auditorium seated some 500 guests in plush comfort, and was equipped with "state of the art" TV studio equipment. At the opening ceremony for the building, several very senior Princes and Generals attended, as Prince Sultan (then Deputy Prime Minister) performed the opening. The Academy Commander mounted the stage and walked to the lectern, to greet the Royal Guests.

He took off his beret and dropped it on the lectern, which had a touch screen lighting control panel. All the lights went out. Panic set in. Luckily, a lone BAe man was still in the control booth, high above the room. He quickly reset the lighting. A modification to the lectern was urgently needed, to prevent a further embarrassment. The Greek contractor came up with a simple and cheap answer. He simply covered the glass touch screen with a neatly cut piece of plywood.

Kuala Lumpur

Dave Kilner, my assistant in Minna, Nigeria, had started work in Kuala Lumpur and Jane and I thought that, as we were half way there already, we should visit them. His son, Edward is my Godson. In February 1994, we flew to Malaysia and stayed

in KL. Dave, Sue and Edward took us out for a meal the first night, to a street market. Jane was not impressed when a multitude of unrecognizable dishes were served up on a dustbin lid. After visiting their flat, Dave took me to see his job. He was working for a German Consultant, building the TV Tower. This high tower was built by slipform and had just reached the underside of the restaurant floor at the top. The view was fantastic, looking down into the excavations for the new Petronas Towers. At the 380 metre level we stepped outside onto thin perforated metal sheeting and held onto the thin wire handrail. Health and Safety UK would have had convulsions. The TV Tower overall height is less than Petronas Towers, but it stands on a hill, so the finished top is above the top of the Petronas Towers.

TV TOWER - KUALA LUMPUR

We went off to Penang to have a beach holiday. We stayed at the Rasa Sayang Hotel on the north coast for three nights. The Tour Guide who picked us up from the airport was Chinese. We arranged a few hours sightseeing with him. He took us into a private home to see the Lion Dance. This is an annual ritual for blessing the house and occupants with prosperity in the coming year. There were lots of very loud drumming and firecrackers, which are banned by Malaysian Law but essential if the Dance is to be effective. It was interesting seeing Buddhist Temples next door to Mosques, Catholic Convents and Hindu temples. All religions live in harmony and share all the religious holidays, and it is an example to other parts of the world.

We had a further four days in K.L. and saw a lot of Dave, Sue and Edward. There was lots of shopping, for fake designer labels and cheap Rolex imitations. We had a day trip to Malacca, the old Dutch port opposite Sumatra. This turned out into a real farce. It rained more than usual. The motorway rest area toilets were beyond imagination, having coped with the Chinese New Year travellers the day before. On arrival in Malacca, we were herded into a Chinese Restaurant and food was dumped on the table. We and the Japanese girls just stared at the group of Germans wolfing down hot chilli and asking for more! The coach had, by now developed a puncture, so we were all taken in the rain to the guide's friend's shop to buy jade while we waited. No one bought jade, but we all got wet. A taxi arrived to take us (in 6 trips) to the Old Fort. Here the guide tried to make me responsible for the group while he tried to find the coach. The group promptly split up into couples that went in all directions!! When the guide got back, he asked us all "to hold the imaginary rope and not to let go" and to follow him through China Town. What a farce! The long lost coach appeared and we were all taken to see the old Portuguese area, and the Portuguese cultural centre. It was closed for the Chinese New Year, so he tried to interest us in a solitary mud skipping fish on the mudflats. (Yes, even the tide had gone out).

We flew on to Singapore for one night where we stayed in the Hyatt Regency, just off Orchard Road. Singapore is exceptionally clean, and everything works. Orchard Road shops can outclass Bond Street, Paris, and Rome for top quality goods. Luckily, by this time we had no cash left, but the window shopping was excellent. We promised ourselves lunch at Raffles Hotel the next day, and ate in the famous Long Bar. The hotel had been beautifully restored, (for £80M, I was told), and is well worth a visit. The Metro is excellent, efficient, clean and very attractively integrated into the City. Most of the top construction management from the Singapore Metro went on to complete the Jubilee Line in London. We flew by Saudia, via Bangkok, direct to Riyadh. The flight was delayed by two hours, due to Saudia insisting that they do an additional full security check in the departure lounge. There were about 200 pilgrims travelling to Mecca with us, and it was still during Ramadhan. As the plane was chasing the sunset, and not actually catching up with darkness, the Muslims were unable to break their fast at dusk for several hours, while we ate quite happily, at a normal time.

Jane's health was deteriorating in 1994. She had lost a lot of weight and tests showed that there was some damage to her immune system, and she had a major stomach ulcer. All this was not helped by the Company Doctor mis-prescribing drugs after she contracted Helicobacter pylori. Two drugs are needed. One is required to kill the bugs, and another to flush out the bugs. The doctor only gave her the flushing drug, and she spent months on the toilet before the doctor admitted his mistake. Endoscopy examinations had to be done according to Muslim customs. She lay on the couch fully encased in a black Abaya throughout the procedure. That summer we flew to UK and replenished her wardrobe, as she had dropped at least two dress sizes. My mother gave me a lace Altar Cloth made for my grandfather, a First World War Army Chaplain, by the army wives of the Yorkshire Division, showing all of the cap-badges of the Regiments. On the way back to Riyadh, we spent a few days in Cyprus, at a beach hotel. It was August Bank Holiday and the air conditioning failed. No mechanics could be found for days. Jane sweltered and got some relief by opening the sealed windows. Outside was a crane used for Bungy Jumps. One day a man had a heart attack during a jump and his body was dangling for hours outside our window while the police checks proceeded. We managed two short drives into the hills for relief from the heat, and then we returned via Bahrain. On arrival at Riyadh, two of the four suitcases were missing. The Altar Cloth was lost. I spent the next week chasing airlines to locate the bags, without success. I was asked to go into the lost baggage stores, every morning before work, in all three terminals at Riyadh airport to search for my bags, and soon I was able to go into each terminal, without a pass or escort. I never did get the bags but was offered 14 Canadian Ice Hockey sticks that were forlornly waiting to be claimed. Not much use in the desert! Although Jane had carefully bought lots of replacement clothes, she was now in Riyadh without them and I had to fight an Insurance Claim and two Airlines for the money to buy more replacements. Still, as there is nothing much to do in Riyadh, it gave Jane an excuse for endless shopping trips.

On Riyadh Airbase, the Americans shared a large hangar with BAe staff. While BAe maintained light aircraft for initial student pilot training, the Americans maintained the AWAC four engined monsters with the rotating radar dome. One was in the hangar, with the dome cover removed when disaster struck. The firefighting sprinkler system is very powerful, and is triggered by sensors. The hangar door was partly open, to allow some air to circulate and for part of the AWAC to stick out. A flash of light from the windscreen of a passing car was enough for the sensors to think that there was a fire in the hangar. The exposed radar dome was drenched, and the electronics ruined.

Three "state of the art" Minehunter ships were supplied to the Royal Saudi Naval Force, under the Project. We became involved in the construction of the jetty, the covered dry dock, depth charge storage buildings and a number of other facilities. Mike Mead had to get a new 132 Kv electricity supply into the Naval Base at Jubail, to improve the power supply. These three Glass Reinforced Plastic (GRP) ships were non-magnetic, and all design work had to take this into account. The dry dock roof and walls also had to be non-magnetic, so the largest GRP roof in the world had to be built, with the attendant problems of expansion in the heat. The jetty was made of 40 ton mass concrete blocks. These blocks were initially piled up three layers higher than required to force the necessary settlement in the seabed, before the extra weight was removed. Casting of the blocks left some small local high spots, but these were within the specified tolerance, and these high points could cause a pressure point to split the blocks. The Navy Brigadier (Commodore) in charge complained that some blocks had cracked and should be removed. He even had underwater video footage to prove the claim. I was sent to Jubail to sort out the problem. Yes, some hairline cracks existed, but mass concrete block walls in harbour works do deform and crack when settling into the sea bed, increasing the interlocking strength. There was no way these blocks were going to be replaced, unless the whole jetty was dismantled. The Commodore (Brigadier) did not agree with me. He went on to tell me that these cracks would allow White Ants or Termites to eat the concrete under water. At this point I could no longer hide my disbelief, and I smiled. I was thrown off the site and told never to come back.

This man was difficult to deal with at the best of times. For his visits to site, he was given a 12ft x 10ft office, but it had no carpet. After many trips into town to select a carpet, he eventually settled on a very expensive Persian carpet.

316

Unfortunately, the carpet was too large for the office, so a new office had to be built for it. He was often the guest of the Royal Navy in UK, visiting Mine Warfare establishments, and hotel bills were paid by the UK MoD. A large number of £160 Beluga Caviar tins, ordered on room service, were found in his luggage. He was a repeat offender and eventually this resulted in having his bags examined on every visit and the "contraband" removed. Having thrown me off site, and refusing to have anything to do with me, he telephoned the office on a Thursday (a Saudi weekend) and I answered. A Minehunter was in the dry dock and the BAe engineer had gone home for the weekend with the keys. The Navy wanted the boat back in the water and they were locked out of the building. After a few telephone calls, the boat was released. Although I helped him out, he still did not like me. He even arranged for his unemployable nephew to become an assistant in my office!

The one good thing about the trip to Jubail was that I was able to meet a Fellow of the Institution. Jerry May was the Sir Alexander Gibb representative in Saudi Arabia, and had been a leading light in the engineers group that met in Riyadh. He agreed to sign my application for Fellowship of the Institution. He was also able to tell me about an identical mass concrete jetty built for the civil port at Jubail, which helped me considerably in convincing Eng Mohammed that the Navy Brigadier was talking through his hat.

Our next door neighbour on the compound was an ex-Group Captain, Ben Ball, whose son was a Red Arrows pilot. The team were due to return from the Far East and wondered whether they could overnight in Riyadh and visit my neighbour? Ben contacted the Defence Attaché, who made an official request, and permission was granted for them to land in Riyadh. The team were due to arrive about noon on a Friday, when the airport normally was closed down. The Air Traffic Controller had been dragged in on his day off and was not pleased. Ben and the Defence Attaché were allowed into the Control Tower and watched the radar screen. A dot appeared and steadily grew larger. This mystified the Controller, who had expected nine separate dots on the screen! He shouted that he had been mis-informed and mis-led and was going to declare the airport closed. He was persuaded to wait a few minutes, and was contacted by radio from the incoming team leader. Only at the last moment did the dot break up into separate dots on the screen as the team prepared to land. They had been flying in their usual close formation, producing the single radar image. The whole crew came to the party next door, and we all met them that night. Ben's son asked me to get him some copies of software for his computer from the souk, which I did.

We managed to get four days leave over Christmas at the end of 1994. This was my first introduction to the "Dubai" set. On arrival, we headed for the bar for our first legal drink in months. It was early afternoon, and an Oil rig expat slid onto the next stool. He flipped a Gold Card at the barman and said "Fill me up". We went off shopping and a meal, and returned just before midnight. He was still on the same stool, being "filled up". On Christmas Day, we ate in the hotel, not wanting to be seen celebrating Christmas in an Arabic country. Saudi brain washing had worked. A Gulf Arab at the next table came over and, after handshakes, wished us "A Happy Christmas" and a pleasant stay in Dubai. The opposite of what would have happened in Riyadh.

Change of employer

In 1995, more pressure was put on Pell Frischmann by BAe to remove themselves from the project. By this time, our little group had built up a good reputation with the Saudi Airforce. Our Director had left Saudi Arabia, leaving just three of us in post. We suggested to Eng Mohammed that a solution would be to sack Pell Frischmann, and hire us as direct employees. This idea would save the 100% "mark-up" on the existing costs of our employment. The plan would satisfy BAe's demand to rid themselves of Pell Frischmann, but would retain our services (which was not what BAe wanted). Prince Sultan, the Minister of Defence and Aviation, liked the idea and I drafted the letter for him to sign, ordering BAe to pay our salaries from the Project Budget and provide us with all benefits that equivalent BAe staff received. However, this arrangement meant that most BAe staff then assumed that we were actual BAe staff, subject to BAe discipline, and questioned us when we made decisions against BAe. To get our Annual Bonuses, a complicated computerized tick-box form had to be completed for the BAe HR department in UK. This involved the BAe Construction Director coming to our office to be told what he should put in the "recommendation" box! My UK Solicitor seemed confused when I asked him to explain our legal position, muttering "there could be a conflict of interest".

Bombs

1995 continued with the occasional bomb going off. There was a low level terrorist threat but expat life continued normally. Jane and I managed a holiday in Thailand, visiting Bangkok and Chang Mai, in February, and had a brief stop-over in Zurich at the end of August on the way back from seeing our mothers. My initial one year employment contract had long expired but the Saudis just assumed that I would carry on working. If "one's face fitted" you were retained. The Arab puts trust at the basis of any relationship, but it can take a while for this trust to be established.

Another responsibility we had was for the UK based training of Saudi Navy Officers for the Minehunters. The agreement was that a fixed number of officers would be trained, and that included an actual pass mark, not just an attendance certificate. When one Saudi student pulled a pistol on the RN Police on a UK base, he was returned swiftly to Riyadh. However, this left the Saudi Navy one short on the list of trained officers. The Invoice was queried by UKMoD and I had to explain to the Saudi Navy that certain rules were expected to be followed while in UK. A separate extra course had to be set up for the replacement officer. The RN were very mindful of a previous incident when officers from another foreign navy were returned to their home country without achieving a pass certificate. They were promptly executed as an example to following students!

Jane had a much better year, health wise, in 1996. She was busy teaching young Saudi Princesses and Princes some English, and enjoying contact inside the Palace. She joined Corona Worldwide; an organization originally formed by a group of Ambassadors wives to get to meet ladies of different cultural backgrounds. It took up a lot of her time, as she was on the committee as a caterer or "Tea Lady", along with the wife of the Canadian Charge D'Affairs. She organised the ~~Christmas~~ Seasonal Festive Lunch for 70 ladies again that year. Ambassador's wives from UK, Malta, Sri Lanka, Canada and Ireland attended. Corona had monthly meetings, with guest speakers, or visits to Children's Hospitals and the like.

Following a successful visit by Corona, the Institution of Civil Engineers arranged a visit to the King Fahd Cultural Centre. This imposing building was built in 1990 to support the Saudi bid to host the Olympic Games. The bid failed because the Islamic clerics banned the idea of the games because female athletes would not be allowed to compete. Built nearby, at the same time, is a state of the art Sports Hospital. Five years after completion, the building contractors were still operating and maintaining the buildings, which cost of some US$120,000,000. The Cultural Centre has a 3000 seat theatre, another with 500 seats, a lecture theatre, a library, and a full sized Planetarium. All these buildings are clad in marble and gold, including a marbled car parking area, which was treacherous in the wet. A wonderful set of buildings, but wasted because of the Mutawwa (Religious zealots). Two years later, the French contractor was sent away and the buildings were left unused and unattended.

We enjoyed our 1996 spring holiday in Bali, and would recommend it to everyone. My water engineer from Oman had just been sent to stay in Indonesia for 2 years, and we were jealous!!! Such friendly people and the tranquillity had to be experienced

More bombs

In July 1996, terrorists detonated a large bomb in Dhahran, killing a large number of US troops. The bomb had been delivered to the apartment block in a large water tanker. To disguise the bomb, and make it invisible to a search, the remainder of the tank was filled with water. On detonation, the water layer forced the majority of the blast downwards. A massive crater was made, and the façade of the apartment block was blown away. Had the water not been in the tanker, the blast would have travelled upwards and outwards and, possibly, flattened the whole building with a much higher death toll.

BAe and UKMoD immediately started to take steps to secure all our offices and accommodation. A large blast wall was erected round my office block. Compound entrances had concrete chicanes erected to prevent a "ram-raid" attack, and RSAF and Army guards were stationed at all locations. Armoured cars guarded approaches, under suitable vehicle sunshades. All personnel were issued with new security passes, and all vehicles were fully inspected. Later, more secure "lift-up" barriers were installed. These were lowered into a concrete trench hydraulically when the guard allowed a vehicle to pass. Initial teething problems included unexpected raising of the barrier while a car was passing, leaving the car some feet up in the air. Apparently, the same problem happened at the Pentagon, USA, when the Phillipino Navy Commander was on an official visit!

In September, we were invited to the UKMoD compound for a "Battle of Britain" Cocktail Party, and we all had to submit details of our vehicle, passengers, and other details, so that we would be allowed through the gate. While the car in front was being searched, with lady passengers in best cocktail dresses standing outside while seats were lifted, I noticed that a water tanker was in the queue behind me. This was a bit worrying, as there were a large number of senior invited guests at this function. My car was searched and allowed through the gate, followed immediately by the tanker. It had not been inspected. Visions of another Dhahran bomb flashed past me. I questioned the senior RAF officer, responsible for security, about this. "It's alright, the guards know him!" I was not reassured.

Each month, I arranged for guest speakers to give a lecture to the ICE Local Association on engineering subjects. This went a long way to providing the Continued Professional Development (CPD) training required by all UK Institutions. Because of the security upgrade work being carried out across the Kingdom, experts had been flown in to advise BAe and UKMoD and I took advantage and got them to speak to the ICE members. The US National Fire Protection Code author gave his opinion on how to evacuate people quickly from high buildings and build in fire protection. The next week, W. S. Atkins gave a talk on strengthening buildings against bomb and terrorist attacks. One wanted all ground floor doors to allow clear and speedy egress, and the other wanted all ground floor exits blocked or barricaded. The client had to decide which was the biggest threat.

Another purely Saudi problem concerned air conditioning. An old Saudi Decree stated that if the air temperature exceeded 50^0C, then all work should cease. As a result, there were no thermometers available for sale showing a scale above 50^0C. To properly calculate the heat loads for a building's air conditioning, the highest temperatures needed to be known. All temperature records rose from January to April, when it reached 50^0C. The graph remained flat at 50^0C until the cooler weather started in September. A HVAC Engineer had to make an inspired guess of temperatures in the summer months, and he was not allowed to acknowledge the higher temperatures in his calculations.

World Trade Organization

Saudi Arabia was trying to join the World Trade Organization, and some of the laws of the country did not align with WTO requirements. In particular, free movement of workers was not really possible into the Kingdom. I met with British Embassy Commercial Attaché and the Saudi Engineering Committee to discuss this. I pointed out that the UK Chartered Engineer qualification was part of the Washington Treaty signed by some 97 countries, and the Treaty allowed mutual recognition of qualifications. The Saudis wanted to "do their own thing" and this would be much more difficult to integrate with the WTO concept. I proposed to the Saudi Engineering Committee that the Kingdom examine qualifications systems for engineers in place in other countries, and model their new system on one of those. This would allow much more easy integration and would allow Saudi qualified engineers to work in neighbouring Arab countries more easily. I spelt this out in a paper that I submitted to a conference on qualifications for engineers held at The King Fahd University of Petroleum and Minerals in Dhahran. The Saudis later made modifications to the draft Royal Decree for qualification of engineers, but many years passed before it was even discussed or signed.

Expat engineers were jealous of Saudi graduates being immediately accorded the title "Engineer", while we UK engineers did not have the same privilege in our own country. In Saudi, I was addressed as "Engineer Dick". Historically, at the time of the granting of the first Royal Charter to The Institution of Civil Engineers in 1828, the subject of titles was dismissed. 20 years later, the medical profession decided to take the title of "Doctor" into the wording of their Charter that they had copied from the civil engineers.

As an example of the small expat world, I found myself sitting next to a nurse at a dinner party in Riyadh. She had shared a room, as an Army nurse, in Nepal with a nurse I met in Salalah and who had married my Superintendent there. Her husband was a Royal Signals Major who was working under the Military Attaché, in Riyadh. Previously, the Military Attaché had been the Sultan of Oman's Head of Military Training!! While in Oman, I worked on his big Exercise at Ras Al Hadd, and several others.

Mysteriously, I got a telephone call in Riyadh from the proposed future Jordanian Ambassador to Oman, asking me whether he should accept the job! Lord knows where he got my name from! I can only assume that it was from one of the Gulf diplomats I had met at the Maltese Embassy.

We spent Christmas 1996 in Dubai, with Hugh and his girlfriend. Hugh was very impressed with the Computer Souks and spent money on hardware and software that was unobtainable in UK. We all were impressed by the skills of Gulf Arab families ice-skating in national costume on the hotel rink. Both our mothers were in good health, although there had been worrying times. My mother, then 86, had a cataract operation and managed to break a wrist in hospital. As the other wrist was affected by a stroke that she would not admit had happened, life was difficult! Jane's mother, then 97 continued to have mini-strokes at almost regular intervals. She was getting much more possessive, and objected to us leaving Cardiff for Cornwall, let alone Riyadh! Family health problems are a constant worry for all expats.

We planned a trip to Malta for the summer of 1997, to see George, the ex-Maltese Ambassador to Riyadh, who was now the Ambassador in Tripoli. This was to be the second time that I had stayed at The Phoenicia Hotel; the last time was the trip to school in 1954. We had a relaxing holiday, but failed to meet up with George as he had been called back to Tripoli to talk to Col Gadhafi. Saudia Airline telephoned us to say that our return flight to Riyadh had been cancelled and would we please find our way to Milan to catch a different flight a day earlier! We rushed to Rome and stayed overnight so that we could catch the early morning Air Italia to Milan. On arrival, we were told that Saudia were operating a Hajj flight as a test out of the new and not yet commissioned Malpensa Airport, some 50 kilometres away. We had very little Lira left and had not expected a taxi fare of that size. At that time, Malpensa had not been formally accepted by the Italian Civil Aviation Authority, and was still undergoing test and trials. Some 350 European Muslims had arrived to board the Hajj flight. Jane and I, and a lone Swedish engineer, were swamped. One of the only two ground staff in the building took pity on us three. He took our tickets and asked us to wait in the First Class lounge, throwing us the keys to the bar of which we made very good use. So much so, that they had to get a car to take us to the aircraft steps! We had all been upgraded to First Class, but the flight was to Jeddah only, not Riyadh. The European hajjis were all trying to dress themselves into the hajj costume of two towels, but could not manage to tuck the bits in securely and were constantly exposing themselves. This embarrassed Jane and the Air Hostesses. Arriving in Jeddah, at midnight, on Thursday night, during Hajj, is every expats worst nightmare. We were unceremoniously whisked off to the waiting Riyadh flight without our baggage, but it did arrive later!

In September 1997, we returned from our UK leave via Vienna. We had booked into the Intercontinental Hotel and our taxi attempted to drop us at the door. The police and Israeli security made us walk 100 yards with our heavy bags. Israeli Prime Minister Benjamin Netanyahu was also staying there! We did most of the tourist things except for the Spanish Riding School, as Jane's ulcer flared up that morning. Our sleep was disturbed one night by loud shouting. Mrs Netanyahu had demanded coffee at 3:00 am and a waiter tried to deliver it. Apparently this waiter had not been security cleared by the Israeli forces months before the visit, and was just replacing another who was absent that night. He was nearly shot by the Israeli guards.

Al Kharj Airbase

In 1998, the Airforce decided that a major new airbase was needed and that it should now be located in Al Kharj, only 150km south of Riyadh. There was a small scale airbase already there, mainly used by the Americans and the French for the Iraq No Fly Zone air patrols. The Al Yamamah Project was given the task of providing the new works in several phases. We had a site with a land area equal to that of Greater Manchester, with a 100 km fence line! 50% of the site was outside the range of mobile telephones and land lines did not exist. There was lots of open desert to play with. The eventual cost of our Al Kharj Project works exceeded some £3 billion. The approved works included a second runway, 1000 married quarters, shops, 8 schools, 13 mosques, bachelor accommodation for 3000, several large headquarter buildings, a major water supply scheme, two clinics and a hospital, 50 km of dual carriageway roads, irrigation, drainage, and a complete power and telephone network.

The design work followed the routine now firmly established by Eng Mohammed over the past few years. Firstly, the prime contractor (BAe), using the civil contractor (Joannou & Paraskiviades), provided a "Concept Design" outline, including brief written descriptions. These were examined for technical problems and then offered to various RSAF users for comment. When any required changes had been made, the three man RSAF/AYPO committee assembled to formally sign off each page of the Concept design. The committee consisted of Eng Mohammed, a Colonel from RSAF Headquarters, and the Colonel in command of the Operations and Maintenance Squadron on Al Kharj Airbase. I was the committee secretary. Three copies had to be signed, on each page, and this document was the basis of all detailed further work. The initial set of documents for the Master Plan had also to be countersigned by the Al Yamamah Project Officer himself, HRH Prince Major General Turki bin Nasser Al Saud. He only became available late one Friday night, so I was dragged away from a poolside barbeque to assemble the documents.

Luckily, I had not been drinking that day! J&P mobilised almost immediately, building up to some 4000 staff living on site.

Detailed designs for the individual buildings now had to be provided and approved by the AYPO/RSAF committee. All buildings were to be provided with full Furniture, Fittings and Equipment (FF&E). Every drawing, structural calculation, mechanical equipment, sign, colour scheme, curtain and carpet fabric, and FF&E item specification had to be approved. All required the three committee signatures on each separate sheet of paper. Once signed and dated, I had to send the approved papers (or comments for rejection) to BAe to action. I had to talk the two Colonels through all technical points before they would sign. These three made, to my mind, outrageous choices in colours and fabrics to be used. This approval process was more or less full time at first; culminating in a day when I got 1276 signatures, making the three very senior Saudis work a full 6 hour stretch.

While the 1000 houses were of only 2 basic designs, all the other 241 structures were individual. I rapidly learnt about the design of, and how the equipment fitted into, Fire Stations, Hospitals, Jails, Mosques, Clinics, Schools, some very technical specialist Headquarter buildings, a Religious Library, an abattoir, a supermarket, telephone exchange and many other strange buildings. Catering equipment for kitchens dealing with 1500 men was a challenge. Sports facilities and parade grounds were built.

The beauty of this job was that, for the first time, I was allowed full access to the site and could be part of the team. No more operating in the dark, fed with incomplete information. Although detailed site inspection was carried out daily by BAe resident site staff, and periodic visits by UKMoD staff, the ultimate "signing – off" could only be done by the AYPO/RSAF committee after I had approved the works.

The first 1000 pupil school, Boys Secondary, took 13 months from approval of the Concept document to "doors open for students". The school included many networked computer classrooms, a high-tech auditorium, and outdoor (covered) play areas. It was a remarkable achievement, and set the standard for the rest of the works.

Lying in the middle of the desert near our part of the Airbase was a three storey air-conditioned barracks complex for 4,000 US troops. This had been funded by the US Congress and built by Bin Laden Construction Company. Lying on the centreline of the proposed new runway was a vast tented camp of US Army and Airforce personnel. They had limited air-conditioning, rudimentary water and sanitation, and were very unhappy at sitting there, baking in the sun. The US Congress would not let them move into the vacant barracks, because they feared that Osama had booby-trapped the complex. When I tried to clear the runway site, a very annoyed US Colonel waved his pistol in my face and demanded that I get Congress to change its mind. Some months later, Congress was induced to allow the troops into the barracks and release the runway land to us.

Under some previous contract, a 50,000 person sewage treatment plant had been constructed and moth-balled. It was in four parallel units. With the move of the Americans into the barracks, there was now sufficient volume of sewage to commence the operation of one quarter of the treatment plant. For a year this operated successfully, with flow increasing as more buildings were completed and occupied. The 50Km of roads had landscaped borders and palm trees planted in the central reservations. All landscaping was supplied with irrigation water from the Treated Sewage Effluent coming from the Sewage Plant. Planting commenced, with palm trees each requiring 200 litres of water a day until established.

As the Iraqi threat diminished in the late 1990's, it was decided that the second runway was not required and the money saved was to be spent on further buildings. About this time, King Fahd ordered the Americans out of Saudi Arabia, under political pressure from the Wahabi leaders. They all moved to Qatar, leaving the big barrack block empty. The flow to the sewage works dwindled to below a usable volume and the plant had to shut down. A very agitated O & M Colonel came into my office, demanding that I "bring back those arseholes, because we need them to run the plant". He was technically correct, but it may also have been a Saudi comment on the US forces. We were forced to run a 3 Km pipe out into an empty patch of desert and pump raw sewage away to dry in the sun. As the supply of Treated Sewage Effluent had died, and in spite of tanker spraying, plants died and there was a large amount of re-planting required.

To supply water to this Airbase, with its rapidly increasing population, six deep drilled wells were constructed at the east end of the site, some 20 Km from the nearest facility, and 30 Km from the housing area. These wells tapped into an aquifer that also supplied two enormous Dairy farms. The nearest, and smallest, only had 20,000 head of cattle under covered accommodation. Vast circular fields grew fodder, and were watered by deep wells. We had to reach an agreement on water abstraction with the farms. The farm across the highway to the north was, at that time, in the Guinness Book of Records as the largest Dairy Herd in the world.

All this construction was initially managed using only two mobile telephones. Part of the project involved providing 5000 telephone lines to various buildings on the base and linking these to the outside world. Saudi Telecomms and the Airforce took a long time to reach an agreement on whether the link would be by fibre-optic or by satellite dishes. Meanwhile everyone on the base struggled to communicate. Eventually, it was decided to use fibre-optic cables from the town some 30 km distant. Up to this time, I was unable to certify payment for any building because the internal telephone systems could not be tested without a link to an outside source. We started asking the technical people in Saudi Telecomms about standards and specifications that would be acceptable to them, and which would allow them to make connections. Saudi Telecomms would not release this information (due to the obsession with secrecy), and no amount of Saudi on Saudi pressure helped. However Jane had a friend whose husband was the CEO of AT&T in Saudi Arabia and had a major contract with Saudi Telecomms. I was able to get his staff to, secretly, talk to BAe staff and details were exchanged, allowing design to go forward. We had to provide an exchange building, with a standby generator, and obtained the standard design details. In order to ensure that Saudi Telecomms would accept what we built, I arranged a site visit to a building under construction by Saudi Telecomms. BAe reported back that "they could not build down to that standard!" We went ahead and provided the 20 x 40 foot building and the required standby generator. When the actual equipment finally arrived, it was smaller than a suitcase! All that wasted and air-conditioned space was unnecessary, and could have been saved with better co-operation.

Away from work in 1998, we managed to have brief but enjoyable trips to Venice & Lugarno in the Spring, and to Montreux and Geneva in September. Jane was still teaching English to young Princesses in a Palace. She was still organising refreshments for the Woman's Corona Society, including a May Ball and Christmas lunch for over 100 ladies. It gave Jane great pleasure because they raised over £2000 for charity.

I was getting more deeply involved with the Institution of Civil Engineers. The Local Association membership had grown to over 250, and included all professions now. A successful Poppy Day Dinner raised £200 for the Royal British Legion. I was involved with getting Saudi university degrees accepted by the UK Engineering Council, so that young Saudi engineers could try for Chartered Membership of UK Institutions. A number of expat civil engineers were persuaded to apply for Fellowship of the Institution of Civil Engineers. As Local representative, I was consulted by the ICE in London on applications or had supported the applications. London had difficulty believing the enormous value of the works the applicants had responsibility for, which were well in excess of the UK norm.

Jane's health problems meant that we had a simple holiday in Prague in the Spring. This was shortly before the river overflowed and the city was flooded. Our hotel basement and ground floor was shown on TV fully immersed. The flood gates to the underground railway system were not closed in time and all signalling and electrics were ruined.

In November, 1999, I organised the annual Poppy Day Dinner for the Institution of Civil Engineers. The Project Manager of the Millennium Dome designers (Buro Happold) was the Speaker at our Annual dinner, with 100 guests including the British Ambassador.

Also, in November, the International Director of ICE came to discuss accreditation of Saudi Universities and to talk to the Saudi Engineering Committee about the setting up of a scheme for professional qualifications. We arranged for the Director to visit the Al Faisaliah Tower, (designed by Norman Foster), then under construction. At that

Al Faisaliah Tower - Riyadh

325

time, the top was at about 290 metres. We reached this level just before sunset. The Director insisted that we wait until he had taken some photos of the sunset, over the glinting gold domes of the Royal Palace. As expected, at dusk, all Muslims go to prayer and all plant is shut down. Neither the lift, nor the temporary lighting system was left working. We had to descend the unfinished staircases, over builder's rubble, under head high electrical wires, in the dark. By the time we had negotiated the full 290 metres, our knees had given up and we were very thirsty. We were late for another reception, arranged for the Director to meet local engineers. We had been escorted up the tower by an engineer who had also worked for the same Project Manager as me in Kenya.

For New Year Eve, 1999, Hugh and his partner joined us in Goa for the Millennium Celebrations. The Indian Navy, across the river, fired off a year's worth of signal flares to mark the moment. The Riyadh Travel Agent I had been using for many years was Goan and fixed us up with a very good hotel, the new Goa Marriott Hotel. The hotel was honoured by a visit from the President of India one night. Hugh had been to Goa before, on the hippy trail, and showed us round. We met up with the Goan travel agent, and visited his home and his local office. His three year old daughter had been brought up in a very clean Riyadh, on good international food. She just hated the filth, and local food, of her native country.

We worked out that, after January 2000 and allowing for the Hijra calendar, we had been working in Saudi Arabia during eight decades, three centuries and two millennia. It sometimes felt like it!!! Over the years, we continued to enjoy the theatre, and concerts at the Canadian Embassy. A local theatre group ran plays, and arranged presentations by professional actors. Visas for actors and musicians had to be obtained for "visiting experts" by various sympathetic companies, and the actual theatre locations were kept secret until the last moment. One actor said to me that it was a little like "walking into a Paris bar during the War and asking for the Resistance". Had the Religious Police found an organiser, he would have had major problems. The Canadian Embassy had Diplomatic protection and could import world class musicians. Similarly, a Christmas Service was held at the British Embassy each year. The RAF Chaplain from Cyprus came as a signals expert to fix the Embassy radios. Most weekends, the local hotels often seem to see us on Thursday night, or Friday lunchtime (or both), together with friends, "to save cooking".

In April, 2000, my mother died. Jane and I were able to be with her for the last few days. My sister, Elizabeth, and I sorted out the Probate with her solicitor. One problem we had was the number of obscure Swiss accounts and bonds. A long time ago, when my parents were leaving Kenya, there was a Law saying that only £100 (2000 Kenya Shillings) could be taken out of the country. A friend wanted to stay in Kenya, so a swap was arranged. All my parents' money in Kenya was given to the friend, and all her Swiss money was transferred to us.

Saudi Vets

Once again, BAe asked us to change compounds and our Siamese cat, Charlie, had settled in to the new villa but refused to make friends with the other feline residents. Mano, our Hindu steward, would take him for walks in the grounds and rescue him from fights. Charlie developed a fur ball blockage and we had to find a vet. The only expat vet allowed in Riyadh was only allowed to deal with Falcons and cattle. Domestic animal vets were considered not necessary. I was told of a company that had a sort of vet responsible for the airport sniffer dogs and we visited these Philllipinos. After Charlie was filmed on the airport baggage x-ray machine, several attempts were made to remove the blockage using medicines. Eventually, surgery seemed the only answer. The "vet" said that he would like to try just one more method. He returned with a wire coat hanger, which he was straightening with a pair of pliers. He intended to probe the blockage via the cat's throat. We picked up the cat and fled. The problem resolved itself naturally shortly afterwards.

We were on leave in UK when the terrible events of 9/11 took place. When it became known that several of the terrorists were from Saudi, our relatives tried to persuade us not to return to Riyadh. Life in Riyadh became much more restricted. Virtually no one left their compounds at night for social reasons, but we still attended concerts at the Canadian Embassy and risked visiting the local supermarket (even if it meant having the car searched several times just to buy a pint of milk). BAe set up an SMS system to advise all employees of threats by text messages, so that they could rapidly advise us when to avoid certain areas or to stay in "lock-down" safety. Up to then, a mobile phone was not essential, but now everyone carried them.

In 2001, I managed to get two prominent Saudi Civil Engineers accepted as full Fellows of the Institution of Civil Engineers. I asked the Ambassador, Sir Derek Plumbly, to make the formal presentations and he took the advantage to tell the Saudi people of the co-operation between our two countries and there was massive press and TV coverage. One Fellow was the King's nephew, and the other was my boss. The Saudi Engineering Committee was invited, together with several high ranking Princes from the Shoura Council. This did a lot to help the Saudi Engineering Committee push the Royal decree for engineering qualifications up the agenda.

Life started to get really awkward early in January 2002, after President Bush made his "Axis of Evil" speech. We all kept very low profiles and spent a lot of time apologizing to Saudi friends about the one-sided Western press coverage of Middle Eastern matters. We all thought that the Bush and Blair combination was dangerous, and could lead to unimaginable problems, not only for Iraq, but also for the whole Middle East and in outward ripples over the Muslim countries. So it turned out.

We were able to spend a few quiet and peaceful days in Northern Thailand in April 2002. We visited the Burmese border, the Golden Triangle, the Hill Tribes, and spent a most memorable day in the late Queen Mother's Da Tung Gardens. Bangkok's new elevated Metro is very efficient and allowed us to make the most of our 48 hours in the capital. Jane was back in Wales at the end of July for her mother's 100th Birthday. No telegram is sent by the Queen now, but (in Cardiff) a senior Post Office man in 19th century uniform delivers the signed Birthday Card at 6:00am. Jane had been up talking to Hugh until 3:00am, and was not prepared for this, and the man nearly got sent away with a flea in his ear! Jane had to stand on the step, in her dressing gown, while he went through his 15 minute prepared speech, before making her sign for the delivery!! Jane's Mum had a very enjoyable day with all the family, and had two successful cataract operations in the following year. In September 2002, we had four days in Berlin. We purchased 3-day Transport Passes and roamed the whole city at leisure on U-Bahn, S-Bahn, and buses (it was too cold for the river boats). Afternoon tea at the Hotel Adlon, next to the Brandenburg Gate, was a highlight. The parks were most attractive, as the trees were turning golden.

Hugh left for Mauritania in December 2002, where he was learning to use a three-wheel buggy, towed behind a kite. He had found some old Russian satellite photos, revealing wide areas of almost flat desert in Morocco, on the Algerian border. These could give him up to 60 miles kiting in a straight line, subject to his support vehicle keeping up with him. He emailed me for help in identifying the Algerian minefields along this border. The Defence Attaché in Riyadh found that his maps only reached half way across Libya, so I was unable to help him. Hugh was investigating a possible new business venture, running trips for people looking for miles of flat surfaces to race three-wheeled buggies, towed by hand-held kites. He wrote up the trip and published this on the internet. The UK magazine "Geographical" wrote a feature on him, following an invitation for Hugh to join the Royal Geographical Society. The Morocco car bombs caused the Mauritanians to close the border again, putting a temporary halt to Hugh's plans to take tourists south from Morocco. The border has only been open for 10 months in 25 years! Still, he was getting bookings for trips! His campervan, an ex-Royal Navy ambulance, survived all the way back to Belgium, when the gearbox gave up. There had been very heavy snow in Europe and he was the only vehicle on some motorways. He got the AA to bring it back to Wales on a transporter, but they dropped it into a ditch when the winch broke during unloading. Later, he found that the garage which had prepared the vehicle for the trip had left a spanner inside the clutch bell-housing. It was very fortunate that the spanner had not caused damage in the depths of the Sahara. As the local garage had helped Hugh with sponsorship for the trip, it was not a good advertisement for the garage.

Gulf War II

By this time, so very few of the old friends that we made over the years were still here in Riyadh. We spent New Years Eve with the last of our "inner circle", as they left in January 2003. On 19th March 2003, the second Gulf War started and things were getting a lot more difficult. BAe issued all of us with a 12 page manual on security and defensive driving. They hired extra security experts, to work with the Saudi Army, Airforce, and different Police units (Secret, plainclothes and uniformed). We had to vary routes and times of our journeys, visually check under vehicles, and have the security call centre number on speed dial.

There were a lot of worried and nervous dependants thinking of leaving Saudi Arabia and some 7% of our 2200 dependants took advantage of the relaxation of employment contract restrictions, designed to allow easier departures. The US Air Attaché told me that only 25% of US dependants had left, which disappointed Washington. The US wanted all dependents and non-critical personnel out of the Kingdom. Many people did not have homes to go to, or schools for the kids to swap into, so they found it difficult to decide. BAe still had a contract to supply personnel to the Saudi Airforce, so a large "Danger Bonus" was paid out to all remaining workers to maintain staff levels.

As an example of our daily worries, a colleague called Robert Dent went to buy some milk for his family breakfast and died. He was returning from the Supermarket near his compound, when a pedestrian shot him at the traffic lights. The assailant leapt into a van and was driven off. Some Saudis took the vehicle number, and the assailant was picked up at a road block. The Saudis were shocked and horrified, and really worried for us all.

At the end of 2003 we spent a very enjoyable short break in Sri Lanka over Christmas and New Year. Colombo was under armed guard during this time as the female President was accusing the female Prime Minister of making assassination attempts. Jane managed to persuade the Navy guards to allow her to walk past the Presidential home and take photos of the machine gun posts. A charming driver took us up to Kandy where we stayed four nights, and on to visit tea plantations further up in the Highlands.

Terrorist attacks

In May 2003, this time, the terrorists, did a bit more research before they attacked. They hit Al Hamra, Cordoba, Jedawel compounds and the Vinnel/Syanco complex. These are mostly American areas. The Syanco bachelors block contained Philllipinos working for National Guard, and it was on the Vinnell compound near the Football Stadium. We were storing boxes for an American who was returning to take up work with Vinnell in June. His accommodation block was demolished, including the room reserved for his return. At Cordoba, they approached the rear gate, as the front was well guarded, but did little damage. At Jedawel, the terrorists had to shoot the Saudi gate guards to get in. An RSAF policeman then killed three of them before being killed himself when the pick-up truck blew up. At Al Hamra, the site of the worst bombing, the majority of the victims were not American! In fact, most were Muslims. At the gate, the terrorists asked for a resident by name and villa number from a saloon car. When the gate was opened, the car together with a pick-up truck rushed in and drove down to the restaurant. The Saudi son of the landlord was entertaining friends in the restaurant and had been alerted by the gate guard. He rushed out to deal with the intrusion but was mown down by machine gun fire. The truck blew up, and as residents rushed out of doors they were also shot. Jane's friend at Al Hamra had just got in from the UK flight and was in a taxi waiting to get into the compound, behind the pick-up truck, when she realised that all was not correct and ordered the driver to take her to another compound. 10 minutes later the bomb went off. Casualty numbers were hard to confirm but continued to grow as people succumbed to wounds, and this sent a shockwave through the community. Thankfully, the hospitals in Riyadh were first class, and had all the modern equipment. Even so, an extra 190 plus patients put a strain on the system. All 400 houses in Al Hamra were evacuated to hotels, as water and electricity supplies were damaged. The adjoining British School lost all of the glass in the windows and the steel frame of the multi-purpose hall was "distorted", and was closed until further notice. Other schools closed for security reasons. A lot of school staff and residents on the affected compounds left. The next empty airline seat was three weeks away.

BA decided that it was too dangerous for crews to stay overnight in Riyadh, and changed crews at Larnaca, in Cyprus.

BAe now had to decide whether to send all the dependents home, possibly for good! Dependents already in UK, following the voluntary repatriation for Gulf War II, were banned from returning. Any family member wanting to go on normal leave was worried that they may not be allowed back! It was all very worrying. "Bachelor staff only" seemed to be the way that BAe was thinking. This would reduce the number of compounds, and make it easier to safeguard people, while maintaining the contract with the Saudi Airforce. BAe had, by then, 37 empty villas. Talk had started, before the bombing, of closing BAe five compounds. The detailed plans were confirmed to us by our houseboy Mano!! One thing that BAe would not consider was doing away with the need to serve out the three months notice contractually required by Royal Saudi Air Force. This made it difficult for families to leave together easily. Dependents still had to wait for husbands to get out. It was thought that the only sure way to leave quickly was to insult an Arab, or hit a senior manager. Leaving early also came with a heavy financial penalty in loss of all the End of Service benefits such as a year's salary.

I had only 15 months to go to retirement at this time and elected to stay, although I had very little work to do now. A very large proportion of the 1250 buildings at Al Kharj had been handed over to RSAF users for the 12 month period before the Final Acceptance inspections could take place and I had nothing to do during the waiting period.

On 12th May 2003, three large car bombs exploded in Riyadh and our lives and way of living changed completely. We knew several of the injured, but none of those killed, and all expats started to feel very nervous. Compound security was immediately improved, with the addition of light tanks, armoured cars, Army and National Guard troops, plain-clothed Security Services (scary), and police cars.

Villa protection Riyadh 2003
Before razor wire and more concrete barriers added

Later, we got concrete barriers, razor wire fences, CCTV and proper access barriers. The various security forces did not always recognise each other, which lead to fun and games. The CCTV were sophisticated enough to have 6 months storage of film. "This means that we do not have to watch the monitors until the end of 6 months" said the guard on our compound! A lot more families decided to leave, although husbands had to stay, and expat life after dark has all but ceased. All shops and hotels increased security and shopping malls were deserted. We still managed to enjoy life, but only in daylight.

I was still running the monthly engineering meetings for the Institution of Civil Engineers. When the terrorist situation first started up, I was still holding these meetings in the British Embassy. One speaker, a Saudi, failed to show up. He was the Project Manager on the construction of the Kingdom Tower; Saudi Arabia's tallest building at the time. This was owned by Prince Waleed Bin Talal bin Abdulaziz al Saud, a very rich Saudi business magnate and investor. During the very large concrete pour for the tower foundation, at night, a Mercedes saloon drove onto the site. A prince got out and ordered all the workers off the site as he considered the land to belong to him. He waved a sub-machine gun and fired into the sky to emphasise his orders. This terrified the tower crane operator, who refused to come down for two days. The concrete pour was aborted and the prince padlocked the gates with the chains that he had brought with him. It took Prince Salman, the Royal Family enforcer,

Kingdom Tower - Riyadh

some time to sort out the title to the land and to sort out the wayward prince. My absent speaker had been fully occupied in trying to rescue the aborted concrete pour and discuss the delay with Prince Waleed.

Jane flew to Cardiff in June 2003, and I arrived in July, in time to attend the wedding of the son of very good ex-Riyadh friends. We had two glorious days in Torquay, in the best of weather. Jane decided on her new kitchen in Cornwall, with installation planned for April 2004. The highlight of the leave was the 101st Birthday of Jane's mother. Jane put on a good spread for the family. As British Airways could not decide whether they were flying to Riyadh or not, we got to Heathrow a day early to be safe, but we had no problem. From then on, we chose Saudia!!! We spent our final Christmas leave in Malaysia over the Christmas and New Year period, including Kuala Lumpur, Cameron Highlands, and Langkawi.

British Embassy

The British Embassy often had Royal visitors from the U.K, and expats were invited to meet the visitors. Although I had held monthly meetings in the Embassy for some years, and worked with the Commercial Attaché with regard to the Kingdom joining the World trade Organisation, I could not get onto the Embassy invitation list, which was carefully controlled by the Embassy "in-set". Jane was a personal friend of Ambassador Sir Andrew Green's wife Jane. She noted that my Jane never got invited. Andrew is now Lord Green and founder of Migration Watch UK. When it was announced that the Duke of Edinburgh was to visit, I wrote to the

Institution of Civil Engineers in London and suggested that, as the Duke was the senior Fellow of the Institution, he might want to meet ICE members resident in Saudi Arabia. The Embassy was duly instructed to invite me. On the morning of the Embassy cocktail party, a Royal Navy Captain visited our offices on business and kept muttering "I must not say that". I stood next to him waiting to be introduced to the Duke. The Captain, when introduced, said "Sir, I had the misfortune to have your son serve onboard my ship". The Duke just glared and walked on, and I never got my introduction. At another Embassy function, the Commercial Attaché introduced me to Prince Andrew.

During my 13 year stay in Riyadh, there were several Ambassadors and I met them all. The first one was Sir David Gore-Booth, who left in 1996 to be posted to Delhi as High Commissioner and who was later rejected by the India Government. He was followed by Sir Andrew Green (of Migration Watch) from 1996 to 2000. His successor was Sir Derek Plumbly (2000 – 2003) who presented Institution of Civil Engineers Fellowship certificates to two Saudi Civil Engineers. In my final year, Sir Sherard Cowper-Coles looked after British interests while terrorists tore Riyadh apart. This was good training for his next posting in Kabul.

In 2004, I finally set up the Institution of Civil Engineers Joint Group, with IMechE, IStructE, and RICS. This was to be called "The Professional Engineers Group of Saudi Arabia", or PEGSA. Our multinational membership stood at over 650. Due to the security problems, we were no longer able use the British Embassy as a meeting place, but held meetings in local hotels.

For a long period, I had been almost in sole charge of the British Embassy for these monthly meetings. I would supervise the gate security and, at times, liaise with the Diplomatic Quarter Police. This all changed as the situation deteriorated and our membership increased. More Arab engineers came to realize the benefits of learning more about the work of other engineering professions. I started to mentor two Saudi BAe Mechanical Engineers for full Membership of the Institution of Mechanical Engineers. The Saudi University BSc did not satisfy the requirements of the UK Engineering Council, so they were required to take further academic exams before applying. They both subsequently became full Members, after taking a Professional Interview in Riyadh.

Jane continued through 2004 to teach the Saudi Princesses in Prince Salman's Palace. His Lincoln Continental saloon with its blacked out windows was known to every law officer in the city and Jane was ferried to and from the Palace at great speed. However, the Palace was not in one of the best neighbourhoods. Frank Gardner, a BBC correspondent, visited Riyadh and wanted to meet Al Qaeda sympathisers known to be in this area. He was told by the Saudis not to attempt this under any circumstances as the area was known to be dangerous, but he went ahead. His cameraman was shot dead and Frank got a bullet through the spine. Jane drove down this street to the Palace each day.

In May we had to return unexpectedly to Cardiff for the funeral of Jane's mother. She died at the grand old age of 104, still with all of her faculties, and only suffering from osteoarthritis.

Our final leave from Riyadh was in July and we used this to transfer our Siamese cat to quarantine in UK, so that his 6 months stay would see him released soon after we returned for good. Also, we sent an advance consignment of household goods home. We were able to sort out and store these items at home in Cornwall before the final consignment at the end of the contract. That leave was spent on house alterations, a new kitchen and other works.

Boscastle floods

We left to return to Riyadh in early August, letting Jane's niece, Fiona, use the house for a holiday. No sooner than we had got back, neighbours telephoned to ask us to watch Sky TV news, showing the Boscastle floods. Knowing that Fiona loved to visit Boscastle, we tried to see if her car was one of those being swept out to sea from the car park. We tried to telephone her but there was no answer from the house phone or her mobile. With the time difference of three hours, it was well past 3:00am Saudi time before we got a reply. They had been marooned in a Tintagel pub by flood waters and had left her mobile in the house! We were very relieved to hear from her.

Management training

Eventually it was time to start the retirement process, and fill in the necessary forms to get my End of Service payments sorted. Under Saudi Law this included a year's salary. BAe, who process the salary payments, told me that I was illegible for any payments because I "had never been trained as a manager". It appeared that BAe Human Resources Department, in UK, had a computer system which insisted on all boxes being checked before money could be released! There were several others caught in the same trap, all senior ex-military officers and others with a long history of holding down senior management jobs. But no exceptions could be made. We had to undergo a training course before the UK HR department could "tick the box". A UK based Training Company was contracted to train us up to the required standard. However, the security situation caused problems with insuring the training staff, who were not allowed to travel to Saudi Arabia. Would we be willing to spend two weeks in a five star hotel in Dubai, and have the training outside Saudi Arabia? Of course we would! So, in my last three months of a long time in management, I set off to Dubai to learn how to be a manager. Another colleague and I realised that there was an Immigration rule that said that wives could not stay in Saudi Arabia when the husband was outside the Kingdom, so BAe had to also pay for wives to accompany us. These poor, bored, wives had to spend their time all day in glossy shopping malls and jewellery shops. It cost the husbands a fortune. On our return, there were still some modules of management training to be completed, and these were held in The Riyadh Intercontinental Hotel. My wife and I had used the outside Catering department for years and knew the staff very well. On the first morning, the management training staff had not managed to arrange the coffee break and ran around like headless chickens. I was able to rub their noses into it by simply calling up the right man and getting the coffee break delivered. What did they know about management?

At the end of October, I had finally got the remaining Al Kharj facilities handed over to the Royal Saudi Airforce, all except for one Clinic. We had built two identical clinics, one for families and another for bachelors. The standard medical equipment was the same for both. However, the ultrasound kit caused a major problem. The manufacturer included a standard set of attachments, which included a vaginal probe for use on female patients. When the medical authorities found that we had issued a vaginal probe for the bachelor clinic, they suspected that it was our secret intention that this be used on male patients! They refused to accept the clinic. When I proposed, that to solve the impasse, this extra probe simply be transferred to the Family Clinic as a spare and free of charge but this was not accepted. The medical authorities were heavily influenced by the religious people and took this matter as a religious slight. It was not helped when, earlier, a wheelchair access had to be added to both clinics. In the family clinic, the contractor put the ramp directly outside a consulting room, opposite a full length clear glass window. The consulting room was the Obstetrics/Gynaecology examination room, and the stirrups were in clear view from the ramp!

It was sad to finally say Goodbye to work and income, and all our friends still left in Saudi Arabia. Life in Riyadh had deteriorated considerably and was no longer the fun that expat life had been for so many years. The Saudis gave me a very good send off party, with the usual "mutton grab" menu. A lot of very kind words were said and I found it difficult to reply properly.

Far East trip

We left Riyadh at the end of September and had four great weeks visiting old haunts in Dubai, Singapore and Bangkok. We also included Hong Kong and Cambodia. Jane's nephew, Chris, worked for DFiD in Cambodia. He met us in Siem Reap, where he had arranged for us to be driven from the airport in the pride of the hotel's fleet. It was a 1926 Citroen and had a top speed of about 10 miles per hour. Cyclists were overtaking us! After visiting some of the magnificent temples of Angkor Wat over two days, we tried to fly to Phnom Penh. Our Saudi Travel Agent had overlooked the fact that the Thai airline that he had used did not have pick up rights for an internal Cambodian flight. We shuttled between the Domestic and International Terminals, trying to sort out flights. Each move meant going through a complete baggage security check, just to talk to ground staff! Jane had a large bottle of whisky that was open. She had to take swig at each check to prove that the content was actually whisky, with the obvious effect! I had bought a lot of electronics and computer stuff cheaply in Singapore, and this looked like spy equipment, to the security staff. Eventually, I got two seats on an internal flight and we got to Phnom Penh, to be met again by Chris. We stayed with him for several days and visited many interesting sights. The Russian Market, with its stalls selling fried cockroaches and honey dipped locust was a prime attraction. We were there for the Abdication and Coronation of the new King, who was a homosexual and had been a ballet dancer in Paris. Our final stop was a week in Phuket, in a very nice beachside hotel and we really unwound. There was a baby elephant giving rides to children. It was sad to see this hotel appear on TV during the Boxing Day Tsunami. It was totally destroyed. The baby elephant did manage to save some children.

Retirement 2004

On our return to Cornwall, we had to buy a car, collect the cat from quarantine, build a conservatory, and prepare for our first full Christmas family gathering as hosts in twenty years. Hugh's stepdaughter, Amelia, was coming up to school age and the teaching in North Wales was all in Welsh. Hugh decided to relocate to Cornwall "to look after the oldies". This meant that they put their house on the market and moved in with us. In January, 2005, we bought a Border Terrier pup called Titch, and trained him to get along with the much older Siamese cat. Hugh, Laura and Amelia moved down to Cornwall, house hunting while the Welsh house was up for sale. During the summer, Hugh and family took off to South Africa for six weeks camping, while we frequently travelled to North Wales to meet potential buyers. This needed a round trip of over 700 miles for a ten minute viewing. We quickly arranged for the estate agent to take on this job. Our Grandson, Daniel, was born in November, in Bossiney and should qualify for Cornish citizenship in years to come. The house eventually sold and we found a bungalow for Hugh near Jamaica Inn, on Bodmin Moor for him to buy, and the sale was completed in January 2006. A large amount of structural work was required before it was habitable or even mortgageable.

Tintagel Sewage

In early 2005, I got involved with other concerned villagers to try and get South West Water Ltd to provide the correct grade of sewage treatment for the village. SWW had, under pressure from Ofwat and EU regulations, started a massive upgrade of some 220 waste water treatment plants with sea outfalls. Bathing water standards in this tourist area needed attention. By the time the programme reached Tintagel and Boscastle, funds were running out and the barest minimum of work was proposed. SWW proposed a scheme for Boscastle positioned in the carpark which had just been flushed into the sea by the flood. At least they were offered primary treatment, whereas the Tintagel proposal only added screens to the raw outfall. The Tintagel population is greater than Boscastle and should have been given better treatment. I suggested to the Member of Parliament that common sense called for a single treatment plant that could serve both communities, and that the level of treatment required by EU regulations was a minimum of Secondary Treatment. Our campaign started with an Appeal against the Planning Permission granted for the Tintagel outfall upgrade. Previously, the contractor had tried to start work but was run off site by a group of women volunteers from the village. A police sergeant was called by the contractor and I met him on site. When I asked why the contractor was working within sight of a badger sett without the necessary permit, he agreed with the ladies. Eventually, the Planning Inspectorate held a Public Inquiry, at which SWW was represented by lawyers and experts at great expense, and we villagers only had assistance from a barrister hired by an affected caravan park company. I proved that the size of plant proposed would become too small for the population within only two years, and that the population would reach the magic 2000Pe (Population equivalent) in three years, requiring the much more comprehensive treatment. The Inspector agreed with us.

Meanwhile, Boscastle also put up a spirited defence and even bought shares in SWW. At the SWW Annual General Meeting they objected to the renewal of the CEO's contract. They also had found that SWW had seriously underestimated the "Pe" so that a lesser plant would satisfy EU requirements. SWW dug their heels in and spent considerable effort in trying to force their ideas through. There were many public meetings and consultations with SWW but they would not budge. We joined forces with Boscastle and it was revealed that SWW had a secret list of all the outfalls and the estimated "Pe" figures for each. An examination of this list showed that small villages had big "Pe" numbers and big villages had small "Pe" numbers. It appeared that SWW originally prepared this list of "Pe" figures and then gave it to the Environment Agency. Thereafter, the list became an official EA document and SWW insisted that they were unable to deviate from official EA doctrine. SWW blamed the EA, at the Inquiry, for the mistakes in the list! At the Royal Cornwall Show in June, our MP dragged me out of a Hotdog stall queue for a talk about sewage. On another occasion, the MP held up a check-out queue in the local supermarket to talk to me about sewage, to the amusement of other shoppers.

By November, we had forced SWW to accept that we would challenge the Planning Application for Boscastle and challenge the overall design of the two individual schemes. A new Planning Inspectorate Public Inquiry was ordered and SWW insisted that the Environment Agency also attend. This time, we had no legal help. Our team all lived in the village, the chairlady had protested at Greenham Common, our chemist (for environmental concerns with smells) had been Chief Chemist at the Royal Mint, I provided the civil engineering input, a local architect also lectured in Planning Law, a lady solicitor went on to run the World Wild Life legal team. SWW and the EA shared a London QC, and hired several experts, one of whom I had met in Saudi Arabia. The SWW case depended on the interpretation of the shape of the village under the wording of the EU regulations. By proving that it could be split into two areas, a lesser scheme could be supplied. The village plumber's son happened to be a Cambridge Don who had researched the Doomsday Book and his evidence showed that the village was one entity. I found that the SWW Population Equivalent (Pe) amount had been calculated from billing records, without a site survey to prove accuracy. Only some 60% of households had been listed, much reducing the actual Pe number. Further, I had commissioned a Consulting Engineer to report on whether we could have a combined scheme for the combined communities of Tintagel and Boscastle, and to provide estimated costs of various options for comparison. Other team members made similar holes in the SWW/EA arguments. The Inspector found, again, in our favour. The decision could only be formally handed down by the Secretary of State, and the Labour Government had three Secretaries in quick succession, delaying the approval of the decision!! Meanwhile, a number of staff changes had taken place within SWW and a very sensible engineer was appointed to Project Manage our scheme. He took my Consultants Report and saw that there was merit in my suggestion. Eventually, in July 2008, a Secretary of State found time to read the Inspectors Report and it was formally released in our favour. This was two years after the Public Inquiry. Finally, in 2009, the village sewage system was constructed. After all the public Inquiries and obstruction from South West Water, they built exactly the scheme that I first proposed to the MP in December 2004. As I have said before, things take too long in UK because of excessive legislation.

Hugh, having bought his house, spent the rest of 2006 making it structurally sound. The previous owner, an Elvis impersonator, had no DIY skills and had removed 4 metres of wall supporting the roof without replacing any support. We also decided to remove the central chimney and some walls. Very long oak beams were bought in Belgium, complete with WW1 shrapnel embedded in them, and sawn to shape. Using climbing ropes, Land Rover jacks, and skills that I had learnt overseas, we put two sets of beams in place, and builder friends could only marvel at how we had managed as there was no direct, straight line, access into the building for the 20 foot beams. Work continued through a cold and snowy winter and eventually the family moved in. The hole in the roof where the chimney had been was inexpertly patched with plywood, and the lounge filled with snow in February.

In February 2006, we were lent a flat in Spain, owned by some Riyadh friends. Jane and I toured Seville and Granada, spending the middle weekend with our hosts, who had flown out to see us. June saw us visiting west Cornwall including Lands End and other little places, a super trip. Then our summer visitors started arriving, making us wonder why we chose to live in a tourist area. My sister was followed by Jane's niece, then more Riyadh friends. I had a heart pacemaker fitted in July and this helped me to feel less tired every day. In September we travelled to Glasgow in September, to see other Riyadh friends. We had a great time, and even managed to catch up with Dr Doug Edmunds from Nigeria days. He used to run the "World's Strongest Man" competitions on TV until he sold the franchise, and he gave me a copy of his autobiography in which I get a mention!

In February 2007, we were invited to a Birthday Party by Dave Kilner, my assistant from Nigeria days, and he told the assembly that I was the only man he knew who could walk into a Nigerian Police Station and order them to demolish it. Most of the guests did not believe the story. We took the opportunity to visit several sets of friends who lived in the Midlands. In March, we again borrowed the Fuengirola flat from our Riyadh friends for a few days. We drove down to Gibraltar to visit to meet other friends who transferred from Riyadh to Gibraltar, where he worked for UK MoD.

We managed to have a short break in August. We had three nights in Dorchester while we explored the area. I had planned to show Jane all the places on the South Coast that I knew from TA soldiering days. The coast was blanked out by fog for the whole journey from Weymouth to Exeter and we could not see a thing! In October, we went to Dublin, from our local airport, Newquay, for four nights. We had hoped to catch up with Capt Denis Gray who worked for the Saudi Ports Authority Riyadh early 1990's and was present when I had my heart attack, but we failed to contact him. He called me after our return. We went to the cinema and watched a film called "The Kingdom". It was a CIA story about bombings in Riyadh and it brought back a lot of suppressed emotions. We had no idea that we had been traumatized until the film brought it all back into focus.

In April 2008, Hugh and Laura got married, with Amelia as Bridesmaid. We looked after the children for the Honeymoon, and then we went off to Spain for a week's break. We stayed in the Fuengirola flat and met up with the Gibraltar friends again. They drove up from Gibraltar, and as we were still on UK time, we were an hour late. They nearly gave up meeting us! In May, our friends from Scotland came south to visit their daughter at her new job in Bournemouth, and we had lunch with them. In June our ex-Mombasa friends came to North Devon and we had lunch with them. It was the first time that Jane had met the son since he was in her Reception Class in Mombasa!

We had a few days in Bruges early in July. It is a lovely place to visit. I went on a WW1 Battlefield tour and helped unearth three live 18lb shells from a farmer's field. Farmers only plough down to 9 inches, and these were at 12 inches! We struggled to eat all the chocolate, and really chilled out. We spent the last morning in Brussels before flying back. My sister came for a few days in July, to get some advice on being a Grandmother. Our Great niece was born in October. September saw us having a very enjoyable week in the Cotswolds, based in Cirencester. We last spent time here when we lived in Gloucester some 30 years ago.

2009 Marrakech

In November 2008, some friends came down to see their friends who were emigrating to Malta, and we had a day in Exeter with them. About this time, Jane started going for medical tests, and she was booked for a major operation early in January. Hugh and Laura decided that a family holiday together in Marrakech would cheer up Jane before her operation and we all flew out and arrived the day before Christmas Eve. That night, Hugh showed us the main square, where he had earned money by juggling when he was much younger and penniless. We went into town for a lunchtime snack and Jane suffered what we subsequently discovered was the first of two strokes. A local doctor prescribed pills and we put her to bed.

Christmas day was spent in the apartment, tending to Jane, who did not look at all well. She perked up on Boxing Day and insisted on another trip into town. She had another stroke and, after getting her back to the apartment and summoning a doctor, she was transferred to a hospital.

We started making arrangements to end the holiday and get Jane home. Laura took the children to Cornwall and handled all the UK end of the negotiations. Hugh and I dealt with the Medical Evacuation insurance company. Eventually, the Geneva based Air Ambulance agent called and Hugh had to explain to him about Moroccan regulations and which air routes could be used. He, as an expedition leader, had done several medical evacuations from. Eventually, a flight was arranged and Jane was flown via Spain to Plymouth. She was admitted to Derriford Hospital, where she died three weeks later. Throughout the stay in hospital, we were very well supported by friends, some of whom helped me by driving the 100 mile daily round trip. After her death, Jane's GP told me that Jane had been booked in for a Bowel Cancer operation, and she had never told me that she had cancer. Typically, she had not wanted to worry me!

So many neighbours and friends from all over UK came to her Funeral. In the large window at the Bodmin Crematorium, there was a lovely view of the forested hill opposite. Two birds of prey, Jane's favourite birds, gave an aerial display for the whole of the ceremony. She would have loved that.

2009 and after

I had two trips to Budapest in the summer of 2010 for Dental treatment. My local private dentist was too expensive, and I had been unable to get on a NHS Dental list. Including fares and hotels, I saved £1000 on the UK price! After complaining to the Press, I was given an NHS Dentist!

I attended Loughborough University in 2009 to be awarded an Honorary Bachelor of Arts degree. This was part of the University Centenary Celebration, and some 1,000 old students, who graduated pre 1974, were awarded either a BA or a BEng. I met several students that I remembered. A very enjoyable weekend, which I combined with visits to Les & Jacqui Painting, Neville & Mavis Goldsby, and Angela & Ben Guest. I also attended a class reunion in 2010 for all Civil Engineering graduates of my year, and many old friends were able to attend.

I joined the Royal Engineers Bomb Disposal Officers Club (REBDOC) and have attended several meetings. On two occasions, I attended dinners in The House of Lords, hosted by one of our members. He is an MP and a TA Bomb Disposal Officer, who spent his parliamentary holidays defusing bombs in Afghanistan. There have been many visits to Army facilities to keep us in contact with injured servicemen and women, and to show us old fogies the new equipment and training.

I spent two years researching and drawing up the Martin Family Tree. I had an old, coffee stained, family tree and some old family records to start the project. I found that two ancestors had been sent to the Tower of London as traitors. One was arrested because Robert Walpole trumped up a charge against him, involving his supposed support for Bonnie Prince Charlie.

The other traitor was caught between Charles II and the King of France. While England was at war with France, my ancestor was Chancellor and was funding the war against France, he was tasked by Charles to ask the King of France for a personal loan! Something went wrong and he was arrested.

Both survived, one being exiled and the other was later released by James II. A third "traitor" was honoured for his service to William the Conqueror against England!

The End